# Advanced Legal
# Writing

# Advanced Legal Writing

## Theories and Strategies in Persuasive Writing

MICHAEL R. SMITH

Associate Professor of Law
Mercer University
Walter F. George School of Law

ASPEN LAW & BUSINESS
A Division of Aspen Publishers, Inc.
New York   Gaithersburg

Permissions
Aspen Law & Business
1185 Avenue of the Americas
New York, NY 10036

Printed in the United States of America.

1 2 3 4 5 6 7 8 9 0

ISBN 0-7355-2014-3

**Library of Congress Cataloging-in-Publication Data**

Smith, Michael R., 1961-
    Advanced legal writing : theories and strategies in persuasive writing / Michael R. Smith.
        p. cm.
    Includes bibliographical references and index.
    ISBN 0-7355-2014-3
    I. Legal composition. I. Title.

    KF250 .S58 2002
    808'.06634--dc21

                                             2001058380

# About Aspen Law & Business
# Legal Education Division

With a dedication to preserving and strengthening the long-standing tradition of publishing excellence in legal education, Aspen Law & Business continues to provide the highest quality teaching and learning resources for today's law school community. Careful development, meticulous editing, and an unmatched responsiveness to the evolving needs of today's discerning educators combine in the creation of our outstanding casebooks, coursebooks, textbooks, and study aids.

**ASPEN LAW & BUSINESS**
**A Division of Aspen Publishers, Inc.**
**A Wolters Kluwer Company**
*www.aspenpublishers.com*

To Lois Ann

For the support. For the faith.
For the sacrifice.

# Summary of Contents

# Contents

# *Preface*

As the title indicates, this book covers *theories and strategies in persuasive writing*. It is designed to build on the introductory persuasive writing instruction offered in most first-year legal writing courses by exploring specific strategies and techniques that lawyers can employ to make their writing more persuasive.

The persuasive strategies presented here are based not merely on anecdotal advice but on theoretical principles of human nature that are relevant to the process of persuasion. A tremendous amount of research and scholarship has been undertaken in other disciplines—such as cognitive psychology, literary theory, and classical rhetoric theory, to name a few—regarding aspects of human nature that are important in persuasion. Accordingly, lawyers, as persuasive writers, have much to learn from these disciplines. This book analyzes persuasive writing strategies that are designed to tap into and account for some of the human behavioral tendencies that have been identified and explored in these other disciplines.

Chapter 1 explains the book's general focus and approach. After this introductory discussion, the book is divided into five parts. Part I (Chapters 2 through 5) begins the analysis of specific persuasive writing strategies by examining the many functions of *literary references* in persuasive legal writing. Part II (Chapters 6 through 8) examines the fundamental, yet crucial, *processes* of persuasion recognized in classical rhetoric. Building on Part II, Part III (Chapters 9 and 10) covers *stylistic* persuasive devices recognized by classical rhetoricians. Part IV (Chapters 11 and 12) then examines persuasive writing strategies based on principles of psychology. Finally, Part V (Chapter 13) examines the ethical and moral implications of being a "professional persuader."

This text has two main goals. The first is to provide legal writers with specific techniques they can use to make their legal documents more persuasive. The second, more general, goal is to introduce students to the "hidden world" of powerful forces underlying effective persuasive writing, a world that the legal profession is just beginning to explore and understand.

*Michael R. Smith*
January 2002

# *Acknowledgments*

I owe thanks to many people who generously contributed their ideas and time to this project. I am especially grateful to three legal writing directors with whom I have been fortunate to work and who provided unwavering support for this book: Linda H. Edwards of Mercer University School of Law, Jan Levine of Temple University School of Law, and Deidre Alfred of the University of San Diego School of Law. Without their encouragement and guidance this book would not have been possible.

I also owe special thanks to two deans, Lawrence Dessem of Mercer and Robert Reinstein of Temple, for providing the generous research funds necessary for me to write this book.

I am also grateful to many colleagues for their support, inspiration and wisdom. Among them are my Mercer colleagues Susan Bay, Patrick Longan, Adam Milani, Jack Sammons, and David Walter; my Temple colleagues Jane Baron, Susan DeJarnatt, Ellie Margolis, and Kathy Stanchi; my San Diego colleagues Joe Hnylka and Patty Shaffer; and my colleagues at large Barbara Busharis, Elizabeth Fajans, Mary Falk, Debra Green, Richard Neumann, and Amy Sloan.

I am also thankful for research assistance by Temple students Mark Anderson and Cheryl Garber and Mercer students Sheila Baran and Frances Clay, as well as administrative assistance by Barbara Blackburn and Jane Burns of Mercer, Freddie Sanford of Temple, and Susan Miller and Mary Vicknair of San Diego.

I am especially indebted to Carol McGeehan, Ellen Greenblatt, Melody Davies, Betsy Kenny, Barbara Roth, Susan Boulanger, and their colleagues at Aspen Law and Business, as well as the anonymous reviewers who provided insightful comments on my initial proposal for this book and on drafts of the chapters.

Finally, I must thank my support system: Barbara Anderson, Michael, Jamie, and Sarah Batchelor, Paul and Sheri Lewis, Bill and Kathy Kaminski, Jed and Lisa Rhodes, Otto and Lois Theirgart, and Bart and Tonya Warner. I would not have been able to write this book without their friendship and encouragement.

## Copyright Acknowledgments

# Chapter 1

# Introduction

## I.  THE IMPORTANCE OF PERSUASIVE WRITING TO THE PRACTICE OF LAW

Why should a law student or a lawyer be concerned with studying persuasive writing theories and strategies? The answer is simple: *Persuasive writing is essential to the practice of law.*

One of a lawyer's primary functions, by definition, is to serve as an advocate for his or her clients. And as an advocate, a lawyer's job is to persuade. As John Dernbach, Richard Singleton, Cathleen Wharton, and Joan Ruhtenberg have pointed out:

> The lawyer as advocate is the counterpart of the lawyer as counselor. To the client, the lawyer is a counselor; to the outside world, the lawyer is an advocate. As an advocate, the lawyer exercises persuasion in a variety of ways to achieve results favorable to the client. Many times, a lawyer will help a client avoid lawsuits by convincing a potential adversary that the client's position is solid. At other times, a lawyer may convince a government agency to adopt a more favorable attitude toward the client's position. While effective advocacy can help keep a dispute out of court, it can also increase the likelihood of success if litigation is necessary.[1]

Much of the persuasion that lawyers achieve is done through writing. Contrary to the popular perception of lawyers (garnered in part, no doubt, from their depiction on television), legal advocates spend a great deal more time persuading through the written word than they do through the spoken word. And, while most of us may think of the formal genres of persuasive legal writing—such as trial briefs and appellate briefs—when we envision persuasive legal documents, lawyers routinely produce many additional types of persuasive documents, such as correspondence to potential adversaries or opposing counsel and written proposals to business organizations and governmental entities. Because lawyers act as advocates for their clients in legal matters, and because most legal matters today (litigation-oriented or otherwise) are handled in writing, lawyers are frequently called upon to use their writing skills to persuade on behalf of their clients. In short, whatever their area of practice, lawyers must write persuasively.

---

[1] John C. Dernbach et al., *A Practical Guide to Legal Writing and Legal Method* 215 (2d ed. 1994).

## II.    BUILDING ON BASIC PERSUASIVE WRITING SKILLS

Because persuasive writing is so integral to the practice of law, most law schools include instruction on persuasive writing in their first-year legal writing curricula. In fact, most law schools dedicate the entire second semester of introductory legal writing to persuasive writing.

The typical introductory persuasive legal writing course introduces a number of foundational concepts: the *purposes* of persuasive legal writing; the *types* of persuasive documents lawyers produce; the nature of legal *audiences* to whom persuasive writing is directed; the basic *tone*, *terminology*, and *conventions* of persuasive legal writing; and fundamental *ethical considerations* relevant to persuasive writing. Additionally, because most of the instruction on persuasive writing is taught in the context of a specific type of legal document such as a trial brief or an appellate brief, considerable time is spent on the *format requirements* of these types of documents. That is, much of the instruction introduces and explains how to draft the various parts of a brief, such as the Questions Presented, the Summary of Argument, the Statement of Facts, the Table of Authorities, the Table of Contents, and the Statement of Jurisdiction, in addition to the "heart" of the brief —the Argument section.

Introductory persuasive writing courses also, of course, provide some instruction on *basic techniques and strategies* of persuasive writing. However, the voluminous background material that must be covered necessitates that instruction on specific strategies and techniques of persuasive writing be fairly basic and often very brief. Furthermore, most of this instruction is either anecdotal (that is, based on the text author's or instructor's experiences of what is effective) or only loosely based on theoretical principles of persuasion. Rarely is detailed explanation given for why the suggested persuasive writing strategies are effective.

This book builds on the introductory persuasive writing instruction provided in most first-year legal writing programs in three ways: (1) by focusing on specific persuasive writing strategies, (2) by combining theory with practicality, and (3) by avoiding a document-based approach.

### A.    *Focusing on Specific Persuasive Writing Strategies*

As previously mentioned, introductory persuasive writing courses, by necessity, treat their subject in *breadth* rather than *depth*. Because persuasive legal writing is completely new to students in these courses, the courses are designed to introduce a whole host of general concepts relevant to persuasive legal writing.

This book supplements the instruction of introductory persuasive writing courses by focusing on one aspect of persuasive writing—*persuasive writing strategies*—and analyzing it in detail. This text assumes that you have taken an introductory persuasive writing course and possess a solid foundation in persuasive legal writing. Consequently, the focus here is on depth rather than breadth, exploring in substantial detail specific strategies and techniques that legal writers can use to make their written arguments more persuasive.

### B.      *Combining Theory with Practicality*

This book also differs from and builds on introductory persuasive writing instruction by incorporating more *theory*. Whereas most of the persuasive writing strategies covered in introductory legal writing courses are based on anecdotal advice, the strategies here are based on recognized theoretical principles of other disciplines.

A number of disciplines outside of law have developed research and scholarship exploring aspects of human nature that are relevant to the process of persuasion. This scholarship is important to persuasive legal writers because it offers insight into why and how people are persuaded. Consequently, much of this text analyzes the theoretical principles of these other disciplines and explores the persuasive writing strategies that these principles suggest. It not only teaches persuasive writing strategies, but it also allows you to explore *why*, based on the underlying theoretical principles, the strategies are effective.

Although the strategies covered in this book are based on underlying theoretical principles, this book is not exclusively theoretical. The strategies themselves are concrete and practical and are directly applicable to the day-to-day writing of practicing lawyers. Thus, this book combines theory with practicality.

### C.      *Avoiding a Document-Based Approach*

Finally, this book supplements introductory persuasive writing instruction by covering persuasive writing strategies without linking them to specific types of documents. As was noted above, much of the instruction in introductory persuasive writing courses involves the parts and format requirements of specific types of persuasive documents such as trial briefs or appellate briefs. The instruction in this book, however, is not tied to specific document formats. Rather, it covers strategies for making writing more persuasive whatever the context or document involved.

Thus, the strategies covered in this book are relevant and applicable to many of the types of persuasive documents lawyers routinely produce, including demand letters, correspondence to opposing counsel, trial briefs, appellate briefs, written proposals, and others. Regardless of the area of practice you intend to pursue, you will benefit from the instruction in this book.

## III.   THERE IS NO SUBSTITUTE FOR EFFECTIVE LEGAL RESEARCH AND ANALYSIS

At the outset, it must be emphasized that the writing strategies discussed in these pages are designed merely to complement basic effective legal argumentation. Legal audiences are persuaded first and foremost by effective legal analysis supported by effective legal research. These basic skills, learned in introductory legal research and writing courses, are at the core of any effective legal argument. The instruction in this book assumes that you have solid skills in legal research, legal analysis, and basic persuasive writing and offers advanced guidelines for honing the persuasive impact of a written argument. When it comes to legal persuasion, nothing can replace effective research and effective legal analysis: Advanced persuasive strategies will not carry a fundamentally flawed legal argument.

## IV.  JUDICIAL OPINIONS AS EXAMPLES OF PERSUASIVE WRITING

The discussions in this book include numerous examples of persuasive writing. Some come from actual documents, such as appellate briefs written by attorneys in real cases. Others have been created specifically for this book. Still others are excerpts from published judicial opinions. While it may be clear to you how the first two categories of examples serve as illustrations of persuasive writing, it may be less clear to you how judicial opinions can serve as illustrations of persuasive writing. Thus, before we begin, we should examine how judicial opinions are a form of persuasive writing and why excerpts from judicial opinions make particularly good illustrations of specific persuasive writing strategies.

Although judicial opinions are not what legal writers typically think of when they hear the phrase "persuasive writing," judicial opinions are, nevertheless, a form of persuasive writing. A judicial opinion is written by a judge to *persuade* his or her audience that the judge decided the matter in question correctly. As D. W. Stevens explains:

> The purpose of the written opinion is not, after all, for the judge to arrive at a conclusion. He has already done that. Rather, it is for him to protect his conclusion and his reasons for holding it to those audiences who need to know about it. . . . The written opinion is not a set of notes written by a judge for his own use. Rather, it is a persuasive essay directed outward toward specific audiences.[2]

In his famous essay "Law and Literature," Benjamin Cardozo stresses not only that judicial opinions are persuasive documents, but that they are necessarily so. According to Judge Cardozo, for a judicial opinion to win acceptance as authority and as precedent, it must employ all available means of persuasion. As Judge Cardozo states: "[An] opinion [needs] persuasive force, or the impressive virtue of sincerity and fire, or the mnemonic power of alliteration and antithesis, or the terseness and tang of the proverb, and the maxim. Neglect the help of these allies, and it may never win its way."[3]

Moreover, because judicial opinions are easy to access, they serve as particularly good sources for *illustrations* of specific persuasive writing strategies. Most forms of persuasive writing, like trial or appellate briefs, are not readily available for inspection and study. Judicial opinions, however, are published publically, both in print and electronically. Thus, we can readily access the actual documents in which the strategies were used.

---

[2] D. W. Stevens, *Writing Effective Opinions*, Judicature, Oct. 1975, at 135, *quoted in* Haig Bosmajian, *Metaphor and Reason in Judicial Opinions* 28 (1992) (alteration in original).

[3] Benjamin N. Cardozo, *Law and Literature*, in *Selected Writings of Benjamin Nathan Cardozo* 342 (1947).

## V.   A FEW COMMENTS ABOUT THE EXERCISES IN THIS BOOK

### A.   *Learning to Write by Writing about Writing*

This book contains three general types of exercises. The first type is the typical *performance* exercise in which you will be asked to employ a specific writing strategy under discussion. This type of exercise is very common in legal writing books and undoubtedly is familiar to you.

The second type of exercise may be less familiar to you. Exercises of this type ask you to *analyze* the use of a strategy by another writer in an existing legal text, such as a judicial opinion. That is, they require you not to employ a specific writing strategy but to compose an essay critically analyzing another writer's use of the strategy. Such exercises help you to think critically about the strategy in question—its characteristics, its communicative and persuasive functions, and the effectiveness of its use in the document under analysis. These exercises are typically used to introduce you to a new strategy before you are asked to employ the strategy yourself. Much can be learned about the nature and functions of a writing strategy by critically analyzing its use by another writer. Once you have a better appreciation of the nature of a strategy, you will be able to employ the strategy more effectively in your own writing.

The third type of exercise involves a combination of the first two. On some occasions, you will be asked (1) to employ a specific writing strategy that we have discussed and (2) to write a separate essay analyzing your effort to employ the strategy. Being comprehensive, these exercises typically come at the end of a discussion of a particular writing strategy. By consciously assessing the characteristics and functions of a persuasive strategy in a document of your own, you will gain a deeper appreciation of that strategy. This is true for three reasons. First, the process of employing a strategy provides insight about the strategy that is not gained merely by evaluating another writer's use of the strategy. Through trial and error, through writing and rewriting, you will come to appreciate nuanced dimensions of the strategy. An essay supplementing a performance exercise serves as a vehicle through which you can express what you learned about the strategy in the process of employing it. Second, employing the strategy yourself, rather than simply analyzing another writer's use of the strategy, motivates you to learn about the internal workings of a persuasive strategy. By being personally invested in the strategy, you will be more inspired to understand its qualities. The supplementing essay gives you an opportunity to communicate this deeper understanding. Third, these two-part exercises typically give you an opportunity to do some "reverse engineering." Knowing that you will have to analyze an effort to employ a specific strategy allows you to draft the effort with the characteristics and functions of the strategy in mind. Employing a strategy while consciously considering its characteristics solidifies your understanding of the strategy and inevitably results in a better effort.

As we will see then, the exercises in this text not only require you to write persuasively, but they also require you to write about writing persuasively. The combination of these approaches allows you to appreciate more fully the strategies covered and the theoretical principles underlying them.

## B.      Exercises Involving the Writing of a Judicial Opinion

As was previously mentioned, this book does not address persuasive writing in the context of any specific type of document. Rather, it addresses how lawyers can write more persuasively generally, regardless of the context or the document involved. That being said, however, employing a strategy that we have discussed must be done in the context of *some* type of legal document. That is, for you to have an opportunity to try to use a specific writing strategy, some writing vehicle—some tangible form of written expression—must be used. Accordingly, the performance exercises in this book use two types of writing vehicles. For some exercises, you will be asked to employ a strategy in the context of a *trial or appellate brief* in a hypothetical case. The focus of these exercises is not on the various parts or formatting aspects of briefs, as it likely was in your introductory persuasive writing courses. Rather, the focus is on employing the strategy in question in the argument section of the brief. Thus, while a court brief may serve as a vehicle for testing your use of a covered writing strategy, the focus of the exercise is not brief writing, but the strategy itself, which is a general skill applicable to various types of persuasive legal documents.

   For other exercises, you will be asked to employ a specific writing strategy in the context of writing a *judicial opinion*. Although you may not have had instruction on judicial opinion writing, that should not pose a problem for you in the completion of these exercises. Remember that judicial opinions are a form of persuasive writing. The text of a judicial opinion is indistinguishable from the text of a court brief in the sense that both involve legal argumentation supporting a legal conclusion. Granted, the format requirements of a judicial opinion differ from those of a court brief. However, for those exercises in which you are asked to write a judicial opinion, the focus will be on your legal argument and your use of the strategy in question, not on whether judicial opinion format requirements have been followed. Thus, the fact that an argument may take place in the form of a fictitious judicial opinion should be of little consequence, for the focus of the exercise will be on your use of a specific persuasive writing strategy, which, again, is transferable to many types of persuasive legal documents.

# VI.    ANOTHER BENEFIT: EMPOWERING YOU AS A SOPHISTICATED "LEGAL READER"

The primary goal of this text is to teach you to be a better legal writer. At the same time, much of the instruction will train you to be a better legal *reader*.

   In this book, we will identify and analyze specific devices that writers can use to make their writing more persuasive. For each strategy we discuss, we will analyze in some detail the communicative and persuasive functions of the strategy and the theoretical bases for those functions. With a more sophisticated understanding of how a writer can persuade a reader, you will better equipped to critically analyze documents for which you are the targeted audience. The more cognizant you are of the processes of persuasion, the more effective you can be at analyzing a piece of persuasive writing.

   Some of the discussions in this book, in fact, are aimed at the student-as-legal-reader just as much as they are aimed at the student-as-legal-writer. Chapter 8, for example, discusses methods by which a writer may endeavor to convince his or her reader that the writer is intelligent and therefore credible. Some of the strategies presented here are common in legal writing, yet not particularly effective. Why address ineffective as well as effective strategies of evincing intelligence? First, this discussion will teach you as a legal *writer* what strategies to avoid. Second, and more important to the present point, it will teach you as a legal *reader* what strategies to watch for in the legal documents you read.

Upon reading this book, you will immediately be able to spot techniques of persuasion in the cases and other legal texts you read. Just as immediately, you will experience the sense of empowerment that flows from this newfound knowledge. You will see that the ability to identify the efforts of persuasion in a legal document and to consciously choose whether to accept or resist them is a powerful skill that unquestionably provides an advantage to the sophisticated legal reader.

# PART I

## THE FUNCTIONS OF LITERARY REFERENCES IN PERSUASIVE WRITING: A MULTIDISCIPLINARY ANALYSIS

[This case involves an appeal under 42 U.S.C. Sec. 1988, which provides that in federal civil rights actions "the court, in its discretion, may allow the prevailing party, other than the United States, a reasonable attorney's fee as part of the costs."] In systemic terms, attorney's fee appeals take up lawyers' and judges' time that could more profitably be devoted to other cases, including the substantive civil rights claims that Section 1988 was meant to facilitate. Regular appellate scrutiny of issues like those in this case also generates a steady stream of opinions, each requiring yet another to harmonize it with the one before or the one after. Ultimately, Section 1988's straightforward command is replaced by a vast body of artificial, judge-made doctrine, with its own arcane procedures, which like a Frankenstein's monster meanders its well-intentioned way through the legal landscape leaving waste and confusion (not to mention circuit-splits) in its wake.

> — *Hensley v. Eckerhart*, 461 U.S. 424, 455 (1983) (Brennan,
> J., concurring in part and dissenting in part)

The Court today approves warrantless helicopter surveillance from an altitude of 400 feet. While Justice O'Connor's opinion gives reason to hope that this altitude may constitute a lower limit, I find considerable cause for concern in the fact that a plurality of four Justices would remove virtually all constitutional barriers to police surveillance from the vantage point of helicopters. The Fourth Amendment demands that we temper our efforts to apprehend criminals with a concern for the impact on our fundamental liberties of the methods we use. I hope it will be a matter of concern to my colleagues that the police surveillance methods they would sanction were among those described 40 years ago in George Orwell's dread vision of life in the 1980's:

> The black-mustachio'd face gazed down from every commanding corner. There was one on the house front immediately opposite. BIG BROTHER IS WATCHING YOU, the caption said. . . . In the far distance a helicopter skimmed down between the roofs, hovered for an instant like a bluebottle, and darted away again with a curving flight. It was the Police Patrol, snooping into people's windows.

*Nineteen Eighty-Four* 4 (1949).
     Who can read this passage without a shudder, and without the instinctive reaction that it depicts life in some country other than ours? I respectfully dissent.

> — *Florida v. Riley*, 488 U.S. 445, 466-67 (1989) (Brennan, J.,
> dissenting)

As these two excerpts from judicial opinions by U.S. Supreme Court Justice William Brennan illustrate, literary references can add force to persuasive legal writing. The first excerpt is from *Hensley v. Eckerhart*, a case involving a narrow issue concerning an interpretation of Section 1988, which provides for attorney's fees in civil rights litigation. Justice Brennan, concurring in part and dissenting in part, argues that allowing appeals on the award of attorney's fees unnecessarily adds to the morass of appellate decisions interpreting Section 1988 and thus "increases the delay, uncertainty, and expense of bringing a civil rights case, even after the plaintiffs have won all the relief they deserve."[1] Justice Brennan further argues that the body of case law resulting from such appeals creates an unintended destructive force that threatens

---

[1] *Hensley*, 461 U.S. at 456.

judicial efficiency and consistency. To add power to this argument, Justice Brennan likens this body of case law to Frankenstein's monster, a reference to Mary Shelley's well-known novel of the same name.

The second excerpt is from *Florida v. Riley*, a case in which the U.S. Supreme Court held that police helicopter surveillance was not unconstitutional. Again Justice Brennan adds persuasive force to his dissent by incorporating a literary reference, this time to George Orwell's chilling political novel, *Nineteen Eighty-Four*.

It has long been recognized that literary references, also called literary allusions, can "add substantially to the subtlety and effectiveness of writing."[2] Little, however, has been written about the specific nature of literary references and the particular functions they can serve in persuasive discourse. In Part I of this book, we will explore literary references in substantial detail, covering several different types of literary references used in legal writing and the unique functions of each. We will also examine how and why these references can improve the persuasive impact of legal writing, using theoretical principles drawn from other disciplines such as classical rhetoric, psychology, literary criticism, and philosophy. Finally, we will explore the potential pitfalls of using literary references inappropriately or carelessly.

## I.    WHY START WITH LITERARY REFERENCES?: DISCOVERING THE "HIDDEN WORLD OF FORCES" UNDERLYING EFFECTIVE PERSUASIVE WRITING

You may be wondering why we are starting our discussion of persuasive writing strategies with what seems to be the purely ornamental concept of literary references. You may also have noticed and wondered about the four full chapters dedicated to this apparently narrow aspect of our subject. A number of reasons—admittedly more pedagogical than substantive—contributed to this decision.

First, starting with such a limited topic allows us to ease into our sophisticated analysis of persuasive writing strategies. In this book, we will be digging deep into the *hows* and *whys* of persuasive writing strategies and will be evaluating the strategies in terms of potentially confusing theoretical principles. Starting with a narrow and concrete topic such as literary references provides an easy entry into what will be an increasingly sophisticated analysis of persuasive legal writing strategies.

Second, because we will examine the functions of literary references in terms of theoretical principles of other disciplines, this topic gives us an opportunity to explore, in a fairly narrow context, the difference between a "theoretical" as opposed to an "anecdotal" approach to persuasive writing strategies. As was explained in the Introduction chapter, our coverage of persuasive writing strategies will include an examination of *why* the strategies are effective based on theoretical principles of other disciplines. This approach of examining the theoretical underpinnings of persuasive writing strategies is markedly different from the primarily anecdotal approach taken in most introductory legal writing courses and, as such, will likely be unfamiliar to most students. Starting with literary references allows us to first experience this

---

[2] Bryan A. Garner, *A Dictionary of Modern Legal Usage* 342 (1987).

different approach in the context of a limited and, therefore, manageable topic.

Third, literary references are unique in that their functions in persuasive writing can only be explained by looking at a number of different disciplines, including psychology, classical rhetoric, literary theory, morality theory, and narrative theory, whereas some persuasive strategies are best explained using only a single theoretical principle. By starting with literary references, we can get an immediate, brief glimpse of many of the different disciplines we will cover in more detail in later chapters.

Lastly, literary references are fun to read. Starting here grabs your attention from the beginning—a persuasive strategy with which we are all familiar!

Why dedicate four chapters to literary references? First of all, it is *not* because they are the most important persuasive writing strategy around. Instead, the answer lies in what a detailed discussion of literary references lets us discover about persuasive writing generally. This book is designed to help you discover the "hidden world of forces" underlying effective persuasive writing. We will learn that effective persuasive writing, far from being haphazard or accidental, is effective for concrete, identifiable reasons. Identifying and examining these reasons, however, requires that we look at persuasive writing under a microscope. In Part I, we focus our microscope on literary references.

We do not have room in this book to completely dissect every persuasive writing strategy; that would take volumes and volumes of text. The most that we can accomplish here is to *introduce* the "hidden world" underlying persuasive writing. And the best way to do this, the best way to change the way you look at persuasive writing, is to choose a specific persuasive writing device and examine it very closely. By analyzing a single, isolated device you will begin to appreciate the extent of the forces underlying persuasive writing. Thus, Part I encompasses both a small-scale and a large-scale goal. Our small-scale goal is to learn about literary references and how they can add to the communicative and persuasive force of our writing. Our large-scale goal is potentially more transformative: It is to see persuasive writing in a whole new way.

## II.   FIVE EFFECTIVE USES OF LITERARY REFERENCES IN PERSUASIVE LEGAL WRITING

Literary references abound in legal writing. When the use of literary references in legal writing is analyzed in detail, however, it quickly becomes clear that not all such references are alike. Literary references do not serve a single function in legal writing; many different types of literary references appear in legal writing, each serving different functions.

In the next four chapters, we will explore the five most effective types of literary references used by persuasive legal writers. As indicated in the outline below, four of these types fall within two general categories; the fifth itself constitutes a distinct category of reference.

> A. Literary References for Nonthematic Comparison
>> Type 1: Literary References for Nonthematic Metaphoric Comparison
>> Type 2: Literary References for Nonthematic Hyperbole

B. Literary References for Borrowed Eloquence
    Type 3: Literary References for Direct Borrowed Eloquence
    Type 4: Literary References for Creative Variation
C. Type 5: Literary References for Thematic Comparison

The terminology used in these titles may at this point be unfamiliar and awkward. Their different characteristics and functions will become clear, however, as you read the various explanations and examples.

# Chapter 2

# Literary References for Nonthematic Comparison

The first general group of literary references that we will discuss are *literary references for nonthematic comparison*. In these types of literary references, a legal writing makes reference to a literary work in an effort to draw a comparison between some person or event in his or her legal case and a character or scene in a literary work. The comparison, however, is nonthematic; that is, it is not made to evoke the general theme of the literary work. This nonthematic use distinguishes this category of literary references from literary references for thematic comparison, discussed in Chapter 4.

Literary references for nonthematic comparison can be subdivided into two categories: *literary references for nonthematic metaphoric comparison* and *literary references for nonthematic hyperbole*. For both of these categories, we will explore their characteristics and the functions they serve in persuasive discourse and consider some cautions regarding their use.

## I.   TYPE 1: LITERARY REFERENCES FOR NONTHEMATIC METAPHORIC COMPARISON

### A.   *The Characteristics of Literary References for Nonthematic Metaphoric Comparison*

The first category of literary references we will explore is *literary references for nonthematic metaphoric comparison*. As the name suggests, this category of literary references has three essential characteristics. First, they are literary references by which a legal writer *compares* some aspect of his or her case to a character, scene, or event from a literary work. Second, the comparison is *metaphoric;* that is, the comparison is figurative or symbolic, not literal. It is important to note, however, that in this context the term "metaphoric" includes both *metaphors* and their close cousins, *similes.* Edward P. J. Corbett and Robert J. Conners offer this helpful explanation of metaphors and similes:

> [A metaphor is] an *implied* comparison between two things of unlike nature that yet have something in common. . . . [A simile is] an *explicit* comparison between two things of unlike nature that yet have something in common. . . . The difference between metaphor and simile lies mainly in the manner of expressing the comparison. Whereas metaphor says, "David was a lion in battle," simile says, "David was *like* a lion in battle." [For both metaphor and

simile] . . . although the comparison is made between two things of unlike nature (*David* and *lion*), there is some respect in which they are similar (e.g., they are courageous, or they fight ferociously, or they are unconquerable in a fight). The thing with which the first thing is compared is to be understood in some "transferred sense": *David* is not literally a *lion*, but he is a lion in some "other sense."[1]

Third, the comparison is *nonthematic*. It is nonthematic because either (1) the aspect of the literary work being alluded to is a minor or incidental aspect of the work, not a major theme of the work, or (2) the literary allusion is being used by the legal writer to support a minor or incidental point in the writer's document, not a major theme of the document.

Let's consider a concrete example:

*Example 2.1*

In the case of *Save Our Cumberland Mountains, Inc. v. Hodel*, 857 F.2d 1516 (D.C. Cir. 1988), the United States Court of Appeals for the D.C. Circuit addresses an issue regarding an award of attorney's fees in a suit under the Surface Mining Control and Reclamation Act. One precedent case for the issue is *Laffey*, a case previously decided by the D.C. Circuit. In its majority opinion in *Hodel*, the D.C. Circuit overrules *Laffey*. In a dissent, Judge Starr writes that, while *Laffey* was severely criticized when it was first decided, its approach to the issue has proven over time to be a good one. Judge Starr also points out that the approach taken in *Laffey* is consistent with the approach taken by the U.S. Supreme Court in later cases. In making this point, Judge Starr states:

> [T]he question remains whether *Laffey* itself faithfully echoes Congress' intent. That may have been a marginally closer question at the time *Laffey* was handed down. But the subsequent decisional law leaves me with not the slightest doubt that *Laffey* vindicates admirably the true Congressional purpose, as divined by the Supreme Court . . . . The clear message of the Supreme Court in its recent cases is precisely to that effect, and therein lies *Laffey*'s normative strength. What some have been tormenting as an ugly duckling has turned out to be a swan.

*Id.* at 1528 (Starr, J., dissenting).

In this excerpt from *Hodel*, Judge Starr uses a nonthematic metaphoric comparison to the children's story, "The Ugly Duckling," by Hans Christian Andersen. Judge Starr includes the reference in an effort to *compare* the *Laffey* case to the famed ugly duckling. The comparison, however, is *metaphoric*, not literal.

---

[1] Edward P. J. Corbett and Robert J. Conners, *Classical Rhetoric for the Modern Student* 396 (4th ed. 1999).

Obviously a precedent case is not literally like a duck. However, like the ugly duckling, who was criticized early in life yet turned out over time to be a beautiful swan, the *Laffey* case over time went from being the subject of criticism to being praiseworthy. Furthermore, the comparison is made in the form of a *metaphor,* rather than a simile. Judge Starr does not explicitly say that *Laffey* is like the ugly duckling; he implies this comparison. In the middle of his discussion of *Laffey,* seemingly out of nowhere, Judge Starr inserts this strange sentence about a duck and a swan, relying on his context to clarify the purpose and meaning of this figurative reference. Had Judge Starr explicitly said that *Laffey* is "like" the ugly duckling, the reference would have been a simile.

Finally, the comparison is *nonthematic*. The theme or moral of "The Ugly Duckling" condemns bigotry and discrimination based on appearance. Clearly, Judge Starr does not evoke that theme in this discussion. He merely compares the transformation over time of the *Laffey* decision to the transformation of Andersen's duckling.

Consider these other examples of literary references for nonthematic metaphoric comparison.

*Example 2.2*

From *People v. Craig*, 581 N.Y.S.2d 987, 989 (N.Y. Sup. Ct. 1992):

> In the instant case the People ask this Court to cross a state boundary to conduct a proceeding to which the defendant has not even consented. A judge of this state who crosses a state line instantly undergoes a transformation as dramatic as Cinderella's midnight metamorphosis; the judge turns into an ordinary citizen traveling in another state, with no more power to hold court or administer oaths and affirmations than any other private person might have.

This opinion writer compares a judge crossing a state line to Cinderella at midnight. The comparison is figurative rather than literal: Clearly, a judge is not literally like Cinderella. Like Cinderella, however, who automatically and suddenly is transformed from princess to scullion at the stroke of twelve, a New York judge automatically and suddenly transforms into an ordinary citizen upon crossing the state border. The writer here uses a simile, as signaled by the phrase "as dramatic as," which makes the comparison explicit. Had the judge written something like, "A judge who crosses a state line becomes Cinderella at midnight," the statement would have been a metaphor. Finally, the comparison is nonthematic. This allusion to the Cinderella story has nothing to do with the fairy tale's theme or moral.

*Example 2.3*

In the case of *State v. Muhammad*, 678 A.2d 164 (N.J. 1996), the New Jersey Supreme Court upholds the constitutionality of New Jersey's "victim-impact" statute. The statute deals with the sentencing stage in capital prosecutions. Under the statute, evidence about a murder victim's character and background and about the impact that the murder had on the victim's survivors may be introduced in connection with the determination of whether the defendant will be sentenced to death or sentenced to some other form of punishment. In a dissent, Judge Handler argues, among other things, that the statute leads to race discrimination in the administration of the death penalty. According to Judge Handler,

> The introduction of victim-impact evidence unacceptably exacerbates the racial disparities evident in capital sentencing. Victim-impact evidence encourages jurors to examine and use, both consciously and unconsciously, the comparative worth of the defendant and the victim. Race unquestionably influences our perceptions. This evidence will therefore set back our attempts to eliminate racial disparities in capital sentencing. Such discriminatory sentencing cannot be tolerated in New Jersey. "[W]hen an institution of justice fosters either overt or hidden use of constitutionally forbidden criteria such as race, social standing, religion, or sexual orientation, it cannot be defended as just." Victim-impact evidence will be the Trojan horse that will bring into every capital prosecution a particularly virulent and volatile form of discrimination.

*Id.* at 203 (Handler, J., dissenting) (citations omitted).

In this excerpt comparing New Jersey's victim-impact statute to the Trojan horse from Homer's *Iliad,* Judge Handler argues that, while the language of the statute appears to be innocent enough on its face, it nevertheless stealthily introduces racial discrimination into the administration of the death penalty in New Jersey. Judge Handler adds force to his argument by likening the statute to the hollow wooden horse filled with Greek soldiers that the citizens of Troy brought into their fortress during the Trojan War. Fooled by the horse's apparently benign purpose, the Trojans did not suspect its hidden destructive force.

The comparison is metaphoric in both the senses we have been discussing: It is figurative, rather than literal; it is implied, rather than explicit. Furthermore, the comparison with the Trojan horse is used nonthematically: Its appearance in the *Iliad* is incidental to the work's complex examination of the themes of *hubris,* civic obligation, and piety.

*Example 2.4*

From *Pipe Liners, Inc. v. American Pipe & Plastics, Inc.*, 893 F.Supp. 704, 706 (S.D. Texas 1995):

> [T]he Court notes to its great dismay that since the filing of the original Motion to Dismiss and Plaintiffs' Reply, additional Motions and Surreplies have found their way to this Court. The Court has denied Defendants' Leave to File Additional Authority for its failure to follow Local Rules, and it now denies leave for Plaintiffs' Surreply.
>
>     This Court, which has one of the largest civil dockets in the

country, finds this paper battle to be a preposterous waste of time for the Court, the attorneys in this case, and their clients, who have to pay for it all. Indeed, it is only one more example of the litigation deficiencies that have clouded the reputation of intellectual property attorneys in this and other trial courts. This endless, and utterly pointless, paper trail makes this extraordinarily busy Court feel like Gulliver bound by the wispy, but multiple, threads of the Lilliputians, and the Court wishes to make as clear as possible to all parties in this case that it has no intention of becoming captive to the glacially slow and relentless litigation maneuvers counsel may have in mind.

*Example 2.5*

From *Harrison v. PPG Industries, Inc.*, 446 U.S. 578, 591 (1980):

The respondents also rely on what the Committee and the Congress did not say about the 1977 amendments to Section 307(b)(1). It is unlikely, the respondents assert, that Congress would have expanded so radically the jurisdiction of the courts of appeals, and divested the district courts of jurisdiction, without some consideration and discussion of the matter. We cannot accept this argument. . . . [I]t would be a strange canon of statutory construction that would require Congress to state in committee reports or elsewhere in its deliberations that which is obvious on the face of a statute. In ascertaining the meaning of a statute, a court cannot, in the manner of Sherlock Holmes, pursue the theory of the dog that did not bark. [FN8]

FN8. Arthur Conan Doyle, *The Silver Blaze*, in *The Complete Sherlock Holmes* (1938).

*Example 2.6*

From *Sieck v. Russo*, 869 F.2d 131, 134 (2d Cir. 1989):

In effect, the defendants' argument is that somewhere between the imposition of a $2,000 fine and the entry of a $1 million default there exists a sanction that would have convinced them to appear for deposition. Apparently, defendants perceive that the function of a reviewing court is to search, like Goldilocks, for a sanction that is not too hard, not too soft, but one that is just right. We, however, prefer to play the other role in that story, and provide the teeth to enforce discovery orders by leaving it to the district court to determine which sanction from among the available range is appropriate. After reviewing the record, we have no doubt that the entry of default judgments against each of the defendants was an entirely proper exercise of the court's discretion.

**Exercise 2.1    Identifying and Understanding Literary References for Nonthematic Metaphoric Comparison**

Choose one of the last three examples above (Example 2.4, 2.5, or 2.6) and explain in a few paragraphs why it is an example of a literary reference for nonthematic metaphoric comparison. Explain (1) how it involves a *comparison*, (2) why the comparison is *figurative* rather than literal, (3) whether it is a *metaphor* or a *simile*, and (4) why the comparison is *nonthematic*. Use the discussions of Examples 2.1, 2.2, and 2.3 as guidelines. If necessary or helpful, look up the full case from which the quote was taken or the literary work referenced.

**Exercise 2.2    Identifying and Understanding Literary References for Nonthematic Metaphoric Comparison**

Expand the assignment described in Exercise 2.1 above to include a discussion of all three of Examples 2.4, 2.5, and 2.6.

## B.    *The Functions of Literary References for Nonthematic Metaphoric Comparison*

Now that we have an understanding of the characteristics of literary references for nonthematic metaphoric comparison, we will explore the communicative and persuasive functions they serve in legal writing. In this book, our discussions of persuasive writing strategies will use various theoretical structures to explore in depth how and why they work. Regarding literary references for nonthematic metaphoric comparison, we will explore their functions in terms of several theoretical principles from discursive psychology, literary criticism, and classical rhetoric.

### 1.   Discursive Psychology Theory

Discursive psychology involves the study of the mental processes involved in human discourse and communication.[2] One theoretical principle of discursive psychology is known as Shared Knowledge Theory. According to Shared Knowledge Theory, communication between people commonly involves brief allusions and references to concepts previously known to both parties. References to this shared knowledge

---

[2] *See, e.g.,* Derek Edwards, *Discourse and Cognition* (1997).

allow the discourse participants to consider that prior knowledge and to bring it to bear on the current topic of conversation. Thus, according to this theory, communication often involves a kind of "shorthand" whereby people in a conversation briefly refer to concepts of shared knowledge.[3]

Shared Knowledge Theory provides significant insight into why literary references for nonthematic metaphoric comparison are effective in persuasive discourse. This type of literary reference helps communicate the substance of an argument quickly and efficiently. Because the literary work alluded to is (or should be) familiar to the reader, it is part of the "shared knowledge" of the writer and the reader. With a brief reference to this literary work, the writer is able to conjure up relevant preexisting knowledge in the mind of the reader which the reader can then use in considering the matter at hand. Thus, this type of literary reference allows a writer to communicate an idea in a very immediate way by tapping into the reader's own prior experiences, in this case, literary ones.

Let's consider an example. In Example 2.1 above, Judge Starr sought to communicate forcefully that over time the *Laffey* case went from being criticized to being praiseworthy. He communicated his point quickly and efficiently by alluding briefly to a literary analogy: the well-known children's tale of the supposed ugly duckling who grew into a beautiful swan. Thus, Judge Starr was able to take advantage of the reader's prior literary knowledge to communicate his point.

## 2.  Literary Theory

Very similar to discourse psychology's theory of "shared knowledge" is the concept of "intertextuality," taken from contemporary literary theory. According to literary theory, every reader has a "mental storehouse" of past literary experiences accumulated throughout their lives. Intertextuality is the process that occurs when readers consciously connect a new text, such as a case opinion, with their past literary experiences. According to literary theorists, bringing past literary knowledge to bear on the analysis of a new text helps readers to better and more fully understand that text. Joel Wingard explains the process this way:

> Often, one text in an intertextual relation with another sheds light on the other or gives you a handle on it. Sometimes there's a contrast that helps you understand the text you're reading. Sometimes you can see common themes or approaches to a topic.[4]

Intertextuality, like shared knowledge, helps to explain what makes literary references for nonthematic comparison so effective in legal writing. By making this type of literary reference, the writer hopes to tap into the reader's mental storehouse of past literary knowledge, thus enabling the reader to bring that information to bear on the new text. This past information can be used by the reader to more fully

---

[3] *See, e.g., id.* at 114-41.

[4] Joel Wingard, *Literature: Reading and Responding to Fiction, Poetry, Drama, and the Essay* 30-31 (1996).

understand the analysis at hand.

### 3.   Classical Rhetoric Theory

Classical Rhetoric Theory, discussed in more detail in Chapters 6 through 10, involves the study of the art of persuasion. Not surprisingly, classical rhetoric can help us significantly in our attempt to understand the communicative and persuasive functions of literary metaphors.

**a. The *Logos* Function.** One process of persuasion recognized by classical rhetoricians is that of *logos*. Logos refers to the process of persuading through substance and logical argument. (For more on logos, see Chapter 6.) Logos encompasses most of the persuasive arguments lawyers routinely employ: arguments based on mandatory rules, arguments based on analogies to precedent cases, and arguments based on policy, to name a few.

Classical rhetoricians have long recognized that metaphors—including literary metaphors—can help communicate the substance (logos) of an argument. This is particularly true when the argument or point is difficult to explain in literal terms and can more effectively and efficiently be explained through a metaphoric analogy. Consider, for example, our previous discussion regarding Example 2.3. In Example 2.3, we saw that Judge Handler wanted to communicate to the reader that New Jersey's victim-impact statute, although benign on its face, introduces a dangerous type of racial discrimination into the administration of the death penalty. To help communicate his point, Judge Handler analogized the statute to the well-known story of the Trojan horse. The comparison was, clearly, metaphoric rather than literal; the victim-impact statute is not literally like a giant wooden horse. Yet, the statute is similar to the Trojan horse in terms of the precise point Judge Handler was endeavoring to communicate: An innocent outward appearance can disguise an underlying destructive force. Thus, this metaphoric literary reference helped Judge Handler communicate the substance (logos) of his argument.

It is, in fact, a combination of "logos theory" from classical rhetoric, "shared knowledge theory" from discursive psychology, and "intertextuality" from literary theory that helps us to fully understand the communicative power of literary metaphors. Being a type of metaphor, literary metaphors provide readers with analogies that help communicate substance—according to logos theory. Furthermore, because literary metaphors (as opposed to nonliterary metaphors) involve references to literary characters or events, such references allow the writer to tap into the readers' mental storehouse of literary texts. As a consequence, according to shared knowledge theory and intertextuality theory, the reader is able to bring his or her prior knowledge of the literary work to bear on the issue to fully appreciate the analogy being made.

**b. The *Pathos* Function.** A second process of persuasion recognized by classical rhetoricians is that of *pathos*. Pathos refers to persuasion through emotional argument, which classical rhetoricians recognize as being coequal with logical arguments using logos.

Moreover, as we will explore more fully in later chapters (see especially Chapter 6), the concept of *pathos* actually encompasses two separate elements relevant to persuasion through emotion. The first, "emotional substance," refers to the process of persuading by arousing emotional reactions in readers regarding the substance of the matter under consideration. This is the type of emotional argument with which attorneys are most familiar. Any arguments designed to arouse emotions such as pity, hate, anger, fear, compassion, regret, guilt, patriotism, and the like are arguments involving "emotional substance."

The second element, "medium mood control," refers to aspects of a writer's document that affect a reader's mood. That is, it refers to aspects of the *medium* used to communicate a concept, rather than the substantive concept itself, that affect the mood or disposition of the reader. Classical rhetoricians recognize that the medium of a message—in addition to the message itself—can have an emotional impact on a reader. Writers who can, through their writing style, put readers in a contented and receptive mood have an advantage over writers whose writing style irritates or bores their readers.

Both "emotional substance" and "medium mood control" are relevant to understanding the persuasive force of literary metaphors. Literary metaphors used in substantive emotional arguments can greatly enhance the argument's inherent emotional force. In Example 2.3, Judge Handler sought to elicit feelings of fear and dread in his audience regarding the racial discrimination resulting from New Jersey's victim-impact statute. By incorporating the reference to the Trojan horse, Judge Handler used shared knowledge and intertextuality to evoke the fear and dread the readers of that story felt when they originally read the *Iliad* and imaginatively experienced the fate that befell Trojans when they opened their fortress to the Greeks' deadly ploy. The literary allusion thus enhanced Judge Handler's substantive emotional argument.

Literary metaphors can also contribute positively to "medium mood control." There are several things about literary metaphors, as stylistic writing devices, that help put a reader in a positive and receptive mood. First, as we saw in the discussion of logos above, metaphors make understanding a writer's point easier for the reader. This undoubtedly has a pleasing effect on the reader. Second, because metaphors involve symbolic or figurative comparisons, they are like "riddles" to be solved by the reader. Solving these riddles—making the mental connection between two seemingly dissimilar things—is often pleasing to a reader. Third, metaphors—particularly clever ones—unexpectedly juxtapose two things that the reader may not have thought about as having a symbolic similarity. This unexpected comparison can be entertaining to the reader. Finally, literary metaphors, unlike nonliterary metaphors, evoke pleasing memories of the literary work referenced. For all these reasons, literary metaphors can help becharm a reader. Once the reader falls into this positive and receptive mood, the writer's substantive point will be more welcome.

**c. The *Ethos* Function.** A third process of persuasion recognized by classical rhetoricians is that of *ethos*. Ethos (covered in more detail in Chapters 6 through 8) refers to establishing and maintaining credibility in the eyes of the audience. The more credible a writer appears to a reader, the more weight the reader will give to the writer's views.

According to classical rhetoricians, including Aristotle, Cicero, and Quintilian, literary metaphors help establish a writer's credibility by demonstrating his or her creativity and resourcefulness. As Aristotle put it, the skill of constructing effective metaphors "is, in itself, a sign of genius."[5] Similarly, Cicero stated that good metaphors are a "mark of cleverness."[6] Finally, Quintilian, in a particularly insightful statement, said, "[B]y the employment of skillful ornament (including metaphor) the orator commends himself at the same time (as he commends his argument)."[7]

Literary metaphors also serve an additional ethos function. Because the referenced work is part of the "shared knowledge" of the writer and the reader, an allusion to it operates like an "inside joke" between the two. The "joke" is only accessible to those who share the knowledge of the referenced work. Because the reader can appreciate the shorthand represented by the literary reference, the literary allusion helps to create a positive "bond" that will often encourage the reader to trust the writer.

Finally, literary metaphors—unlike nonliterary metaphors—can serve one additional ethos function: They demonstrate that the writer is educated and well-read. A writer, however, should be careful not to use overly obscure or sophisticated literary references in an attempt to impress readers. As we will see, few things more annoy readers than encountering unknown literary references. Overreaching for sophisticated literary references will actually do a writer's argument more harm than good.

**d. The Rhetorical Style Function.** Finally, classical rhetoricians recognize the importance of *style* for drawing emphasis in persuasive writing. (See Chapters 9 and 10.) From a stylistic standpoint, metaphors, including literary metaphors, allow a writer to present ideas in unexpected and clever ways, thus serving to emphasize points and make them more memorable to the reader.

## C.     *Cautions and Suggestions Regarding the Use of Literary References for Nonthematic Metaphoric Comparison*

Now that we have discussed the characteristics and functions of literary references for nonthematic metaphoric comparison, we will consider some cautions and suggestions regarding their use.

### 1.   Obscure Literary References

The first and perhaps most important issue when considering using a literary

---

[5] Aristotle, *Aristotle's Poetics: A Translation and Commentary for Students of Literature* 41 (Leon Golden trans. 1968), *quoted in* Michael Frost, *Greco-Roman Analysis of Metaphoric Reasoning*, 2 Legal Writing 113, 127 (1996) (hereinafter "Frost's *Metaphoric Reasoning*").

[6] Cicero, *De Oratore* 125 (E. Sutton trans. 1942), *quoted in* Frost's *Metaphoric Reasoning*, *supra* note 5, at 127.

[7] III Marius Fabius Quintilianus, *Institutio Oratoria* 213 (H. E. Butler trans. 1954), *quoted in* Frost's *Metaphoric Reasoning*, *supra* note 5, at 127.

reference for nonthematic metaphoric comparison is whether the literary work referenced will be known to the writer's audience. If the reference is obscure or pretentious, the writer risks confusing, alienating—or worse, offending—the reader. Some legal writers insert obscure literary references into their argument, partially to impress the reader and partially, perhaps, to amuse themselves. Such a strategy, however, unwisely focuses on the needs, concerns, and desires of the writer, not the reader. Persuasive writing should be "reader-based." It is unwise for a writer selfishly to include arcane literary references for his or her own self-gratification. Even if readers can understand the writer's point without understanding the literary reference, they are likely to be put off by the writer's pretentiousness and lack of concern for the reader. It should go without saying, but much legal writing demonstrates that it cannot: It is not a good idea to insult the very person you are trying to persuade.

In terms of the "functions" of literary references discussed previously, obscure references defeat the ethos and pathos functions. Obscure literary references damage the writer's credibility in the eyes of the reader and, by frustrating and perhaps even insulting the reader, they create a negative emotional reaction that undermines the writer's medium mood control over readers.

Furthermore, an obscure reference defeats the communicative functions this writing strategy is designed to serve. As we saw previously, literary metaphors serve important communicative functions according to discursive psychology's shared knowledge theory, literary theory's concept of intertextuality, and classical rhetoric's concept of *logos*. These functions are served, however, only when the literary work alluded to is known to the reader. Obscure literary references hinder rather than facilitate communication.

Consider the following example.

*Example 2.7*

From *ITT v. Vencap, Ltd.,* 519 F.2d 1001, 1015 (2d Cir. 1975), discussing 28 U.S.C. Section 1350:

> This old but little used section is a kind of legal Lohengrin; although it has been with us since the first Judiciary Act, . . . no one seems to know from whence it came.

Few readers—other than those well-versed in German mythology or opera—would know the reference to Lohengrin in this excerpt. For those who do not know it (and I would have included myself among them until I looked it up), Lohengrin was a knight of the Holy Grail in Germanic legend who refused to reveal to anyone the mystery of his origins. This knight was also the subject of an opera by the same name by German composer Richard Wagner. It is only by knowing this information that the reader can appreciate and make sense of this literary allusion in *ITT v. Vencap*. Granted, given this knowledge, the allusion becomes a particularly clever one, comparing the statute's unknown origins to those of Lohengrin. The cleverness of the metaphor aside, however, obscure literary allusions such as this are not effective, because most readers will not understand the references or appreciate them.[8]

Moreover, including an explanation of an obscure reference—either in the text or in a footnote—is not the answer. If the allusion has to be explained to the reader, many of the functions such references are designed to serve are defeated. If in drafting a literary reference you find yourself tempted to include an explanation of it, delete both the explanation and the reference. The desire to include an explanation indicates that even you at some gut level believe that the reference is too obscure.

The question then becomes, what should you do if you are unsure as to whether your readers will know a particular literary reference? There is no easy answer to this question. Obviously, the more information you have about your audience, the better equipped you will be to make this decision. Also relevant is the level of concern that you as the writer have about offending your reader. You would want to be less adventurous, for example, if you were an attorney writing to a judge, as opposed to an attorney writing to a fellow attorney. Judges, on the other hand, have much more freedom. As Bryan A. Garner points out, "It is perhaps easier for judges than for practicing lawyers to use literary allusions, for judges have a guaranteed readership and do not suffer directly if anyone (or everyone) fails to appreciate their allusions."[9]

In the end it comes down to a judgment call. You would be well advised to err on the side of conservatism and omit references about which you are doubtful. If, however, it is a close call, and you really want to include the reference, you should, at a minimum, follow the advice of Charles Alan Wright. Professor Wright suggests that, if any chance exists that readers may not recognize a literary reference, the text of the discussion should be arranged so that they can understand the point without necessarily understanding the literary reference.[10] Consider again Example 2.7 above. Despite my prior criticism of the Lohengrin allusion, its presentation in this instance does satisfy Professor Wright's guideline. The text of the discussion is arranged so that readers can understand the writer's point: The origin of Section 1350 is a mystery. Consequently, the possible damage the obscure reference might cause is minimized.

---

[8] Criticism of the allusion to Lohengrin in *ITT v. Vencap* is not universal among legal writing experts. In fact, two such experts, Bryan A. Garner and Charles Alan Wright, cite this exact excerpt from *ITT v. Vencap* as an example of effective literary allusion. *See* Bryan A. Garner, A Dictionary of Modern Legal Usage 343 (1987); Charles Alan Wright, *Literary Allusion in Legal Writing: The Haynsworth-Wright Letters*, 1 Scribes J. Legal Writing 1, 3-4 (1990).

[9] Garner, *supra* note 8, at 342.

[10] Wright, *supra* note 8, at 4-5.

## 2. Be Conscious of Cultural Differences Between Writer and Reader

Related to the warning to avoid "obscure" literary references is a warning to avoid literary references that may be culture-specific and hence unknown to a reader from a different culture. Like society in general, legal writing audiences, such as judges, other attorneys, governmental officials, and business leaders, are becoming increasingly more multiethnic and multicultural. One cannot assume that all cultures in our society will have been exposed to the same body of literary works. Literary works that may be pervasive in one culture may be completely unknown in another. Thus, when evaluating a reader's potential appreciation of a literary reference you are considering including in a legal document, consider carefully any cultural differences that may render the reference obscure to your targeted audience.

## 3. Forced Literary Metaphors

"Forced" literary metaphors, that is, those "'where there is no real resemblance' or which are 'too far-fetched,'"[11] should also be avoided. Consider the following, for example:

*Example 2.8*

From *Brush v. Office of Personnel Management*, 982 F.2d 1554, 1559 (Fed. Cir. 1992):

> The language of this statute is as clear as a glass slipper, there is no shoehorn in the legislative history, and the government, just as surely as Cinderella's step-mother, cannot make the fit.

In this example, it takes two similes and a metaphor—all in one sentence—to complete the writer's metaphoric analogy. In an effort to incorporate an allusion to Cinderella, the writer has to equate the statute at hand with the glass slipper, the legislative history to a shoehorn, and the government to Cinderella's step-mother. If a literary reference takes that much work, it's not worth it. In this situation, the literary analogy—like the step-sister's foot—is forced where it doesn't easily and effectively fit. As a consequence, the literary metaphor seems contrived, awkward, and unpersuasive. (This excerpt also involves a mixed metaphor. First the glass slipper is alluded to for its properties as "glass"—that is, it is as clear as the language of the statute in question. Then the glass slipper is alluded to for its properties as a "shoe"—that is, it is incapable of accommodating a "forced fit." This mixing of metaphorical meanings adds to the confusion created by the allusion.)

---

[11] Frost's *Metaphoric Reasoning*, *supra* note 5, at 127 (quoting Cicero, *supra* note 6, at 129).

## 4.  Overly Simplistic or Overly Grand Literary Metaphors

Overly simplistic, obvious, trite, or cliched literary metaphors should also be avoided. By way of example, referring to someone suddenly lifted from obscurity to a position of esteem as a "Cinderella," or referring to someone prone to sounding false alarms as "crying wolf," is not so much cleverness as it is cliche. Hackneyed literary metaphors like these add very little persuasive force to your writing.

As a related matter, overly grand literary metaphors should be avoided. If a point is a rather minor one in your document, avoid including an overly grand or dramatic literary metaphor in explaining it. Such references confuse and distract readers more than they help.

## 5.  Overuse of Literary Metaphors

It is also important not to overuse literary metaphors. The impact of literary metaphors, like that of most stylistic devices, comes in large part from their unexpectedness. Used too frequently, literary metaphors lose this quality and wear the reader out. As Thomas Haggard states (appropriately phrased in the form of a simile): "[Metaphors] are like strong seasoning: a dash will enhance the flavor enormously, but too much will ruin the dish."[12]

## 6.  Allusions to Children's Books

As you have probably noticed, several of the examples in this section have used references to children's stories. All of these examples came from judicial opinions and, as we discussed previously, judges have much more latitude in their writing. Thus, you may be wondering whether such references are appropriate for lawyers drafting serious legal documents, such as appellate briefs. Light-hearted or mock-serious references are definitely inappropriate, as are any other references that might be interpreted as showing a lack of respect for the court or other recipient of the document or lack of serious regard for the matter at hand.

This being said, attorneys need not automatically rule out the use of children's books or other popular writing as sources for the literary references in their documents. First, because such works are widely distributed and known, references to them are likely to be understood by most if not all readers. Second, although many such works may have been primarily meant for children, they often carry important universal messages. Finally, these works—with their ugly ducklings, wish-granting fairy godmothers, bed-sleeping bears, and various other fantastic creatures—offer dramatically vivid characters and scenes that can serve as great resources for metaphoric analogies.

Again, the writer must make a judgment call, evaluating the situation and targeted audience. If, in drafting a legal document, you are tempted to include a clever literary reference to a children's book, yet are concerned that some readers may think it too informal or childish, consider the strategy used by the writer of the following appellate brief submitted to the U.S. Supreme Court:

---

[12] Thomas R. Haggard, *Rhetoric in Legal Writing, Part I*, 8-Jun S. C. Law. 13 (1997).

*Example 2.9*

From Brief of Tax Executives Institute, Inc., as Amicus Curie in support of Petitioners, 1998 WL 778386, at *21, *South Central Bell Telephone Company v. Alabama*, 526 U.S. 160 (1999) (No. 97-2045):

> In this case, the Supreme Court of Alabama embraced a bogus theory of res judicata to deny taxpayers a refund of illegally extracted monies. If Alabama's judicial alchemy succeeds, state courts will become Wonderland, a place where the rules no longer matter. If taxpayers win by the rules, the States—like the Queen of Hearts in her game of croquet—will consider themselves free to change them. The stakes here, however, are much greater than those encountered in a fanciful game of croquet. Accordingly, the Court should end its willing suspension of disbelief concerning the State's commitment to protect the constitutional rights of business taxpayers and thereby vivify the core values of the federal system and the Supremacy Clause.

In this excerpt, the brief writer compares the state courts' treatment of tax issues to the Queen of Hearts in Lewis Carroll's *Alice's Adventures in Wonderland*, who felt free on a whim to change the rules of her croquet game. To avoid any possible negative reaction by the court to this arguably "childish" literary reference, the attorney follows the reference up by stating: "The stakes here, however, are much greater than those encountered in a fanciful game of croquet." This statement assures the court that, despite the attorney's reference to Wonderland, the attorney is not taking the matter lightly. (Additionally, this statement helps to emphasize the importance of the issue to the court.) While such qualifying statements are not always necessary when using popular literary references, they are an option available to hesitant brief writers.

### 7.   "Premeditation" versus "Inspiration" in the Creation of Literary Metaphors

You may be thinking to yourself that all of this information on literary references may be interesting, but that it has little relevance to your writing. You may feel that their use demands creativity, that you have no—or, at least, very few—creative bones in your body, and that effective literary references can only be drafted by the artistically gifted. In other words, you may feel that drafting literary metaphors is not a learned but an innate skill.

This couldn't be farther from the truth. As in the case of most stylistic writing devices, effective use of literary allusion comes from conscious effort and hard work; it is not limited to those with natural creativity. Classical rhetoricians have long emphasized that effective persuasive writing derives from the conscious deployment of well thought out writing strategies. According to them, effective persuasive writing style involves two steps: (1) deciding which point in a discussion to emphasize using a stylistic device, and (2) coming up with an effective stylistic device to accomplish the task. (For more on stylistic devices, see Chapter 10.) As Michael Frost has stated, "[drafting an effective metaphor] is more a matter of premeditation than it is of inspiration. Good advocates do not just hope that an apt metaphor will occur to them; instead they consciously seek or create the proper metaphor to achieve a specific rhetorical effect."[13]

Any writer can draft effective literary metaphors. The key lies in knowledge and commitment: knowledge of what constitutes effective literary allusion, and commitment to undertaking the work necessary to apply this knowledge. This section has supplied the necessary knowledge. Using it is up to you.

**Exercise 2.3     Evaluating the Functions and Effectiveness of Literary References for Nonthematic Metaphoric Comparison**

From the examples of literary reference for nonthematic metaphoric comparison set out earlier (Examples 2.4, 2.5, and 2.6), choose one and write a few paragraphs (1) explaining the communicative and persuasive functions the reference serves in the judicial opinion from which it was taken, and (2) evaluating the effectiveness of the reference in terms of the cautions discussed above. If necessary or helpful, look up the full case from which the quote was taken or the literary work referenced.

**Exercise 2.4     Evaluating the Functions and Effectiveness of Literary References for Nonthematic Metaphoric Comparison**

Expand the assignment described in Exercise 2.3 above to include a discussion of all three of Examples 2.4, 2.5, and 2.6.

## II.     TYPE 2: LITERARY REFERENCES FOR NONTHEMATIC HYPERBOLE

*Literary references for nonthematic hyperbole* constitute the second category of effective literary references. As for the first category, we will explore the characteristics of these literary references and the functions they serve in persuasive legal writing and offer suggestions for using them to greatest effect.

### A.     *The Characteristics of Literary References for Nonthematic Hyperbole*

---

[13] Frost's *Metaphoric Reasoning*, *supra* note 5, at 126.

This category of literary references is very similar to the first in that it involves *comparison* between some aspect of a legal case and a character, scene, or event in a literary work. Also like the first category, this category involves comparisons that are *nonthematic*. The primary difference between this category of literary references and the first is that the comparisons at issue here are not metaphoric, symbolic, or figurative; rather, they are made to express an exaggeration. That is, these comparisons involve *hyperbole*.

Hyperbole is defined as the intentional and dramatic use of exaggeration. As Theodore M. Bernstein explains:

> [Hyperbole involves] exaggeration to intensify what is being mentioned. . . . [H]yperbole "lies without deceiving." When we say, "I'm eternally grateful" or "His Cadillac is as long as a Pullman car" we are indulging in hyperbole. We don't expect anyone to take what we say literally; we are lying but not deceiving. Hyperbole is usually thought of as an isolated expression inserted into speech or writing to heighten the effect.[14]

The literary references we are discussing under this category involve "literary hyperbole." That is, they involve instances where a legal writer likens the attributes of a person from his or her real case to those of a comparable yet exaggerated literary character, or where a legal writer likens a real situation to a comparable yet exaggerated literary scene. Literary works often involve exaggerated characters and scenes. Consequently, comparisons to literary works often involve exaggeration—hence, hyperbole.

It is true that the first category of literary references—literary metaphors—can also involve exaggeration. Consider, for example, the comparison between New Jersey's victim-impact statute and the Trojan horse in Example 2.3, or the comparison between attorneys' motions and the ropes of the Lilliputians that bound Gulliver in Example 2.4. Both of these comparisons are exaggerated. However, these comparisons are also metaphoric and figurative. Literary hyperbole, on the other hand, refers to exaggerated, yet nonmetaphoric, comparisons.

Let's consider some examples.

*Example 2.10*

From *Lanier v. State*, 709 So.2d 112, 117 (Fla. 3d Dist. Ct. App. 1998) (Levy, J., concurring):

> "[O]verwhelming" evidence was presented which implicated the Defendant. That evidence included the eyewitness identification of the victim, the fact that the Defendant was found in the passenger seat of a car which had been observed by police at a location consistent with the direction of travel of the assailant's get-away vehicle, and [the fact that] the Caprice was identified by the victim

---

[14] Theodore M. Bernstein, *The Careful Writer: A Modern Guide to English Usage* 396 (1982).

as the car used in the robbery. If that were not enough, the roadway between the victim's home and the location where the Defendant was apprehended was littered with the victim's property in a fashion reminiscent of the famous bread crumbs and pebbles left along the path of Hansel and Gretel.

In this example, Judge Levy humorously *compares* the defendant's trail of dropped loot to the trail of pebbles and bread crumbs left by Hansel and Gretel in the children's story familiar from the fairy tale collections of the Brothers Grimm. The comparison here is not metaphoric or figurative. In fact, the comparison is almost literal: Both scenes involve dropped items that create a trail. Hansel and Gretel left pebbles and crumbs to help them find their way home from the forest; the defendant in *Lanier* inadvertently dropped portions of the victim's property, leaving a trail that authorities could follow. The comparison is not literal, however, because it involves an *exaggeration*. The trail left by the defendant was not as clearly marked as that left by Hansel and Gretel. To suggest that it was constitutes an exaggeration. Yet, the reader is not deceived by this exaggeration because from the context the reader can see that the writer makes the comparison simply to emphasize the unusual fact that the defendant left a trail—any trail—that the authorities could follow. This is the essence of hyperbole.

Finally, the comparison is *nonthematic*. This allusion to the tale of Hansel and Gretel has nothing to do with the theme or moral of that story; the scene alluded to is an incidental detail of the story.

*Example 2.11*

From *Reebok International Limited v. Sebelen*, 959 F.Supp. 553, 557-58 (D. Puerto Rico 1997) (citations omitted):

> In light of defendants' tactics in this case—openly violating the Preliminary Injunction, tampering with evidence, flooding the docket with frivolous motions, stalling any and all discovery for over a year, answering the sanctions order with yet another frivolous motion, and ignoring the Court's order to pay sanctions—this Court has no other recourse but to enter default judgment against defendants. The Court in particular marvels at counsels' continuous and recalcitrant insistence regarding the Court's lack of subject matter jurisdiction, an issue upon which the Court ruled not once, but twice, and after which the Court expressly ordered defendants to engage in discovery proceedings. Time and again during the February 25 hearing, counsel [for defendants] . . . refused to provide a cogent and persuasive justification for the defendants' failure to comply with the discovery proceedings, to timely pay the Court-imposed sanctions and to account for the missing Subject Shoes. Like a modern-day Bartleby, counsel [for defendants] . . . , upon the Court's repeated inquiries regarding the breach of the preliminary injunction and the noncompliance with discovery orders, figuratively replied, "I would prefer not to address those issues but rather talk about the

lack of jurisdiction." Such nonchalant behavior, this Court will not tolerate.

In this example, Judge Casellas of the Puerto Rico District Court compares the behavior of the defendants' attorney to the behavior of Bartleby the Scrivener from Herman Melville's classic tale of the same name. In the *Reebok* case, the defendants' attorney continuously fails to respond to the court's orders and requests, much to the dismay of the court. Similarly, in "Bartleby the Scrivener," a lawyer becomes exasperated with his assistant scrivener because the assistant, whenever he is asked to perform a task, always replies: "I would prefer not to." Clearly, this comparison is direct, not symbolic or figurative. The comparison is an exaggeration, however. The character in Melville's tale continues saying "I would prefer not to" in response to every request made of him—even eating—until he ultimately dies in prison. Obviously, the defendants' attorney in the above case does not go this far in his refusal to respond to the court's requests. Nevertheless, the reader is not deceived by this exaggeration. The reader can see from the context that the judge makes this comparison in an effort to highlight the unusual and unacceptable behavior of the defense lawyer in this case. Again, the writer's point is emphasized through literary hyperbole.[15] The Bartleby reference is also nonthematic: The writer does not mean to evoke the theme or moral of Melville's tale.

*Example 2.12*

In the case of *Ahring v. Truck Insurance Exchange*, No. 95-16838, 1997 WL 525161 (9th Cir. Nov. 4, 1996), the Ninth Circuit affirms a judgment awarded against an insurance company based on insurer bad faith. In a separate opinion, Judge Farris criticizes the majority's logic in reaching its conclusion. In the beginning of the opinion, Judge Farris states:

> The majority upholds the $500,000 insurer bad faith award on an illogical theory that Lewis Carroll's Mad Hatter would have been proud of. . . .

*Id.* at *9 (Farris, J., concurring in part and dissenting in part).

*Example 2.13*

From *Sanford v. State*, 589 A.2d 74, 81(Md. Ct. Spec. App. 1991):

> The appellant, finally, protests with a sense of offended dignity

---

[15] A different question is whether the average reader would know this reference to "Bartleby the Scrivener." Even Judge Casellas had some doubt. In the *Reebok* opinion, Judge Casellas includes not one, but two separate explanations of Melville's tale. *See Reebok*, 959 F.Supp. at 554-55, 558 n.1. As we saw in our discussion above of obscure references, if a reference has to be explained to the reader, many of the functions it is designed to serve are defeated.

that: "A mantel clock, on a mantel, is not of such a distinctive character so as to immediately lead one to believe that it is stolen. Mantel clocks are routinely found in business settings without creating the assumption that they are stolen."

That may be true—in a vacuum. The scene at Ted's Lounge, however, did not exist in a vacuum but was one lifted straight from the pages of Oliver Twist. It is one thing to accept with benign equanimity an antique clock sitting on a mantel in a business establishment. It is something quite different to fail to see the significance of just such a clock sitting on a mantel if the business establishment is Fagin's den of thieves and you are armed with the knowledge that Bill Sykes and Nancy have stolen such a clock within the [last] month and have confessed, moreover, to having just fenced the clock with Fagin.

---

**Exercise 2.5     Identifying and Understanding Literary References for Nonthematic Hyperbole**

Choose one of the last two examples, 2.12 or 2.13, and write a few paragraphs explaining why it is a literary reference for nonthematic hyperbole. Explain (1) how it involves a *comparison*, (2) why the comparison is *direct* rather than metaphoric, (3) why the comparison involves *hyperbole*, and (4) why the comparison is *nonthematic*. Use the discussions of Examples 2.10 and 2.11 as guidelines. If necessary or helpful, look up the full case from which the quote was taken or the literary source referenced.

---

**Exercise 2.6     Identifying and Understanding Literary References for Nonthematic Hyperbole**

Expand the assignment described in Exercise 2.5 above to include a discussion of both Example 2.12 and 2.13.

---

## B.     The Functions of Literary References for Nonthematic Hyperbole

The characteristics of literary references for nonthematic hyperbole are similar to those of the literary metaphors discussed previously. Not surprisingly then, many of their functions, too, are the same. The main difference, as we will see, involves the relative importance of the various functions.

### 1.   Classical Rhetoric Theory: Rhetorical Style

As we have seen, the main function of literary hyperbole is to add emphasis to a specific point in a written document. According to classical rhetoric theory, hyperbole—including literary hyperbole—adds emphasis to a point through exaggeration. By comparing an aspect of a real case to an exaggerated literary character or scene, a legal writer highlights that aspect. Effectively used, hyperbole is not deceptive; the reader can tell from the context that an exaggeration has been incorporated to make a rhetorical point. Examples 2.10 and 2.11 illustrate the prominence and effectiveness of this function of literary hyperbole.

### 2.   Discursive Psychology Theory and Literary Theory: Shared Knowledge and Intertextuality

Like literary metaphors, literary hyperbole helps to communicate the substance of an argument quickly and efficiently. References to literary characters or scenes allow writers to tap into their readers' mental storehouses of literary experience, thus enabling readers to bring that prior knowledge to bear on the analysis at hand.

### 3.   Classical Rhetoric Theory: Logos

Also like literary metaphors, literary hyperbole aids in communicating the substance of a point by providing the reader with an understandable and vivid analogy. The only difference is that literary hyperbole makes direct rather than indirect or symbolic comparisons.

In fact, literary hyperbole is particularly helpful in communicating substance for two reasons. First, because the comparison is not metaphoric or symbolic, the analogy is more direct and thus easier for the reader to understand. Second, because the literary character or scene alluded to is exaggerated, the analogy becomes even clearer to the reader. What better way to explain a point than to provide a direct, yet exaggerated, analogy? Because the literary event alluded to is exaggerated in terms of the exact concept the writer is attempting to communicate, the reference assists greatly in achieving the desired communication.

### 4.   Classical Rhetoric Theory: Pathos

Literary hyperbole also serves some *pathos* functions. In terms of "emotional substance," literary hyperbole can add significantly to the emotional reaction generated by a substantive emotional argument. Consider Example 2.11. Judge Casellas was there attempting to elicit feelings of disbelief and incredulity in his readers to highlight the intolerable behavior of the defense attorney. To assist in generating these feelings, the judge compared the attorney to the exaggerated literary character, Bartleby the scrivener. By doing so, the writer evoked the reader's stored feelings of incredulity over Bartleby's actions and character. As a consequence, the writer enhanced his emotional argument.

Literary hyperbole can also serve some "medium mood control" functions. Although not as dramatic as literary metaphors, literary hyperbole can be pleasing to the reader, leading to a positive *emotional* impact. Literary hyperbole can be pleasing to a reader for a number of reasons. First, direct, yet exaggerated, analogies make it easier for readers to get the writer's point, which undoubtedly has a pleasing effect on them. Second, the mental exercise of considering the similarities between a real situation or person and a literary scene or character can be refreshing and entertaining to readers, especially when the reference involves a clever comparison or amusing exaggeration. In addition, literary hyperbole reminds readers of a presumably pleasurable literary experience.

### 5.   Classical Rhetoric Theory: Ethos

Again like literary metaphors, literary hyperbole can help establish writers' *credibility* by demonstrating their creativity and resourcefulness. Like skill in drafting metaphors, the skill of drafting effective literary hyperbole can be viewed as a mark of brilliance.

Moreover, because literary hyperbole, like literary metaphors, involves shared knowledge between the writer and the reader, the use of such devices creates an impression in readers that a bond exists between them and the writer. Like literary metaphors, literary hyperbole can operate as an "inside joke" to which the writer and reader are both privileged.

## C.   *Cautions and Suggestions Regarding the Use of Literary References for Nonthematic Hyperbole*

### 1.   Use Literary Hyperbole with Caution

Despite the foregoing discussion regarding the communicative and persuasive functions that literary hyperbole can serve, lawyers should use it with caution for several reasons. First, by its nature, literary hyperbole involves exaggeration. In fact, as we saw in the beginning of this section, Theodore M. Bernstein describes hyperbole as a type of "lying." Granted, effective hyperbole does not deceive, because readers can tell from the context that the exaggeration is intended to emphasize, not mislead. But legal writing is, by necessity, very precise and accurate. In fact, an attorney's credibility rests in large part on the precision and accuracy of his or her writing. Intentionally including exaggeration in one's writing seems to contradict this. Thus, it should be done only knowingly and with caution.

Second, as we saw in some of the foregoing examples, literary hyperbole often mocks, belittles, or satirizes the target of the comparison. By way of illustration, in Example 2.10 we saw Judge Levy poke fun at the defendant in that case by comparing his getaway route to the trail of pebbles and bread crumbs left by Hansel and Gretel. While such mocking comments may be permissible from a judge writing a judicial opinion, they should be used more carefully by attorneys.

Third, literary hyperbole is in no way subtle. In fact, literary hyperbole often brings with it an aggressive, highly dramatic tone. As Aristotle wrote, "Hyperboles . . . betray vehemence. And so they are used, above all, by men in angry passion."[16] Hyperbole will not be an effective persuasive writing device if the writer's goal is to be subtle.

---

[16] Aristotle, *The Rhetoric of Aristotle* 216 (Lane Cooper trans. 1932).

Again, the decision whether to use literary hyperbole comes down to a judgment call. Before using it, carefully consider your audience and whether the hyperbole will damage your credibility and professionalism in the eyes of that audience. Also consider whether the point under discussion is best argued through the aggressive tone of literary hyperbole or through more subtle methods. If you decide to include literary hyperbole, take steps to minimize any possible negative impact. First, use your context carefully to make clear to readers that the exaggeration is intended not to deceive, but to emphasize. Second, minimize the mocking or satirical tone that often accompanies literary hyperbole.

## 2.  Other Cautions and Suggestions

If you do determine that literary hyperbole is appropriate in your document, consider the other cautions and suggestions described fully above under literary metaphors and summarized in the list below.

1. Avoid obscure literary references.
2. Consider any cultural differences between the writer and the reader.
3. Avoid forced literary references.
4. Avoid cliches or comparisons that are overly grand for the point being made.
5. Avoid overusing literary hyperbole.
6. When considering using references to children's books, be sure your context exhibits the necessary degree of seriousness and respect for your audience.

**Exercise 2.7     Evaluating the Functions and Effectiveness of Literary References for Nonthematic Hyperbole**

From the literary references for nonthematic hyperbole set out in Examples 2.12 and 2.13, choose one and write a few paragraphs (1) explaining the communicative and persuasive functions the reference serves in the judicial opinion from which it was taken, and (2) evaluating the effectiveness of the reference in terms of the cautions discussed above. If necessary or helpful, look up the full case from which the quote was taken or the literary work referenced.

**Exercise 2.8     Evaluating the Functions and Effectiveness of Literary References for Nonthematic Hyperbole**

Expand the assignment described in Exercise 2.7 above to include a discussion of both Example 2.12 and 2.13.

# Chapter 3

# *Literary References for Borrowed Eloquence*

The second general group of literary references that we will discuss are *literary references for borrowed eloquence*. With these types of literary references, a legal writer borrows a well-known or eloquent passage from a literary work or creatively alters such a passage to enhance or punctuate the borrower's own writing.

We will discuss two categories of literary references for borrowed eloquence: *literary references for direct borrowed eloquence* and *literary references for creative variation*. As we did for the previous categories of literary references, we will explore the characteristics of these two types of literary references and the functions they serve in persuasive discourse and offer suggestions and cautions regarding their use.

## I.   TYPE 3: LITERARY REFERENCES FOR DIRECT BORROWED ELOQUENCE

### A.   *The Characteristics of Literary References for Direct Borrowed Eloquence*

Literary references for direct borrowed eloquence are much less involved and much less complicated than are the first two categories we discussed. In simple terms, this strategy involves a legal writer directly quoting an eloquent phrase or passage from a literary work such as a poem, essay, short story, play, or novel. The quote can be as short as a word or phrase or as long as several lines or paragraphs.

Unlike the first two categories of literary references, it is not necessary when using this type of literary reference that readers have prior knowledge of the quoted material or of the work from which it was taken. As we will see, however, the functions served by such quotations will differ depending on whether the source is known or unknown to the reader.

Consider this example of direct borrowed eloquence:

> *Example 3.1*
>
> From *Kay v. First Continental Trading, Inc.*, 976 F. Supp. 772, 776 (N.D. Ill. 1997) (commenting on the statistical evidence offered by the plaintiff and the plaintiff's expert statistician):
>
> > Though the art or science (take your choice) of statistics has evolved considerably during the intervening three-quarters of a century, what [plaintiff] Kay and [plaintiff's expert] Moffitt have tendered remains

> evocative of Mark Twain's sardonic comment in his 1924 *Autobiography*: "There are three kinds of lies—lies, damned lies and statistics."

In the above example, the writer of the *Kay* opinion expresses scepticism over the reliability of the statistical evidence offered by the plaintiff's expert statistician. To enliven this point, the writer "borrows" (that is, quotes) a relevant clever statement from Mark Twain. This is the essence of literary references for direct borrowed eloquence: stating one's point by borrowing another's eloquence. Literature offers a rich mine of clever and unique expressions of ideas. Resourceful legal writers can make excellent use of it.

Consider the following additional examples:

*Example 3.2*

From *Nilssen v. Motorola, Inc.*, No. 93C6333, 1998 WL 513090, at *1 (N.D. Ill. Aug. 14, 1998):

> This long-in-the-tooth action between Ole Nilssen ("Nilssen") and defendants Motorola, Inc. and its subsidiary Motorola Lighting, Inc. ("Lighting") . . .—the third oldest case on this Court's calendar—has been stretched almost beyond belief by the litigants' successful efforts to deforest a substantial part of our nation's timber resources by the papers that they have filed in a host of areas. . . .
>
> Both the press of other matters and, it must be confessed, the unpleasant prospect of wading through highly combative sets of materials for a third time, prevented the motions from being addressed as promptly as this Court would have preferred. But after last week's generation of two lengthy opinions in other intellectual property cases, this Court has undertaken the task of scaling the peak of the mountain of accumulated papers. On examination, what had presented such a formidable appearance turned out in large part, with full apologies to the Bard of Avon, to be "full of sound and fury, signifying nothing." [FN4] Nonetheless, as will be seen, bulk tends to generate bulk, so that this opinion too has caused a tree to be felled.
>
> FN4. William Shakespeare, *Macbeth* act 5, sc. 5, lines 27-28.

*Example 3.3*

From *Guidry v. Steel Metal Workers National Pension Fund*, 39 F.3d 1078, 1089 (10th Cir. 1994) (Brorby, J., dissenting):

> The rain it raineth on the just
> And also on the unjust fella:
> But chiefly on the just, because
> The unjust steals the just's umbrella.

Charles Bowen, Thad Stem Jr., and Alan Butler, *Sam Ervin's Best Short Stories* (1973).

. . . The majority has concluded a faithless servant, an embezzler, a man who steals from the hard earned labors of the workers, is entitled to keep the fruits of his crime. I do not believe the Colorado legislature or the Colorado courts would permit such an unconscionable result. It is nonsensical to assume Colorado would want a thief to keep ill-gotten gains. Like Mr. Bumble of *Oliver Twist*, [FN2] I believe "[i]f the law supposes that, . . . the law is a ass—a idiot," and I am not willing to believe Colorado law to be either.

FN2. *Oliver Twist,* Charles Dickens 520 (Dodd, Mead & Co. 1941) (1838).

*Example 3.4*

In *Japan Whaling Association v. American Cetacean Society*, 478 U.S. 221 (1986), the United States Supreme Court dismisses an action brought by wildlife conservation groups for declaratory and injunctive relief against certain federal officials alleging that the officials breached their statutory duty to enforce international whaling quotas. In a dissenting opinion, Justice Marshall writes:

Since 1971, Congress has sought to lead the world, through the repeated exercise of its power over foreign commerce, in preventing the extermination of whales and other threatened species of marine animals. I deeply regret that it will now have to act again before the Executive Branch will finally be compelled to obey the law. I believe that the Court has misunderstood the question posed by the case before us, and has reached an erroneous conclusion on a matter of intense worldwide concern. I therefore dissent. . . .

I am troubled that this Court is empowering an officer of the Executive Branch, sworn to uphold and defend the laws of the United States, to ignore Congress' pointed response to a question long pondered: "whether Leviathan can long endure so wide a chase, and so remorseless a havoc; whether he must not at last be exterminated from the waters, and the last whale, like the last man, smoke his last pipe, and then himself evaporate in the final puff." H. Melville, *Moby Dick* 436 (Signet ed. 1961).

*Japan Whaling*, 478 U.S. at 241-42, 249-50 (Marshall, J., dissenting).

In Examples 3.2 through 3.4, the opinion writers express their points by borrowing from literary works. In Example 3.2, the writer of the *Nilssen* opinion states that the matter under discussion, while seemingly overwhelming at first glance, is actually rather basic upon closer examination. The writer expresses this point by borrowing an eloquent quote from Shakespeare. Similarly, in Example 3.3, the dissent writer borrows passages from both a poem and Charles Dickens's *Oliver Twist* to express the idea that the law is not so impractical as to provide that a thief may keep the fruits of his crime. Finally, in Example 3.4, Justice Marshall adds force to his dissent in the *Japan Whaling Association* case by quoting a moving passage from Melville's *Moby Dick*.

Sometimes legal writers borrow metaphoric language from literary works. In this context then, we must distinguish Type 1 literary references (literary references for metaphoric comparison) from Type 3 literary references (literary references for borrowed eloquence). Consider the following example:

*Example 3.5*

In *Baylson v. Disciplinary Board of the Supreme Court of Pennsylvania*, 975 F.2d 102 (3d Cir. 1992), the issue on appeal was "whether Rule 3.10 of the Pennsylvania Rules of Professional Conduct, which was adopted by the federal district courts in Pennsylvania, may be enforced against federal prosecutors practicing before the federal district courts in that state. The rule requires a federal prosecutor to obtain prior judicial approval before serving a grand jury subpoena on an attorney where the attorney would be asked to testify about past or present clients." *Id.* at 104. The *Baylson* court held that "Rule 3.10 may not be enforced against federal prosecutors because . . . its enforcement as state law violates the Supremacy Clause of the United States Constitution." *Id.* In reaching this conclusion, the court stated:

> Both parties seem to place a great deal of importance on the name assigned to Rule 3.10. The Board calls it a rule of professional conduct. Baylson calls it a rule of procedure. But as Shakespeare asked:
>
> > What's in a name? That which we call a rose by any other name would smell as sweet.
>
> For purposes of determining whether Rule 3.10 violates the Supremacy Clause, it matters not at all what the Board or Baylson choose to call it. What matters is whether the substance of Rule 3.10 actually conflicts or is incompatible with federal law.

*Id.* at 111 (quoting William Shakespeare, *Romeo and Juliet*, act 2, sc. 2).

In this example, the opinion writer points out that it does not matter what label is given to Rule 3.10; what matters is what the rule accomplishes substantively. In expressing this idea, the writer includes a metaphor: "That which we call a rose by any other name would smell as sweet."

Despite the use of a metaphor, this passage is not a Type 1 literary reference (literary reference for metaphoric comparison). In this example, the opinion writer did not *create* the metaphor. The opinion writer merely *borrowed* a metaphor created by Shakespeare. Accordingly, this literary reference is "borrowed eloquence," and does not qualify as a literary reference for "metaphoric comparison." Literary references for metaphoric comparison require that the writer compose an original metaphor by figuratively relating people or events in a case to a literary character or scene. If a writer merely quotes a pre-existing metaphor from a literary work, the literary reference is of the "borrowed eloquence" variety.

## B.   The Functions of Literary References for Direct Borrowed Eloquence

The functions of literary references for direct borrowed eloquence are much more limited than those of the first two types we discussed. Literary references for borrowed eloquence are primarily used for *stylistic* purposes, although they can also serve some *ethos* and *pathos* functions.

### 1.   Classical Rhetoric Theory: Rhetorical Style

The main function of literary references for direct borrowed eloquence is to help a writer state a point memorably. They do this in two ways. First, the eloquence of the borrowed statement itself can make a point memorable. That is, the phrasing of a borrowed quote may be so effective and eloquent that a legal writer's adoption of the quote makes his or her own point more memorable. This, in fact, is the most common reason for using these types of literary references: They allow legal writers to emphasize particular points in their documents by "borrowing" a particularly eloquent phrasing of the idea. It should also be noted that this function is served even if the reader is unfamiliar with the referenced literary work or has never heard the borrowed quote before.

The second way borrowed eloquence can make a point more memorable to a reader only applies if the borrowed phrase is famous or otherwise known to the reader. If a borrowed quote is previously known to the reader, the writer's use of it allows the reader to associate the writer's point with the well-known and memorable quote.

### 2.   Classical Rhetoric Theory: Logos

In some circumstances, a legal writer may insert a literary quote into a document to help communicate a particularly complicated point. That is, a writer having difficulty wording a concept may search for a literary quote that expresses the idea clearly. This is not the typical use of literary quotes, however. As we discussed above, literary quotes are most often used to incorporate eloquence and artistry into a document, not for purely communicative—that is, logos—purposes.

### 3.   Classical Rhetoric Theory: Pathos

Literary quotes can also serve *pathos* functions. In terms of "emotional substance," eloquent literary quotes can enhance the emotional reaction generated by an argument. Consider Example 3.4. In that example, Justice Marshall argues in his dissent that the continued existence of whales on earth depends on the enforcement by the United States federal government of international whaling quotas. Justice Marshall adds force to his emotional argument by incorporating an eloquent and moving quote from Melville's *Moby Dick*.

Literary quotes can also serve some "medium mood control" functions. Literary references for borrowed eloquence can be pleasing to the reader, and thus have a positive *emotional* impact. First, an unexpected or clever use of a literary quote can be entertaining to a reader. Second, if the work from which the quote is taken is previously known by the reader, an allusion to it can be pleasing to the reader as a welcome reminder of a former enjoyable literary experience.

### 4.   Classical Rhetoric Theory: Ethos

Although not as artistically demanding on a writer as literary metaphors or literary hyperbole, the use of literary quotations can help establish a writer's credibility. The incorporation into a legal argument of a particularly apt and eloquent literary quote suggests to a reader that the writer is a creative and resourceful communicator.

The effective use of literary quotes can also demonstrate to a reader that the writer is well read. In our discussion of the first two types of literary references, we saw that references to sophisticated literary sources can help establish credibility by demonstrating to the reader that the writer is educated and possesses broad knowledge. However, this strategy for establishing credibility was discouraged under the first two types of literary reference because the reader's knowledge of the referenced literary work is integral to the functions those types of references are designed to serve. Literary references for borrowed eloquence, on the other hand, do not require that the reader have prior knowledge of the referenced work. Quotations even from obscure or sophisticated literary works can thus be used to help establish credibility without the risk of alienating the reader or otherwise defeating the functions these types of literary references are meant to serve.

Finally, if a literary quote is known to the reader, the use of the quote involves "shared knowledge" between the writer and the reader. Consequently, the use of such quotes—like the use of other types of known literary references—can serve to create a kindred bond between the writer and reader.

### C.   *Cautions and Suggestions Regarding the Use of Literary References for Direct Borrowed Eloquence*

Because with literary references for direct borrowed eloquence it is not imperative that a literary quotation be known to a reader prior to its use by a legal writer, fewer cautions are needed regarding their use. In fact, one warning will suffice: Do not overuse literary quotations. Literary quotations, like other stylistic devices, derive their power from unexpectedness. If they are used too frequently, the surprise is lost. Furthermore, the overuse of literary quotations (or indeed any type of quotation) may suggest to readers that the writer lacks communication skills and eloquence of his or her own. Thus, use literary quotes sparingly and selectively.

## II.  TYPE 4: LITERARY REFERENCES FOR CREATIVE VARIATION

### A.  *The Characteristics of Literary References for Creative Variation*

The fourth category of literary references that we will explore is called *literary references for creative variation*. This type of literary reference, like direct literary quotations, involves allusion to the literary language of others. Rather than providing a direct quote from a literary work, however, writers using literary references for creative variation adapt or alter the quotation to better suit their own contexts. That is, rather than making a faithful quotation of the original material, the legal writer creatively alters a well-known literary passage to support his or her particular argument.

Consider this example:

> *Example 3.6*

> From *Lokeijak v. City of Irvine*, 76 Cal. Rptr. 2d 429, 430 n.1 (Cal. Ct. App. 1998):

>> It is uncertain why the court calls it a "policy." . . . The trial court may call it a policy, but as Shakespeare might say, a rule by any other name is still a rule.

In this example, the opinion writer creatively alters a well-known quote from Shakespeare. In fact, the quote alluded to here is the same Shakespearian quote that we already discussed in connection with Example 3.5: "What's in a name? That which we call a rose by any other name would smell as sweet." Indeed, the difference between the allusion to Shakespeare's quote in Example 3.5 and the allusion to this quote in Example 3.6 highlights the difference between literary references for direct borrowed eloquence and literary references for creative variation. In Example 3.5, the quotation was direct and unaltered. In Example 3.6, the quotation was creatively adapted to suit the writer's context. Consider the following additional example of a literary reference for creative variation in which the writer alludes to and creatively alters Mark Twain's famous witticism: "The reports of my death have been greatly exaggerated."

> *Example 3.7*

> From *U.S. v. Jackson*, 48 M. J. 292, 297 (C.A.A.F. 1998):

>> To paraphrase Mark Twain, the report of the demise of the rules concerning privacy of servicemembers has been greatly exaggerated.

Literary references for creative variation must be distinguished from literary metaphors (that is, Type 1 literary references for metaphoric comparison). While literary references for creative variation involve the alteration of an original literary quote, the quote as altered is still used for its original meaning. If, however, the writer uses a literary quote and adapts it into a new metaphor, the reference is a Type 1 literary metaphor rather than a Type 4 creatively altered quote. Consider this example:

*Example 3.8*

From *Aoude v. Mobil Oil Corporation*, 862 F.2d 890, 890-91 (1st Cir. 1988):

> [Appellant] polemizes mightily against a preliminary injunction issued by the United States District Court for the District of Massachusetts in favor of [Appellee] Mobil Oil Corporation (Mobil).
>
> In the end, [Appellant] huffs and puffs, but he fails to blow down the edifice which the district court competently constructed from the facts of record and the applicable law. Cf. The Three Little Pigs 16-18 (E. Blegvad ed. 1980) (house three).

In this example, the opinion writer creatively alters a phrase familiar from the children's story, "The Three Little Pigs," by stating that the Appellant "huffed and puffed, but fail[ed] to blow down" the judgment of the lower court. This example, however, constitutes a Type 1 literary metaphor rather than a Type 4 creatively altered quote. While the wolf in the story "huffed and puffed" literally in his attempt to blow down the pigs' houses, the writer's use of this phrase is metaphoric. The Appellant did not literally "huff and puff"; the phrase merely symbolically refers to the Appellant's fervent efforts to invalidate the lower court's opinion.

A particularly creative and sophisticated subcategory of literary references for creative variation is *encoded literary references*. Consider this example:

*Example 3.9*

From *Jones v. Fisher*, 166 N.W.2d 175, 182 (Wis. 1969):

> The road that has brought us to the present state of affairs in regard to punitive damages in Wisconsin courts is a long one, paved with good intentions.

In this example, Justice Robert W. Hansen of the Wisconsin Supreme Court, speaking in a type of "literary code," suggests that the status of the law on punitive damages in Wisconsin is "hell." As Bryan A. Garner explains, "Justice Hansen here subtly suggests that this is the road to hell, conjuring up the saying 'The road to hell is paved with good intentions.'"[1] By alluding to this well-known quotation attributed to

---

[1] Bryan A. Garner, *A Dictionary of Modern Legal Usage* 342 (1987).

Samuel Johnson, the writer creatively uses an encoded literary reference to communicate his point.

Consider this additional example:

*Example 3.10*

From *In the Matter of Israel-British Bank (London) Ltd.*, 401 F.Supp. 1159, 1175 (S.D.N.Y. 1975):

> In reaching this conclusion we make no attempt to pronounce what Congress' action might have been had it ever considered whether foreign banks should be accorded the right to file voluntary petitions. To do so would be to rush in where angels fear to tread.

Here, the opinion writer alludes to Alexander Pope's famous line, "Fools rush in where angels fear to tread." By making this allusion, the writer—through an encoded literary message—conveys his point that any efforts by the court to guess what Congress might have done in an area in which Congress has not yet spoken would be the efforts of a *fool*.

*Example 3.11*

From *First English Evangelical Lutheran Church of Glendale v. County of Los Angeles*, 482 U.S. 304, 340-41 (1987) (Stevens, J., dissenting) (emphasis added):

> The policy implications of today's decision are obvious and, I fear, far reaching. . . . Were this result mandated by the Constitution, these serious implications would have to be ignored. But the loose cannon the Court fires today is not only unattached to the Constitution, but it also takes aim at a long line of precedents in the regulatory takings area. It would be *the better part of valor* simply to decide the case at hand instead of igniting the kind of litigation explosion that this decision will undoubtedly touch off.

**Exercise 3.1   Identifying and Understanding Encoded Literary References**

Write a few paragraphs explaining why the highlighted language in Example 3.11 above is an example of an encoded literary reference. (1) Explain the original literary quotation alluded to and identify the literary work from which it was taken; and (2) explain the encoded message being expressed by the opinion writer.

### B.        The Functions of Literary References for Creative Variation

Literary references for creative variation are primarily used for *stylistic* purposes. As we will see, however, they also serve important *pathos* and *ethos* functions.

#### 1.   Classical Rhetoric Theory: Rhetorical Style

Not surprisingly, the main function of literary references for creative variation is stylistic. They add emphasis by allowing a writer to state a point in a clever and memorable way. Moreover, because the literary quote alluded to is known to the reader, the reader can associate the writer's point with the memorable quote.

#### 2.   Classical Rhetoric Theory: Pathos

In terms of *pathos*, creative variations can serve some "medium mood control" functions. First, because these types of literary references involve quotes that have been creatively altered from their original version, they operate like "riddles" to be solved by the reader. Solving these riddles—figuring out the famous quote that is being played with—can be entertaining and pleasing to the reader. Second, they can remind the reader of the pleasing literary work referenced.

#### 3.   Classical Rhetoric Theory: Ethos

Because literary references for creative variation require creativity, their use can affect positively the reader's impression of the writer. This is especially true of encoded literary references, which can seem particularly impressive to readers

Like the other types of literary references we have discussed, creative variations can also help establish or enhance a bond between writer and reader. In fact, this function is even stronger for this type of literary reference than for some of the other types because understanding the reference may require a bit of work on the part of the reader. To be "in the know," to understand the allusion, the reader has to work to make the mental connection between the writer's words and the original quote the writer means to evoke. Encoded literary messages require even more effort from readers. Not only must readers mentally conjure up the source quotation, they must also decode the writer's hidden message. Not surprisingly then, readers who make the connection will often feel a sense of kinship with the writer.

### C.        Cautions and Suggestions Regarding the Use of Literary References for Creative Variation

#### 1.   The Original Quote Must Be Known to the Reader

It should be clear from the foregoing discussion that literary references for creative variation work only if the quote being creatively altered is well known to the reader. Unlike direct quotations from literary works (that is, literary references for direct borrowed eloquence), which can be effective regardless of whether the reader has heard the statement before, creative variations are only effective if the reader knows the literary phrase being altered. What makes the point memorable (in terms of the *stylistic* function), what makes the point a clever and entertaining riddle to be solved by the reader (in terms of *pathos*), what makes the point impressively creative and the source of a kindred bond between writer and reader (in terms of *ethos*)—that is, what gives the reference its persuasive power—is the reader's ability to figure out the original quote that the writer is alluding to. If the reader doesn't know the quotation being played with, the functions of this type of literary reference are completely defeated.

### 2.  Do Not Overuse Creative Variations

As for the other forms of literary references, a legal writer should not overuse creative variations. Too much of a good thing hurts more than it helps. Use this and all types of literary references sparingly and selectively.

### 3.  Use Encoded Literary References Cautiously

Finally, encoded literary references should be used cautiously by legal writers. In Chapter 2, we discussed that lawyers should use literary hyperbole (Type 2 literary references) cautiously because exaggeration can be seen as inconsistent with the precision required in legal writing. Similarly, encoded literary references state their points indirectly, by implication, rather than explicitly. While judges may be able to get away with hiding messages in their writing, such a tactic should be used carefully by lawyers, for lawyers should generally state their points as clearly as possible to avoid the risk of misinterpretation or confusion.

# Chapter 4

# Literary References for Thematic Comparison: Summoning Dreams and Swords

All books are either dreams or swords.
— Amy Lowell

The fifth, final, and arguably most powerful category of effective literary references that we will discuss is *literary references for thematic comparison*. This type of literary reference involves referring to a literary work for the purpose of evoking its theme.

## I.   THE CHARACTERISTICS OF LITERARY REFERENCES FOR THEMATIC COMPARISON

The *theme* of a literary work is the main "idea or concept with which . . . [the work] seems to be concerned. Theme in a text may be a general principle, a moral point, an ethical point, or a logical or aesthetic resolution of a conflict."[1] When we speak of the "point" of a literary work—asking, for example, "What is the point of that book?" or "What point is that book making?"— we are referring to the theme of the work. A literary work typically has a dominant main theme, but may have several subthemes as well.

In a literary reference for thematic comparison, a persuasive writer, in making an argument, includes a reference to a literary work the theme of which supports the writer's argument. These types of literary references often come in the form of brief references to a literary work. It is important to note, however, that they can also come disguised as one of the other types of literary references we have discussed: literary metaphors (Type 1), literary hyperbole (Type 2), or direct or altered literary quotes (Types 3 and 4). What separates this type of literary reference from the others is that the reference is designed to evoke a theme or value represented in the referenced literary work. That is, it involves "thematic comparison": The reference is designed to force the reader to compare the societal value at issue in the legal matter at hand to a literary work involving the same societal value or theme.

This category of literary references can usefully be analyzed in terms of two subcategories: (1) Thematic Literary References to Works Involving Obvious

---

[1] Joel Wingard, *Literature: Reading and Responding to Fiction, Poetry, Drama, and the Essay* 1714 (1996).

Political or Social Commentary; and (2) Thematic Literary References for General Societal Values.

## A.     *Thematic Literary References to Works Involving Obvious Political or Social Commentary*

The first subcategory of literary references for thematic comparison involves references to literary works that contain obvious *political or social commentary*. In employing this type of literary reference, a legal writer alludes to a literary work that has as its theme the condemnation of (or, less frequently, the praise of) a political or social situation or phenomenon relevant to the writer's issue. Not surprisingly, the allusion is strategic, in that the reference is to a literary work that has a theme consistent with and supportive of the writer's position on the issue under discussion. Consider the following examples:

*Example 4.1*

In the case *In re Carlos P.*, 358 N.Y.S.2d 608 (N.Y. Fam. Ct. 1974), Judge Stanley Gartenstein takes dramatic steps to ensure that a troubled and neglected youth will be admitted to a vocational school that was fighting the youth's enrollment. Arguably the judge exceeds his authority in the case, a fact that the judge himself recognizes. Knowing that his decision will be appealed and subjected to much scrutiny, the judge endeavors to justify his decision with an eloquent and persuasive written opinion. Judge Gartenstein begins his opinion as follows:

> "I am invisible man. No, I am not a spook like those who haunted Edgar Allan Poe . . . I am invisible, understand, simply because people refuse to see me. . . . When they approach me they see only my surroundings, themselves, or figments of their imagination . . . anything except me. It is . . . often . . . wearing on the nerves . . . you doubt if you really exist. . . . It's when you feel like this that . . . you ache with the need to convince yourself that you do exist in the real world . . . and you strike out with your fists, you curse, and you swear to make them recognize you. And, alas, it's seldom successful."

*Invisible Man*, by Ralph Ellison. . . .
   Perhaps a history of our time will someday define the function of the law and its courts as the intervenor between an individual struggling to be recognized as human and the vast bureaucracy which tends to dehumanize him.
   Bureaucracy and red tape have a way of feeding on themselves. When they trap a human being, he is categorized; placed on the assembly line; labeled, packaged and delivered at the end of this treadmill wholly anesthetized as a neat stack of reports, each of which has picked up its requisite complement of marginal initials on

the way. When the frustration becomes intolerable, this human being is often impelled to perform some act affirming that he is in fact alive and unique. In his rage, the delinquent youth who is promised but receives no treatment might well become the misfit of tomorrow. It is tragic enough that Society's insoluble problems contribute to this process. But it is criminal when we are given a chance to intervene and let it pass us by. The court is here given this opportunity, indeed, the positive statutory duty to do so. In the light of the unsatisfactory choice of dispositional alternatives which Society at large has made available to this court, a condition for which Society has the temerity to blame the court itself, it will not allow this opportunity to slip through its fingers.

*Id.* at 609.

In this example, Judge Gartenstein quotes from Ralph Ellison's powerful and critically acclaimed novel, *Invisible Man*. *Invisible Man* is a novel about racism in America and the African-American experience. More specifically, it is a book about an individual's struggle for identity and the societal forces that can dehumanize and render that individual socially invisible. Judge Gartenstein quotes from this novel not only to "borrow" Ralph Ellison's eloquence (although that may in part be his purpose), but more importantly to evoke Ellison's theme. Judge Gartenstein does so to support his drastic and unprecedented efforts to give the youth in the case at hand "the best opportunity to realize his potential as a useful member of society and break the vicious cycle which has trapped his parents and siblings."[2]

*Example 4.2*

The case of *Kruse v. Village of Chagrin Falls, Ohio*, 74 F.3d 694 (6th Cir. 1995), involves certain landowners (the "Kruses") who filed suit against their municipality (the "Village") seeking compensation for a portion of their property taken by the municipality. After years in the Ohio state court system without relief, the Kruses filed suit in federal court. In granting relief to the Kruses, the Sixth Circuit expressed dismay regarding the defendant's protracted procedural tactics in defending the action. In its conclusion, the court stated:

After reviewing this record and listening to counsel at oral argument, it is obvious to us that, left to the devices of the Village's counsel, this case will become another Jarndyce v. Jarndyce, with the participants "mistily engaged in one of the ten thousand stages of an endless cause, tripping one another up on slippery precedents, groping knee-deep in technicalities, running their . . . heads against walls of words, and making a pretence of equity. . . ." Charles

---

[2] *In re Carlos P.*, 358 N.Y.S.2d at 615.

Dickens, *Bleak House* 2 (Oxford University Press ed. 1989) (London 1853). For nearly ten years, the Kruses have endeavored to vindicate their property rights guaranteed by the Constitution and by state statutes. The Village's actions threaten to turn the Kruse family into generations of "ruined suitors" pursuing legal redress in a system "which gives to monied might, the means abundantly of wearying out the right; which so exhausts finances, patience, courage, hope" as to leave them "perennially hopeless." *Id.* at 3-4. Enough is enough, and then some. . . .

For these reasons, the judgment of the district court is reversed and the case is remanded with instructions. On remand, the district court will enter judgment for the Kruses and conduct a trial to award them damages.

*Id.* at 701.

In this example, the opinion writer makes reference to Charles Dickens's *Bleak House*. *Bleak House* involves a fictional probate suit, *Jarndyce v. Jarndyce*, which drones on for generations due to the abuse of procedural tactics by all of the parties involved. Dickens wrote *Bleak House* as a condemnation of both lawyers and the legal system. The opinion writer in *Kruse* evokes this theme from *Bleak House* in support of the court's criticism of the defendant and of the long-delayed judgment for the plaintiff.

This excerpt from *Kruse* not only provides us with another example of a literary reference for thematic comparison, but it also helps illustrate the difference between this type of literary reference and some of the others we have discussed. In the *Kruse* case, the opinion writer criticizes the delaying tactics employed by the defendant and evokes the theme of *Bleak House* in support of this point. In Chapter 2, in Example 2.4, we saw a similar point being made by the court. In that case, the court criticized the attorneys in the matter for their "glacially slow and relentless litigation maneuvers." In that opinion, the writer used a literary simile and compared the court, inundated with procedural motions by both parties, to "Gulliver bound by wispy, but multiple, threads of the Lilliputians."

Example 2.4 and Example 4.2 involve similar substantive points, and in both the writers incorporate literary references in arguing those points. They differ, however, in terms of the *types* of literary references used. In Example 2.4, the writer's reference is nonthematic; that is, the referenced work—Jonathan Swift's *Gulliver's Travels*—does not have as its theme the point being made by the opinion writer. The writer includes this reference as a metaphoric comparison only. Conversely, in Example 4.2, Dickens's *Bleak House* offers direct thematic support for the writer's point. While both literary references are effective, they differ in type and function.

Moreover, the reference to *Bleak House* in Example 4.2 is hyperbole. Clearly the comparison between the *Kruse* case and the decades-long *Jarndyce v. Jarndyce* is an exaggeration. It is not a Type 2 literary reference (literary reference for nonthematic hyperbole), however, because the comparison is also thematic. The reference may look like a Type 2 literary reference, but it is actually a Type 5 (literary reference for thematic comparison). As we discussed at the beginning of this chapter, literary references for thematic comparison can come disguised as other types of literary references. Example 4.2 serves as good illustration of this.

The works referred to in Examples 4.1 and 4.2—Ralph Ellison's *Invisible Man* and Charles Dickens's *Bleak House*—embody obvious political or social themes. The list below includes a number of other well-known literary works with overt political or social themes often relevant to legal issues. This list is not meant to be exhaustive but merely to illustrate the range of works that can be used in connection with this type of literary reference in persuasive legal writing.

> *Animal Farm,* George Orwell
> *Brave New World,* Aldous Huxley
> *Catch-22,* Joseph L. Heller
> *The Crucible,* Arthur Miller
> *Fahrenheit 451,* Ray Bradbury
> *The Handmaid's Tale,* Margaret Atwood
> *Hard Times,* Charles Dickens
> *The Ox-Bow Incident,* Walter Van Tilburg Clark
> *The Scarlet Letter,* Nathaniel Hawthorne

**Exercise 4.1     Understanding the Strategy of Literary References for Thematic Comparison**

From the list of literary works above, choose one and write a brief essay describing a legal issue for which it could be used as thematic support. In your essay, (1) describe a legal issue that would give rise to an allusion to the literary work in question; (2) describe a possible factual scenario in which the issue could arise; (3) explain which side of the issue would likely use the literary work for thematic support; and (4) explain how that side might use the literary reference.

**Exercise 4.2     Writing a Literary Reference for Thematic Comparison**

From the list of literary works above, choose one and find a past legal case involving a legal issue for which the literary work could have served as thematic support. Write or rewrite an opinion as a judge in the case, incorporating a thematic reference to the selected literary work, using one of the following methods. (1) If the theme of the literary work supports the majority opinion in the case, rewrite a portion of the majority opinion incorporating the literary reference or, alternatively, write a separate concurring opinion incorporating the reference. (2) If the theme of the literary work contradicts the majority opinion, rewrite a portion of any workable dissenting opinion, incorporating the literary reference; if no dissenting opinion (or no workable dissenting opinion) exists, write a separate dissenting opinion incorporating the reference. Attach a copy of the original case to your opinion.

## B.     *Thematic Literary References for General Societal Values*

The second subcategory of literary references for thematic comparison involves literary references reflecting *general societal values*. The term "societal values" refers to beliefs commonly held in a society regarding what is moral or ethical, good or bad, right or wrong, proper or improper. Societal values include the importance of honesty, family, hard work, or tolerance, to name a few. General societal values often play a role in deciding legal issues. Moreover, many literary works have as their theme (or as a subtheme) a general moral or societal value. Consequently, Thematic Literary References for General Societal Values occur when a legal writer incorporates a reference to a literary work that has as its themes a general societal value supportive of the writer's argument. Let's consider some examples:

*Example 4.3*

In *Mileski v. Locker*, 178 N.Y.S.2d 911 (N.Y. Sup. Ct. 1958), the court invalidates two deeds executed by a woman to her two children, finding among other things that the deeds were procured through fraud. In reaching this conclusion, Judge Nicholas M. Pette writes:

> Virtues and vices are all put in motion by interest. When interest is at variance with conscience, any pretense that seems to reconcile them cannot satisfy the principles of Equity. It is regrettable, if desire for the earthly possessions that are involved in this action have transcended spiritual and moral values, and that they should be cause for this litigation, and the inevitable cleavage apparently caused between this old mother and her children. It would seem that in her declining years and her poor condition of health she should be blessed with that measure of harmony and peace, the love and respect of all her children should certainly bring to her, instead of her having to resort to the Court for redress and the adjudication of

her rights in this matter. Plaintiff, could she read and understand English, might feel as Shakespeare did when he wrote:

> "How sharper than a serpent's tooth it is to have a thankless child. Filial ingratitude! Is it not as this mouth should tear this hand for lifting food to it."

*Id.* at 917.

In Example 4.3, Judge Pette uses the theme from Shakespeare's *King Lear* to support his decision to invalidate deeds executed by a woman who was a victim of fraud at the hands of her own children. *King Lear* is not what one would call political or social commentary. Nevertheless, *King Lear* has a theme relevant to the issue in the *Mileski* case: the importance of family loyalty and of respect for one's parents and the tragedy of having disloyal, ungrateful children. Thus, this excerpt is an example of a thematic literary reference for a general societal value.

*Example 4.4*

In *Shearer v. Shearer*, 448 S.E.2d 165 (W. Va. 1994), the West Virginia Supreme Court reverses the decisions of a special family court judge and a West Virginia circuit court and grants custody of a minor child to its mother. The Supreme Court reaches this decision even though the mother had moved to a separate city and the family court judge and the circuit court found that the father had been the child's primary caretaker for an extended period of time leading up to the filing of the action. In a dissent, Justice Neely writes:

> In the children's book by Dr. Seuss, *Horton Hatches the Egg,* Horton the elephant devotedly sat on a bird's nest while Mayzie, a lazy bird, went on an extended vacation returning months later, when the egg was hatching, and demanded custody. The elephant prevailed, and in the words of Dr. Suess:
>
> > And it should be, it should be, it SHOULD be like that!
> > Because Horton was faithful! He sat and he sat!
> > . . . And they sent him home
> > Happy,
> > One hundred per cent!
>
> (Emphasis in original.)
> Mr. Shearer sat on the "nest" alone for the past two years, and this court sent him home empty handed. I have no doubt that "but for" Mr. Shearer's gender, the outcome in this case would have been different, and for this reason I dissent.

*Id.* at 171 (Neely, J., dissenting).

*Example 4.5*

In *United States v. Harrington*, 947 F.2d 956 (D.C. Cir. 1991), the D.C. Circuit Court of Appeals addresses several issues concerning the Federal Sentencing Guidelines. In a concurring opinion, Judge Edwards advocates major changes in the guidelines themselves. Judge Edwards writes in part:

> The two clever swindlers had a good laugh as they got ready to leave the city. The nobles who were to carry the train were clutching at the air. Neither dared to admit that he couldn't see the Emperor's clothes.
>
> And so the Emperor walked through the city under a magnificent canopy, and all the people cried, "Oh!" and, "Ah! The Emperor's new clothes are splendid!"
>
> Not one person was willing to say that he was stupid or unfit for his job. Each pretended the Emperor's clothes were a great success.
>
> "But he doesn't have anything on!" cried one little child in the crowd.
>
> "Just listen to the voice of the innocent!" said the father, trying to hush his child.
>
> Whispers began to buzz about: "A child says the Emperor has nothing on."
>
> "Yes!" cried all the people at last. "He doesn't have anything on!"
>
> The Emperor's heart almost stopped beating. He knew the little child was right. But he thought, "The procession must go on." So he stood a little straighter and walked a bit faster. And the nobles hurried to keep up with him, carrying a train that wasn't even there.

Hans Christian Andersen, *The Emperor's New Clothes* (Picture book ed., Random House, 1978).

. . . Like the Emperor's new clothes, the Sentencing Guidelines are a bit of a farce. . . . We continue to enforce the Guidelines as if, by magic, they have produced uniformity and fairness, when in fact we know it is not so. In the view of many, myself included, the Guidelines merely substitute one problem for another, and the present problem may be worse than its predecessor. Nonetheless we, the district courts, the U.S. Attorney's Office and the defense bar are forced to press on—through contorted computations, lengthy sentencing hearings and endless appeals—in the service of a sovereign who can be neither clothed nor dethroned.

*Id.* at 963-64, 967 (Edwards, J., concurring).

**Exercise 4.3    Identifying and Understanding Thematic Literary References for General Societal Values**

Choose one of Example 4.4 or Example 4.5 and write a short essay explaining why it is an example of a thematic literary reference for general societal values. (1) Explain the relevant theme of the literary work alluded to; that is, state and describe the general societal value the work embodies. (2) Describe how the writer uses this theme to support the legal argument. To the extent that the literary reference may also involve metaphor or hyperbole, explain how, while differentiating the allusion from Type 1 and Type 2 literary references. Use the discussions of Examples 4.1, 4.2, and 4.3 as guidelines for your essay. If necessary or helpful, look up the full case from which the quote was taken or the literary work to which it alludes.

**Exercise 4.4    Identifying and Understanding Thematic Literary References for General Societal Values**

Expand the essay described in Exercise 4.3 above to include a discussion of both Examples 4.4 and 4.5.

## II.    THE FUNCTIONS OF LITERARY REFERENCES FOR THEMATIC COMPARISON

Literary references for thematic comparison serve many of the same functions that we discussed in connection with the other types of literary references. As we shall see, however, they also serve a unique function, one that arguably makes this type of literary reference the most powerful available for persuasive writing. Literary references for thematic comparison have the potential to affect a decision-maker's value system.

### A.    *The Function of Influencing Value Hierarchies*

As we discussed briefly above, societal values often play a role in deciding legal issues. In fact, reaching a decision in a legal matter often requires the decision-maker to choose between *competing* values. Consider, for example, an issue involving the exclusion in a criminal matter of evidence arguably obtained in an illegal search. Societal values regarding the desire to reduce crime and punish criminals would support one result. Societal values regarding the right to privacy or the right to be free from unreasonable searches would, however, support the opposite result. As further illustrations, consider the conflicting values represented by each side of such controversial issues as abortion rights, the right to assisted suicide, censorship, the death penalty, and gun control. Decisions in such cases, and even in less controversial cases, often require the decision-maker to choose between competing and conflicting societal values. Furthermore, such decisions are often difficult for a decision-maker because the decision-maker may believe strongly in the values represented by both sides of the issue. Thus, the decision-maker must choose between two or more closely held but conflicting values.

In these situations, the value or values that the decision-maker personally considers to be the most important will have a greater influence on the decision. Thus, it is not an individual value that influences the decision; it is the *relative importance* of the various values implicated by an issue in the mind of the decision-maker that actually influences the ultimate decision. Roy Stuckey explains this concept more fully:

> Individual values do not usually control our behavior. Instead, our decisions are determined by the manner in which our values are organized, our *value systems*. . . . Personal values are organized into hierarchical systems that evolve from individually acquired values as we gain experience and maturity. . . .
>
> Since a given situation will typically activate several values within a person's value system rather than just a single one, it is unlikely that he will be able to behave [i.e., decide] in a manner that is equally compatible with all of them. A given situation may, for example, activate a conflict between behaving independently and obediently or between strivings for salvation and hedonic pleasure or between self-respect and respect from others. A value system is a learned organization of principles and rules to help one choose between alternatives, resolve conflicts, and make decisions.
>
> . . . Each value in a person's value system is ordered in priority or importance relative to other values. When multiple values become relevant to a decision, lower ranked values will be disregarded to accommodate higher ranked values. "When we think about, talk about, or try to teach our values to others, we typically do so without remembering the other values, thus regarding them as absolutes. But when one value is actually activated along with the others in a given situation, the behavioral outcome will be a result of the relative importance of all the competing values that the situation has activated."[3]

For some issues, a decision-maker's value preference is so strong that the role of values in reaching a decision is clear and unalterable. If, for example, an issue involves two competing values and one value is ranked low in the decision-maker's hierarchy of values and the other ranks high, the higher ranked value will

---

[3] Roy Stuckey, *Understanding Casablanca: A Values-Based Approach to Legal Negotiations*, 5 Clinical L. Rev. 211, 220-21 (1998) (quoting Milton Rokeach, *The Nature of Human Values* 14, 6 (1973)).

undoubtedly have greater influence on the decision-maker's ultimate decision. In this situation, the lower ranked value will be disregarded in favor of the higher ranked value, and any attempts to elevate the lower ranked value over the higher ranked value will be unsuccessful. In many situations and for many issues, however, the decision-maker does not have a clear or overwhelming preference for any one of the values implicated by the issue. In such situations—when an issue involves competing values of approximately equal rank in the decision-maker's hierarchy of values—the role of the values in the ultimate decision is less certain and predestined. Here, the value that will have the most influence on the decision will be the value most highly "activated" by the situation.[4] If the circumstances surrounding the decision-maker's deliberations on an issue somehow activate or emphasize one of the values more than the competing values, the accentuated value will have greater influence on the ultimate decision.

One strategy of persuasion for situations in which the competing values are of approximately equal rank in the decision-maker's value system is to attempt to activate favorable values in the mind of the decision-maker and to deactivate unfavorable ones. If an advocate can somehow influence the hierarchy of values held by the decision-maker and increase in the mind of the decision-maker the degree of importance awarded the favorable values as opposed to the competing values, the advocate can convince the decision-maker that the greater good is served by a decision in the advocate's favor. The question then becomes, how does one influence a decision-maker's value system? Nimble writers call on the strategy of literary references for thematic comparison.

It has long been recognized that literary works play an important role in the formation of a person's values. As Teresa Godwin Phelps has stated,

> Our social and moral selves are . . . formed and developed through narrative. We learned from *Cinderella* that virtue and patience are rewarded, that cruelty and envy result in amputated toes; we learned from *Little Red Riding Hood* not to talk to strangers; from *Peter Pan* that we would have to grow up; and from the *Wizard of Oz* that there is no place like home.[5]

Mark Johnson explains why and how literary works help to shape our values and morals:

> Why is it that we turn to literary texts for our moral education? . . .
> We learn from, and are changed by, such narratives to the extent that we become imaginatively engaged in making fine discriminations of character and in determining what is morally salient in particular situations. We actually enter into the lives of the characters, and we perform acts of perception, decision, and criticism. We find ourselves judging of a character that she shouldn't have done X, or wishing that he had seen a particular

---

[4] *See id.* at 235.

[5] Teresa Godwin Phelps, *Narratives of Disobedience: Breaking/Changing the Law,* 40 J. Legal Educ. 133, 133 (1990).

situation differently than he did. We want to stop the characters and tell them, "Oh, no, don't do that!" or "No, that's not what she meant." Just as in life, we find ourselves surprised by what happens, or disappointed in ourselves for not having seen something earlier. We explore, we learn, and we are changed by our participation in the fiction that creatively imitates life.
. . .

John Gardner has argued that fiction is a laboratory in which we can explore in imagination the probable implications of people's character and choices. . . . His point is that in a fictional setting we can explore the way a person with a certain character, placed within certain circumstances, might live his life. We can see how his self-knowledge, or lack of it, determines what he does and how that affects others. We can see how his care, or lack of it, determines the quality of his relationships and the morality of his actions. . . .

Fictional narratives provide us rich, humanly realistic experimental settings in which we can make our own moral explorations.[6]

Considering the role that values play in decision-making, and considering the role that literary works play in the formation of values, it's not hard to see how a reference to a literary work in a persuasive document can be a powerful persuasive device. As we discussed above, one strategy in persuasion is to attempt to elevate in the mind of the decision-maker the importance of the value supporting an advocate's position over the competing values. If literary works helped to form the favorable value in the mind of the decision-maker in the first place, then an allusion to one of these literary works can serve to activate and enhance the importance of that value among and in relation to the various other values in the decision-maker's value system. Referring to a literary work that is part of the decision-maker's mental storehouse of literary texts allows the decision-maker to "relive" the original experience of reading that text. As Professor Johnson explained above, the decision-maker's original reading of the text helped to form the value in question by allowing him or her to see the implications and consequences of that value within the "experimental setting" of literary fiction. A later allusion to that text in a persuasive document allows the decision-maker to reexperience that imaginary journey of discovery and to again appreciate the importance of the value or lesson learned on that journey. Thus, for issues that implicate competing yet equally ranked values in the mind of the decision-maker, the incorporation of a reference to a literary work that aided in the original formation of one of those values has the power to enhance the importance of that value over the competing values. Consequently, that value will likely play a greater role in the ultimate decision by the decision-maker. This is the essence of literary references for thematic comparison.

It is important to emphasize that this persuasive strategy only works for issues that involve competing values of approximately equal rank in the decision-maker's hierarchy of values. If the decision-maker has a strong preference for one specific value implicated by an issue, that value will influence the result, and no thematic

---

[6] Mark Johnson, *Moral Imagination: Implications of Cognitive Science for Ethics* 196-98 (1993).

literary reference will overcome it. In these situations, a thematic literary reference will have little or no affect on the decision-maker's conclusion. If a decision-maker does not have a strong value preference, however, thematic literary references can be valuable persuasive strategies in attempting to favorably influence the decision-maker's value system. Moreover, for many issues, we as persuasive writers have very little prior knowledge about our audiences' value systems and, therefore, have no idea if the decision-maker has a strong preference for one value or ranks the various values implicated by the issue equally. Thus, thematic literary references are often worth a try.

Let's consider all of this in terms of a concrete example. In Example 4.2, the court faced the issue of whether to grant relief to the Kruses for the taking of their property by the municipality. The Kruses had endured years of suits and procedural steps in pursuit of relief. Among the various values implicated by the matter were two competing values: the importance of following procedure versus the inequity of protracted litigation. The court decided to grant the Kruses relief. In order to persuade the court's audience that it had reached the correct decision, the opinion writer sought to elevate in the mind of the reader the importance of the supporting value over that of the competing value. That is, knowing that a reader of the opinion likely has strong beliefs about both the importance of procedure and the inequity of protracted litigation, the opinion writer sought to influence the reader's hierarchy of values by increasing in his or her mind the importance of avoiding protracted litigation over the competing value of following procedure. To accomplish this task, the opinion writer incorporated a thematic literary reference to *Bleak House*. This novel may have played a role in the original formation of the reader's value regarding the inequity of protracted litigation. Accordingly, a reference to this novel in the opinion can cause the reader to relive the original experience of reading that book and can thereby revive the value it represents in the mind of the reader. Thus, the literary reference serves to activate and enhance this value within the reader's hierarchy of values, and by doing so it helps persuade the reader that the court's decision was the correct one.

Similarly, in Example 4.3, the court decided to invalidate two deeds executed by a mother as the result of fraudulent behavior on the part of her own children. Among the societal values implicated by the matter were the competing values of (i) respect for one's parents and (ii) the binding nature of a signature (or more generally, the importance of keeping a promise). To persuade the audience of the opinion that the court had reached the correct result, Judge Pette incorporated a thematic literary reference to *King Lear*, the theme of which supports the value of parental respect. The story of *King Lear* was very likely instrumental in the reader's development of this value in the first place. Thus, a reference to it helps to activate and enhance that value among the reader's hierarchy of values. This in turn helps the opinion writer to persuade the reader that the court chose correctly between the competing values and reached the right decision.

**Exercise 4.5     Understanding How Thematic Literary References Influence Value Hierarchies**

Choose one of Example 4.4 or Example 4.5 and write a short essay explaining how the literary reference in that example influences the reader's hierarchy of values in an effort to support the opinion writer's conclusion. Explain (1) the conflicting values implicated by the case, and (2) how the writer uses the literary reference to enhance in the reader's mind the importance of one value over that of the competing value. Use the foregoing discussions of Examples 4.2 and 4.3 as guidelines for your essay. If necessary or helpful, look up the full case from which the quote was taken or the literary source referenced.

**Exercise 4.6     Understanding How Thematic Literary References Influence Value Hierarchies**

Expand the essay described in Exercise 4.5 above to include a discussion of both Examples 4.4 and 4.5.

## B.     Discursive Psychology Theory and Shared Knowledge: Literary Theory and Intertextuality

Shared knowledge theory from discursive psychology and the similar literary theory of intertextuality help us significantly in understanding how thematic literary references work. As we saw above, thematic literary references can actually influence a reader's value system. They accomplish this by allowing a writer to tap into prior knowledge held by the reader. Because the referenced literary work is part of the "shared knowledge" held by both the writer and the reader, the writer can conjure up the literary work and its theme using only a quick reference. The writer is thus able to make strategic use of the reader's prior knowledge by encouraging the reader to "relive" a past literary experience and return to its attendant values. Furthermore, through intertextuality, the reader is encouraged to see the connection between the theme of the referenced literary work and the values implicated by the legal issue and to bring the thoughts and feelings from the experience of reading the referenced literary work to bear on that issue. Thus, thematic literary references work, in large part, by taking advantage of "shared knowledge" and "intertextuality."

## C.     Classical Rhetoric Theory: Logos

Like literary metaphors (Type 1 literary references) and literary hyperbole (Type 2 literary references), thematic literary references aid in communicating the substance (logos) of a point by providing the reader with an understandable and vivid analogy. A thematic literary reference evokes a situation from a literary work that is analogous to the case at hand and thus can help the reader to understand the writer's point. Consider Example 4.2, in which the opinion writer wanted to communicate to the reader that the Kruses had suffered unfairly in enduring years of procedural steps to pursue the recovery they sought. To help communicate this point, the writer analogized the Kruse's plight to that of the parties in Dickens's *Bleak House.*

## D.      *Classical Rhetoric Theory: Pathos*

Thematic literary references also serve some *pathos* functions. In terms of "emotional substance," thematic literary references contribute greatly to the emotional reaction generated by a substantive emotional argument. When a thematic literary reference evokes a theme from a literary work, it also evokes the emotions associated with that theme and with the value the theme represents. Consider Example 4.3. In that illustration, Judge Pette, attempting to elicit feelings of pity for the victimized mother and of anger towards her deceptive children, compared the mother's situation to that of King Lear and his disloyal children. By doing so, the writer not only evoked the theme of *King Lear,* but also the reader's stored feelings of pity and anger regarding Lear's plight. As a consequence, the writer enhanced the emotional aspect of this argument.

Thematic literary references can also serve some "medium mood control" functions. Although not as dramatic as literary metaphors or creative variation of literary quotes, thematic literary references can be pleasing to the reader and, therefore, can have a positive *emotional* impact. First, thematic literary references, as helpful analogies, can be pleasing to readers by making it easier for readers to understand a writer's point. Second, being reminded of a similarity between a real-life situation and a scene or character in literature can be mildly entertaining to readers. Finally, such references remind readers of their original pleasurable literary experiences.

## E.      *Classical Rhetoric Theory: Ethos*

Again, like other types of literary references, thematic literary references help establish the *credibility* of a writer by demonstrating his or her creativity and resourcefulness. Moreover, because thematic literary references involve "shared knowledge" between the writer and the reader, use of such devices provides evidence of a bond between the writer and reader.

## III.   CAUTIONS AND SUGGESTIONS REGARDING THE USE OF THEMATIC LITERARY REFERENCES

### A.    *Thematic Literary References Cannot Overcome Strongly Held Competing Values*

As we discussed previously, thematic literary references have the unique power to influence a reader's value system. As we also discussed, however, this function is only possible when the matter in question implicates values that are ranked relatively equally in the reader's hierarchy of values. If the matter implicates a very highly ranked value, this value will likely have a determining influence in the reader's decision and inferior competing values will be disregarded. In this situation, thematic literary references supporting inferior-ranked values will not be able to influence the reader's decision.

Nevertheless, it is often worth the effort to incorporate a thematic literary reference into a persuasive argument for two reasons. First, we as persuasive writers often have very little prior knowledge about our reader's value systems and thus we cannot know whether a thematic literary reference will have a significant impact. Second, little harm can be done by incorporating a literary reference, even if that reference is disregarded by a reader who holds a strong preference for a competing value.

## B.   *The Reader Must Have Read the Referenced Literary Work*

For thematic literary references to accomplish their persuasive and communicative functions, the reader must have read the literary work in question. Thus, when drafting thematic literary references, you must avoid using obscure literary works, and you must take into account any cultural differences between you and your reader that might render your source unfamiliar.

## C.   *Other Cautions and Suggestions*

Finally, consider the other cautions and suggestions discussed more fully in the Cautions and Suggestions section under Type 1 Literary References. These other cautions are summarized below.

1.   Avoid forced literary references.
2.   Avoid cliched or overly grand comparisons.
3.   Avoid overusing thematic literary references.
4.   When considering using references to children's books, be sure your context exhibits the necessary degree of seriousness and respect for your audience.

**Exercise 4.7    Writing and Analyzing a Literary Reference for Thematic Comparison**

Look up and read the case of *In re Dubreuil*, 629 So. 2d 819 (Fla. 1993). This case involves a mother of four children (including a newborn) who wanted to refuse a life-saving blood transfusion because of her religious beliefs. The issue in the case pits the interests of the hospital and state on one side against the interests of the mother on the other side.

1.    Make a list of the societal values implicated by both sides of the *Dubreuil* case. More specifically, make a list of the societal values that support a decision in favor of the hospital/state. Make a separate list of the societal values that support a decision in favor of the mother.

2.    Choose one of the values from your lists and write a dissenting or concurring opinion in the *Dubreuil* case, arguing that this value dictates a particular result in the case. In making this argument, incorporate a thematic literary reference to a literary work whose theme supports the value you are advocating. Whether you write a concurring or dissenting opinion will depend on whether the result you advocate agrees or disagrees with the majority's decision in the case.

3.    Write a separate essay analyzing your opinion. (1) Explain the value you advocate and your strategy in advocating it. (2) Analyze the *functions* that your thematic literary reference serves in your opinion. (3) Evaluate the *effectiveness* of your literary reference.

**Exercise 4.8    Writing and Analyzing a Literary Reference for Thematic Comparison**

1.    Find a case (like the *Dubreuil* case referred to in Exercise 4.7) that involves two or more competing societal values. Chose one of those values and write a dissenting or concurring opinion for the case advocating how that value requires a particular result in the case. In making this argument, incorporate a thematic literary reference to a literary work whose theme supports the value you are advocating. Whether you write a concurring or dissenting opinion will depend on whether the result you advocate agrees or disagrees with the majority's decision in the case.

2.      Write a separate essay analyzing your opinion. (1) Explain the various values implicated by the case. (2) Explain the value you advocate in your opinion and your strategy in advocating it. (3) Analyze the *functions* that your thematic literary reference serves in your opinion. (4) Evaluate the *effectiveness* of your literary reference.

# *Chapter 5*

# *Final Thoughts on Literary References*

In Chapters 2 through 4, we analyzed five types of effective literary references used in persuasive writing.

> Type 1: Literary References for Nonthematic Metaphoric Comparison
> Type 2: Literary References for Nonthematic Hyperbole
> Type 3: Literary References for Direct Borrowed Eloquence
> Type 4: Literary References for Creative Variation
> Type 5: Literary References for Thematic Comparison

In connection with each type of literary reference, we explored its characteristics and its communicative and persuasive functions and offered suggestions and cautions regarding its use. There are two purposes behind this in-depth coverage of literary references in persuasive writing. From a small-scale perspective, learning about the different types of literary references is meant to help you use them to add force to your persuasive writing. Our broader perspective, however, has been to reveal a new dimension in persuasive writing. By dissecting literary references, we have been able to peer beneath the surface of persuasive writing and to glimpse the forces that give it power. Our comprehensive discussion of five different categories of literary references, each serving differing important persuasive functions, reveals their basis in theoretical principles from psychology, classical rhetoric, literary theory, morality theory, and narrative theory. Thus, in addition to teaching you how to use persuasive literary references in your writing, Part I has been meant to give you an appreciation of the sheer vastness of the "world of forces" underlying effective persuasive writing.

## I.   TWO INEFFECTIVE USES OF LITERARY REFERENCES IN PERSUASIVE LEGAL WRITING

The five types of literary references we have discussed are but a few of the many types that can appear in persuasive writing. They are, however, the most effective types. While it is beyond the scope of our coverage to discuss all of the other types, two ineffective ones should be noted and avoided: literary references for lay authority and contrived literary references.

### A.   *Literary References for Lay Authority*

In making a literary reference for lay authority, a legal writer "cites" a literary work as authority for a general proposition, such as a scientific or historical fact, an attribute of human behavior, or a societal phenomenon. Consider these examples:

*Example 5.1*

From *Ganzy v. Allen Christian School*, 995 F.Supp. 340, 351 (E.D.N.Y. 1998):

> Premarital and extramarital sexual activity in early America was subject to both social disdain and criminal sanctions. *See, e.g.,* Nathaniel Hawthorne, *The Scarlet Letter* (1850).

*Example 5.2*

From *Capps v. Atiyeh*, 559 F.Supp. 894, 917 (D. Or. 1983):

> The diagnosis of mental illness is made tougher still because it is easy for inmates tired of their boring, "restrictive even harsh" routines to feign the symptoms of mental illness to effect a change in their environment. *See* K. Kesey, *One Flew Over the Cuckoo's Nest* 44-45 (1962).

*Example 5.3*

From *Arizona v. Moran*, 784 P.2d 730, 733-34 (Ariz. Ct. App. 1989):

> Defendant was insubordinate; he declined to perform a duty that arose from his employment with ITT. Such behavior is no stranger to the workplace. *See* H. Melville, "Bartleby, The Scrivener," *Great Short Works of Herman Melville* (1966). Often it interferes with the employer's efficient use of facilities and equipment. Yet employers have deterrent powers as potent as termination and demotion. And we do not believe the legislature intended by the passage of A.R.S. Sec. 13-1602 to march the criminal law into the workplace to bolster employers' directives with the punitive machinery of the state.

*Example 5.4*

From *Utah v. Maycock*, 947 P.2d 695, 698 (Utah Ct. App. 1997):

> Totally aside from the remote possibility that an officer would deliberately fabricate, claiming he had smelled marijuana knowing he had not, an officer might subjectively sense that he smells marijuana without objectively realizing that his conclusion, however honest, is more a product of hope, conjecture, exaggeration, self-suggestion, or imagination than of a keen olfactory sense. [FN2]
>
> FN2. Ebenezer Scrooge aptly commented on the limitations of human senses. When the ghost of Jacob Marley, perceiving that Scrooge did not believe in his existence, asked, "Why do you doubt

your senses?," Scrooge answered: "Because . . . a little thing affects them. A slight disorder of the stomach makes them cheats. You may be an undigested bit of beef, a blot of mustard, a crumb of cheese, a fragment of an underdone potato. . . . I have but to swallow this [toothpick], and be for the rest of my days persecuted by a legion of goblins, all of my own creation." Charles Dickens, *A Christmas Carol*, in *A Christmas Carol and The Cricket on the Hearth* 3, 19-20 (J.M. Dent & Sons Ltd. 1963) (1843).

In all of these examples, the writers "cite" to literary works as "authority." In Example 5.1, the writer cites Nathaniel Hawthorne's *The Scarlet Letter* as authority for the "historical" proposition that premarital and extramarital sexual practices were punished in colonial times in this country. In Example 5.2, the writer cites Ken Kesey's *One Flew Over the Cuckoo's Nest* for a "medical" proposition regarding the diagnosis of mental illness. In Example 5.3, the writer cites to Herman Melville's "Bartleby the Scrivener" as authority for a "sociological" proposition regarding employee behavior patterns in the workplace. Finally, in Example 5.4, the writer cites Charles Dickens's *A Christmas Carol* as authority for the "scientific" proposition that the human senses are fallible.[1]

Literary references for lay authority are not particularly effective in persuasive writing. The referenced literary works are, by their nature, fiction. However realistic the setting of the works might be, and however compelling the language, literary works of this type are works of fiction and thus have limited authoritative strength for proving a historic or scientific fact or general phenomenon. In such circumstances, a writer is much better off citing legitimate authoritative sources such as professional articles and books from the sciences, the social sciences, economics, history, and the like.

An exception to this guideline is that literary works can be (and often are) cited for propositions of linguistics, grammar, and usage. A legal writer will sometimes cite a literary work, not for its substance, but for its form of expression when advocating an interpretation of specific language in a statute or other document. Rather than (or in addition to) citing a linguistics text or a manual of grammar and usage, some legal writers will cite similar language in a literary work. This is a permissible use of a literary work for lay authority. Consider this example:

*Example 5.5*

From *Muscarello v. United States*, 524 U.S. 125, 128-29 (interpreting the phrase "carries a firearm" in a criminal statute):

---

[1] If the writer of this opinion was referring to *A Christmas Carol* as authority for the idea that the human senses are fallible, this reference is for "lay authority." If, however, the writer made the reference primarily to borrow Dickens's creative expression in describing this concept, then the reference is for "direct borrowed eloquence" (a Type 3 literary reference). Accordingly, this reference fits under more than one category, a phenomenon we discuss in more detail below.

[T]he . . . basic meaning of the word "carry" includes conveyance in a vehicle. . . .

The greatest of writers have used the word with this meaning. *See, e.g.,* the *King James Bible*, 2 Kings 9:28 ("[H]is servants carried him in a chariot to Jerusalem"); *id.,* Isaiah 30:6 ("[T]hey will carry their riches upon the shoulders of young asses"). Robinson Crusoe says, "[w]ith my boat, I carry'd away every Thing." D. Defoe, *Robinson Crusoe* 174 (J. Crowley ed. 1972). And the owners of Queequeg's ship, Melville writes, "had lent him a [wheelbarrow], in which to carry his heavy chest to his boarding-house." H. Melville, *Moby Dick* 43 (U. Chicago 1952). . . .

These examples do not speak directly about carrying guns. But there is nothing linguistically special about the fact that weapons, rather than drugs, are being carried. Robinson Crusoe might have carried a gun in his boat; Queequeg might have borrowed a wheelbarrow in which to carry, not a chest, but a harpoon.

## B.     *Contrived Literary References*

The final category of literary references we will discuss is literary references that serve little or no function at all. Bryan A. Garner warns against the use of what he calls "contrived uses of literature":

> Some judges and advocates, in their quest for originality, go off the deep end. Perhaps the worst manifestation of this phenomenon is what we might term "literary foppery," consisting in the legal writer's going to absurd lengths to display the breadth of his literary knowledge. . . . Contrived allusions and references invariably detract from the message being conveyed.
>
> In a striking example of artificially engrafted literariness, an American judge recently peppered one of his opinions with wholly impertinent allusions and references to William Faulkner. The opinion itself treats . . . the constitutionality under the Fourth Amendment of a lessor's inspection of his land to determine whether the lessee has wrongfully diverted oil production. The first sentence of the statement of facts reads: "The event underlying Auster's claim could have arisen in Yoknapatawpha County, Mississippi, but most of them happened in Calcasieu Parish, Louisiana, where Stream owned the surface and mineral rights in oil-producing property." A footnote, of course, explains that Yoknapatawpha County is the fictional setting of many of Faulkner's novels. . . . The contrivance has neither purpose nor subtlety.
>
> Worse yet, however, are the headings and subheadings throughout the opinion. We begin with "The Sound and the Fury," which is followed by "Lease in August" (*Light in August*), "The Reivers," "Intruders in the Dust" (*Intruder in the Dust*), "Auster's Gambit" (*Knight's Gambit*), "Go Down, Auster" (*Go Down, Moses*), "Requiem for a Plaintiff" (*Requiem for a Nun*), "Sanctuary," "Microchip! Microchip!" (*Absolom! Absolom!*?), "Trooper's Pay" (*Soldier's Pay*), "As the Wells Lay Pumping" (*As I Lay Dying*), and "The Unvanquished." In short, the references and allusions to Faulkner are entirely factitious.

To some, such contrivances may be appealing. For them, one can only point to the advantages of developing a more discerning literary sensibility.[2]

## II.   A SINGLE LITERARY REFERENCE CAN FALL INTO MORE THAN ONE CATEGORY

Most of the examples of literary references that we discussed in Chapters 2 through 4 clearly fell within only one of the five categories of effective literary references. This approach was intended to clarify the differences between the various categories upon first encounter with them. Literary references are not always so easy to categorize, however. In fact, a single literary reference can fall into more than one category. A legal writer might quote a literary passage that not only expresses the writer's point eloquently (a Type 3 literary reference for direct borrowed eloquence) but also expresses a theme relevant to the writer's argument (a Type 5 literary reference for thematic comparison). The possibility that a single reference can fall into more than one category and can, thereby, serve multiple communicative and persuasive functions, should be kept in mind when analyzing and evaluating literary references in legal writing.

**Exercise 5.1    Identifying and Analyzing Different Types of Literary References**

Reread the two examples of literary references written by Supreme Court Justice William Brennan set out in the introduction to Part I. Write an essay (1) identifying the category into which each of these literary references falls; (2) explaining the functions that each reference serves in the opinion from which it was taken; and (3) analyzing the effectiveness of these references.

---

[2] Bryan A. Garner, *A Dictionary of Modern Legal Usage* 343-44 (1987).

**Exercise 5.2      Identifying and Analyzing Different Types
                    of Literary References**

1.      For each of the five categories of effective literary references discussed
        in Chapters 2 through 4, find one example in a judicial opinion. Hint: One
        easy way to locate literary references in judicial opinions is to do
        computer searches of judicial opinion data bases using literary authors,
        titles, and characters as key words or phrases.

2.      Write an essay analyzing the five examples of literary references you
        located. In your essay, (1) explain why each example fits into the category
        you assigned it; (2) explain the functions each example serves in the
        opinion from which you took it; and (3) analyze the effectiveness of each
        example. Attach copies of the five judicial opinions to your essay.

# PART II

# PERSUASIVE WRITING STRATEGIES BASED ON CLASSICAL RHETORIC THEORY: PERSUASIVE PROCESSES

What is Classical Rhetoric? While many of you have heard the term "rhetoric," it is likely that few of you have a clear understanding of what it means. Undoubtedly, much of this confusion stems from the shifting and rather loose use of the term in recent years.[1] In some contexts, the term "rhetoric" is used to mean "general English composition," encompassing the principles relevant to effective writing generally. In other contexts, rhetoric refers to a "flowery" writing style that overuses strategies such as metaphor, alliteration and personification. In still other contexts, the term has an even more negative connotation, referring to "empty, bombastic language, as implied in the familiar phrase 'mere rhetoric.'"[2]

None of these modern conceptions of rhetoric accurately reflects its original, traditional meaning. In classical terms, rhetoric referred to "the use of language for *persuasive* purposes."[3] Originating around 450 B.C., classical rhetoric involved the comprehensive and systematic study of the art of persuading through written and verbal expression. In fact, Aristotle—one of the first and best known of the classical rhetoricians—defined rhetoric as the power "of discovering in the particular case what are the available means of persuasion."[4]

The following passage by Michael Frost describes the origins of classical rhetoric in fifth century B.C. Greece and its importance in Greco-Roman culture until the fall of the Roman Empire in 410 A.D. This discussion demonstrates not only that classical rhetoric has from its origins focused on the art of persuasion, but also that the materials its originators developed were extremely comprehensive—even by modern standards:

> In 400 A.D. if an ordinary Roman citizen of the educated class had a legal dispute with another citizen, he usually argued his own case before other Roman citizens and did so without the advice or help of a lawyer. Even so, he analyzed and argued his case with a near-professional competence and thoroughness. In preparing his case, he first determined the proper forum for his argument and identified the applicable law. He then determined which facts were most important, which legal arguments were meritorious, and which arguments his adversary might use against him. When choosing his strategies for the trial, he also decided how he would begin, tell the story of the case, organize his arguments, rebut his opponent, and close his case. Before actually presenting his arguments, he would carefully evaluate the emotional content of the case and the reputation of the judges. And finally, he would assess how his own character and credibility might affect the judges' responses to his legal arguments. In effect, he was analyzing and preparing his case in a lawyerly fashion.

---

[1] *See* Edward P. J. Corbett and Robert J. Connors, *Classical Rhetoric for the Modern Student* 15 (4th ed. 1999).

[2] *Id.*

[3] *Id.* (emphasis added).

[4] Aristotle, *The Rhetoric of Aristotle* 7 (Lane Cooper trans. 1932).

In making these preparations, he was not depending solely on native intelligence or good instincts. Instead, he was relying on a lengthy, highly structured, formal education in the art of rhetoric which featured the most comprehensive, adaptable, and practical analysis of legal discourse ever created. In fact, the art of rhetoric was originally created as a flexible technique for training advocates to present cases in Greek and Roman law courts. Moreover, for nearly 1,000 years, the study of rhetoric was at the core of both Greek and Roman education and, in one form or another, has been part of most formal education since that time. . . .

The study of rhetoric was central to the Roman education system from the first century B.C. until the fall of the Empire in 410 A.D. Before that, rhetorical education had also been a key component in Greek education from at least 450 B.C. Thus, the formal study of rhetoric, especially as reflected in Aristotle's *Rhetoric,* Cicero's *De Oratore*, and Quintilian's *Institutio Oratoria,* had a virtually continuous 1,000 year history in the Greco-Roman world. Although all Roman citizens did not complete the full course of study, most completed a substantial part of the ten- to twelve-year rhetoric course which "carried boys from beginning alphabet exercises at six or seven through a dozen years of interactive classroom activities designed to produce an adult capable of public improvisation under any circumstances." Designed for use by all members of the educated classes, the rhetoric course included, among other things, detailed instructions for discovering and presenting legal arguments in almost any context and to almost any audience. A student's rhetorical education prepared him to meet all his public speaking obligations, especially his legal obligations.[5]

Edward P. J. Corbett and Robert J. Conners offer further insight into the history, development, and traditions of classical rhetoric. In particular, Corbett and Conners explain how classical rhetoric expanded beyond its original focus on persuasive *oratory* to persuasive *writing*:

> From its origins in 5th century B.C. Greece through its flourishing period in Rome . . ., rhetoric was associated primarily with the art of oratory. During the Middle Ages, the precepts of classical rhetoric began to be applied to letter-writing, but it was not until the Renaissance, after the invention of printing in the fifteenth century, that the precepts governing the spoken art began to be applied, on any large scale, to written discourse.
>
> Classical rhetoric was associated primarily with persuasive discourse. Its end was to convince or persuade an audience to think in a certain way or to

---

[5] Michael Frost, *Introduction to Classical Legal Rhetoric: A Lost Heritage*, 8 S. Cal. Interdisciplinary L.J. 613, 613-16 (1999) (quoting James J. Murphy, *Roman Writing Instruction as Described by Quintilian*, in *A Short History of Writing Instruction from Ancient Greece to Twentieth-Century America* 19-20 (James J. Murphy ed. 1990) and citing *id.* at 19, 20, 38); Edward P. J. Corbett, *Classical Rhetoric for the Modern Student* 596 (2d ed. 1971); Aristotle, *The Rhetoric of Aristotle* (Lane Cooper trans. 1932); Marcus Tullius Cicero, *De Oratore* (E. W. Sutton trans. 1942); Marius Fabius Quintilian, *Institutio Oratoria* (H. E. Butler trans. 1954)).

act in a certain way. . . .

For extended periods during its two-thousand-year history [from 450 B.C. to the Renaissance in the fifteenth century], the study of rhetoric was the central discipline in the curriculum [of our schools]. Rhetoric enjoyed this eminence because, during those periods, skill in oratory or in written discourse was the key to preferment in the courts, the forum, and the church.[6]

As the foregoing discussion shows, rhetoric has traditionally involved the arts of argumentation and persuasion, traditions that have existed since 450 B.C. It is within this history of classical rhetoric that we find the genesis of the modern legal advocate. In fact, lawyering today is essentially the modern version of a noble practice that has existed for 2500 years. It is not surprising, then, that classical rhetoric has much to offer the modern advocate.

Parts II and III of this book will explore many of the theories and strategies of persuasion analyzed by classical rhetoricians and their implications for the persuasive efforts of today's legal writers. Specifically, in Part II (Chapters 6, 7, and 8), we will examine the fundamental *processes* of persuasion recognized by classical rhetoricians, focusing on the various *substantive means* of persuasion analyzed in classical rhetoric. In Part III (Chapters 9 and 10), we will turn our attention to *persuasive style*, exploring how writing style, in addition to substance, can affect an argument's persuasive impact.

---

[6] Corbett and Conners, *supra* note 1, at 15-16.

# Chapter 6

# Logos, Pathos, and Ethos in Television Commercials: Understanding Fundamental Persuasive Processes

Life today is about selling: selling products, selling ideas, selling ourselves. Selling is the language of our time and advertising is its boldest manifestation.
– Bernice Kanner, *The 100 Best TV Commercials . . . and Why They Worked*

Classical Rhetoric is a discipline that systematically studies the art of persuading through written and verbal expression. In Chapter 2, we learned that classical rhetoricians have traditionally recognized three general means of persuasion: *logos*, *pathos*, and *ethos*. *Logos* refers to persuading through logic and rational argument. *Pathos* involves persuading by appealing to the audience's emotions. *Ethos* refers to persuading by establishing credibility in the eyes of one's audience. In this chapter, we will explore logos, pathos, and ethos in more detail. In particular, we will examine how these three modes of persuasion operate in persuasive discourse, how they differ from each other, and how they can work together and complement one another.

Rather than turning directly to legal writing to see how these three processes operate, we will first explore these processes in terms of a different form of persuasive discourse: television advertising. As the quote above from Bernice Kanner indicates, advertising is the "boldest manifestation" of persuasion in our society. Companies spend billions of dollars a year trying to come up with the most effective, the most persuasive, advertising possible. Billboards, flyers, and print, radio, and television ads all compete for our attention as consumers and attempt to persuade us to do this or buy that. Moreover, because consumers have short attention spans, advertising must persuade quickly and efficiently. Ads must be bold, dramatic, and overt in their efforts to persuade. Legal writing, on the other hand, employs persuasive processes much more subtly. Because of the nature of legal writing's subject matter and audiences, the employment of logos, pathos, and ethos in legal writing must be less overt. Consequently, advertisements serve as a better source than legal writing for initially exploring the fundamentals of logos, pathos, and ethos because these processes are amplified in advertising. The philosophy here is that the best way to gain a fundamental understanding of these three separate persuasive processes is to examine them in an exaggerated form. Examining them initially in the context of television advertising rather than legal writing allows us to do just that.

After we explore logos, pathos, and ethos in TV commercials, we will explore their general implications in legal writing. We will see that the same basic persuasive forces underlying advertising also underlie legal writing. While the level of "boldness" (and the operative ethical constraints) may differ, we will nevertheless see that the same basic persuasive processes used to sell goods and services to consumers are also used to "sell" ideas, arguments and positions in legal matters.

As you read, you may find that you are already familiar with many aspects of these processes as they relate to legal writing. Logos and pathos, in particular, are customarily taught in most introductory legal writing courses, although often under other names. Indeed, you may already be applying many of the skills discussed here. Of the three, ethos commonly receives the least coverage in introductory legal writing courses, and you may consequently have little familiarity with it. For that reason, we cover ethos in more detail in Chapters 7 and 8, analyzing the more sophisticated aspects of its function in legal writing.

# I.    HOW LOGOS, PATHOS, AND ETHOS OPERATE IN TELEVISION COMMERCIALS

## A.    *Logos*

Logos, the process of persuading through logical argument and reason, not surprisingly plays an important role in television advertising. Whenever an ad attempts to convince its audience to purchase a product or service based on logic or rational arguments, logos is being employed. Ads that explain what a product does or how a product works—like a dandruff shampoo or a carpet cleaner—are employing logos to sell the product. Similarly, ads that compare a product to a competitor's product in an effort to show the product's superiority are persuading through logical argumentation. Ads that rely on statistics or authority—such as "four out of five dentists" or "J.D. Powers and Associates" or a ranking from *Car and Driver* magazine—are also using logos to persuade.

Perhaps the most obvious example of logos in product marketing is the "infomercial." Infomercials are extended television commercials—typically running from five to thirty minutes—that explain in detail how a product works, provide demonstrations of the product in action, and show the results of tests comparing the product to competitors' products. Marketing through infomercials became popular in the 1990s, and industry statistics indicate that they now account for more than $900 million in sales each year.[1] The success of infomercials demonstrates the power of logos to persuade consumers.

## B.    *Pathos*

Pathos, persuasion through an appeal to an audience's emotions, encompasses two separate processes: *emotional substance* and *medium mood control*. Persuading

---

[1] Reon Carter, *Give Infomercials a Hard Look; Those Contraptions on TV Account for Millions in Sales, But Not Everything Is Fit for Consumption*, Cincinnati Enquirer, Feb. 7, 2000, at C3 (citing Infomercial Marketing Report).

through emotional substance involves eliciting an emotional response from the audience regarding the substance of the matter under consideration. In the context of marketing and television commercials, emotional substance refers to efforts to convince consumers to purchase a product or service based on an appeal to emotions rather than an appeal to logic or reason. Pathos plays an important role in television advertising.

Perhaps the emotion most often appealed to in television ads is envy. Television commercials that try to make us envious of the people they portray are persuading through pathos. An ad, for example, that makes us wish we were as cool, as wealthy, as beautiful, or as well-dressed as the actors in the ad is employing pathos.

Another emotion frequently used to persuade in television commercials is love. Many commercials, for example, encourage us to purchase products by suggesting that they will help us to take better care of a loved one such as family member, child, or pet.

Public service announcements frequently make emotional appeals. Ads advocating the use of seat belts or condoms often use fear to persuade. Consider also the well-known ad depicting a Native American shedding a tear over pollution and careless littering. This ad, which was one of the most successful public service campaigns in history, employs guilt and patriotism in an effort to convince us to "Keep America Beautiful."

The second aspect of pathos—medium mood control—refers to the effect that the medium of a message, as opposed to the substance of the message, has on the on the audience's mood or emotions. Classical rhetoricians have long recognized that if the medium used to communicate a message can entertain or otherwise please the audience, the audience will be more receptive to the substance of the message.

Medium mood control plays a very significant role in television commercials. Because an ad must grab the attention of busy consumers, most successful television commercials are designed to entertain, not just inform, their audience. To the extent that a commercial entertains and amuses watchers, the commercial is employing medium mood control. By making commercials funny, dramatic, or thrilling, advertisers help to assure that the audience will watch the ads and pay attention.

We can see many examples of medium mood control in television commercials. Perhaps the most prevalent type involves humor: Many ads are entertaining to watch because they are funny and amusing. Other ads use sex to entertain their audiences. It is axiomatic in the ad industry that "sex sells." Accordingly, advertisers frequently use erotic images to draw the attention of television viewers. Other commercials entertain by telling a dramatic "story" that gives us a warm feeling or brings a tear to our eyes. Still others entertain with thrilling graphics or special effects. Finally, some commercials depict impressive feats that are entertaining to watch. Perhaps the best known of this type in recent years is the ad in which golfer Tiger Woods impressively bounces a golf ball on the end of a golf club. Many people flock to the television whenever this ad is on to watch in amazement. By employing medium mood control, Nike Golf is assured that people will watch and enjoy its commercial.

Interestingly, some advertisers emphasize medium mood control so much in their commercials that nothing substantive, neither logical nor emotional, is said about the product. In these ads, the advertisers focus exclusively on medium mood control in an effort to establish the product's name firmly in the minds of the audience. Product recognition is the main goal of these commercials. To achieve it, the advertisers make the commercials as entertaining as possible hoping that consumers will watch the ad repeatedly and remember it. Because nothing substantive is said about the product, however, no persuasion occurs based on logos or emotional substance. While such ads can be effective for achieving product recognition, their approach is unduly limited. Better commercials do not engage in medium mood control to the exclusion of other forms of persuasion. Better commercials do more than entertain; they entertain *and* persuade.

## C.     Ethos

The third process of persuasion—ethos—involves efforts on the part of a persuader to establish credibility in the eyes of the audience. Classical rhetoricians have long recognized that an audience's perceptions of a speaker or writer's credibility plays a significant role in how it will respond to the message presented. The more credibility the speaker or writer has, the more receptive the audience will be.

Like logos and pathos, ethos plays an important role in television advertising. In fact, ethos has two dimensions in television advertising: the credibility of the advertiser's spokesperson and the credibility of the company itself. Many ads feature a person who represents the company producing the ad. This spokesperson can be a real person actually affiliated with the company—like Dave of Wendy's Restaurants—or an unaffiliated person, like a celebrity or a expert, hired by the company to endorse its products or services. Alternatively, the spokesperson can simply be an actor playing the role of someone who uses the product. To the extent that an ad portrays a spokesperson as being a credible source of information, the ad is employing ethos.

Televison advertisers employ various means to establish the credibility of their spokespersons. Some advertisers employ scientists or other experts knowledgeable in relevant fields to promote their products. Other advertisers pay sports or entertainment stars to promote and endorse their products, investing in the credibility these stars have amassed in the eyes of the public. When an actor is hired to play the role of someone who uses the product, the ad will often strive to make the character seem as credible as possible by giving them attractive traits such as intelligence, friendliness, ability, helpfulness, and so on. All of these approaches reflect efforts to persuade through ethos.

An interesting recent phenomenon in some television commercials has been the use of an "antihero" as a spokesperson. In a number of recent commercials, the character using or advocating use of the product is portrayed, not as credible, but as amusingly incompetent or obnoxious. Consider, for example, the recent Volkswagen commercial in which a Volkswagen owner and his friends attempt to tie a mattress to the car's roof while stopped at a traffic light. They manage to accomplish the task in time, only to discover they have tied the car doors shut. Similarly, in a series of commercials for 1-800-ATT, a bumbling, inept spokesperson encourages strangers to use this long distance dialing service. Many other recent commercials depict rude and obnoxious spokespersons. Such commercials elevate medium mood control—use of an entertaining form—over spokesperson ethos. Focusing primarily on making the commercials amusing and entertaining, these advertisers minimize and perhaps even sacrifice altogether persuasion through spokesperson ethos. While medium mood control can be an effective way to gain and keep an audience's attention, better commercials accomplish this end without sacrificing ethos. Better and more persuasive commercials find a way to entertain the audience while also establishing credibility for the spokesperson.

The second aspect of ethos relevant to television commercials is the process of establishing the ethos of the company itself. That is, apart from the credibility of a spokesperson, a commercial can help establish the credibility of the company producing the commercial. This can occur in several ways. First, companies often create or hone their public images by emphasizing desirable traits in their commercials. Ads for luxury cars or expensive jewelry, by way of illustration, are often presented with an air of sophistication. This type of ad suggests to consumers that the company itself is sophisticated. Similarly, ads for perfume and clothing are often stylish and chic, suggesting that the company itself is stylish and chic. Ads that use spokespersons who are "common folk" are meant to suggest to consumers that the company has down-home values and is not a cold, faceless, uncaring corporation.

A second way that commercials lend credibility to a company is by showing it is creative and innovative in its marketing. A particularly entertaining or impressive ad "speaks" highly of the company itself. Companies that produce such ads gain a reputation for being clever, creative, and intelligent. Thus, an effective ad not only "sells" the product, it also "sells" the company.

Finally, an ad can show that a company has taken a position on a significant social issue, such as the environment or race relations. Such ads can enhance the public's perception of the company and, consequently, enhance the operation of ethos in the company's advertising.

## II.   ANALYZING SOME SPECIFIC TELEVISION COMMERCIALS

Now that we have explored how logos, pathos, and ethos operate generally in television commercials, we will see how these processes can work together in specific television commercials. In the discussion that follows, we will analyze three highly acclaimed and highly successful television commercials: Snap.com's "New Friend" (1999), Volvo's "Take My Car, Please" (1976), and Discover Brokerage's "The Tow Truck Driver" (1999). As we will see, the success of these commercials is due in large part to their effective use and integration of logos, pathos, and ethos.

### A.   *Snap.com's "New Friend" (1999)*

*The commercial opens by showing a school bus stopped at a bus stop. The bus is carrying children of grade school age, and it has stopped to pick up another child. Among the children on the bus is a boy named Tommy, who is seated next to a window. While looking out the window, Tommy sees a boy about his age or younger engaging in a sign language conversation with a woman who appears to be the boy's mother. The boy then hugs the woman and nervously gets on the bus. The boy walks past Tommy and makes his way to the back of the bus, where he sits alone. The scene suggests that the boy is deaf and riding the bus for the first time. (Perhaps it is his first day at a new school.)*

*The next scene shows Tommy coming in the front door of his house and running up the stairs to his bedroom. There, Tommy sits down at his computer and uses Snap.com to search the Internet for "sign language."*

*The final scene again takes place on the school bus. While Tommy is sitting on the bus, the other boy walks down the aisle and takes a seat across from him. Tommy approaches the boy, who looks up inquisitively. Simultaneously using sign language and speaking aloud, Tommy says, "My name is T-o-m-m-y." Delighted, the boy replies in sign and spoken language, "Nice to meet you." A new friendship has been formed.*

Snap.com is an Internet portal, owned in part by NBC, that offers several services, including a search engine and a web site directory. "New Friend," produced by Snap.com, won the Emmy Award for best commercial for 1999. Its success is largely due to its effective use of logos, pathos, and ethos.

In terms of logos, the commercial persuades consumers to use Snap.com by illustrating its ability to help people find information quickly and efficiently. In the ad, Tommy was able to use Snap.com to find out all he needed to know about the specialized topic of sign language. The ad illustrates that, with Snap.com, a world of information is at one's fingertips. The ad also suggests that Snap.com is user-friendly, considering how quickly and successfully it was used by the child in the commercial. Thus, by showing what Snap.com is and what it can do, the ad persuades by appealing to consumers' logic and reason.

The ad also employs pathos. In particular, the ad invokes medium mood control. The commercial tells a heart-warming story of a boy who senses the trepidation of a newcomer and goes out of his way to communicate with and befriend him. The story is sweet and emotional. Because many people find such stories entertaining, the ad employs medium mood control that ensures that consumers will watch and enjoy the ad.

Finally, the commercial employs ethos. In the ad, Tommy is the company "spokesperson." He is the character in the ad who uses and who is tacitly advocating the use of Snap.com. Tommy is portrayed as someone with tremendous credibility. First, Tommy is friendly, as evidenced by his willingness to go out of his way to make new friends. Second, he is caring and sensitive. Tommy senses that the other boy is anxious about riding the school bus with strangers, and he takes it upon himself to assist the newcomer. Third, Tommy is industrious, as evidenced by his innovative and effective approach to the situation. Fourth, he is intelligent and a quick learner. All of these attributes cause the audience to view Tommy as being credible in terms of both character and ability. (One may argue that the fact that Tommy is a child as opposed to an adult reduces his credibility as a spokesperson for something as technical as an Internet portal. However, considering that children of Tommy's age are viewed as the "computer generation" and are typically seen as the most knowledgeable segment of our society when it comes to computers, Tommy's age does not seem to negatively impact his credibility as the product spokesperson.)

The ad also has an effect on the image (that is, the ethos) of the company itself. Snap.com, by implication, is portrayed as being sensitive and caring. Moreover, this creative, award-winning ad encourages consumers to view the company as innovative and intelligent.

The only persuasive process not employed in this ad is the "emotional substance" aspect of ethos. While the ad is emotional, the emotion is for entertainment purposes only. Nothing in the ad persuades consumers to use Snap.com based on emotion. By contrast, the next ad that we will evaluate includes a strong dose of emotional substance.

### B.      Volvo's "Take My Car, Please" (1976)

Advertising expert Bernice Kanner describes this classic commercial:

> *A worried father and his wife pace the living room while a thunderstorm rages outside. The father frets about his daughter going on a date in such horrible weather. "It's crazy to let them go out on a night like this," he grumbles agitatedly to his wife. "But she waited months for tonight," the mother replies understandingly.*
> *The doorbell rings. "Mom, is that Jeff?" the young girl asks expectantly.*
> *Indeed it is and Mom greets him with "Hello, Jeff."*
> *Jeff greets the parents: "Mrs. Stewart. Mr. Stewart."*
> *After some feet-shuffling greeting, Dad makes a decision—the next best thing to preventing his daughter from going out.*
> *"Jeff, do me a favor, will you?" he says. "Take my Volvo."*
> *Voice-over: "Over the years, safety has been an obsession with Volvo. Because of all the things that go into a Volvo, the ones we've always valued most are people."*
> *[Superimposed wording]: "Volvo."*
> *Mother has the last word: "Be careful," she calls as they leave the house.*[2]

Volvo's "Take My Car, Please" was incredibly successful when it was released in 1976, and Kanner lists it as one of the 100 best commercials of all time. The commercial's success can be attributed to its effective combination of logos and pathos.

In terms of logos, the ad tacitly informs consumers that Volvo is a safe vehicle. By asking Jeff to use his Volvo in such dangerous weather, Dad (the product spokesperson) is suggesting to consumers that Volvo is safer than other cars. The ad need only tacitly refer to the car's safety because, at the time the ad came out, Volvo was widely perceived as being one of the safest cars on the market. Because this reputation was so ingrained in the minds of the public, the ad needed only to include a brief reminder to consumers of the logic behind purchasing a Volvo.[3] Thus, the logos aspect of this ad relies heavily on the product's preexisting reputation.

Because of this preexisting reputation, the ad's primary process of persuasion is pathos. Rather than redundantly explaining that Volvos are safe, the company decided to persuade through emotion by demonstrating *why* a safe car is desirable. In the ad,

---

[2] Bernice Kanner, *The 100 Best TV Commercials . . . and Why They Worked* 204 (1999).

[3] *See id.* at 204-5.

Dad's actions illustrate that a safe car will protect loved ones more effectively. Thus, the ad persuades consumers to buy a Volvo out of love for their families. The ad taps into and takes advantage of consumers' love for their families and their desire to keep their families safe. In this way, the ad is a compelling example of persuasion through emotional substance.

A comparison between Snap.com's "New Friend" and Volvo's "Take My Car, Please" helps to illustrate the difference between the "emotional substance" aspect of pathos and the "medium mood control" aspect of pathos. Both ads are highly emotional. "New Friend" involves a sweet and touching story of a boy going out of his way to befriend a newcomer. Similarly, "Take My Car, Please" involves a sweet and touching story about a father who wants his daughter to be both happy and safe. Both of these ads are entertaining to watch, and, in this way, both involve medium mood control. However, the emotion generated by Volvo's ad is more than just entertainment. The emotion—love for family—also helps to persuade consumers to purchase the product. By watching the ad, consumers are persuaded to purchase a Volvo to keep their loved ones safe. Conversely, the emotion generated by "New Friend" is for entertainment purposes only. The emotions evoked by the ad are heart-warming to the audience and ensure that people will watch and enjoy the ad. However, nothing about these emotions substantively compels consumers to use Snap.com.

Finally, "Take My Car, Please" persuades viewers through ethos. Volvo's spokesperson—Dad—is portrayed as being caring, friendly, and understanding. Moreover, Volvo (the company) is portrayed, not as a cold, faceless company, but as a caring company committed to keeping families safe.

## C.    *Discover Brokerage's "The Tow Truck Driver" (1999)*

*The scene opens with a tow truck towing a luxury car down an isolated desert highway. It is daylight on hot sunny day. Painted on the side of the truck is "Al's Towing." Inside the truck are two men. The first man is Al, the tow truck driver. He has longish, unkempt hair and is wearing work clothes, including a shirt with a name patch reading "Al." The second man, the passenger, is dressed as a businessman. He has short hair and is wearing the pants of a business suit, a dress shirt, and a tie. The jacket of the suit is draped over the seat between the men; the businessman's shirt sleeves are rolled up; his top shirt button is unbuttoned; and his tie is loosened. Because of the heat, the windows of the truck are rolled down. Several sounds can be heard: the roar of the truck's engine, the wind whipping in the windows, and the hum of the tires on the road. The scene suggests that the businessman had car trouble in the desert and is being towed to safety.*

*As the truck drives down the highway, the businessman notices a copy of* Barron's, *a financial newspaper, on the seat by the driver. In a mildly surprised tone, the businessman asks the driver if he reads* Barron's. *In a friendly and matter-of-fact tone, the driver tells the businessman that he does read* Barron's, *that he invests online with Discover Brokerage Direct, and that* Barron's *has named Discover Brokerage the best online broker for three years in a row.*

*With a smirk on his face and in a condescending tone, the businessman asks the driver if he invests a lot. In the same friendly tone, the driver explains that he used to invest a lot, but that he is retired now. Noticing the surprised look on the businessman's face, the driver explains that he doesn't have to drive a tow truck; he just enjoys helping people.*

*Changing the subject, the businessman points to a picture on the driver's sun visor and asks if it is a vacation spot. Somewhat embarrassed, the driver explains that the picture actually shows his house. Confused, the businessman remarks that the picture is of an island. The camera shows a close-up of the picture. It is an aerial shot of a beautiful tropical island. The driver, in a sheepish tone, says "Technically, it's a country."*

*An announcer then states in a voice-over: "Discover Brokerage. Discover the advantages of investing online."*

*In a final tag line, the driver explains that the problem with owning your own country is that you've got to name it.*

"The Tow Truck Driver" was produced by Discover Online Brokerage Services, now operating under the name of Morgan Stanley Dean Witter Online. This commercial was one of the most popular commercials in 1999, and it won numerous awards. It was also one of only five commercials in 1999 to be nominated for an Emmy award. This commercial, perhaps even better than the first two commercials, effectively illustrates the integration of logos, pathos, and ethos in persuasion.

In terms of logos, "The Tow Truck Driver" informs consumers that they can use Discover Online Brokerage Services to invest in the stock market. It also informs them that they can make money doing this. Moreover, by portraying the product spokesperson, Al, as an average, ordinary guy, the ad suggests that Discover is user-friendly for the average consumer. Finally, by citing an "authoritative source," *Barron's* financial newspaper, the commercial conveys to potential investors that Discover has been consistently ranked higher than its competitors. These aspects of the commercial tell consumers what the product is, what it can do for them, and how it is better than similar services. Thus, these aspects of the commercial serve to persuade consumers to use Discover Online Brokerage Services based on logic and reason.

In terms of pathos, the commercial employs both emotional substance and medium mood. The product's spokesperson is portrayed as being very wealthy, wealthy enough, in fact, to retire at a young age and to own his own tropical island—an island big enough to be its own sovereign nation. Furthermore, it is suggested through the ad that Al acquired his wealth by using Discover's services. In this way, the ad persuades through emotional substance. Consumers who watch the ad envy Al and desire his wealth. While they may spend the money in different ways, consumers see Al's life and covet it. And the ad suggests that consumers can have what Al has if they use Discover's services. Thus, the ad persuades by tapping into one of the most basic human emotions—*envy*.

The ad also employs the medium mood control aspect of pathos. Much about the ad makes it entertaining to watch. First, the ad is humorous. Watchers of this ad find it particularly amusing to learn not only that this tow truck driver is wealthy enough to own his own country, but that one of the biggest dilemmas in his life is naming his country home. Second, the ad involves an "underdog" theme. In the ad, Al is portrayed as a regular guy who becomes incredibly wealthy. History shows that audiences love this theme, as evidenced by the perennial popularity of such stories as Cinderella and Rocky. Third, the ad involves a condescending snob being "taken down a notch." In the ad, the pompous businessman learns that this "lowly" tow truck driver is actually much more successful than he is. Again, audiences tend to find such themes very entertaining. Thus, several things about this ad make it enjoyable to watch, and in this way the ad effectively employs medium mood control.

Finally, the ad effectively employs ethos. Discover's spokesperson, Al, is portrayed as being very credible. Al is successful, yet humble and friendly. He is patient, even when confronted by the condescending businessman. He is a hard worker, even though he doesn't have to be. And he is helpful and has a good heart, as evidenced by the fact that he drives a tow truck simply because he "enjoys helping people." All of these things contribute to Al's credibility in the eyes of consumers. Moreover, the ad helps to establish the credibility of Discover itself. The ad's humor and cleverness reflect well on Discover, painting it as a creative, innovative, and intelligent company.

## III.   A SUMMARY OF THE PERSUASIVE PROCESSES OF LOGOS, PATHOS, AND ETHOS

The following outline summarizes what we have learned so far regarding the three fundamental processes of persuasion recognized by classical rhetoricians.

---

**An Outline of the Three Fundamental Processes of Persuasion Recognized by Classical Rhetoricians**

- **Logos**   Persuasion through logic and rational argument.

- **Pathos**   Persuasion through emotion; its two aspects are

  - *Emotional Substance:* Persuasion by arousing an emotional reaction in the audience regarding the substance of the matter under consideration.

  - *Medium Mood Control:* Use of the medium of a message to generate positive emotional reactions in the audience.

- **Ethos**   Persuasion by establishing credibility in the eyes of the audience.

---

**Exercise 6.1     Analyzing a Television Commercial in Terms of
Logos, Pathos, and Ethos**

1.     Make a presentation to the class analyzing a television commercial of
your choice in terms of logos, pathos, and ethos.

2.     Write an essay based on your presentation.


**Exercise 6.2     Analyzing a Print Advertisement in Terms of
Logos, Pathos, and Ethos**

On the next two pages you will find reproductions of two print advertisements,
one for Colgate Sensitive Toothpaste, the other for Tropicana Orange Juice with
Calcium. Choose one of these ads and write an essay analyzing the ad in terms of
logos, pathos, and ethos.

I scream.

You scream.

No scream.

Clinical tests prove new Colgate Sensitive Maximum Strength* Toothpaste delivers significantly more pain relief than Sensodyne. Our advanced formula soothes sensitive nerves inside your teeth, so the only sound you'll make is Mmmm.

## MAXIMUM STRENGTH RELIEF FOR SENSITIVE TEETH

**Exercise 6.3      Analyzing a Print Advertisement in Terms of
                    Logos, Pathos, and Ethos**

Locate a print advertisement in a magazine or newspaper that you feel serves as
a good specimen for analyzing logos, pathos, and ethos. Write an essay analyzing
the ad in terms of these three processes of persuasion. Attach a copy of the ad to
your essay.

**Exercise 6.4      Analyzing the Dominant Persuasive Process
                    in Print Advertisements**

For this exercise you are to locate three separate print advertisements—one
representing each of the three processes of persuasion. The first ad should be an
ad that has as its *dominant feature* the process of logos. The second should be an
ad that has as its *dominant feature* the "emotional substance" aspect of pathos.
The third ad should have ethos as its *dominant feature*. Write an essay analyzing
the three ads. The essay should explain: (1) the dominant persuasive process in
each ad, and (2) the other persuasive processes that may be reflected in each of the
ads.

# IV.   LOGOS, PATHOS, AND ETHOS IN
#       PERSUASIVE LEGAL WRITING

In the preceding sections, we analyzed how the persuasive processes of logos, pathos,
and ethos operate in television advertising. Because of the exaggerated nature of
television ads, we were able to see clearly how these three persuasive processes
operate, how they differ, and how they can work together. Although persuasive
writing in a legal context is much more understated than television advertising, these
same persuasive processes exist in persuasive legal writing.

## A.     *Logos*

It will likely come as no surprise to you that the primary process of persuasion
employed in legal writing is logos. Legal writing audiences are persuaded first and
foremost through logical reasoning and analysis. Consequently, law students and
lawyers learn early on how to persuade through logical analysis based on legal
authorities. In fact, most of what law students learn about persuasive writing in
traditional introductory legal writing courses involves strategies and techniques for
persuading through logos. Among the "logos skills" taught in introductory legal

writing courses are the following:

- The skills involved in *researching* primary and secondary sources to find the legal authority relevant to an issue.

- The skills involved in *analyzing* a legal issue in terms of the relevant authority. These skills include (1) the ability to read and comprehend cases, statutes, and other legal authorities, (2) an appreciation of the "weight" and interrelationship of authorities, and (3) an appreciation of the various types of legal analysis, such as rule-based analysis, analogical analysis, and distinguishing analysis.

- The skills involved in *communicating* legal analysis in writing. These skills include (1) the ability to organize an argument logically and persuasively, (2) the ability to explain effectively the relevant law on an issue and apply it to the case at hand (which typically involves the use of the IRAC paradigm or one of the other basic paradigms taught in the general legal writing texts), and (3) an appreciation of effective citation form.

As this list indicates, the skills involved in persuading through logos in legal writing are essentially the basic writing skills taught in most general legal writing programs. This is no coincidence. Because legal writing audiences are persuaded most by logical reasoning based on legal authorities and precedent, most of the foundational instruction in persuasive legal writing focuses on logos skills. Accordingly, we will not delve further into logos skills here in this text.

## B.    *Pathos*

The second general process of persuasion—pathos—is also employed in legal writing. In fact, both aspects of pathos—emotional substance and medium mood control— are relevant to legal writing.

### 1.  Emotional Substance

Legal writers use the "emotional substance" aspect of pathos whenever they attempt to persuade their audiences using an emotional appeal, as opposed to an appeal to logic. Helene S. Shapo, Marilyn R. Walter, and Elizabeth Fajans explain how and why persuasive legal writers use emotional arguments:

> Many people believe that emotion is inappropriate for a lawyer, at least for certain types of argument. But an appeal to emotion can be proper and effective, if it is restrained. You can evoke sympathy for your client's suffering, anger at the defendant's cruelty, or respect for the values of fairness and justice. An emotion that is inappropriate is hostility towards the opposing counsel and parties. Most important, you should convey your conviction for the merits of your client's case, and positive feelings towards your client. You want to make the judge, even an appellate judge, care who

wins the case.[4]

Similarly, Richard K. Neumann, Jr., explains how, in the development of argument strategies, emotional arguments (called "motivating arguments") can be (and should be) used to support and supplement legal arguments (called "justifying arguments"):

> Include both motivating arguments and justifying arguments. Both are needed to persuade.
>
> A motivating argument is one that causes a judge to *want* to decide a case in a particular way. It causes the judge to feel that any other decision would be unjust. Motivating arguments tend to be centered on facts or a combination of facts and policy. . . .
>
> A justifying argument is one that shows that the law either requires or permits the result urged by the arguer. Justifying arguments are centered on legal rules or on a combination of rules and policy. . . .
>
> Why do you need both motivating arguments and justifying arguments? A motivating argument alone is not enough because even a motivated judge is not supposed to act without a solid legal justification. Judges understandably want to feel that they are doing a professional job of judging, and they can be reversed on appeal if they fail to justify their actions within the law.
>
> And a justifying argument alone is not enough because, in a large number of cases, a justifying argument, without more, will not persuade. The law can usually be interpreted in more than one reasonable way. When a judge is given a choice between two conflicting justifying arguments, each of which is reasonable, the judge will take the one she or he is motivated to take. (Judges are, after all, human.)[5]

"Emotional substance" arguments in legal writing typically involve arguments that focus on the *facts* of a client's case. These types of arguments involve explaining and emphasizing particular facts in the case that will evoke emotions that persuade the decision-maker to decide in the client's favor. As Professors Shapo, Walter, and Fajans indicated above, such arguments could involve explaining facts that evoke sympathy for a client's plight or anger towards an opposing party's behavior. They can also involve many other types of "motivating" emotions such as love (for family, animals, the environment, and so on), patriotism, hope, among many others. Such arguments are designed to act differently on a decision-maker than do arguments based on legal authorities and legal reasoning. As Neumann points out, while arguments based on authority and logical reasoning serve to "justify" a conclusion, arguments based on emotion serve to motivate the decision-maker into *wanting* to reach that conclusion.

---

[4] Helene S. Shapo et al., *Writing and Analysis in the Law* 278 (4th ed. 1999).

[5] Richard K. Neumann, Jr., *Legal Reasoning and Legal Writing: Structure, Strategy, and Style* 289-91 (4th ed. 2001).

Emotional substance arguments in legal writing can be implied or express. An express emotional substance argument would involve an argument in the argument section of a brief or other legal document that expressly tells the reader why certain emotional facts, and the values they implicate, dictate a result in the case. While such express emotional arguments are sometimes used, many attorneys only imply emotional arguments in their legal writing. The most common example of an implied emotional argument occurs in the Statement of Facts section of a trial or appellate brief. As you undoubtedly learned in your introductory legal writing courses, the Statement of Facts section of a trial or appellate brief is the section where the legal writer sets out the facts of the case under consideration. As a general rule, a legal writer is not allowed to "argue" in the Statement of Facts section.[6] The ostensible purpose of the Statement of Facts is merely to inform the reader of the basic facts relevant to the issue under consideration. Nevertheless, the Statement of Facts also provides a legal writer with the opportunity to make an implied emotional argument through the strategic inclusion, organization, and phrasing of certain facts. An effective Statement of Facts contains implied emotional substance arguments by including with the legally relevant facts helpful emotional and background facts and by organizing and phrasing the facts in a way that evokes the desired emotion in the reader. As Neumann has stated, "The ulterior purpose [of the Statement of Facts in a brief] is to imply your motivating arguments through the way the facts are presented."[7]

As they do for logos skills, most introductory legal writing texts include instruction on how legal writers can make emotional arguments in their documents. Consequently, we will not cover these skills in any detail in this text. For our purposes, it suffices simply to identify as we have done which of the various skills that are taught in introductory legal writing courses fall under the "emotional substance" aspect of pathos.

## 2.   Medium Mood Control

The second aspect of pathos—medium mood control—also plays a role in persuasive legal writing. Unlike the "emotional substance" aspect of pathos, however, the "medium mood control" aspect of pathos is not usually covered in much depth in most introductory legal writing courses. Consequently, we will explore it here in some detail.

As we discussed earlier, medium mood control refers to aspects of the *medium* used to communicate a message (as opposed to the *substance* of the message) that have an effect on the audience's mood or emotions. In the area of television advertising, we saw that advertisers employ medium mood control by making their commercials as entertaining as possible. Such strategies assure the advertisers that audiences will watch their ads and be receptive to their message. In persuasive legal writing, medium mood control involves *stylistic* strategies and techniques used by a writer to capture a reader's attention and put a reader in a contented and receptive

---

[6] *See, e.g., id.* at 342.

[7] *Id.* at 341.

mood. That is, medium mood control in legal writing focuses on how a writer's writing style, as opposed to the substance of an argument, affects the mood or emotions of a reader. Classical rhetoricians have long recognized that writers whose style captivates and charms their readers will have an advantage over writers whose style irritates or bores their readers.

Obviously, the medium mood control strategies employed by legal writers must be more subtle than those employed by television advertisers. Conspicuous and exaggerated attempts at humor, for example, do not go over very well in legal writing. Instead, legal writers are limited to three relatively conservative strategies for engaging their readers and for putting their readers in a contented mood through their writing style.

First, legal writers can please their readers by effectively organizing their arguments and by using simple and understandable language. Few things put readers off more than being made to struggle through a disorganized discussion or through overly complicated prose. While an unclear writing style obviously hurts the substance (that is, the logos) of an argument by risking confusion and misunderstanding on the part of the reader, it also hurts the medium mood control aspect of pathos by irritating and frustrating the reader. Conversely, writers who use a clear writing style not only communicate the substance (logos) of their argument more effectively, but they also take advantage of medium mood control. Readers of well-written prose are more contented than those who must struggle to read a document; they are therefore more receptive to the substance of the message being communicated. Thus, the first and most important strategy of medium mood control in legal writing is a clear, organized writing style.

The second strategy of medium mood control relevant to legal writers is to avoid stylistic techniques or devices that may irritate or offend a reader. A legal writer, for example, should not use insulting language, condescending comments, and obscure allusions. Our discussion in Chapter 2 provided a concrete example of this strategy. In discussing the use of literary references in legal writing, we saw that, while such references can be an effective device, writers should not include obscure references that are likely to be unknown to readers. Such obscure references offend readers by suggesting that the writer does not care if they understand. Thus, to take advantage of the medium mood control aspect of pathos, legal writers should be sensitive to stylistic strategies in their documents that might adversely affect the reader's mood.

The third and most aggressive way for legal writers to regulate medium mood control is by using stylistic devices that produce rhetorical flair. As previously mentioned, legal writers cannot go to the extremes that television advertisers can to entertain and amuse their audiences. Nevertheless, legal writers can "entertain" through a more subtle form of amusement—artistic and eloquent language. Some legal writers are able to capture the attention of their readers and charm them through the use of stylistic devices that make their writing entertaining to read. In Chapters 2 through 4, for example, we saw how literary references in persuasive legal writing can entertain readers and thereby make readers more receptive to the writer's message. In Chapters 9 and 10, we will explore other effective rhetorical stylistic devices, such as metaphor, alliteration, and personification. Because such stylistic devices can enhance a reader's emotional reaction to a legal writer's writing style, they help writers take advantage of the medium mood control aspect of pathos.

## C.    *Ethos*

The final process of persuasion—ethos—also plays a significant role in legal writing. Ethos, as we have discussed previously, involves efforts on the part of an advocate to establish credibility in the eyes of the decision-maker. The more credibility that an advocate has, the more weight a decision-maker will give to the advocate's position.

While ethos is at least as important as, if not more important than, logos and pathos, it typically receives the least coverage in introductory legal writing courses. Consequently, Chapters 7 and 8 will explore ethos in some detail, covering both its general nature and its specific implications for persuasive legal writing.

# Chapter 7

# *Ethos in Legal Writing: Character and Good Will*

> [P]ersuasive discourse depends as much on the advocate's character and credibility (*ethos*) as it does on the logic of the argument or the emotional content of the case.[1]
> — Michael Frost

In the preceding chapter, we learned that one of the three basic processes of persuasion recognized by classical rhetoricians is that of *ethos*, persuading by establishing credibility in the eyes of one's audience. According to classical rhetoricians, one who seeks to persuade another must present himself or herself as a credible source of information. An advocate who lacks credibility in the eyes of a decision-maker will have very little chance of persuading that decision-maker to adopt the advocate's position.

In this chapter we will examine the process of ethos in detail. In this analysis, we will discover that there are actually several different aspects of ethos, each being very important to the credibility of an advocate. We will also explore with specificity the relevance of these classical rhetoric principles to persuasive legal writing.

## I.   AN INTRODUCTION TO ETHOS

### A.   *The Importance of Ethos to the Persuasive Process*

A strong argument could be made that ethos is more important to persuasive legal writing than either logical argument (logos) or appeals to emotion (pathos). In fact, the effectiveness of both emotional and logical arguments depends in large part on perceptions of the advocate's credibility. Consider, for example, the role of credibility in an emotional appeal. A highly emotional argument, if presented by someone with little credibility, will likely be met with skepticism rather than acceptance. When an emotional argument is made by someone who possesses little credibility, it often comes across as an effort to manipulate or distract the decision-maker. Conversely, when an advocate who possesses credibility makes an emotional argument, the audience is more likely to receive it as it was intended, as a supplement to the arguments based on logic and reason.

Likewise, credibility is important in arguments based on logic and reason. The law relevant to any particular legal issue is often susceptible to multiple interpretations, many of which could be reasonable. Arguments based on the logical

---

[1] Michael Frost, *Ethos, Pathos & Legal Audience*, 99 Dick. L. Rev. 85, 104 (1994).

application of legal authorities rarely point to a single clear conclusion. Not surprisingly, then, when a decision-maker is forced to choose between alternative logical conclusions, an advocate's credibility can play a significant role in the decision-maker's deliberations.

## B.    Establishing Credibility Through One's Writing

In our analysis of ethos, we will focus exclusively on ways in which a legal advocate's written document impacts his or her credibility in the eyes of a reader. The significance of this statement is threefold. First, we are not discussing here how an advocate's pre-existing reputation may affect the persuasive process. In some situations, an advocate may be seen as a credible source of information based on his or her general reputation in the community or on previous dealings between the advocate and the decision-maker. Such aspects of credibility, however, are beyond our coverage. Frequently, a decision-maker will have no prior knowledge of an advocate. In these situations, an advocate's credibility will depend completely on how the advocate presents himself or herself in the written document submitted to the decision-maker in the present matter. Even where an advocate has established a reputation with a decision-maker, the latter's impression of the advocate's credibility will still be affected to a significant extent by the document at issue. Thus, while it is important for an attorney to develop a general reputation for credibility among practicing attorneys and judges in the community, we focus here on how an advocate can evince credibility in a specific written document.

Second, this discussion will focus only on how advocates can evince credibility in writing; we will not focus on the related subject of how an advocate can evince credibility in a speech or other oral presentation. Ethos—defined as the process by which an advocate establishes credibility in the eyes of his or her audience—clearly applies to both written and oral advocacy. Yet, while there is much overlap between how a persuasive writer evinces credibility and how an oral advocate evinces credibility, significant differences exist between the two. In this text on persuasive *writing* strategies, we will limit our discussion of ethos to concepts and strategies applicable to written advocacy.

Third, this text goes beyond a discussion of whether an advocate *is* credible to discuss how an advocate actually *evinces* credibility to a reader. It is not enough for an advocate to actually be credible; the reader must have specific knowledge of the aspects of an advocate's character that indicate credibility. Thus, our focus will be on aspects of a written document that impact the reader's impression of a writer's credibility. Our discussion will not be phrased in terms of what makes an advocate credible; our discussion will be phrased in terms of how an advocate projects and evinces credibility to a reader through his or her written product. This is not to say, however, that it is enough for a writer to *appear* credible regardless of whether he or she actually is. As we will see, in many incidences, an advocate can only evince a trait of credibility if he or she actually possesses it. Furthermore, as we will discuss in several places, many dangers confront an advocate who attempts to feign credibility or who attempts to establish a trait of credibility deceitfully.

### C.   *The Three Components of Ethos: Intelligence, Character, and Good Will*

Although the word "credibility" is frequently used as a general term for those traits of an advocate that inspire confidence and trust in an audience, classical rhetoricians have long recognized three separate components to credibility. According to these classical rhetoricians, the three qualities that help to win the confidence of a reader are *intelligence*, *character*, and *good will*. Aristotle explained these aspects of ethos as follows:

> As for the [writers] themselves, the sources of our trust in them are three, for apart from the arguments [i.e., logos] there are three things that gain our belief, namely, intelligence, character, and good will. [Writers] are untrustworthy in what they say or advise from one or more of the following causes. Either through want of intelligence they form wrong opinions; or, while they form correct opinions, their rascality leads them to say what they do not think; or, while intelligent and honest enough, they are not well-disposed [to the audience], and so perchance will fail to advise the best course, though they see it. That is a complete list of the possibilities. It necessarily follows that the [writer] who is thought to have [intelligence, character, and good will] has the confidence of his [audience].[2]

In the rest of this chapter, we will explore in detail the implications of two of these qualities—character and good will—for persuasive legal writing. An in-depth discussion of the third aspect of ethos—intelligence—is found in Chapter 8.

## II.   EVINCING GOOD MORAL CHARACTER IN LEGAL WRITING

Classical rhetoricians recognize *character* as one of the three fundamentals of ethos. To gain the confidence of their audiences, legal writers must demonstrate that they are of good moral character, or at least that they are not of questionable moral character. If a reader believes that a writer is, to use Aristotle's word, a "rascal," that is, if a reader believes that a writer is not above lying, cheating, deceiving, or misleading, then the reader will view the writer's arguments with skepticism and doubt. Conversely, if a reader believes that a writer possesses good character—or at least if the reader has no reason to question the writer's character—then the reader will be more receptive to the writer's arguments and assertions.

There are several traits or characteristics that legal writers should project through their writing to demonstrate that they are of good moral character. These traits include:

---

[2] Aristotle, *The Rhetoric of Aristotle* 91-92 (Lane Cooper trans. 1932) (some alterations in the original translation). Because Aristotle's *Rhetoric* focuses on oral persuasion rather than persuasive writing, the actual quote uses the word "speakers" not "writers." I have inserted the word "writers" because our discussion is limited to legal writing and because these concepts are as applicable to persuasive writing as they are to oral persuasion.

Truthfulness
Candor
Zeal
Respect
Professionalism

In the following discussions, we will analyze each of these traits and examine how what a legal writer does or says in a document affects the projection of these traits.

## A.     Evincing Truthfulness

Arguably, the most important character trait for legal writers to project to their readers is *truthfulness*. If a reader believes that an advocate is untruthful, the reader will view what the advocate writes with doubt and skepticism, giving the advocate's arguments minimal consideration.

Legal writers can evince truthfulness in their writing in two main ways: by explaining the *facts* of the matter under consideration accurately and honestly and by explaining the *law* relevant to the matter accurately and honestly. Stated in the reverse, there are two main ways that a legal writer can cause a reader to doubt the writer's truthfulness: by misstating or misrepresenting the facts of the matter or by misstating or misrepresenting the law relevant to the matter.

As you undoubtedly learned in your introductory legal writing courses, it is an express violation of the ethical rules regulating the practice of law for an attorney knowingly to make a false statement of law or fact to a court.[3] Such conduct can result in severe sanctions as an ethical violation. Apart from and in addition to the ethical implications of such conduct, however, misrepresenting the law or facts damages an advocate's credibility and negatively affects his or her effectiveness. Thus, legal writers should seek always to evince truthfulness in their writing by accurately and honestly explaining the facts of the matter and the law on which they rely.

The following two cases clearly demonstrate how, apart from the ethical implications, misrepresentations of fact or law in court briefs can undermine an advocate's credibility.

### 1.   Misstatement of Fact in an Appellate Brief: *Howells v. Pennsylvania Unemployment Compensation Board of Review*

In *Howells v. Pennsylvania Unemployment Compensation Board of Review*,[4] the petitioner was a worker seeking unemployment compensation benefits, arguing that the termination of his employment was not voluntary, but a dismissal.[5] The Unemployment Compensation Board of Review found that the worker had repeatedly

---

[3] Model Rules of Professional Conduct Rule 3.3(a)(1) (1996).

[4] 442 A.2d 389 (Pa. Commw. Ct. 1982).

[5] *Id.* at 390.

been late for work prior to the end of his employment and that he had been warned by his employer that "'he would be discharged' if such actions continued."[6] The record further indicated that the worker testified to the Board that "'about a week before' the end of the employment, he had come in late and 'was told that, if I missed time or come in late, more or less right from my foreman, that I might as well pick up my check.'"[7]

On the day that the worker's employment ended, he knew that he was going to be late for work and, therefore, decided not to go in at all. The worker testified:

> I would have been like fifteen minutes' late. . . . I remembered what the man had said to me, and I felt, well, I may as well not go in, because they don't need me anymore. So I considered myself laid off from the job. This is because of what my foreman told me. . . . In other words, he gave me a warning, and I wouldn't go against him.[8]

In light of this evidence, the Board refused to award the worker unemployment compensation benefits on the ground that the worker was not discharged, but had voluntarily quit.[9] The worker petitioned to the Commonwealth Court of Pennsylvania for review of the Board's decision. The Commonwealth Court affirmed the Board's decision. The court held:

> Where a claimant does not report to work in the face of a discharge warning, the cessation of employment is viewed, not as a firing, but as a voluntary quit, unless the evidence establishes that discharge would be a certainty. Here the claimant himself characterized as a "warning" the information that he "might as well pick up [his] check" if he was absent or late. In view of the employer's previous toleration, discharge was not a certainty. . . .
> Hence, the board's denial of benefits is affirmed.[10]

Aside from the substantive issues involved in the case, the *Howells* court discussed certain misstatements of fact made by the petitioner's counsel in a brief submitted to the court. The court pointed out that the petitioner's counsel had undermined his credibility as an advocate by misstating in his brief that the petitioner had gone to work on the day his employment terminated and "was told to go home." This statement was clearly contrary to the worker's own testimony that he decided not to go to work that day because he knew he would be late and because of the prior warning he had received from his foreman. After setting out a quote of the worker's testimony, the *Howells* court stated:

---

[6] *Id.* (quoting the Board's findings).

[7] *Id.* (quoting the claimant's testimony).

[8] *Id.* (quoting the claimant's testimony).

[9] *Id.*

[10] *Id.* at 390-91 (citations omitted).

In the face of this evidence, counsel for the claimant has seriously undermined his professional credibility with this court by submitting . . . a brief in which he stated that the claimant "appeared for work at his place of employment and was told by the foreman to go home," and, in another part of the brief, that claimant "appeared for work and was told to go home. . . ." At still another point in the brief, counsel averred that claimant "testified that he appeared for work at Bechtel where he was employed and was informed by the foreman to go home." Such misstatement or carelessness, in view of the actual testimony quoted above, is a breach of counsel's duty to this court and to the client.[11]

The *Howells* case provides us with a good illustration of how misrepresentations of fact in legal writing can affect an advocate's credibility.[12] Although we cannot know for sure how much this misstatement by the petitioner's counsel affected the court's ultimate decision, we do know through the court's express statements that it did affect the court's impression of the brief writer. Based on this we can reasonably speculate that the petitioner's counsel, with his credibility tarnished, was less effective in his efforts to persuade the court to adopt his viewpoint. Consequently, it comes as no surprise to readers of this opinion that, in the end, the court decided against the petitioner and his counsel.

### 2.   Misstatement of the Law in an Appellate Brief: *In re Citric Acid Litigation*

The matter of *In re Citric Acid Litigation*[13] involved an allegation of price fixing in the citric acid industry.[14] "Citric acid is a corn derivative with a wide variety of uses in the manufacture of food, soft drinks, detergents, and pharmaceuticals. The citric acid market is dominated by a small number of major producers."[15] Four major citric acid producers pled guilty under federal antitrust law to conspiring to raise the price of citric acid by limiting sales. After these criminal proceedings, several separate civil law suits were brought by purchasers of citric acid against these four citric acid producers and a fifth producer, Cargill, who had not been indicted in connection with

---

[11] *Id.* at 390 n.1.

[12] It is difficult to tell from the opinion whether the *Howells* court believed that the misstatement by the petitioner's counsel was an effort to deceive the court or an unintentional mistake. If the court felt that the misstatement was intentional, its impression of the attorney's truthfulness and general moral character would be affected, as discussed above. If, however, the court felt the misstatement resulted from carelessness, its impression not of the advocate's character but of his *intelligence* would be most affected, as we will discuss in Chapter 8. In either event, the misstatement clearly had a negative impact on the advocate's credibility in the eyes of the court.

[13] 996 F. Supp. 951 (N.D. Cal. 1998).

[14] *Id.* at 953.

[15] *Id.*

the conspiracy.[16]

Because Cargill was never charged with involvement in the conspiracy, it brought a motion for summary judgment in the civil cases.[17] The plaintiffs challenged the motion asserting that, although Cargill was not indicted along with the other four producers, it had nevertheless been involved in the conspiracy and was liable for civil damages along with the other conspirators.[18] After reviewing the record, the United States District Court for the Northern District of California granted Cargill's motion for summary judgment. The court held that "no reasonable jury could, on the basis of this record, conclude that defendant Cargill was a member of the conspiracy."[19]

As part of its analysis, the court had to consider, among other things, the significance of the fact that Cargill's prices for citric acid during the times in question paralleled the prices of the conspirators. The court recognized the general rule that, in an industry such as the citric acid industry that is dominated by a few major producers (a situation known as a "concentrated market"), "parallel pricing, by itself, is generally insufficient to prove an antitrust conspiracy."[20] After reviewing the facts of the case, the court found that the fact that Cargill's prices paralleled the prices of the other major producers in the concentrated citric acid industry was not evidence of conspiratorial behavior on the part of Cargill.[21]

It is in connection with this discussion of parallel pricing that the *Citric Acid* court expressed its concern over certain misstatements made in the plaintiff's brief submitted in opposition to the defendant's motion for summary judgment. As stated previously, the general rule for a *concentrated* market is that parallel pricing is generally insufficient by itself to prove an antitrust conspiracy. The converse of this rule is that "'when a market is highly *unconcentrated*, parallel pricing alone may be all the proof that is required [to prove an antitrust conspiracy].'"[22] In their brief, the plaintiffs' counsel misquoted this rule, "asserting that parallel pricing is all that is required when a market is highly *concentrated*."[23] In a footnote, the *Citric Acid* court identified this misquote on the part of the plaintiff's counsel and stated, "Such an egregious error on a central point of law diminishes plaintiffs' credibility and borders

---

[16] *Id.*

[17] *Id.*

[18] *Id.* at 954.

[19] *Id.* at 962.

[20] *Id.* at 956.

[21] *Id.*

[22] *Id.* at 956 n.1 (quoting *In re Coordinated Pretrial Proceedings in Petroleum Products Antitrust Litigation*, 906 F.2d 432, 445 n.9 (9th Cir. 1990)) (emphasis added).

[23] *Id.* (quoting Plaintiffs' Memorandum in Opposition to Motion for Summary Judgment, at 25).

on a violation of Federal Rules of Civil Procedure 11(b)(2)."[24]

The *Citric Acid* case provides a compelling example of how misrepresentations of the law relevant to a matter in a legal document such as a brief can negatively impact the credibility of the advocate submitting the document. By making this misstatement, the counsel for the plaintiffs severely damaged their credibility in the eyes of the court, not only regarding the "parallel pricing" argument, but with regard to all of the plaintiffs' arguments. The summary judgment motion required the court to analyze more than ten separate sub-issues.[25] Although the plaintiffs' counsel misrepresented the law on only one of these sub-issues, this single misrepresentation undermined their credibility generally, thus potentially undermining the effectiveness of all of their arguments. When an advocate's character is brought into question, his or her entire argument is affected. We cannot know the extent of the impact this misstatement had on the court's ultimate conclusion. Yet, based on the court's express statement, it clearly hurt the plaintiffs' position. And the court did ultimately decide against the plaintiffs.

---

### Exercise 7.1    Analyzing the Implications of Ethos on an Appellate Court's Decision

Find and read the case *Sobol v. Capital Management Consultants, Inc.*, 726 P.2d 335 (Nev. 1986). Write an essay explaining this case and analyzing the implications of the advocates' ethos on the Nevada Supreme Court's decision. Use the preceding discussions of the *Howells* and *Citric Acid* cases as guidelines for your essay.

---

## B.    *Evincing Candor*

Candor, the second general character trait that legal writers should project through their writing, is related to truthfulness, and yet differs from it significantly. Untruthfulness involves deceit by express misrepresentation. A lack of candor, on the other hand, involves deceit by *omitting* information.[26] As we saw in the previous section, in the context of legal writing, untruthfulness involves an express

---

[24] *Id.* Federal Rules of Civil Procedure 11(b)(2) provides that, by presenting a signed document to a court, an attorney is certifying that "to the best of the [attorney's] knowledge, information, and belief, formed after an inquiry reasonable under the circumstances, . . . the claims, defenses, and other legal contentions therein are warranted by existing law."

[25] *See id.* at 954-61.

[26] "Truthfulness" and "candor" are actually sub-traits of the more general character trait of "honesty." Rather than discussing honesty generally, this discussion has been divided into the two sub-traits in order to clarify as much as possible the various ways legal writers can risk damaging their credibility.

misrepresentation of facts or law. In contrast, a lack of candor in legal writing involves deceiving readers by omitting legally significant information from a document.

There are two main ways that a legal writer can damage his or her credibility through a lack of candor. First, a legal writer could fail to include in his or her document legally significant facts that are damaging to the advocate's position. As we discussed in the previous section, it is an express violation of the ethical rules regulating the practice of law for an advocate knowingly to make a false statement of fact to a court.[27] This prohibition applies both to express misrepresentations of facts and tacit misrepresentations accomplished through the omission of facts. Thus, misrepresenting facts by the omission of damaging facts is an ethical violation punishable by sanctions. However, aside from and in addition to the ethical implications of misrepresenting facts through omission, such conduct can also severely damage an advocate's credibility in the eyes of a court. Linda Holdeman Edwards explains how, apart from the ethical implications, lack of candor regarding the facts of a case can undermine an advocate's credibility:

> [A] lawyer must not misrepresent facts. Misrepresentation includes both stating facts untruthfully and omitting material facts when the result of the omission is to create a false inference. . . .
>
> In virtually every case, you'll find some facts you wish weren't there, generally because they are unfavorable for your client's case. The more material the facts are, the more you wish they didn't exist. But they exist nonetheless, and leaving them out of your Fact Statement won't make them go away, for they will certainly appear in the opposing brief. Omitting them from your brief will only damage your credibility before the judge, causing the judge to wonder how much she can rely on the other facts you assert. Few things make a judge angrier than feeling misled by a lawyer. . . . Therefore, both ethics and good strategy require inclusion of all material facts, whether favorable or not.[28]

The second way that legal writers undermine their credibility through lack of candor is by failing to disclose adverse legal authority when required to do so by ethical rules. As you probably learned in your introductory persuasive writing course, an advocate is required under the rules of ethics to disclose to a court adverse authority from a controlling jurisdiction known to the advocate and not disclosed by the opposing counsel.[29] This does not mean that an advocate is required to (or expected to) disclose all unfavorable law relevant to an issue. However, if the adverse authority is from a controlling jurisdiction and it has not been disclosed to the court

---

[27] *See supra* note 3 and accompanying text (discussing Model Rules of Professional Conduct Rule 3.3(a)(1) (1996)).

[28] Linda Holdeman Edwards, *Legal Writing: Process, Analysis, and Organization* 338-39 (2d ed. 1999).

[29] *See* Model Rules of Professional Conduct Rule 3.3(a)(3) (1996).

by the opposing counsel, an advocate has an obligation to inform the court of the authority. Moreover, this obligation applies not only to legal authorities that existed at the time the advocate submitted his or her brief to the court, but also to authorities that may arise after the submission of the brief and before the court renders a decision. As Beverly J. Blair explains, "[An] advocate must not only relate cases accurately at the time of filing the initial brief but must stay abreast of the status of cases on which the advocate relies and affirmatively advise the court of any changes pending the resolution of the case before the court."[30] Failure to disclose adverse authority under any of these circumstances is an ethical violation. More importantly for our purposes, however, it can also severely damage the credibility of an advocate by evincing a lack of candor and forthrightness on the part of the advocate.

In summary, legal writers should make an effort to evince candor and forthrightness by disclosing adverse facts and law as required by ethical rules. Failure to disclose such information, apart from being an ethical violation, can severely undermine the writer's credibility. If a decision-maker feels that a writer has been less than candid, the decision-maker is likely to view the writer's arguments generally with doubt and skepticism. Under such a cloud of skepticism, an advocate can hardly be effective in persuading a decision-maker to adopt his or her viewpoints.

### 1. Failure to Disclose Damaging Facts in an Appellate Brief: *Hickman v. Fraternal Order of Eagles, Boise #115*

In *Hickman v. Fraternal Order of Eagles, Boise #115,*[31] the plaintiffs-appellants brought a negligence action against a fraternal organization alleging that the organization negligently served alcohol to a driver who subsequently caused an automobile collision that injured one of the plaintiffs and killed family members of the other plaintiffs.[32] At the trial court level, a jury found that the defendant fraternal organization was not negligent, and judgment was entered for the defendant.[33] The plaintiffs appealed to the Idaho Supreme Court. In its brief to the appellate court, the defendant-respondent indicated that, while the intoxicated driver had consumed alcohol at a Christmas party hosted by the organization, the driver had "nine 'whiskey sours'" at his sister's home after he had left the party and before the automobile accident.[34] The plaintiffs-appellants, however, had failed to include these crucial facts in their brief, an omission that the Idaho Supreme Court did not look upon favorably. In a footnote, the *Hickman* court commented on this lack of candor in the plaintiff-appellant brief:

---

[30] Beverly J. Blair, *Ethical Considerations in Advocacy: What First-Year Legal Writing Students Need to Know*, 4 Legal Writing 109, 115-16 (1998).

[31] 758 P.2d 704 (Idaho 1988).

[32] *Id.* at 705.

[33] *Id.*

[34] *Id.*

> We first learned of [the driver's] drinking subsequent to the Christmas party when reading Respondent's Brief. Counsel for appellant Hickman failed to include these facts in his brief, contrary to Idaho Appellate Rule 35, which requires that appellant give an accurate statement of the facts. . . . Counsel for appellant damages both his credibility and his client's position when he fails to state the facts to this Court with the utmost candor.[35]

In the end, the Idaho Supreme Court upheld the judgment for the defendant.[36]

The *Hickman* case provides a compelling example of the negative consequences of a lack of candor in a persuasive legal document. In the *Hickman* case, the appellate court had to analyze a number of important issues raised by the case. Moreover, both attorneys—the attorney for the plaintiffs-appellants and the attorney for the defendant-respondent—submitted briefs to the court arguing their positions on the various issues. Early in his brief, however, the attorney for the plaintiffs-appellants undermined his credibility and damaged his case by failing to be candid regarding the facts of the matter. By being less than forthright, the attorney for the plaintiffs-appellants caused the court to doubt his credibility as a source of information. Although we cannot know how much this lack of candor affected the court's ultimate decision, we do know from the court's express statements that this deception affected its impression of the advocate, and it is a safe bet that it had a negative effect on the advocate's general effectiveness. Again, we as readers of the opinion are not surprised at the end of the opinion when the court affirms the judgment for the defendant-respondent.

### 2. Candid Disclosure of Adverse Authority: *Commonwealth v. Frisino*

In *Commonwealth v. Frisino*,[37] a defendant was convicted in a Massachusetts trial court of breaking and entering, and the defendant appealed to the Appeals Court of Massachusetts on a number of procedural and evidentiary grounds.[38] On one of these evidentiary issues, a case relevant to the issue had been decided by the Massachusetts Supreme Court after the parties had submitted their briefs but before the Appeals Court decided the case. The respondent's attorney—the assistant district attorney for the Commonwealth—notified the *Frisino* court of the case (called the *Weaver* case) both in writing through a supplemental memorandum and orally in oral argument.[39] The assistant DA did this even though *Weaver* supported a proposition directly adverse to the Commonwealth's position. In commending the assistant DA's candor, the *Frisino* court stated:

---

[35] *Id.* at 705 n.1.

[36] *Id.* at 708.

[37] 488 N.E.2d 51 (Mass. App. Ct. 1986).

[38] *Id.* at 53.

[39] *Id.* at 54 n.7.

The *Weaver* case was decided after the briefs were filed in this case. The Commonwealth, commendably, directed the court's attention, by way of memorandum and again at oral argument, to *Weaver* as well as another later decided case. Both decisions supported a position adverse to the Commonwealth. Such advocacy comports with the highest level of professionalism and deserves to be praised as exemplary ethical conduct.[40]

In the end, the *Frisino* court found for the defendant and reversed the conviction.[41] Nevertheless, the attorney for the Commonwealth was able to secure the confidence of the court by evincing a strong moral character. The attorney lost, but not for lack of credibility in the eyes of the court. Thus, the attorney can be confident that the court heard and gave due consideration to his arguments.

---

**Exercise 7.2     Analyzing the Implications of Ethos on an
                   Appellate Court's Decision**

Find and read the case *Alfonso v. State,* 633 So. 2d 126 (Fla. 3d Dist. Ct. App. 1994). Write an essay explaining this case and analyzing the implications of the advocates' ethos on the Florida appellate court's decision. Use the preceding discussions of *Hickman* and *Frisino* as guidelines for your essay.

---

In the preceding discussion, we saw that an advocate can damage his or her credibility through lack of candor both by failing to disclose adverse facts and by failing to disclose adverse law when required to do so by ethical rules. In addition to these two concepts, there is a third concept relevant to the projection of candor in legal writing: conceding factual or legal assertions made by opposing counsel.

When an attorney is in the position of a respondent or appellee—that is, when an attorney is writing second on a matter, responding to assertions made in an opening petition or brief—the attorney must consider which factual and legal assertions to contest rigorously and which, if any, to concede. Many advocates take the position that nothing should be conceded. This, however, is an unwise strategy. Refusing to concede anything, even insignificant or incontestible points, undermines an advocate's credibility. Some points are worth contesting; others are not. Courts often frown upon advocates who steadfastly refuse to concede anything and thereby unnecessarily complicate and lengthen the decision-making process. Such behavior sends the message that the advocate is more interested in being contrary and combative than in being honest and forthright about the legitimate points of contention in the case. On the other hand, an advocate can gain much by candidly conceding "concedable" points, thus narrowing the focus of the dispute. Consider, for

---

[40] *Id.*

[41] *Id.* at 55.

example, this statement by the Fourth District Court of Appeal of Florida regarding the propriety and advisability of lawyers from the Attorney General's Office conceding matters of law and fact under certain circumstances:

> We think it very important to reaffirm that it is entirely appropriate, even preferable, for an appellee's lawyer to accept factual assertions in the statement of facts in the initial brief and to concede facts or law at oral argument. Good lawyers do not waste time in petty quarrels over tertiary details, so long as the ultimate facts and law are accurately stated. In this regard, [appellee's attorney] Mr. Rogers is one of the better lawyers frequently appearing in our court. His briefs for the state usually concentrate on the important matters for our consideration and do not have us counting dancing angels on small promontories. We recognize in his advocacy a lawyer on whom we can usually rely to get it right and do it ethically. We commend Mr. Rogers for his professionalism in this case.
>
> We therefore deem it equally important to emphasize that the lawyers from the Attorney General's office who argue in this or any other appellate court in this state simply must have the authority in the heat of oral argument to concede weaknesses in the state's case. To deprive them of that authority is to severely weaken their effectiveness as advocates. Moreover the failure of a lawyer to acknowledge clearly contrary facts or law is decidedly unethical and unprofessional.[42]

As this statement indicates, conceding points of fact and law can improve an advocate's credibility in the eyes of a court. The question then becomes, when and how should advocates concede. The determination of whether to concede a point is a matter of strategy and judgment involving two variables: (1) how *crucial* the point is to the client's overall case, and (2) how *contestable* the point is. These variables are correlated and involve parallel sliding scales. For example, an attorney should clearly concede a point that is both of minor significance (low on the "crucial" scale) and highly incontestable (low on the "contestability" scale). By the same token, an attorney should not concede any point that is dispositive of a client's whole case (high on the "crucial" scale) yet highly contestable (high on the "contestability" scale). Unfortunately, a vast gray area lies between these two extremes. In these situations, an advocate must make a judgment call. However, in making this call the attorney should keep in mind the rhetorical benefits to be gained by being candid regarding points that are legitimately subject to concession.

If an advocate does decide to concede a point, the advocate should nevertheless engage in "damage control" to minimize the negative impact of the concession. As Carole C. Berry explains, if an advocate concedes a point, the advocate should, in connection with the concession, "indicate to the court the limits of the concession and argue its relative insignificance. The concession must emphasize that the decision should still be in favor of the appellee. . . . [C]ounsel must . . . argue the limits of the

---

[42] *Barnes v. State*, 743 So.2d 1105, 1112-13 (Fla. 4th Dist. Ct. App. 1999). Although this statement from *Barnes* focuses mostly on conceding in oral argument, it applies with equal force to conceding in responsive briefs.

concession and guide the court to what is important and decisive in the case."[43]

## C.     Evincing Zeal

The third quality that an advocate should evince through his or her writing is *zeal*; that is, an advocate should project passion, conviction and confidence in a client's position. Ethical rules provide that, "A lawyer should act with commitment and dedication to the interests of the client and with zeal in advocacy upon the client's behalf."[44] Judges and other readers of persuasive legal writing expect advocates to pursue their client's interests zealously. It follows then, that if a reader receives the impression through an advocate's writing that the advocate is not confident in and committed to the client's arguments, the reader will likely give less weight and attention to those arguments. After all, if a party's own advocate lacks conviction and confidence in the party's position, why then should the impartial decision-maker give it much consideration? A passionate advocate has more credibility than one who appears disinterested or lacking in confidence, and a decision-maker will not give much weight to a half-hearted, lackluster argument.

The manifestation of zeal in a legal writer's document is mainly affected by two things: (1) the substantive effort made by the advocate on behalf of the client, and (2) the language or tone of the argument. If a legal document shows that the writer has not put much substantive effort into investigating, researching, strategizing, analyzing, and/or writing a client's case and arguments, this lack of effort will be viewed by a reader as a lack of confidence and commitment on the part of the writer. Thus, while a lack of effort on the part of an advocate obviously hurts a client's case due to the absence of persuasive substance, and while such conduct may also constitute an ethical violation, it has a third effect, as well: It undermines the credibility of the advocate's position. Conversely, whenever an advocate's document demonstrates through its substance that the advocate is zealously pursuing the client's cause, the advocate receives two benefits: first, the substance itself helps to persuade, and second, the credibility of the advocate's argument is enhanced by the zeal and commitment reflected in the advocate's effort.

The writer's perceived zeal in a case is also revealed by his or her choice of language and by the tone used in the document. An advocate generally should present his or her arguments using forceful and confident language. As John C. Dernbach, Richard V. Singleton II, Cathleen S. Wharton, and Joan M. Ruhtenberg have stated,

> [A lawyer should] use forceful and affirmative language. . . . Word choice is as important as structure in an argument. Words make an argument seem confident or defensive, bold or halting, credible or dubious. . . . Words cannot substitute for good argument, but they can greatly enhance it. The lawyer whose arguments are stated with authority and confidence is the most

---

[43] Carole C. Berry, *Effective Appellate Advocacy: Brief Writing and Oral Argument* 119 (2d ed. 1999).

[44] Model Rules of Professional Conduct Rule 1.3 cmt. 1 (1999).

convincing to the court.[45]

The advocate who evinces confidence through his or her writing gains the confidence of the decision-maker. A confident writer is more credible, and therefore more effective, than one who is not.

The foregoing discussion regarding the importance of evincing zeal in legal writing is subject to a number of important qualifications and warnings. Although an advocate should evince zeal, it should not be overdone, nor should it be done without thinking about what is most appropriate for the specific situation. Advocates should evince zeal, but they should not be overzealous. Overzealousness can hurt an advocate's credibility even more than a lack of zeal. Thus, the foregoing suggestions on how to evince zeal should be tempered with the following guidelines and warnings:

- First, an advocate should not sacrifice truthfulness and candor in an effort to be zealous. As we discussed in the previous two sections, an advocate must evince truthfulness and candor by presenting the law and facts relevant to a matter honestly and accurately. An advocate should not forget or ignore these principles in the name of zealousness.

- Second, an advocate should not be so zealous as to offend a court or other decision-maker by showing a lack of respect. In the following section we will explore ways by which a legal writer can evince a proper amount of respect for a court. An advocate should not violate the suggestions in that section in a effort to be zealous.

- Third, an advocate should not be overzealous to the point of engaging in unprofessional conduct. In the section following our discussion of respectfulness, we will discuss "professionalism" as another character trait that advocates should project in their writing. Advocates should not pursue zeal in any ways that would run afoul of the guidelines regarding professionalism.

- Finally, before incorporating forceful and assertive language in a document, an advocate should consider what level of assertiveness is most appropriate for that situation and for that audience. An advocate should gear his or her assertiveness to the situation. Some situations require more assertiveness and some require less. An effective advocate adapts his or her style to the situation at hand.

---

[45] John C. Dernbach et al., *A Practical Guide to Legal Writing and Legal Method* 233 (2d ed. 1994).

## D.     *Evincing Respect*

The fourth character trait that advocates should project through their writing in order
to establish credibility with the reader is *respect*. Decision-makers, such as judges,
are more receptive to advocates who demonstrate an appropriate amount of respect
both for them and for the legal system. Conversely, disrespectful language in a brief
or other persuasive document undermines the writer's credibility and negatively
impacts the writer's effectiveness as an advocate. Obviously, disrespect toward the
decision-maker is unwise: It is never a good idea to offend the very person you are
trying to persuade. However, even when the disrespect is directed not at the decision-
maker but at other judges or other aspects of the legal system, such conduct can have
negative consequences on the persuasive process. Disrespect generally evinces a lack
of sound moral character and thereby undermines the advocate's credibility as a
source of information.

An advocate's writing can show disrespect in three general ways: (1) by including
disrespectful content, (2) by writing in a disrespectful tone, and (3) by submitting a
messy and unprofessional document. Disrespectful content includes such things as
discourteous and improper comments about a judge. Consider, for example, the
following comment by the First Circuit Court of Appeals in *Scully Signal Company
v. Electronics Corporation of America*[46] regarding disrespectful remarks made about
the lower court in the appellant's brief:

> We must comment on the entirely unacceptable tenor of argument by
> [appellant's] counsel. The right of appeal includes the right vigorously to
> challenge the decision of a lower court and to describe in every proper way
> its alleged errors. But appellate counsel may not give vent to their
> frustrations by undignified or discourteous remarks directed against the
> person of the deciding judge. Never suppressing any fact or proper argument,
> counsel have a professional responsibility to refer to the tribunals from which
> an appeal is taken, as well as those before which they appear, with reasonable
> respect and courtesy. . . . While it might be natural for a layman, embittered
> by a decision, to lash out at a judge, such conduct cannot and will not be
> tolerated from a member of the bar of this court. We only refrain from taking
> some action because of the curious history of this case which, beginning with
> defendant's egregious misconduct, seems to have spawned an unusual
> atmosphere that seems unlikely of repetition. We make it quite clear,
> however, that counsel's personal asides in [appellant's] brief raise serious
> questions in our mind. Should we receive anything approaching this from
> counsel in the future, we shall not hesitate to act.[47]

Although the *Scully* court did not pursue ethical sanctions for the appellant's conduct,
the appellant was nevertheless negatively affected by the incident. By including the
disrespectful comments in his brief that sparked this rebuke by the appellate court,
the appellant's attorney undermined his effectiveness as a credible advocate.

---

[46] 570 F.2d 355 (1st Cir. 1977).

[47] *Id.* at 363 (citations omitted).

In addition to disrespectful content, a disrespectful tone can also damage a persuasive legal writer's credibility. A legal writer can do several things to avoid projecting a lack of proper respect to a court through his or her writing style. First, a legal writer should not be improperly informal when writing to a court. Slang, contractions, informal jargon, and other such overly informal language should be avoided. Second, a writer should not include humor or sarcasm in a document submitted to a court. Third, a legal writer should avoid "lecturing" a court or "demanding" that a court take a particular action. An advocate should not use imperative language that tells a court what it "must" do or what it "cannot" do. An advocate should use less confrontational language in phrasing his or her arguments and should not issue commands to a court.

Finally, submitting a messy or sloppy document can also indicate a lack of respect for the recipient. Advocates should pay attention to detail and should take the time to make their documents as neat and professional looking as possible.[48]

## E.    *Evincing Professionalism*

The last character trait that an advocate should evince in his or her writing is *professionalism*. Professionalism is used here as a "catch-all" term for conduct that epitomizes honor and nobility in the practice of law. The more professionalism an advocate evinces through his or her writing, the more credibility the advocate will establish with the court. Unprofessional conduct includes behavior that is discourteous, undignified, vicious, deceitful, or otherwise inconsistent with high ethical, moral, and professional standards. Admittedly, this definition of professionalism overlaps with the character traits we have already covered. Clearly, a lack of honesty, zeal, or respect in a legal document constitutes unprofessional conduct. "Professionalism," however, also covers various other types of improper conduct. Violations of ethical rules, for example, constitute unprofessional conduct. It would also include behavior that falls short of a technical ethics violation, yet does not comport with the degree of respectability and virtuousness expected of a lawyer. Unprofessional exaggeration or overstatement, express hostility toward an opposing party or opposing counsel, cutting corners on procedural rules—all of these are examples of unprofessional conduct that can occur in legal writing and that can undermine a writer's credibility.

It is not realistic to enumerate in this discussion all the possible examples of unprofessional conduct that could undermine an advocate's credibility. Set out below, however, are a number of excerpts from cases in which the courts criticized the advocates for lack of professionalism. These excerpts will give you an idea of what courts consider unprofessional in appellate briefs. In some of the cases, the advocate's conduct resulted in ethical sanctions. But regardless of the ethical implications, in all of these cases the advocates in question undermined their

---

[48] As we will see in Chapter 8, sloppiness in a persuasive document also indicates a lack of attention to detail, which can undermine a reader's view of the writer's "intelligence." Thus, sloppiness undermines an advocate's credibility in terms of both character and intelligence.

credibility in the eyes of the court and their own effectiveness.[49]

•      From *Bettencourt v. Bettencourt*, 909 P.2d 553, 556-58 (Haw. 1995):

Preliminarily, it appears both necessary and appropriate that we address the form and content of appellant's opening brief. . . . First [Hawai'i Rules of Appellate Procedure (HRAP)] Rule 28(a) provides in pertinent part that, "[e]xcept after leave granted, the clerk will not receive an opening or answering brief of more than 35 typewritten pages[.]" Appellant's brief actually totals thirty-seven pages. Although the last numbered page of the brief reflects the number "35," the brief contains two pages, with different text, that are designated as page "20" and an unnumbered page after the last page numbered 35. Were it not for the "creative" page numbering technique, the opening brief would not have been accepted for filing. . . .

Finally, . . . it is the failure to heed HRAP Rule 28(b)(7) that most warrants comment in this case. Rather than "exhibiting clearly the points of fact and of law being presented, citing the authorities relied upon," HRAP Rule 28(b)(7), the argument section of appellant's brief excoriates individual family court judges personally in a scathingly contemptuous diatribe that has no place in appellate argument. . . .

[T]he argument section [also] consists of lengthy quotations from the hearing transcript and [appellant's counsel's] running sarcastic commentary, carried on in footnotes throughout the opening brief. For example, where the court commented that calling non-party witnesses without a witness list was an unfair surprise, the comment was footnoted with the remark that

If this is not an example of an out-an-out [sic] abuse of power, then the author [appellant's counsel] does not what [sic] is. At this point, the only *surprise* that played in appellant's counsel's thought was "how'd she ever become a judge!" Followed by "why am I putting up with this b-------?" . . .

Additional footnotes (1) refer to the proceedings as "being similar to trying to take a leak at the Pali on a windy day," (2) ask "[i]s this a script right out of Saturday Night Live or what," and (3) refer to a family court judge as "a Rell Sunn Look-alike."

This kind of incivility is demeaning to the legal profession and

[49] For an informative discussion of how courts react to unprofessionalism in documents submitted by legal advocates, see Judith D. Fischer, *Bareheaded and Barefaced Counsel: Courts React to Unprofessionalism in Lawyers' Papers*, 31 Suffolk U. L. Rev. 1 (1997).

should not be tolerated. As we have stated,

> lawyers who know how to think but have not learned how to behave are a menace and a liability . . . to the administration of justice. . . . [T]he necessity for civility is relevant to lawyers because they are . . . living exemplars—and thus teachers—every day in every case and in every court; and their worst conduct will be emulated . . . more readily than their best.

The opening brief, which was filed in this case, is an egregious example of the substitution of rancorous rhetoric for legal and factual analysis in appellate briefs. Not only does this burden the court, but, more importantly, it is adverse to the client's interests, and we view such matters with dismay. It is sound legal and factual argument, rather than vituperative sniping, that is compelling to the court. When an attorney, in briefing the court, foregoes the former to engage in the latter, the client is deprived of an opportunity to persuade the court of the merits of his or her position.

The lack of professionalism and civility demonstrated in appellant's opening brief does not comport with the precepts embodied in the preamble to the HRPC, and we are compelled to refer the supreme court record in this case, as we must pursuant to the Revised Code of Judicial Conduct Canon 3(D)(2) (1992), to the Office of Disciplinary Counsel for its review and appropriate action.

• From *Amax Coal Co. v. Adams*, 597 N.E.2d 350, 352 (Ind. Ct. App. 1992):

We must first discuss the quality of briefing by counsel in this appeal. Throughout the parties' briefs, they have launched rhetorical broadsides at each other which have nothing to do with the issues in this appeal. Counsels' comments concern their opposite numbers' intellectual skills, motivations, and supposed violations of the rules of common courtesy. Because similar irrelevant discourse is appearing with ever-increasing frequency in appellate briefs, we find it necessary to discuss the easily-answered question of whether haranguing condemnations of opposing counsel for supposed slights and off-record conduct unrelated to the issues at hand is appropriate fare for appellate briefs.

At the outset, we point to the obvious: the judiciary, in fact and of necessity, has absolutely no interest in internecine battles over social etiquette or the unprofessional personality clashes which frequently occur among opposing counsel these days. Irrelevant commentary thereon during the course of judicial proceedings does nothing but waste valuable judicial time. On appeal, it generates a voluminous number of useless briefing pages which have nothing to do with the issues presented, as in this appeal.

Further, appellate counsel should realize, such petulant grousing has a deleterious effect on the appropriate commentary in such a brief. Material of this nature is akin to static in a radio broadcast. It tends to blot out legitimate argument.

On a darker note, if such commentary in appellate briefs is actually directed to opposing counsel for the purpose of sticking hyperbolic barbs into his or her opposing numbers' psyche, the offending practitioner is clearly violating the intent and purpose of the appellate rules. In sum, we condemn the practice, and firmly request the elimination of such surplusage from future appellate briefs.

- From *Underly v. Advance Machine Co.*, 605 N.E.2d 1186, 1196 n.8 (Ind. Ct. App. 1993):

  [Appellant's counsel] presented in his reply brief on p. 38 what was purported to be authority "directly on point" from Indiana regarding the appropriate test for the admission of videotaped evidence. However, our research revealed such "dispositive authority" was not from Indiana, but rather, from the state of Illinois. We also note that in citing to this case, [Appellant's counsel] failed to list the appropriate abbreviation designating what state tribunal it was from; [Appellant's counsel] made no such "omission" in the plethora of other citations he presented to this court in both his appellate brief and reply brief. While we cannot be certain this "omission" was intentional, we remind counsel for [appellant] of his duty to this tribunal to exercise candor when citing authority for legal arguments. *See*, Rules of Professional Conduct, Rule 3.3(a)(1).

- From *Arnett v. Pearce*, 45 Cal. Rptr. 2d 593, 595 n.4 (Cal. Ct. App. 1995) (disregarding an entire brief submitted by an amicus curiae due to the lack of professionalism reflected in the brief):

  We pause to note that both parties have cogently and responsibly set forth their respective positions on an issue that is susceptible of meritorious policy arguments for each side. Unfortunately, we do not find the same level of professionalism in the brief of amicus curiae, the Center for Public Interest Law. It misleadingly and illogically portrays the peer review committee as a "wholly private" self-serving organization of colleagues seeking to oust a competitor from the marketplace. It raises new arguments on appeal, distorts the issues, relies on incompetent new evidence, and attributes disingenuous self-protective motives to the Hospital, cast in an unnecessarily shrill and hostile tone. We find the parties' briefs to be entirely adequate for purposes of review, and therefore disregard the brief of amicus curiae.

- From *State v. Gordon*, 948 S.W.2d 673, 676 (Mo. Ct. App. 1997):

On appeal defendant has in his brief made a number of unsupported allegations of perjury by a witness and further allegations of the known use of perjury by the prosecution. Such allegations are very serious charges of criminal activity and misconduct, but when the issue was raised by the court at oral argument no record evidence to support such charges was asserted by counsel. It should not be necessary to remind counsel, but apparently is, that zealous advocacy and professionalism do not encompass unsubstantiated accusations such as those made here against witnesses and prosecutors.

- From *Larson v. Furlong*, 1997 WL 705355, at *3 (Wis. Ct. App. 1997):

We are hard pressed to determine which of the parties has prosecuted the more frivolous appeal. The parties' briefs contain erroneous citations to the record, wholesale extrapolating of arguments from briefs submitted in the trial court without editing for changes in the opposing party's position or the trial court's ruling, argument on issues that are not raised, and argument based on mischaracterization of the record and opposing counsel's arguments and gross exaggeration of the positions being taken by each. The briefs are unnecessarily vituperative and shed more heat than light.

The foregoing excerpts reflect incidents in which an attorney's lack of professionalism in a brief damaged his or her credibility as an advocate. Compare these to the following, which reflect incidences in which appellate courts *praised* advocates for the professionalism embodied in their briefs. We should not underestimate the importance of such comments. The statements made by the courts in the following cases are more than mere compliments to the advocates; they are express indications to the advocates that their efforts to evince a proper ethos were successful. By making these comments, the courts not only praise the attorneys for their professionalism, they also acknowledge the attorneys' effectiveness as advocates, at least from an ethos perspective. There is little doubt that the attorneys to whom this praise was directed were more effective as advocates due to the trust and confidence they were able to instill in the court. All legal writers should strive to project a like amount of professionalism through their writing, not only for ethical and moral reasons, but for strategic, persuasive purposes as well.

- From *Quirk v. Premium Homes, Inc.*, 999 S.W.2d 306, 310 n.5 (Mo. Ct. App. 1999):

We would be remiss if we failed to make public our appreciation for the well written briefs, superior arguments and, above all, exemplary courtesy and professionalism exhibited by counsel for both parties.

- From *Pruett v. Thigpen*, 444 So.2d 819, 828-29 (Miss. 1984) (Robertson, J., concurring):

  [W]e have received excellent briefs from both the attorneys representing [Petitioner] and from the office of the Attorney General on behalf of the state. Indeed, it is appropriate that counsel be commended for the competence and professionalism with which they have presented to the Court this case which, as all know, arises out of one of the most sensationalized and emotionally charged crimes in the recent history of this state.

- From *Commonwealth v. Pignato*, 574 N.E.2d 1018, 1019 (Mass. App. Ct. 1991)

  In conclusion, we think it appropriate to applaud the professionalism of the Commonwealth for its presentation of a competent, careful, and well-crafted brief and to indicate for the record that the defendant's brief barely reaches the level of appellate argument required by Mass. R.A.P. 16(a)(4).

## F.    *A Summary of Traits Indicating Good Moral Character*

The following table summarizes the five traits that legal writers should project through their writing in order to demonstrate that they are of good moral character.

| Trait Indicating Good Moral Character | How the Trait Is Evinced Through Legal Writing |
|---|---|
| **Truthfulness** | • By explaining the *facts* of the matter accurately and honestly.<br>• By explaining the relevant *law* accurately and honestly. |
| **Candor** | • By apprising the decision-maker of damaging, yet legally significant, facts.<br>• By apprising the decision-maker of adverse authority when required to by applicable rules of ethics.<br>• By conceding "concedable" points raised by the opposing party. |
| **Zeal** | • By making a substantial effort in investigating, researching, strategizing, analyzing, and writing the persuasive legal document in question.<br>• By using affirmative and confident language. |
| **Respect** | • By omitting content that is disrespectful to a judge or the legal system.<br>• By writing in a respectful tone.<br>• By presenting a neat and professional-looking document. |
| **Professionalism** | • By avoiding conduct in the writing of a document that is inconsistent with high ethical, moral, and professional standards. |

# III.   EVINCING GOOD WILL IN LEGAL WRITING

In the beginning of this chapter, we saw that classical rhetoricians have identified three components of ethos, or credibility, in persuasive writing: intelligence, character, and good will. We analyzed credibility in the preceding section, examining the various things a legal writer can do or avoid in a persuasive document to give an impression of high moral character. We saw, too, how this impression can affect the readers' confidence and trust in the writer as a source of information. In this section we will similarly explore the role of good will in effective legal writing.

## A.   *Defining Good Will*

*Good will* in the context of persuasion refers to how an advocate feels or is disposed toward others involved in the matter under discussion. According to classical rhetoricians, a decision-maker will doubt the veracity of what an advocate has to say if the advocate does not appear to be "well-disposed" toward the decision-maker or toward another party that may be affected by the decision. If a decision-maker receives the impression that an advocate is angry at, resentful of, or otherwise malevolent toward the decision-maker or an adverse party, the decision-maker will likely be skeptical about the advocate's advice on the matter; the advocate might, after all, be speaking, not out of logic or a sense of justice, but out of spite and anger. In such situations, the decision-maker may feel that the advocate may not advise the best course of action because of the contempt felt by the advocate and motivation it provides to advise otherwise. The concept of good will is based largely on "folk psychology" and common sense: We tend to doubt a person's word if that person has ill-will toward us or toward another person who will be affected by the course of action we are being persuaded to take.

## B.   *Distinguishing Good Will from Character*

The "good will" aspect of ethos is often confused with the "character" aspect of ethos. Analyzing the differences between these two will therefore help us to better understand ethos. "Character" refers to an advocate's general moral makeup and personality. In the preceding section, we saw that a legal writer's general character, as manifested in his or her writing, affects the degree of credibility he or she has in the eyes of a reader. "Good will," on the other hand, does not refer to a general character trait, but to an advocate's disposition toward a specific audience or adversary. Good will is unique to a specific matter and refers to the *motivation* an advocate may have to advise incorrectly, due to ill-will toward the audience or the adversary. An advocate could be of relatively sound moral character generally and yet be untrustworthy in a specific matter because of ill-will toward one of the participants in that particular matter.

The confusion between character and good will occurs largely because both can come into play when an advocate manifests anger or hostility toward a decision-maker or an opposing party in a matter. In the discussion of character earlier in this chapter, we saw that hostility in a persuasive document can impact a reader's impression of an advocate's general character in two ways. First, if the hostility is directed at the decision-maker in the matter, it manifests a lack of *respect*. Second, if the hostility is directed at an opposing party or an opposing party's counsel, it manifests a lack of *professionalism*. In both of these situations, the advocate's credibility is damaged because such behavior suggests that the advocate is "that type of person," that is, of unsound moral character.

Apart from and in addition to the impact of such behavior on the perception of an advocate's general character, however, hostility in a persuasive document also undermines an advocate's credibility under the concept of good will. Hostility not only brings an advocate's general moral character into question, but it also raises questions regarding the *motivation* behind the advocate's advice. Under the principle of good will, the manifestation of malevolence by an advocate causes a decision-maker to doubt the advocate's advice because it may be based less on rational reasoning than on ill-will toward a participant in the matter. In fact, even when an advocate is otherwise known to be of sound moral character, ill-will can undermine the advocate's credibility in a specific matter by bringing the advocate's motivation into question.

## C.     The Relevance of Good Will to Persuasive Legal Writing

Based on the foregoing, the relevance of good will to effective persuasive writing should be clear: Legal writers should avoid projecting ill-will in their documents. An advocate should avoid bringing his or her motivation into question by avoiding manifestations of ill-will toward the decision-maker, an adverse party, or the adverse party's counsel. While legal matters can often generate negative emotions between the parties and their attorneys, and sometimes between a party and a presiding judge, legal advocates should not let their emotions get the best of them. Regardless of the hostility that may exist between the participants in a matter, advocates should not let signs of this hostility seep into their documents and thereby undermine their credibility. Attitudes and emotions that legal writers should avoid expressing in their documents include hate, anger, spite, jealousy, resentment, irritation, impatience, and bitterness. The projection of any of these negative emotions can undermine an advocate's credibility by causing a decision-maker to doubt the advocate's motivation to advise truthfully and accurately.

## D.     The Paradox Between Pathos and Good Will

In Chapter 6 we learned that emotional arguments can be very effective in legal writing. In our discussion of Pathos—the process of persuading through emotion—we saw that legal writers sometimes persuade through emotion by explaining and emphasizing certain facts in the case to evoke emotions in a decision-maker that motivate the decision-maker to decide for the advocate's client. Moreover, while we saw that advocates sometimes persuade by evoking positive emotions such as sympathy for a client's plight or love for family, we also saw that such emotional arguments could involve evoking *anger* toward an opposing party's behavior. Furthermore, classical rhetoricians have long recognized that the most effective way for an advocate to evoke a desired emotion is to exude and project that emotion through his or her writing. As the ancient Roman rhetorician Cicero said: "[I]t is impossible for the [audience] to feel indignation, hatred or ill-will, to be terrified of anything, or reduced to tears of compassion, unless all of those emotions, which the advocate would inspire in the arbitrator, are visibly stamped or rather branded on the advocate himself."[50]

This advice on pathos, however, appears to contradict the preceding discussion of good will. According to classical rhetoricians, arousing an audience's anger requires an advocate to evince anger. Advocates who do this, however, run the risk of damaging their credibility under the rhetorical principle of good will. Thus, a paradox exists between this principle of pathos and the principle of good will. In such situations—that is, when an advocate wants to evoke anger in an audience but is concerned that such a strategy will negatively impact the advocate's good will—the advocate should follow these guidelines:

1.  Focus on the opposing party's behavior, not on the opposing party. When trying to arouse the audience's anger, an advocate should not express hostility toward the *person* of the opposing party, but only toward specific acts of the party. While this may seem a subtle difference, expressions of hostility toward an opposing party can damage an advocate's credibility and bring his or her motivation into question. Projecting anger toward specific acts of behavior lessens this effect. As Shapo, Walter, and Fajans have stated, "You can evoke . . . anger at the defendant's cruelty. . . . [However], [a]n emotion that is inappropriate is hostility towards the opposing counsel and parties."[51]

2.  Focus only on cruel or despicable behavior by the opposing party that relates to the matter under discussion. Advocates seeking to evoke anger in their audience toward the opposing party should not focus on acts of the opposing party that are completely irrelevant to the issue under discussion. In most cases, the discussion of extraneous "bad acts" committed by the opposing party will cause readers to doubt the advocate's motivation more than it will cause readers to develop an unfavorable attitude toward opposing party.

3.  Never evince hostility toward the decision-maker or another attorney, such as the opposing party's counsel. To do so undermines the advocate's credibility in terms of both character and good will.

4.  Make an extra effort to evince other aspects of credibility (ethos) to counter any unwanted effects from emotional appeals that put the appearance of good will at risk. If an advocate knows that an attempt to arouse anger may affect the advocate's good will in the eyes of the decision-maker, the advocate should make sure that all other aspects of credibility—character and intelligence—are strongly established.

---

[50] Marcus Tullius Cicero, *De Oratore* 333 (E. W. Sutton trans. 1959).

[51] Helene S. Shapo et al., *Writing and Analysis in the Law* 278 (4th ed. 1999).

An advocate can minimize the potential negative impact under the principle of good will by solidly establishing that he or she is intelligent and able and of strong moral character.

5.     Realize that it is a judgment call. No one strategy suits all situations. In some situations and with some audiences, any amount of negative emotion projected by an advocate will be received unfavorably. In other situations and with other audiences, evincing and arousing anger may be more appropriate and productive. An advocate must be sensitive to the particulars of both the matter and the audience and must tailor his or her approach accordingly.

**Exercise 7.3     Analyzing the Good Will Component of Ethos**

Locate a example of persuasive writing in which the writer expresses hostility toward his or her audience or toward an opponent or adversary. The example can come from any form of persuasive discourse, such as a dissenting or concurring opinion in a case, an editorial in a magazine or newspaper, or a letter to the editor in a magazine or newspaper. Write an essay analyzing the persuasiveness of the writer's argument in terms of good will. Attach a copy of the item to your essay.

# Chapter 8

# *Evincing Intelligence in Legal Writing*

[Modern] research proves what Aristotle suggested more than 2000 years ago: the importance of knowledge as an element of ethos. A[n] [advocate] who is perceived to be intelligent and authoritative will generally be more persuasive.

— Ronald J. Waicukauski,
JoAnne Epps, and
Paul Mark Sandler

In Chapter 7, we learned that an advocate's credibility plays a very important role in persuasion. In fact, we learned that classical rhetoricians have identified advocate credibility—called ethos—as one of the three main processes of persuasion, along with logical argument (logos) and emotional appeals (pathos). We also learned that classical rhetoricians have identified three separate aspects of credibility: intelligence, character, and good will. In Chapter 7, we explored the last two of these aspects of credibility in some detail. In that discussion we saw how an advocate's credibility is affected by the general character he or she projects through a persuasive document. We also saw how the manifestation of good will—or its opposite, ill-will—toward participants in a legal matter can affect the amount of credibility an advocate has in the eyes of a reader. In this chapter we will examine the remaining aspect of ethos: intelligence.

It will come as no surprise to you that the more capable and intelligent an advocate is perceived to be, the more trust and confidence the advocate will inspire in his or her audience. Ronald J. Waicukauski, JoAnne Epps, and Paul Mark Sandler explain it this way:

> [Another] factor in ethos is knowledge—the perception that the speaker should be believed because she knows what she is talking about. Research confirms this commonsense principle in a variety of contexts. In one study, for example, a message about radioactivity was found to be much more effective when the speaker was identified as a professor of nuclear physics than when the speaker was identified as a student. Similarly, an article describing a cure for the common cold was more likely to be believed if the reader was told that the article had appeared in the New England Journal of Medicine as opposed to Life magazine.
>
> This research proves what Aristotle suggested more than 2000 years ago: the importance of knowledge as an element of ethos. A speaker who is perceived to be intelligent and authoritative will generally be more

persuasive.[1]

While it may seem commonsensical that an intelligent advocate is more persuasive than an unintelligent one, it is not so obvious how an advocate goes about establishing that he or she is intelligent to an audience. In some situations, of course, a prior reputation as an intelligent and capable source of information may be enough to give an advocate's arguments credibility. However, as we discussed in Chapter 7, our focus here is on how an advocate can establish credibility through his or her writing, separate from and independent of any pre-existing reputation the advocate may have in the community or with the audience. Thus, in this chapter, we will analyze how an effective legal writer manifests intelligence through a specific written document and how this in turn affects a reader's perception of the writer as a credible source of information.

# I.      THE TRAITS OF AN INTELLIGENT LEGAL WRITER

Before we analyze how a legal writer evinces intelligence through his or her writing, we must first define what we mean by an "intelligent" legal writer. An advocate is deemed intelligent when he or she possesses a number of important character traits that, taken together, indicate that the advocate is a trustworthy source of information in terms of *ability* (as opposed to being a trustworthy source of information in terms of *moral character*, as discussed in Chapter 7). Listed below are the general traits of intelligence that serve to gain the confidence of a legal audience. Later in this chapter we will define each of these traits and discuss how an effective legal writer evinces each of these through his or her writing.

An intelligent legal writer is perceived as:

1. Informed
2. Adept at legal research
3. Organized
4. Analytical
5. Deliberate
6. Empathetic to the reader
7. Practical
8. Articulate
9. Eloquent
10. Detail-oriented
11. Innovative

# II.     TWO GENERAL MEANS OF EVINCING INTELLIGENCE: SUBSTANCE AND HIGHLIGHTING

---

[1] Ronald J. Waicukauski, et al., *Ethos and the Art of Argument*, 26 Litigation 31, 32 (1999).

## A.    *Evincing Intelligence Through Substance*

Legal writers can indicate their intelligence to readers in two general ways: through substance and through highlighting. Nothing speaks more highly of a writer's intelligence and ability than his or her use of effective substantive arguments.[2] Just as we generally form impressions of other people's intelligence and ability by what they say and how they say it, a reader's impression of a legal writer's intelligence is formed first and foremost by the content of the writer's document. An effective legal argument not only sells the writer's position, it also sells the writer. That is, by presenting effective "substance" in an argument, a legal writer not only persuades a reader through the logic of the argument (logos), but the writer also demonstrates that he or she is an intelligent, credible source of information (ethos). Thus, when a legal writer presents an effective substantive argument in a legal document, two separate processes of persuasion are actually occurring simultaneously.

Generally speaking, evincing intelligence through substance is not something a writer consciously considers and employs. It is a natural and inherent by-product of an informed, logical argument. When presenting what they hope will be an effective argument, writers focus on persuading through substance, usually giving little thought to the potential positive impact on their credibility. Nevertheless, we will analyze this method of evincing intelligence in some detail in this chapter. Understanding and appreciating this subtle yet important persuasive process can help us, as legal writers, to employ these methods more consciously and effectively.

## B.    *Evincing Intelligence Through Highlighting*

### 1.   Defining "Highlighting"

The second general way that a legal writer evinces intelligence through his or her writing is by *highlighting* the fact that he or she possesses characteristics of intelligence. The problem with evincing intelligence through the substance of an argument is that such means are often subtle. Sometimes a reader might not appreciate the intelligence underlying and reflected in a persuasive legal document. In such situations, the writer does not receive the full benefit of the ethos process because of the reader's failure to fully appreciate the intelligence it took to produce the document in question. Highlighting strategies rectify this situation by drawing the reader's attention to specific aspects of the writer's intelligence. Occasionally, highlighting involves the writer expressly telling the reader that the writer possesses a specific characteristic of intelligence. At other times, highlighting involves the writer overtly pointing out to the reader aspects of the writer's document that reflect intelligence. In still other situations, highlighting entails a writer telling the reader that the writer engaged in specific conduct in preparing the written product—out of the reader's view—that is indicative of a characteristic of intelligence.

Consider this example: Suppose the law on a legal issue is particularly disorganized and confusing. Suppose also that an advocate undertakes the task of

---

[2] Unfortunately, the opposite is also true: Nothing betrays an advocate's lack of ability and intelligence more clearly than ineffective substance.

organizing and synthesizing the law and presents a lucid and effective argument on the issue in his or her brief to a court. Unless the judge reading the brief has independent knowledge of the confused and disorganized state of the law on the issue, he or she will not appreciate the advocate's efforts in organizing the material. Consequently, the writer will miss out on the opportunity to improve his or her credibility unless he or she somehow showcases the intelligence it took to organize and write the synthesis presented. By including a statement in the brief indicating the confused state of the law—or more boldly, a statement indicating the skill required to produce the coherent argument—the writer can draw attention to his or her efforts and thereby enhance the court's appreciation of the writer's ability and intelligence. In the discussion of "organization" below, we will see examples of highlighting strategies employed in just this way.

Let's consider a more formal (and, arguably, famous) example of a legal writer highlighting a trait of intelligence. In the case of *Lochner v. New York*,[3] the United States Supreme Court struck down a New York statute that limited the hours of work in bakeries, finding that the statute was a deprivation of liberty without due process of law. Justice Holmes dissented in the decision. Justice Holmes begins his dissenting opinion with the following words:

> This case is decided upon an economic theory which a large part of the country does not entertain. If it were a question whether I agreed with that theory, I should study it further and long before making up my mind.[4]

In the second sentence of this passage, Justice Holmes employs a highlighting strategy by expressly informing the readers of his dissent that he is the type of person who carefully deliberates over an issue before taking a position. This statement is irrelevant and unnecessary to the substance of Holmes' opinion. However, Holmes strategically inserts it to enhance his credibility as a thoughtful and deliberate judge. Later in this chapter we will see that being "deliberate"—that is, carefully considering all sides of an issue before taking a position—is a trait of intelligence that inspires confidence in an audience. Justice Holmes evinces this trait through an overt highlighting statement. He does so in an effort to enhance his credibility and the credibility of his dissenting position.

Holmes' rhetorical strategies in *Lochner* have been analyzed in detail by Judge Richard Posner in his article *Law and Literature: A Relationship Reargued*.[5] What we have called a "highlighting strategy," Judge Posner calls an "ethical appeal." According to Judge Posner, an ethical appeal is a rhetorical device by which an advocate "attempt[s] to convey a sense that he is a person you ought to believe."[6] In Judge Posner's opinion, the above statement by Holmes is an example of a well-

---

[3] 198 U.S. 45 (1905).

[4] *Id.* at 75 (Holmes, J., dissenting).

[5] 72 Va. L. Rev. 1351, 1379-88 (1986).

[6] *Id.* at 1378.

crafted ethical appeal:

> Th[is] . . . sentence in the *Lochner* dissent ("If it were a question . . .") is [an] ethical appeal. An ordinary judge might say, "I deem it irrelevant what my own views on the truth of the majority's view of policy might be." This is the essential content of Holmes's sentence, but by putting it as he does he has slipped in the additional suggestion that he is a man slow to jump to conclusions. This suggestion makes the sentence more credible. It is a masterful touch. . . . Many judges voting to uphold statutes that they personally dislike will say so, to make themselves sound more impartial. This is an ethical appeal, but of a somewhat crass and self-congratulatory sort. Holmes is subtler, and therefore disarming and effective.[7]

As we will see in this chapter, highlighting strategies abound in legal writing. Writers have traditionally used them to add rhetorical power to their documents, but for many this use has been largely intuitive and without a conscious or full awareness of their persuasive function. In fact, you will likely recognize many of the phrases associated with highlighting; you may even have used some of them in your own writing without being fully aware of their rhetorical function. In this chapter, we will identify, analyze, and organize highlighting phrases so that we as legal writers can more fully appreciate their function and, when appropriate, use them more effectively.

## 2.   Cautions Regarding Highlighting Strategies

Although highlighting can be a valuable tool for building credibility, legal writers should keep several cautions in mind when employing these strategies. First, used inappropriately, highlighting strategies can turn readers off. As previously mentioned, the major benefit of highlighting is that it is direct and unambiguous. If it is used incorrectly, however, this asset can be a major liability. A reader may see a writer's use of highlighting strategies as crass and self-congratulatory (to use Judge Posner's words), in which case the reader may question the writer's character and find the writer less credible (the complete opposite effect that was intended). Even worse, the reader may interpret these strategies as an effort to manipulate the reader. Again, this would severely damage the writer's credibility. Writers should, therefore, use these strategies with sensitivity to the writing situation and their audience.

Second, a legal writer should never use highlighting strategies disingenuously. A writer should never feign conduct indicative of a trait of intelligence or give a false impression through highlighting strategies. For example, in connection with the hypothetical situation posed above, a writer should not suggest that the preparation of an argument required unusual organizational skills if that was not the case. Such

---

[7] *Id.* at 1381. It should also be noted that Judge Posner believes this statement by Holmes to be false, which, according to Posner, "is commonly the case with the ethical appeal." *Id.* On this point this chapter disagrees with Judge Posner. As we will discuss in many places, highlighting strategies (or ethical appeals, as Posner calls them) are not generally used, nor should they be used, disingenuously.

disingenuous statements damage an advocate's credibility far more than they can enhance it.

Third, a legal writer should not substitute highlighting strategies for substance. Highlighting strategies alone should not be used to project intelligence. An advocate should always evince intelligence though the substance of a document; highlighting strategies should be used, if at all, merely to supplement substantive means for evincing intelligence.

Fourth, legal writers should be aware that some highlighting strategies have been overused and have thus lost some of their power. As we will see, some of the more common highlighting strategies have become such cliches in legal writing that they no longer have the rhetorical impact they once did.

Finally, legal writers should realize that some readers may view many highlighting phrases as mere excess verbiage. Highlighting language is often extraneous to the substance of an argument. Moreover, modern legal writing pedagogy emphasizes clear, simple language and sentence structures. A dominant aspect of this pedagogy is a call for the elimination of "excess verbiage," "surplus words," "throat clearing phrases," and the like from sentences. Despite the potential rhetorical benefits of highlighting strategies, many legal readers trained in this pedagogy would frown on them as needless language. While such a reaction may be based on a lack of appreciation for the rhetorical functions of such phrases, the reaction is nevertheless real. Thus, before employing a particular highlighting strategy, a writer should consider whether the reader will appreciate its rhetorical design or merely view it as unnecessary wordiness.

### 3.   Why Analyze Highlighting Strategies?

Above, we examined several reasons why legal writers should be cautious when using highlighting strategies. These warnings would suggest that it is rarely appropriate for a legal writer to use highlighting strategies to evince intelligence. In view of this, one may question why we are examining such strategies at all.

There are three reasons why a comprehensive discussion of highlighting strategies has been included in this chapter. First, as we discussed several times, one of the large-scale goals of this text is to assist legal writers in viewing persuasive writing in a whole new way. Underlying persuasive writing is a world of persuasive forces that we are just beginning to explore and appreciate. Furthermore, as we discussed above in connection with the warnings for using highlighting strategies, many legal writers would view highlighting phrases as mere "excess verbiage." This reaction, however, is more than likely based on a lack of appreciation for the subtle rhetorical benefits such phrases serve. Thus, a comprehensive discussion of highlighting strategies has been included in this chapter to give these legal writers an opportunity to reevaluate their impression of such phrases and, more generally, to assist them in viewing persuasive writing in a whole new way.

The second reason why this chapter includes an in-depth discussion of highlighting strategies is to assist you at becoming more sophisticated legal *readers*. As was mentioned above, highlighting strategies for evincing intelligence abound in persuasive legal writing. Many, however, go unrecognized by most legal readers. In Chapter 1, we saw that a by-product of studying specific strategies of persuasive writing is that such a course of study helps students to become more savvy legal readers. Even if you never use highlighting strategies in your own writing, you will encounter such devices in the writing of others. Thus, the discussion of such strategies in this chapter helps you gain a fuller appreciation of persuasive writing from the standpoint of a legal reader, if not as a legal writer.

Finally, although many of the highlighting strategies that we will explore in this chapter are disfavored in legal writing, some are acceptable for evincing intelligence. Thus, at least with regard to the acceptable highlighting strategies, this chapter is designed to help writers convince their readers that they are intelligent and credible sources of information.

# III.   ANALYZING THE TRAITS OF AN INTELLIGENT LEGAL WRITER

## A.    *The Informed Writer*

The first sign of an intelligent, and therefore trustworthy, legal writer is that the writer is *informed*. In general, an informed writer is one who has comprehensive knowledge of the information relevant and applicable to the matter at hand. In the context of legal writing, to be informed means that a writer has a thorough and comprehensive understanding of the *facts* of the matter, the relevant *law*, and any non-legal sources (such as scientific studies and articles) that may be relevant to the matter. An advocate who is perceived by an audience to be well informed on the matter at hand is seen as a trustworthy source of information and is, therefore, able to gain the confidence of the audience. Conversely, readers will be skeptical of the arguments and advice of an advocate who appears to be shaky on the relevant facts or law.

### 1.  Substantive Means of Establishing that One Is Informed

As with most traits of intelligence, the most powerful and effective way for a legal writer to indicate to a reader that he or she is informed is through the substance of the document itself. More specifically, a legal writer establishes that he or she is an informed source of information in the following ways:

   a.  By demonstrating a *mastery of the facts* of the matter. Legal writers do this by including the following in a document:
   
   i.   an accurate statement of all factual details relevant to the matter;
   
   ii.  quotes from the record when appropriate and effective; and
   
   iii. effective citations to specific pages in the record.

   b.  By demonstrating a *mastery of the law* (and, if applicable, non-legal authority) relevant to the matter. Legal writers do this by including the following in a document:
   
   i.   all mandatory legal authority relevant to the matter (such as constitutional provisions, statutes, cases, administrative rules, etc.);
   
   ii.  persuasive legal authority such as dicta, dissenting and

concurring opinions, and authority from other jurisdictions, when appropriate and effective;

iii. persuasive secondary sources when appropriate and effective; and

iv. non-legal sources such as scientific studies and scholarship, when appropriate and effective (as in policy arguments, for example).

By incorporating these substantive aspects into their documents, legal writers establish themselves as well-informed, credible sources of information. As we discussed above, such substantive aspects of a legal document actually persuade readers in two ways simultaneously. First, by including relevant legal and non-legal authorities and explaining how those authorities apply to the facts of the case at hand, a legal writer persuades readers through logical argument (logos). However, separate from and in addition to this logos function, the inclusion of relevant authority and facts in a legal document indicates to the reader that the writer is well informed on the matter and, therefore, a credible source of information (ethos). Thus, the legal writer who accurately and thoroughly incorporates legal authority and facts into a persuasive document receives multiple benefits.

Not surprisingly the converse is also true. When a legal writer fails to state the facts of a matter fully and accurately or fails to locate and incorporate relevant authority, the writer undermines his or her argument in two separate ways. First and most obviously, the inaccurate or incomplete substance itself damages the logos function of the advocate's argument. Second, and more importantly for our discussion here, such mistakes damage the ethos function of the advocate's argument by suggesting that the writer is not fully informed and thus lacking in credibility.

As we also discussed above, legal writers do not typically think much about the ethos function of an effective substantive argument. The credibility-establishing function of incorporating the facts and law relevant to a matter is a natural and inherent by-product of making an effective substantive argument. Nevertheless, legal writers should be aware that such substantive aspects of a legal document affect the ethos function of persuasion in addition to their more obvious role in the logos function. Just as importantly, legal writers should realize that a failure to master the facts or law relevant to a matter undermines their effectiveness as advocates not only in terms of substance or logos, but also in terms of credibility or ethos.

## 2.   Highlighting Strategies for Establishing that One Is Informed

As we discussed earlier, the second general way that a legal writer evinces intelligence in a document is by expressly drawing the readers' attention to behavior on the part of the writer that is indicative of intelligence. Such overt strategies to evince intelligence are called "highlighting strategies."

In the context of establishing that one is an "informed" writer, highlighting involves express statements regarding the writer's grasp of the relevant facts and/or law. Phrases such as "based on a thorough review of the record . . ." or "after exhaustive research . . ." are common examples of such highlighting strategies. The following examples are taken from judicial opinions:

*Example 8.1*

From *Boodoo v. Cary*, 21 F.3d 1157, 1159 (D.C. Cir. 1994) (emphasis added):

> **A thorough review of the record reveals** that [Plaintiffs' expert] Dr. Wu consistently maintained at trial that the accident was rendered unavoidable by the excessive speed of the Metrobus. Reading Dr. Wu's testimony as a whole, we find he did not concede that the Metrobus accident would have occurred even if the bus were moving 30 miles per hour ("m.p.h."). And giving the benefit of all favorable factual inferences to appellants, we believe that a reasonable jury fairly could have found that excessive speed was the proximate cause of the collision.

*Example 8.2*

From *Williams v. Brandt*, 672 F. Supp. 507, 508 (S.D. Fla. 1987) (emphasis added):

> **A thorough review of the record reveals** that all the essentials of the transactions between the parties occurred without the borders of the United States by conscious design of all involved. Whatever the underlying reasons, the participants, including Plaintiff, intended all aspects of their dealings to remain offshore. . . . [T]his Court finds no support for extending the protections of the United States' securities laws to a transaction of the nature herein. From the very inception, the parties went to great lengths to ensure that all of their dealings remained foreign in all material aspects. They successfully insulated their transactions from any rights and obligations which would attach were the negotiations domestic. Having consciously sought relief from any negative implications perceived inherent in U.S. transactions, Plaintiff cannot now contend that he may invoke the protections of U.S. laws for alleged wrongs stemming from this exclusively foreign deal-gone-sour.

*Example 8.3*

From *Life and Casualty Ins. Co. of Tenn. v. Jones*, 328 S.W.2d 118, 122 (Ark. 1959) (emphasis added):

> **Our exhaustive research reveals** the law to be well settled in this state that an insurance company is liable on their policy of accident insurance if death resulted when it did on account of an aggravation of a disease by accidental injury, even though death from the disease might have resulted at a later period regardless of the injury, on the theory that if death would not have occurred when it did but for the injury, the accident was the direct, independent and

exclusive cause of death at the time.

*Example 8.4*

From *Van Tran v. State*, 6 S.W.3d 257, 270 (Tenn. 1999) (emphasis added):

> **Exhaustive research reveals** that the vast majority of jurisdictions apply [the] rule either by statute or case law [that a prisoner is not entitled to have a jury determine the issue of competency to be executed.]

*Example 8.5*

From *Bolton v. United States*, 604 F. Supp. 1219, 1222 (S.D. Miss. 1985) (emphasis added):

> In *Feres v. United States*, 340 U.S. 135, 71 S.Ct. 153, 95 L.Ed. 152 (1950), the Supreme Court held that "the Government is not liable under the Federal Torts Claims Act for injuries to servicemen where the injuries arise out of or are in the course of activity incident to service." *Id.* at 146, 71 S.Ct. at 159. . . . The issue before the Court is whether the *Feres* doctrine operates to bar claims which are not the serviceman's, but are claims which belong to his ex-wife as administratrix of the estate of the deceased son, Ray Scott Jackson. **After exhaustive research of the issue,** the Court has found definitive the case law which holds that the *Feres* doctrine bars recovery by family members where the cause of action is ancillary or derivative to the serviceman's action for his own injury.

The highlighting strategies in bold in Examples 8.1 to 8.5 show the writers' efforts to indicate to readers that they are informed and therefore credible. In Examples 8.1 and 8.2, the writers wanted readers to know that their decisions were based on comprehensive knowledge of the *facts* of the case, and so they expressly included statements indicating that the decisions were based on a "thorough review of the record." Similarly, in Examples 8.3 through 8.5, the writers included statements indicating that their decisions were based on thorough research of the relevant *law*.

Language such as this is inserted into legal writing to emphasize to readers that the arguments and conclusions in the document are the product of "informed" reasoning. Theses phrases could be deleted without affecting the substance of the writers' arguments. The phrases serve merely as rhetorical devices, designed to enhance the writer's credibility by stressing to the reader that the writer is well informed on the relevant facts and/or law.

Such highlighting strategies abound in legal writing. In fact, a computer search of the phrase "thorough review of the record" in case law databases alone results in over 6100 hits. You may even have used such highlighting strategies in your own writing. Granted, many legal writers who insert such language in their documents are not consciously aware of the rhetorical functions of such statements. Frequently, the inclusion of such statements is simply the product of intuition on the part of an experienced persuasive writer. Nevertheless, these statements are examples of writing strategies designed to highlight and enhance the credibility of a writer.

Earlier in this chapter we discussed several general warnings regarding the use of highlighting strategies. Several of those warnings are specifically applicable to the use of the highlighting strategies discussed here.

First, while judges writing judicial opinions like those set out above may be able to get away with expressly stating that they have "thoroughly reviewed the record" or that they have "conducted thorough research," such statements are often less appropriate in an attorney's brief. Judges want advocates to prove through the substance of their arguments that the advocates have a mastery of the law and facts of a matter. Express statements like those set out above, when stated by an advocate, sometimes convey a tone of insecurity. That is, such statements, rather than enhancing the writer's credibility, often sound hollow, contrived, and overly defensive. They often come across to a reader as an effort to conceal shoddy research rather than to highlight legitimate efforts, which is the exact opposite of the effect that is intended. Thus, legal advocates should use such highlighting strategies cautiously. In many cases an advocate is better off letting the substance of a document speak for itself and eliminating highlighting strategies of this nature.

Second, highlighting strategies of this type should be used, if at all, merely to supplement substance; an advocate should never use such highlighting strategies in lieu of substantive means of establishing intelligence. As stated earlier, an advocate should establish that he or she is "informed" on a matter first and foremost through the substance of a document. A reader will not have confidence in the fact that an advocate is well informed on the matter if the substance of the advocate's document itself does not reflect the writer's knowledge, and this is true even if the advocate expressly states that he or she is informed through highlighting strategies.

Third, advocates should be aware that highlighting strategies such as those set out in Examples 8.1 through 8.5 are very common in legal writing and border on being cliche. Consequently, the impact of such statements has been reduced by overuse. While it is quite possible that when these phrases were first used they were capable of enhancing a writer's credibility, their overuse over the years has rendered them virtually impotent. Thus, their impact in modern legal writing would likely be minimal.

Finally, highlighting strategies such as these should never be used disingenuously. If you decide that, despite the previous warnings, such strategies are appropriate in your document, you should never state that you have thoroughly reviewed the record or exhaustively researched the relevant law unless it is true. While an inadvertent misstatement or omission regarding the law or facts on a matter will undoubtedly undermine your credibility, your credibility will be damaged even more if you make such a mistake while expressly averring that you are completely informed on the matter. Moreover, you should never say that you are fully informed in an effort to disguise the fact that you really aren't. This, like all highlighting strategies, should be used only to draw attention to what in reality you have done; you should not use highlighting strategies as a substitute for substantive intelligence.

## B.     *The Writer Adept at Legal Research*

The second trait of intelligence that inspires confidence in a legal audience is that the legal writer is *adept at legal research*. As you well know, the analysis of legal issues predominately involves the analysis and application of relevant legal authority to the case at hand. Consequently, legal research is very important in the resolution of legal disputes. Moreover, courts primarily rely on the advocates themselves to inform the court about the law relevant to a particular matter. It naturally follows that a judge will have more confidence in those advocates who appear to be effective legal researchers, for only those advocates who are adept at legal research will be able to advise the decision-maker effectively. Consequently, the more a legal advocate can establish to a decision-maker that he or she is a skilled legal researcher, the more trust and confidence the decision-maker will place in the advocate's arguments and advice.

This trait is clearly related to the preceding one of being "informed." In the preceding section, we saw that a legal writer should establish to a reader that the writer is well informed on the matter under discussion. We also saw that one way to accomplish this effect is to demonstrate a mastery of the law on the matter. In that context, we saw that such mastery indicates that the writer is adequately prepared to render sound advice on the issue under discussion. Here our focus is similar, yet different in a significant way. Whereas establishing that one is "informed" enhances credibility by indicating the writer is *prepared*, establishing that one is an "adept legal researcher" goes beyond evincing preparation to evincing that the advocate possesses *sound lawyering skills*. That is, establishing that one is an effective legal researcher inspires confidence in an advocate's general skills as an attorney.

The difference between these first two traits of intelligence can best be understood through an illustration. Assume that an advocate's brief fails to advise a court of a favorable case directly applicable to the issue under discussion.[8] Such a mistake will negatively impact the advocate's credibility in two separate ways, corresponding to the first two traits of intelligence. First, failing to mention the favorable authority will cause the court to question whether the advocate is adequately "informed" on the relevant law. In terms of this effect, the court will be skeptical of the advocate's advice because the court will question whether the advocate is adequately prepared to render sound advice. In terms of the second trait of intelligence, the advocate's failure to mention the favorable authority will also cause the court to question the advocate's general skills as an attorney. That is, such behavior, in addition to causing a decision-maker to question the *preparation* of the advocate, causes a decision-maker to question the *general legal skills and ability* of the advocate.

---

[8] The hypothetical posed assumes that the case is "favorable" to the advocate to eliminate the implications of "lack of candor" on the part of the advocate. If the case in question hurt the advocate's position, the failure to mention the case would likely be interpreted by the court as an attempt to deceive the court, rather than a careless mistake. While "lack of candor" will definitely hurt an advocate's credibility, the impact is on the advocate's "general moral character" as we discussed in Chapter 7, not on the advocate's "intelligence."

### 1.   Substantive Means of Establishing that One Is Adept at Legal Research

Legal writers establish that they are effective legal researchers primarily through the substance of their documents. As in establishing that one is informed, legal writers can indicate the quality of their research skills in the following ways.

a.   By including all *mandatory legal authority* relevant to the matter (such as constitutional provisions, statutes, cases, administrative rules, etc.). In particular, this includes incorporating recent revisions to the law that can only be found through effective "updating" skills.

b.   By including *persuasive legal authority* such as dicta, dissenting and concurring opinions, and authority from other jurisdictions when appropriate and effective.

c.   By including *persuasive secondary sources* when appropriate and effective.

d.   By including *non-legal sources,* such as scientific studies and scholarship, when it is appropriate and effective (as in policy arguments, for example).

A legal writer who incorporates these sources into a persuasive document establishes that he or she is a good legal researcher, for only a good legal researcher would have found these authorities. Consequently, their inclusion serves to increase the advocate's credibility in the eyes of the reader.

To summarize, and to incorporate this information into our previous discussion, three separate and important rhetorical benefits are gained by including effective research in a persuasive document. Effective research (1) persuades through logos by identifying and applying relevant legal authorities; (2) persuades through ethos by establishing that the advocate is effectively prepared and informed on the matter (intelligence trait #1); and (3) persuades through ethos by establishing that the advocate possesses effective lawyering skills (intelligence trait #2).

### 2.   Highlighting Strategies for Establishing that One Is Adept at Legal Research

The techniques for highlighting one's adeptness at legal research are rather limited in quantity and rhetorical impact. Basically, a legal writer can highlight that he or she is an effective legal researcher by stating not only *what* authority was found, but also *how* it was found. Consider the following examples:

*Example 8.6*

From *Feola v. Valmont Indus., Inc.*, 304 N.W.2d 377, 382 (Neb. 1981) (emphasis added):

Plaintiff relies heavily upon the case of *Kruzer v. Giant Tiger Stores*, 39 Ohio Misc. 129, 317 N.E.2d 70 (1974), . . . However, **in Shepardizing the *Kruzer* case,** we have been able to locate a very recent case taking the opposite view from *Kruzer*, and whose language, reasoning, and statements of law are persuasive. That case is *Compton v. Shopko Stores, Inc.*, 93 Wis.2d 613, 287 N.W.2d 720 (1980).

*Example 8.7*

From *State v. Schultz*, 205 N.E.2d 126, 129-30 (Toledo Mun. Ct. 1964) (emphasis added):

> **This Court has searched through the Decennial Digest System and the various State Codes** in the hopes of finding a single reported instance in which a legislature in a criminal case enacted a statute containing a presumption on a presumption. It would seem that Ohio's drag racing statute is unique in its wording and that such a statute has never been judicially tested.

The bold language in these examples reflects efforts by the writers to highlight for readers some of the specific research steps taken to locate the authority presented. In Example 8.6, the writer expressly mentioned that important authority was located through Shepards. The writer could have simply discussed and applied the authority without stating how it was found. Including the reference to Shepards was merely a rhetorical device designed to highlight the writer's performance as an effective researcher. Similarly, in Example 8.7, the writer's allusion to the "Decennial Digest and the various State Codes" reflects the writer's effort to enhance his or her credibility as an able researcher.

As you can see from these examples, strategies for highlighting that one is "adept at legal research" are fairly modest. Nevertheless, several important warnings exist for using these highlighting strategies in persuasive legal writing.

First, such highlighting strategies are generally not recommended for legal advocates. While it may be appropriate for judges to use these types of phrases as reflected in the above examples, they are less appropriate for brief writers. At best, such language comes across as self-congratulatory. At worst, it comes across as amateurish and unprofessional. Thus, legal writers should use such highlighting strategies sparingly, if at all.

Second, if a writer does decide to use such highlighting strategies, the writer should not use them disingenuously. Any reference in a legal document to the research steps taken by a writer should accurately reflect how the authority in question was located.

Third, as stated previously, legal writers should realize that the rhetorical benefits of these highlighting strategies are fairly minor. Upon weighing the modest benefits of these strategies against the possible detrimental effects, most legal writers will decide that they are not worth the effort.

**Exercise 8.1    Analyzing the Implications of Ethos on an Appellate Court's Decision**

Find and read the case *Glassalum Eng'g Corp. v. 392208 Ontario Ltd.*, 487 So. 2d 87 (Fla. Dist. Ct. App. 1986). Write an essay explaining the case and analyzing the implications of the advocates' ethos on the Florida Appellate Court's decision. (Hint: Both the "character" and the "intelligence" aspects of ethos are implicated in this case. If necessary, review the coverage of character in Chapter 7.)

## C.    *The Organized Writer*

The third trait of an intelligent legal writer is that the writer is *organized*. In general terms, people who approach and think about problems in an organized way are typically perceived by others as being intelligent and capable. This is also true in the context of legal writing. Legal audiences generally have more confidence in advocates who appear to possess strong organizational skills. Conversely, legal audiences tend to be skeptical of arguments and advice given by an advocate who appears to be confused and disorganized.

### 1.    Substantive Means of Establishing that One Is Organized

There are four main ways that a legal writer manifests skills of organization through the substance of a persuasive document:

a.  By synthesizing and organizing complicated and/or voluminous information relevant to the issue under discussion. Often the law and/or record on an issue is extensive and disorganized. One important way that an advocate evinces skills in organization is by organizing this material and presenting it in a clear and understandable way.

b.  By presenting a clear and organized Statement of Facts.

c.  By incorporating logical and effective large-scale organization in the Argument section of a brief or other document.

d.  By using signposting and other presentational techniques that reflect organizational skills. Such writing techniques include:
    i.   The effective use of headings and sub-headings;
    ii.  The effective use of enumeration, bullet points, and other similar devices that add clarity to the presentation of lists of information;
    iii. The effective use of transitions between separate points in a discussion; and
    iv.  The effective use of introductions and thesis paragraphs to provide readers with "roadmaps" to the ensuing discussions.

The above listed items, when incorporated into a persuasive document, indicate to a reader that the writer of the document possesses strong skills in organization. Thus, as with most substantive means for evincing traits of intelligence, these items serve both logos functions and ethos functions. In terms of logos, an organized document persuades a reader because the substantive arguments themselves are presented in a way the reader can understand. Thus, effective organization helps an advocate to persuade through logic and reason. Second, in terms of ethos, the effective organization of a document helps to establish the credibility of a writer by indicating that the writer is organized and intelligent. Not surprisingly, the converse is also true. A confusing and disorganized argument not only hurts an advocate's effectiveness because it makes the substance of the arguments difficult to understand (logos), but it also undermines an advocate's credibility as an intelligent and capable source of information (ethos).

## 2.   Highlighting Strategies for Establishing that One Is Organized

The most common technique for highlighting that one is an organized legal writer is to include language emphasizing that, while the law and/or record on the issue under discussion may be particularly confusing or disorganized, the advocate's document has untangled and clarified it. Consider these examples:

*Example 8.8*

From *McCloud v. Testa*, 97 F.3d 1536, 1541 (6th Cir. 1996) (citation omitted) (emphasis added):

> We review the denial of summary judgment on grounds of qualified immunity *de novo* because application of this doctrine is a question of law. As we shall see in our discussion of the various rules cited to us by the parties, this is the only rule relevant to our choice of a standard of review in this case. **Nevertheless, because this is a confusing area of the law, we go on to address the other rules invoked by the parties and organize these rules in a useful framework.**

*Example 8.9*

From *Johnson v. Misericordia Community Hosp.*, 294 N.W.2d 501, 505 (Wis. Ct. App. 1980) (emphasis added):

> Counsel for [Appellant] has raised thirty issues for our consideration on appeal. **In the interest of conciseness, we have organized these issues under the four elements of a cause of action in negligence.**

In these examples, the writers have no substantive reason for telling readers about their attempts to organize confusing information. The writers could have simply presented their analysis without drawing attention to their efforts at organization. The writers included the bolded statements merely as a rhetorical strategy for highlighting their ability to organize and thus to add credibility to the opinions.

Few warnings exist regarding the use of such highlighting strategies. While many highlighting strategies can come across as crass and immodest, this is less of a concern for highlighting organizational skills. If an advocate has to synthesize and organize confusing and voluminous information to produce a brief on a matter, a statement to this effect in the brief can be an effective rhetorical device to draw attention to the writer's skills in organization. Only rarely will such statements come across as inappropriate or self-congratulatory. Thus, this type of highlighting strategy can be more effective than many of the others discussed in this chapter.

Perhaps the most important warning regarding these highlighting strategies is that they should never be used disingenuously. Judges and other readers can independently verify whether a particular legal matter required exceptional organizational skills. Consequently, a writer should never suggest in a document that the synthesis and organization of the law and/or record relevant to a matter required unusual skills in organization unless it is true.

## D.    *The Analytical Writer*

The fourth trait of an intelligent legal writer is that the writer possess *strong analytical skills*. This is perhaps the most important trait of intelligence for a legal advocate. Judges, in deciding legal matters, rely heavily on the advocates to provide sound arguments on how the issue under discussion should be resolved based on existing legal authority. Only someone with strong legal analysis skills can render such advice. Thus, an advocate's credibility is heavily influenced by the reader's perception of the strength or weakness of the advocate's analytical skills. The stronger these skill appear to be, the more trust and confidence the court will have in the advocate's arguments and advice. Conversely, if an advocate's analytical skills are suspect, the advocate will have minimal credibility in the eyes of the court.

### 1.  Substantive Means of Establishing that One Is Analytical

The most effective way for a legal writer to convince a reader that he or she possesses strong analytical skills is by presenting strong and effective legal analysis in the document itself. In the beginning of this chapter we discussed generally how a reader's impression of a legal writer's intelligence is formed first and foremost by the content of the writer's document. Nowhere is this more true than in the advocate's efforts to convince a reader that he or she is analytically strong.

Because strong legal analysis permeates effective persuasive documents, summarizing and listing the specific aspects of a legal document that exhibit these skills can be difficult. In general terms, however, a legal writer evinces strong analytical skills through the substantive aspects of a legal document by demonstrating strong skills in reading, synthesizing, interpreting, and applying legal authority. These skills include (1) the ability to read and comprehend cases, statutes, and other legal authorities; (2) an appreciation of the "weight" and interrelationship of authorities; and (3) an appreciation of the various types of legal analysis involved in the application of legal authorities to the facts of the case at hand, such as rule-based analysis, analogical analysis, and distinguishing analysis.

Throughout this chapter we have discussed how effective substance in a legal

Throughout this chapter we have discussed how effective substance in a legal document persuades both in terms of logos and ethos. This point is perhaps best illustrated here in our discussion of how strong analytical substance serves to persuade a reader. When a document contains strong legal analysis, it persuades first and most obviously through the substantive analysis itself, persuading readers through logic and reason, or logos. In addition to its logos function, however, strong analytical substance also persuades through ethos by "selling" the writer along with the writer's position. Legal writers who evince strong analytical skills through their writing are more effective in their efforts to persuade because the strong substance indicates to a reader that they are intelligent and credible sources of information.

## 2.  Highlighting Strategies for Establishing that One Is Analytical

Highlighting strategies for evincing that one possesses strong analytical skills are very common in legal writing. In fact, there are two general categories of such highlighting strategies. The first category involves a writer expressly stating that the analysis of the issue at hand is extraordinarily complex. Such statements serve a rhetorical function by emphasizing to readers that the problem requires analytical precision. This in turn implies that the writer, who is offering advice to resolve the complicated issue, possesses the strong legal analysis skills needed to penetrate it. Thus, such statements subtly enhance the writer's credibility as an intelligent source of information. Consider the following examples:

*Example 8.10*

From *In re Corrugated Container Antitrust Litigation*, 661 F.2d 1145, 1154 (7th Cir. 1981) (emphasis added):

> It is important to distinguish, at the outset of this discussion, two different concepts. The first is the court's remedial power to exclude evidence which violates the Fifth Amendment. The second is the scope of the protection afforded by a grant of statutory immunity—aside from any later effort to remedy a violation of the privilege. The basic error committed by the district court is that it confused, and lumped together, these two concepts.
> **This complex issue requires precise analysis.**

*Example 8.11*

From *Wilson v. O'Connor*, 555 S.W.2d 776, 779 (Tex. Civ. App. 1977) (emphasis added):

> **Article 5236e [regulating the return of lease security deposits] is a complex measure which requires careful analysis.**

*Example 8.12*

From *Marshall v. United States*, 623 A.2d 551, 558 (D.C. App. 1992)

(Ferren, J., dissenting in part and concurring in part) (emphasis added):

> **Unraveling the twisted threads of this complicated murder case requires a thorough analysis of our felony-murder law.**

In Examples 8.10 through 8.12 above, the writers included express language indicating that the issue under discussion is analytically complicated. These writers need not have mentioned this; the language in bold adds nothing substantive to the discussions. However, the writers chose to include this language as a rhetorical strategy for enhancing their credibility as intelligent sources of information. The bold language in these examples indicates to readers that, while the matter involves complex analysis, the writer possesses the skills necessary to resolve it effectively.

The second general category of highlighting strategies for evincing strong analytical skills involves statements that are less subtle and a bit more self-congratulatory than those set out above. Under this category, rather than stating generally that the law on the issue is complicated, a writer states that the specific point he or she is making is subtle or sophisticated. Whereas the first category involves statements that the issue is generally complicated (which merely implies that the writer possesses strong analytical skills), this second category involves statements by which the writer expressly takes credit for sophisticated analysis.

*Example 8.13*

From *Lancaster v. Kaiser Found. Health Plan of Mid-Atlantic States, Inc.*, 958 F. Supp. 1137, 1148 n.34 (E.D. Va. 1997) (emphasis added):

> **A . . . subtle point worth noting** is that the [HMO] Incentive Program [that offers financial rewards to physicians for not ordering tests and treatments for patients] may have the pernicious effect of lowering the standard of care for reasonably prudent practitioners. If a financial incentive was sufficiently robust so as to induce enough physicians to refrain from ordering MRIs and other diagnostic tests in situations such as the one at bar, this cost containment program would effectively diminish the "objective" benchmark for assessing physician competency. Put another way, the denial of benefits on this basis over time might subtly alter the standard by which to measure whether health care providers have rendered adequate medical care.

*Example 8.14*

From *McGautha v. California*, 402 U.S. 183, 308 n.72 (1971) (Brennan, J., dissenting) (bold emphasis added):

> **A peculiarity of California law raises another, more subtle, point.** Juries, as noted, are not required to base their decision [to impose the death penalty] on any particular findings of fact. But if a given jury should determine to impose the death sentence *only* if

it found particular facts that it thought relevant, it still would not be required to find those facts by even a preponderance of the evidence. *People v. Hines*, 61 Cal.2d 164, 173, 390 P.2d 398, 404 (1964). I do not suggest that due process requires such facts to be found beyond a reasonable doubt, or that we could reverse on due process grounds a conviction or sentence that we believed contrary to the weight of the evidence. But there is in my mind a serious question whether a State may constitutionally allow its *chosen trier of fact* to base a determination to kill any person on facts that the *trier of fact himself* does not believe are supported by the weight of the evidence.

*Example 8.15*

From *Herring v. Estelle*, 491 F.2d 125, 127 (5th Cir. 1974) (some citations omitted) (emphasis added):

> In 1965, . . . a panel of this circuit seemed to adopt a different standard [for evaluating a claim of ineffective counsel]. In *Williams v. Beto* the court said:
>
>> It is the general rule that relief from a final conviction on the ground of incompetent or ineffective counsel will be granted only when the trial was a farce, or a mockery of justice, or was shocking to the conscience of the reviewing court, or the purported representation was only perfunctory, in bad faith, a sham, a pretense, or without adequate opportunity for conference and preparation.
>
> *Williams v. Beto*, 5th Cir. 1965, 354 F.2d 698, 704. For several years following 1965, *Williams'* "farce-mockery" language appeared in our opinions with some frequency. **But a close reading of *Williams v. Beto* reveals that** that opinion did not intend to adopt the farce-mockery test in lieu of the reasonably effective assistance standard. The passage quoted above, after stating the general rule, cited eleven cases from other circuits as support; it cited no cases from this circuit. Thus the panel was saying that the farce-mockery test was the general rule in other circuits but not in ours.

*Example 8.16*

From *Overnite Transp. Co. v. Chicago Indus. Tire Co.*, 697 F.2d 789, 794 (7th Cir. 1982) (emphasis added):

> [W]e now address the question of whether the district court abused its discretion when it awarded the defendant costs and attorney's fees. As noted above, the district court based its award of attorney's fees and costs on the application of 28 U.S.C. Sec. 1927 (1981 Supp.) which provides:

> Any attorney . . . who so multiplies the proceedings in any case unreasonably and vexatiously may be required by the court to satisfy personally the excess costs, expenses, and attorneys' fees reasonably incurred because of such conduct.

**A close reading of this statute reveals that** the rule envisions a sanction against an attorney only when that attorney both (1) multiplies the proceedings, and (2) does so in a vexatious and unreasonable fashion.

*Example 8.17*

From *United States v. Martinez*, 949 F.2d 1117, 1120 (11th Cir. 1992) (emphasis added):

> The result we reach today is supported by this court's holding in *United States v. Milian-Rodriguez*, 759 F.2d 1558 (11th Cir.), *cert. denied*, 474 U.S. 845, 106 S.Ct. 135, 88 L.Ed.2d 112 (1985). In that case, the court held that the defendant's sweeping consent to a search of his office authorized government agents to pick the lock on a closet door. *Milian-Rodriguez*, 759 F.2d at 1563-64. [Defendant] Martinez argues that the court in *Milian-Rodriguez* relied not on the defendant's general consent to the search, but rather on his oral statement to the police that he could provide them with a key to the closet. **A close reading of the opinion, however, reveals that** the court relied primarily on the general nature of Milian's consent to the search. The court focused on that issue first, referring to Milian's oral statements about the closet key as merely "additional evidence" of his consent. *Milian-Rodriguez*, 759 F.2d at 1564.

*Example 8.18*

From *Untied States v. Cheska*, 202 F.3d 947, 951 n.1 (7th Cir. 2000) (emphasis added):

> The dissent cites *United States v. Joy*, 192 F.3d 761 (7th Cir. 1999) for the proposition that a prosecutor's remark may be found "appropriate" when viewed in context, even though the remark is literally untrue. **A careful reading of *Joy* reveals that** the court did not find the remark "appropriate." In *Joy*, the prosecutor repeatedly referred to the police as "we" in her closing argument. The defendant argued that this implied the prosecutor was present with the police as events unfolded, and resulted in improper vouching. The court found that the statements were not "innocuous" and admonished prosecutors to be more precise when addressing juries. Rather than finding the statement "appropriate," the court merely upheld the district court's exercise of discretion in refusing to grant a mistrial. The court ultimately held that this was not improper vouching

because no reasonable juror would assume that the prosecutor meant she was literally present with the police as her use of the term "we" implied.

*Example 8.19*

From *Campbell v. Clinton*, 203 F.3d 19, 25 (D.C. Cir. 2000) (Silberman, J., concurring) (emphasis added):

> **[A] careful reading of [the cases cited by appellants] reveals that** the language upon which appellants rely is only dicta.

In Examples 8.13 through 8.19, the writers draw attention to their analytical skills by emphasizing that the points they are making are "subtle" or require a "close or careful reading" of the relevant law. In all of these examples, the bold language could be eliminated and the substance of the discussions would be unaffected. By including this language, however, the writers essentially take "bows" for the clever analysis reflected in their discussions. Consider Example 8.13, in which the opinion writer points out that the HMO's Incentive Program could actually have the effect of lowering the standard of care of health care providers. Obviously, the writer could have made this point without stating at the outset that it is a "subtle" point. By proclaiming the concept to be "subtle," however, the writer draws the reader's attention to his analytical prowess. The bold language in the other examples serves a similar function. In essence, by including these phrases, the writers say to readers "Look how intelligent I am to have seen this subtle or sophisticated point of analysis."

In Examples 8.15 through 8.19, the writers used the phasing "a close reading . . . reveals" or "a careful reading . . . reveals." These two phrases are by far the most commonly used by legal writers for highlighting their analytical abilities.[9] In Examples 8.15 and 8.16, the writers use this phrasing straightforwardly. In Examples 8.17 through 8.19, however, use of the phrases has an added dimension. In those examples, the writers are responding to arguments of one of the parties to the case or, as in Example 8.18, to the arguments of a dissenting member of the court. In pointing out how the other person's arguments are erroneous, the opinion writers use the language "a close /careful reading . . . reveals." In this type of situation, this language has two rhetorical functions that benefit the writer. First, as we have discussed, such language draws attention to the fact that the writer is making a subtle or sophisticated point. Additionally, however, by including this language in a response to an argument made by another, the writer is also implying that the other person did not analyze the

---

[9] The language "a close reading reveals" actually has three rhetorical functions in legal writing. First, it warns readers that the ensuing discussion will be sophisticated or complicated, preparing them for a subtle or complex analysis by suggesting they pay close attention. Second, such language indicates that the writer is using authority in an non-obvious way, thus urging the reader to suspend disbelief or doubt until the writer has finished explaining the subtle point. Its third function, discussed here, is to highlight the writer's analytical skills.

law carefully and precisely. Thus, the use of this language in these situations not only enhances the writer's credibility, but it also has the effect of discrediting an adversary's intelligence and ability. Not surprisingly, this strategy is frequently used by legal advocates in responsive briefs when addressing the "erroneous" arguments made by opposing counsel in an opening brief.

As was mentioned above, the phrases "a careful reading . . . reveals" and "a close reading . . . reveals" are used very frequently by legal writers. In fact, a computer search of the following "terms and connectors" in case law databases results in over 3800 cases, many of which involve the use of these phrases as highlighting strategies:[10]

("close reading" "careful reading") +s reveals

You may have even used such phrases in your own writing. Despite the prevalence of these phrases, however, finding helpful examples has proven difficult, because the phrases, by definition, appear in subtle and complicated arguments that do not lend themselves to use in brief excerpts. Even Examples 8.15 through 8.19 may be a bit complicated to understand in isolation. Thus, to supplement the above illustrations, you are encouraged to look up full examples of cases in which this highlighting strategy appears by doing a computer search of the "terms and connectors" phrase set out above. The prevalence of and circumstances behind the use of these phrases can best be understood by examining their use in the context of full opinions.

---

**Exercise 8.2    Analyzing Highlighting Strategies for Establishing that One Is Analytical**

Conduct a computer search of case law databases using the terms and connectors set out above. From your search results, select a case that effectively illustrates the use of a highlighting strategy for evincing strong analytical skills. Write a short essay explaining the case and analyzing how the opinion writer used the highlighting strategy in question. Attach a copy of the case to your essay.

---

[10] Many of the cases located through this search involve the use of the phrase "a close reading of the record reveals" or similar language indicating that the point under discussion required a careful review of the facts of the matter. While such language may sometimes be used to highlight complex factual analysis, this phrasing is most often used to highlight that the writer thoroughly reviewed the record. Thus, rather than being a strategy for highlighting one's "analytical skills," this phrasing is most often used to highlight that the writer is "informed" (that is, intelligence trait #1).

**Exercise 8.3     Analyzing Highlighting Strategies for Establishing that
One Is Analytical**

Read the following excerpt from *White v. Fraternal Order of Police*, 707 F. Supp.
579, 589 (D.D.C. 1989):

> The law regarding defamation by implication is laced with subtleties and
> riddled with fine distinctions.  The Court finds, however, that making
> sense of this imbroglio is essential to the principled resolution of the
> issues before this Court. Accordingly, one important, but subtle, point
> requires clarification. A communication is not rendered defamatory
> simply because a recipient may draw a defamatory inference from it.
> Rather, the communication itself must be capable of bearing a defamatory
> meaning—the recipient must be able to reasonably understand the
> statement to convey the defamatory meaning. If the communication is not
> capable of bearing a defamatory meaning, it is irrelevant what inferences
> can reasonably be drawn by a recipient.

Write an essay identifying and analyzing the highlighting strategies used in this
excerpt to evince strong analytical skills. If necessary or helpful, look up the full
case from which this excerpt was taken.

**Exercise 8.4     Analyzing Highlighting Strategies for Establishing that
One Is Analytical**

Write an essay analyzing the rhetorical functions of the bold language in the
following case excerpt. If necessary or helpful, look up the full case from which
this excerpt was taken.

From *Tanzman v. Midwest Express Airlines, Inc.*, 916 F. Supp. 1013, 1016-17
(S.D. Cal. 1996) (some citations omitted) (emphasis added):

> Defendants argue that the San Diego Superior Court had jurisdiction
> over the case on September 11th, the day that the San Mateo Superior
> Court made its order granting the motion to transfer venue. Defendants
> cite cases which they argue stand for the proposition that, upon its
> issuance, an order of transfer vests the transferee court with jurisdiction.
> *See Badella v. Miller*, 44 Cal.2d 81, 85, 279 P.2d 729 (1955); *Chase v.
> Superior Court*, 154 Cal. 789, 99 P. 355 (1908); *Refrigeration Discount
> Corp. v. Superior Court*, 91 Cal.App.2d 295, 204 P.2d 932 (1949).

*continued*

> **A more precise reading of these cases, however, suggests that** the cases stand for the proposition that a transferring court does not lose all jurisdiction over a case once the transfer order has been made. *Badella*, 44 Cal.2d at 86, 279 P.2d 729 ("It does not appear that the finality and appealability of an order changing venue, nor the provision that the court to which the transfer is made should thereafter exercise jurisdiction, should preclude the court making the order from considering a motion to vacate such order . . .").

Several of the general cautions and guidelines previously discussed for using highlighting strategies are relevant to their use for evincing strong analytical skills. First, these types of highlighting strategies can sometimes come across to readers as immodest and self-congratulatory. This is particularly true of the second category of highlighting strategies discussed above—that is, the use of language that emphasizes that the point the writer is making is particularly clever. Thus, writers should be wary of using these phrases, remembering that readers may find them offputting.

Second, writers should not use these highlighting strategies disingenuously or in situations where the level of analysis does not justify their use. For example, a writer should not state that the analysis of a particular point is "subtle" or that it requires a "careful reading" of the relevant law, if the point under discussion is rather basic. In fact, using these highlighting strategies when they are not warranted can severely damage a writer's credibility by suggesting to the reader that the writer has had difficulty with a seemingly basic and fundamental point.

Third, legal writers should be aware that, as noted above, the phrases "a close reading . . . reveals" or "a careful reading . . . reveals" have become very common in legal writing. This frequency reduces their rhetorical impact to the point where they border on being cliches. Rather than effectively highlighting the writers' skills, they may simply go unnoticed by experienced legal readers.

## E.   *The Deliberate Writer*

The fifth trait of an intelligent legal writer is that the writer is *deliberate*. In general terms, a person is deliberate if he or she carefully considers both sides of an issue before reaching a conclusion. A deliberate person is not rash, impulsive, or quick to come to a decision. Instead, a deliberate person thoughtfully considers the competing arguments and justifications relevant to a matter before making a decision. People have more confidence and trust in the opinions of deliberate thinkers than of thinkers who seem rash and impulsive.

What does this mean for legal writers? Obviously this concept is relevant to the writing of judges, who should carefully consider the arguments for both sides before rendering a decision. Thus, to the extent that judges can indicate through their writing that the matter in question was carefully considered from all angles, they will be viewed as credible in the eyes of their readers. This concept, however, is also relevant to legal advocates. While it is true that advocates are not expected to be impartial like judges, and while it is also true that advocates represent the interests of only one side of a dispute, advocates should nevertheless strive to appear deliberate rather than rash or impulsive. Effective advocates do not simply focus on their own arguments and ignore the arguments of the opposing party; effective advocates carefully consider the arguments for the opposing party and explain why their clients should prevail *despite* those arguments. Legal audiences have more confidence and trust in those advocates who render advice after careful deliberation of both sides of a matter. The more deliberate an advocate is perceived to be, the more credibility he or she will have in the eyes of a reader.

### 1.  Substantive Means of Establishing that One Is Deliberate

The most effective way for legal writers to convince readers that they are deliberate is to demonstrate through the substance of the document itself that their advice is the product of careful deliberation. More specifically, a legal writer establishes that he or she is deliberate through the following substantive means:

a.  By recognizing adverse authority and adverse facts and explaining why these do not control the outcome of the present case.[11]

b.  When arguing first on a matter, by anticipating and refuting the arguments of the opposing party.

c.  When arguing second on a matter, by refuting the arguments made by the opposing party in the opening brief.

When an advocate not only presents his or her own arguments but also addresses adverse authority and the opposing party's adverse arguments, the advocate benefits in two ways. First, in terms of logos, the advocate persuades through logic and reason by demonstrating that the result advocated is justified, notwithstanding apparently conflicting legal authority and the arguments by the opposing party. Second, in terms of ethos, the advocate enhances the credibility of his or her advice by establishing that the advice resulted from careful and thoughtful deliberation.

### 2.  Highlighting Strategies for Establishing that One Is Deliberate

Legal writers commonly use two strategies to highlight the careful deliberation behind their writing. The first strategy appears most often in judicial writing. It involves an explicit statement that the opinions expressed were the product of thoughtful deliberation. Consider the following examples:

*Example 8.20*

From *NAACP v. Civiletti*, 609 F.2d 514, 515 (D.C. Cir. 1979) (emphasis

---

[11] As we saw in Chapter 7, acknowledging and addressing adverse authority and adverse facts also affects an advocate's credibility in terms of "character." Acknowledging adverse authority and facts evinces candor and honesty and thereby enhances perception of the advocate's general moral character.

added):

> The above-captioned cases are consolidated on appeal because both raise the same central issue—that is, whether the Civil Rights Attorney's Fees Awards Act of 1976, 42 U.S.C. Sec. 1988, permits an award of fees against the United States. **After careful deliberation**, we conclude that the Awards Act does not operate as a waiver of sovereign immunity in this context. Therefore, as to the award of attorney's fees by the courts below, we reverse.

*Example 8.21*

From *Askew v. Firestone*, 421 So. 2d 151, 154 (Fla. 1982) (emphasis added):

> **After careful deliberation**, we find no factual basis for the trial court's ruling and hold that he reached the wrong conclusion and that his order must be reversed.

*Example 8.22*

From *United States v. St. Louis-San Francisco Ry. Co.*, 464 F.2d 301, 311 (8th Cir. 1972) (Matthes, C. J., concurring) (emphasis added):

> **After careful deliberation**, I feel constrained to join the opinion of the Court. However, in doing so, I state some of my views separately.

The writers of these opinions included the phrase "after careful deliberation." This language is a rhetorical device designed to enhance the credibility of the writers' decisions by highlighting their deliberative quality. As stated above, this language, and language like it, is very common in the writing of judicial opinions. However, it is not so common in the writing of legal advocates because it is used most often in connection with the rendering of a final decision. Because attorneys advocate for conclusions rather than render them, language such as this is rarely appropriate in the writing of legal advocates.

The second category of highlighting strategies for indicating that one's advice and opinions are based on careful deliberation involves the use of language conceding that legitimate arguments exist on both sides of the issue. Consider the following case excerpts:

*Example 8.23*

From *Metz v. Transit Mix, Inc.*, 828 F.2d 1202, 1212 (7th Cir. 1987) (Easterbrook, J., dissenting) (emphasis added):

> **My colleagues' treatment of "wage discrimination" under the [Age Discrimination in Employment Act] has the support of several other courts. Fair arguments may be made on both sides.**

But I am persuaded that my brethren, and these other courts, have settled on an approach that is too broad, and I shall try to explain why.

*Example 8.24*

From *District of Colombia v. Patterson*, 667 A.2d 1338, 1348 (D.C. App. 1995) (Wagner, C. J., dissenting) (emphasis added):

There is no disagreement among the panel about the general rule which governs whether a party is entitled to attorney's fees under Sec. 1988. What seems to divide us is the difficult problem of determining when a party fairly may be said to have prevailed on a claim for declaratory judgment for purposes of shifting counsel fees to the opposing party under the controlling precedents. **Although this is a close question**, plaintiffs crossed that threshold, in my opinion.

In the above case excerpts, the writers acknowledge that, notwithstanding their ultimate conclusions, legitimate arguments exist on both sides of the issue under discussion. Such language serves the rhetorical function of emphasizing to readers that the writer's opinion is based on careful consideration of the competing arguments. Although the above examples are from case opinions, language such as this is also used on occasion by legal advocates in their briefs. In brief writing, language such as this emphasizes to a reader that the writer has considered the opposing arguments and that the advocate's advice is not rash or impulsive, but rather is the product of thorough deliberation. Consequently, this language can be used by legal advocates to enhance their credibility.[12]

Some experienced advocates, however, argue that including such language in a persuasive document is unwise, because it unnecessarily legitimizes the arguments of the opposing side. According to these experts, an advocate should never admit that the opposing party has compelling arguments. On the contrary, they maintain, an advocate should concentrate on minimizing the legitimacy of the opposing party's views. While this strategy may be effective in many situations, it should not be considered an absolute. In some situations, the rhetorical advantages of evincing deliberation may outweigh the negative impact of legitimizing the opposition's arguments. This is particularly true in cases in which it is readily apparent to all involved that compelling arguments exist for both sides. In these situations, attempts

---

[12] Language that acknowledges that an adversary has legitimate arguments actually serves two rhetorical functions. First, as discussed above, it indicates that the writer has considered the opponent's arguments and is rendering advice only after careful deliberation of the issue. Thus, it enhances the writer's credibility as an "intelligent" source of information. Second, it enhances the "good will" aspect of credibility discussed in Chapter 7 by showing that the advocate is cognizant and respectful of the opponent's views. That is, by acknowledging an opponent's arguments, advocates demonstrate that their arguments are based on careful deliberation, not on ill-will or malevolence toward the opponent.

to trivialize an opponent's position would undoubtedly undermine an advocate's effectiveness more than enhance it. Thus, rather than saying nothing, an advocate in this situation may want to consider acknowledging that the opponent has legitimate arguments, while ultimately advocating a conclusion favorable to his or her own position. Such a strategy may serve to enhance the advocate's credibility as an intelligent and thoughtful source of information. In the end, use of this strategy comes down to a judgment call. In making this call, however, advocates should be mindful of the rhetorical benefits that can be gained from language highlighting the careful deliberation that went into the advocate's arguments.

## F.    *The Writer Empathetic Toward the Reader*

The sixth trait of an intelligent legal writer is *reader empathy.* One of the most basic principles of effective persuasive writing is an appreciation of one's audience. One aspect of audience appreciation is "reader empathy." Reader empathy refers to a writer's ability to put himself or herself in the position of the reader so that he or she can appreciate what the reader needs to understand the material being presented.

Some writers write in ways that satisfy their own needs and expectations rather than those of their readers. Empathetic writers, however, are sensitive to their readers. They write with an eye on their audience and present their material in ways that accommodate their readers' needs. Reader empathy is a sign of intelligence. Consequently, advocates who demonstrate reader empathy are viewed as being more intelligent, and therefore more credible, than those who do not.

### 1.    Substantive Means of Establishing that One Possesses Empathy Toward Readers

There are many ways that the content of a legal document demonstrates that a legal writer is sensitive to the needs of a reader. In particular, a legal writer evinces reader empathy through the following substantive means:

a.   By including effective "signposting" devices and other devices that prevent a reader from getting lost in a complex legal discussion.[13] These devices include:
i.   The effective use of headings and sub-headings;
ii.  The effective use of enumeration, bullet points, and similar devices that add clarity to the presentation of lists of information;
iii. The effective use of transitions between points of discussion;
iv.  The effective use of introductions and thesis paragraphs to provide readers with "roadmaps" to the ensuing discussions; and
v.   The use of consistent terminology.

b.   By eliminating vague references to external information that the reader does not share with the writer.

---

[13] As we discussed earlier in this chapter, the incorporation of "signposting" devices also indicates that a writer is "organized" (intelligence trait #3).

    c.  By establishing a solid foundation for the analysis presented in the document. A writer establishes a strong foundation by

        i.  Clearly explaining the facts the reader will need to know in order to understand the writer's analysis; and

       ii.  Clearly and fully explaining rules, statutes, cases, and so on, before applying them to the case at hand.

    d.  By setting out clearly the application of legal authority to the facts of the case at hand.

Let's explore items c. and d. more fully, as they are crucial to evincing reader empathy. As indicated in item c., an advocate evinces reader empathy by establishing a strong foundation for his or her analysis. In the context of persuasive legal writing, the audience is typically a judge or a panel of judges. And while a judge presiding over a matter may have a strong understanding of general legal concepts, legal terminology, and procedural rules, he or she will typically have limited knowledge of the facts of the matter at hand and the relevant law. Accordingly, judges rely heavily on the parties themselves to inform the court of the facts of the case and the applicable law.

As part of "reader empathy" a writer must be sensitive to the judge's lack of familiarity with the case. In writing to the judge, the advocate must be sensitive to what the reader needs to know about the facts and the law in order to understand the analysis and conclusion presented in the document. Some writers, however, fail to set out a strong foundation for their analysis. That is, some writers have strong analytical skills yet are not effective advocates because they do not present their analysis so that readers with limited prior knowledge can understand it. For example, they may make vague references to facts they have not adequately explained or apply legal principles they have not effectively defined.

The source of this problem is fairly easy to identify. Legal advocates typically spend hundreds of hours studying the facts of their cases and analyzing the relevant law prior to writing their briefs. They become so familiar with the matter that they forget what it was like to be uninformed on the relevant facts and law. Consequently, when they present their arguments, they may fail to provide the reader—who is new to the matter—with the foundational knowledge necessary to understand their arguments. While the writer's arguments may be sound, they are not understandable to a reader with limited prior knowledge.

Reader empathy is thus essential to effective legal advocacy. A legal writer must be able to put himself or herself in the reader's position and realize and provide the foundational information the reader needs to understand the arguments presented.

As item d. indicates, legal writers must also clearly explain the *application* of the law to the facts of the case at hand. That is, writers must explain to readers each logical step in their analysis. Legal writers should not make leaps in logic or state unsupported conclusions. Rather, they should lead readers to their conclusions step by step. John C. Dernbach, Richard V. Singleton II, Cathleen S. Wharton, and Joan M. Ruhtenberg explain it this way:

> Because [briefs] are written for [law-trained readers], it is safe to assume that the reader will have a basic understanding of the law and the legal process. It is not safe, however, to assume that the reader will be able to see how the cited cases or statutes support your conclusion. It is not enough to state that a particular result [should] occur; you must identify the analytical steps leading to that result. . . . A reader who is able to follow all the important steps of your thought process on paper will be able to evaluate the soundness of your conclusions and act accordingly. Failure to show all the steps of your analysis may give the reader an incomplete understanding of the issue or sub-issue you are discussing and thus little or no confidence in your conclusion.
>
> In a way, writing a . . . brief is like giving directions to your home. You know how to get there, but the directions you give or the map you provide must be complete enough to enable someone else to get there. Each important feature or turn in your analytical map must be clearly identified, or your reader is likely to get lost. . . . Many writers understand their subject so well that they compress several analytical steps into one, make unexplained assumptions, fail to define important terms, and in many other ways obscure their thinking from the reader. Make sure your directions are clear and complete.[14]

An advocate who incorporates the above aspects into his or her writing benefits both in terms of logos and ethos. In terms of logos, a writer who is sensitive to the needs of a reader will be better understood by the reader. That is, to the extent that a writer writes in a way that is reader-friendly, the writer can be more confident that his or her substantive arguments will be understood by the reader. Thus, a writer who possesses reader empathy is more persuasive in terms of substance and reason.

In terms of ethos, reader empathy is a sign of intelligence. A writer whose document reflects a sensitivity to the needs of the reader is generally viewed as intelligent and capable, and is therefore more credible.

### 2.  Highlighting Strategies for Establishing that One Possesses Empathy Toward Readers

Highlighting strategies for evincing reader empathy are common, yet fairly limited in their rhetorical impact. Typically these strategies involve a writer highlighting the fact that he or she is setting out foundational information that the reader needs to know in order to understand a subsequent discussion. Consider these examples:

*Example 8.25*

From *United States v. Castro*, 629 F.2d 456, 458 (7th Cir. 1980) (emphasis added):

---

[14] John C. Dernbach et al., *A Practical Guide to Legal Writing and Legal Method* 133-34 (2d ed. 1994). Although the authors made this point in discussing the writing of objective memos, they later indicate that this concept is also relevant to persuasive writing. *See id.* at 236.

**In order to appreciate the issues raised on appeal, a full discussion both of the factual and the procedural underpinnings of this case is necessary.** . . . [The writer then explains the facts and procedural history of the case.]

*Example 8.26*

From *McKenzie v. Risley*, 842 F.2d 1525, 1544 (9th Cir. 1988) (Fletcher, Pregerson, Canby, and Norris, JJ., dissenting) (emphasis added):

> [T]he [jury] instructions [in this case] were so flawed that the defendant could not have had a fair trial. Harmless error analysis is simply inappropriate in such a case. The instructions in this case are so bad that even the prosecution at trial objected to their use and requested that alternatives be read in their place. They are instructions that the counsel for the State at the en banc oral argument admitted were in some respects the worst he had ever seen. Justice Shea of the Montana Supreme Court called the instructions "the most confusing and inconsistent set of instructions I have ever seen." *McKenzie v. Osborne*, 195 Mont. 56, 640 P.2d 368, 411 (1981) (Shea, J., dissenting). **Because only a complete reading of the instructions will illustrate fully the extent to which they deviate from fair and comprehensible instructions, we append the full text to the end of this dissent. We suggest that the readers of this opinion turn first to the instructions in order to appreciate the dissent's profound disagreement with the approach the majority embraces.**

*Example 8.27*

From *FilmTec Corp. v. Hydranautics*, 67 F.3d 931, 933-34 (Fed. Cir. 1995) (emphasis added):

> Hydranautics, defendant-appellant in this case, competes with plaintiff-appellee FilmTec in manufacturing and selling reverse osmosis membranes. Another competitor is Allied-Signal, Inc. (Allied). FilmTec has sued, separately, both Hydranautics and Allied for infringement of the '344 patent. **It is necessary to describe the parallel litigation between FilmTec and Allied in order to appreciate fully the course of the litigation between FilmTec and Hydranautics**. . . . [The writer then explains the facts and procedural history of the parallel litigation.]

*Example 8.28*

From *Helen v. DiDario*, 46 F.3d 325, 329-30 (3d Cir. 1995) (emphasis added):

**In order to appreciate the scope of the [Americans with Disabilities Act] and its attendant regulations, it is necessary to examine the circumstances leading to its enactment.** . . . [The writer then explains the history of the Act.]

*Example 8.29*

From *Smart v. Leeke*, 856 F.2d 609, 610 (4th Cir. 1988) (emphasis added):

It is of utmost importance to realize that there are two different factors presented here for our consideration. One is known as the elements of the crime, the other is the burden of proof. **In order to appreciate the difference between the two factors, it is necessary to understand the distinction between *Mullaney v. Wilbur*, 421 U.S. 684, 95 S.Ct. 1881, 44 L.Ed.2d 508 (1975), and *Patterson v. New York*, 432 U.S. 197, 97 S.Ct. 2319, 53 L.Ed.2d 281 (1977).** . . . [The writer then explains the distinction between these two cases.]

*Example 8.30*

From *State v. Atkinson*, 751 P.2d 784, 787 (Or. 1988) (Gillette, J., dissenting) (emphasis added):

I should like to think that, were we doing it for the first time, this court would not today decide *State v. Tooley*, 297 Or. 602, 687 P.2d 1068 (1984), the way it was decided in 1984. We now find ourselves entangled in a web woven by that decision, a web of our own creation. . . . I therefore find myself compelled to dissent.
**A complete review of *Tooley* is useful in order to appreciate the problems in the present case.** . . . [The writer then explains the *Tooley* case in detail.]

*Example 8.31*

From *Max Daetwyler Corp. v. Input Graphics, Inc.*, 545 F. Supp. 165, 166 (E.D. Pa. 1982) (emphasis added):

Plaintiffs have brought this action asserting two causes of action: count one of their amended complaint alleges that defendants are infringing plaintiffs' patent for "doctor blades"—a blade-shaped device for wiping excess ink from the printing surface used in photogravure printing techniques—by manufacturing and selling a similar device; and count two asserts that the defendants falsely represented the characteristics of their doctor blade device in violation of Section 43(a) of the Lanham-Trademark Act, 15 U.S.C. Sec. 1125(a). Defendants have now moved for summary judgment on both counts. . . .

> **In order to appreciate the legal issues presented, the technology of photogravure printing and the role played by doctor blades in that art must be understood in some detail**. . . . [The writer then explains these technical concepts.]

In Examples 8.25 through 8.31, the writers demonstrate their sensitivity to their readers' needs by setting out foundational information the readers will need to know in order to understand the analysis presented in the opinions. In Examples 8.25 through 8.27, the writers set out information regarding the facts and procedural history of the cases that readers will need to know in order to understand the subsequent discussions. Similarly, in Examples 8.28 through 8.30, the writers take a moment to clearly explain relevant legal authority to prepare the reader for the ensuing analysis using that authority. Finally, in Example 8.31, the writer explains technical information regarding the printing industry that the reader needs to know in order to understand the opinion fully. Thus, the substance of these opinions reflects reader empathy on the part of the writers.

However, in addition to evincing reader empathy through the substance of the opinions, the writers also employ highlighting strategies to emphasize their empathy for their readers. In all of these examples, the writers use the phrase "in order to appreciate . . ." as a transition to their foundational information. In Example 8.25, for instance, the writer states, "In order to appreciate the issues raised on appeal, a full discussion of both the factual and the procedural underpinnings of this case is necessary." The writer then goes on to prepare the reader for the opinion by explaining the facts and procedural history of the case. Similar transitions, marked in bold type, are used in the other examples.

The bold language in the examples represents a highlighting strategy for evincing reader empathy. By this language, the writers stop communicating the substance of their opinions for a moment and speak directly to the reader. This language is like a "theatrical aside," in that the writer breaks from the substantive discussion to tell the reader *why* certain information has been inserted into the written opinion: They need it "in order to appreciate" the subsequent discussions. By this language the writers expressly indicate their sensitivity to the needs of their readers and their willingness to write the opinions with those needs in mind. Thus, this language serves to highlight the writers' empathy with their readers, thereby enhancing the writers' credibility as intelligent and thoughtful writers.

As mentioned earlier, such highlighting strategies are common in legal writing, both in judicial opinions and in persuasive briefs. When using these highlighting strategies in persuasive briefs, however, writers should remember one important guideline: The phrase "in order to appreciate" can sometimes come across to readers as condescending and patronizing. Thus, before using such language, an advocate should consider whether it unwisely creates an off-putting tone.

## G.    *The Practical Writer*

The seventh trait of an intelligent legal writer is that the writer is *practical*. Some advocates, in arguing their cases, get caught up in sophisticated points of analysis or theoretical principles and lose sight of the practical implications of their positions. Courts, however, depend on advocates to advise them not only as to what is legally right, but also as to what is practical. Consequently, courts have more trust and confidence in those advocates whose advice is both legally sound *and* practical. Carole C. Berry explains it this way:

> Another factor that influences [an advocate's] credibility is the practicality of the relief sought. The desired outcome must make sense from both a legal and a public policy standpoint. An advocate who asks the court to overstep its judicial bounds (be it in terms of separation of powers, standard of review, overruling established mandatory authority, etc.) will be viewed as unknowledgeable or unintelligent. If the request has far reaching negative consequences, it may appear the advocate has not devised a workable solution to the problem.[15]

Advocates who consider the broad implications of their positions are perceived as being wise. Thus, an advocate's document should not only contain sound legal arguments, it must also reflect an appreciation of the public policy and practical implications of the relief sought. Advocates who consider the practical as well as legal implications of a case have more credibility than do those who address only the legal dimensions of a case.

### 1.   Substantive Means of Establishing that One Is a Practical Legal Writer

The most important way in which an advocate evinces to an audience that he or she is "practical" is by expressly considering in the document itself the practical implications of the relief sought. In particular, advocates demonstrate their practicality in the following ways:

a.   By considering and addressing the practical consequences of the relief sought; and

b.   By considering and addressing the broad public policy implications of the relief sought.

An advocate who incorporates these aspects into a persuasive document benefits both in terms of logos and ethos. First, by explaining how the relief sought is not only legally sound but also practical, an advocate enhances the persuasiveness of his or her argument in terms of logos. Second, such discussions enhance an advocate's credibility as an intelligent source of information. The ability to see the "big picture" and appreciate the practical consequences of a course of action is a sign of wisdom. Advocates who evince such wisdom are able to inspire more trust and confidence in their readers, thus furthering the ethos process of persuasion.

---

[15] Carole C. Berry, *Effective Appellate Advocacy: Brief Writing and Oral Argument* 42-43 (2d ed. 1999).

## 2.  Highlighting Strategies for Establishing that One Is a Practical Legal Writer

The most common highlighting strategies for evincing that one is practical involve phrases such as "from a practical standpoint" or "from a public policy standpoint." These phrases and phrases like them are commonly used in legal documents as transitions to discussions of the practical implications of the result advocated. Consider the following example:

*Example 8.32*

From *In re Davis*, 705 N.E.2d 1219, 1221-22 (Ohio 1999) (emphasis added):

> [A] seven-day limit . . . appears in the Revised Code section delimiting the procedure for dispositional hearings for children adjudicated abused, neglected or dependent. . . . R.C. 2151.35(B)(3) requires that after the dispositional hearing is concluded, "the court shall enter an appropriate judgment within seven days." . . .
>
> Appellants argue that the seven-day constraint is mandatory and that the juvenile court's failure to adhere to it deprived the court of authority . . . to determine permanent custody. We, however, view the provision as directory rather than mandatory, leaving the juvenile court's jurisdiction unaffected by the untimeliness of its decision.
> . . .
>
> **Finding the provision directory makes sense from a practical standpoint as well.** If we decided that the time constraint is mandatory and that juvenile courts therefore lack jurisdiction to decide these cases from the eighth day following submission of the issue, we would defeat the very purposes the time limit was designed to protect. If there were jurisdictional consequences, a missed deadline would require either that the child be returned to a potentially risky home situation, or that a new complaint be filed and the process begun anew, delaying the final resolution of the issue even further. Such consequences would not serve the interests of children, who are too often relegated to temporary custody for too long.

In *In re Davis*,[16] a lower Ohio court granted permanent custody of five minor children to a county agency 17 months after the conclusion of the custody hearing.[17] The parents appealed, arguing that the court lost jurisdiction to award permanent custody because the court did not render its final judgment within seven days of the

---

[16] 705 N.E.2d 1219.

[17] *Id.* at 1220-21.

conclusion of the custody hearing, as required by the applicable statute.[18] The Ohio Supreme Court found that the statute imposing the seven-day limit was merely "directory" not "mandatory" and that the lower court did not lose jurisdiction for its failure to comply with the statute.[19] In reaching this conclusion, the court first engaged in sophisticated "legal" analysis, which included an analysis of canons of statutory construction.[20] After the legal analysis, however, the court also considered the practical implications of the issue. As indicated in the excerpt above, the court concluded that, from a practical standpoint, interpreting the statute as merely directory made more sense.[21]

In writing this opinion, the opinion writer evinces intelligence by considering the practical as well as legal dimensions of the issue. By including the practical implications, the writer establishes to the reader through the substance of the opinion that she is practical and wise. Thus, this substantive aspect of the case enhances the writer's credibility as an intelligent source of information. However, the writer also highlights her consideration of the practical implications of the matter by using the transitional phrase "from a practical standpoint." The writer could have presented a discussion of the practical implications without expressly stating the intention to do so. However, by including the bold language, the writer draws attention to the fact that she is addressing the practical consequences of the matter. Thus, the writer not only discusses the practical implications, but highlights the fact that she is doing so through the use of highlighting language.

As mentioned above, the phrases "from a practical standpoint" and "from a policy standpoint" appear very frequently in legal writing as transitions to discussions of the practical implications of an issue. Technically, these phrases can be considered highlighting strategies because they expressly draw a reader's attention to the fact that the writer is discussing the practical implications of the case. However, because these phrases are used so frequently by legal writer, they typically have only minimal rhetorical impact.

---

[18] *Id.* at 1221.

[19] *Id.*

[20] *Id.* at 1222.

[21] *Id.*

**Exercise 8.5     Analyzing How a Legal Writer Evinces Practicality**

Conduct a computer search of case law databases for the phrase "from a public policy standpoint." From your search results, choose a case that you feel effectively illustrates how a legal writer evinces that he or she is "practical." Write an essay explaining the case and analyzing how the writer evinces practicality through both the *substance* of the discussion and *highlighting strategies*. Use the discussion of *Davis* above as a guideline for your essay. Attach a copy of the case to your essay.

## H.     The Articulate Writer

The eighth trait of an intelligent legal writer is that the writer is *articulate*. For our purposes, "articulate" means that a writer has strong skills in written communication. Just as the substantive content of a document affects a reader's impression of a writer's intelligence, the way in which that substance is presented also has considerable effect on readers. A poor writer has very little credibility in the eyes of a reader.

Being an "articulate" legal writer has two aspects. First, a writer must have strong command of the rules of grammar, usage, and punctuation. A demonstrated mastery of these basic skills of English composition is essential to the writer's credibility. A reader will be skeptical of the advice and viewpoints of a writer whose document contains basic errors in grammar and punctuation.

Second, a writer must use a clear and understandable *style*. Sometimes a document may be grammatically correct and yet still difficult to understand because it is unnecessarily complicated. The writers who are most successful at gaining the confidence of their readers are those who can communicate complicated legal concepts in a clear and understandable way. The substance of legal analysis is complicated enough without adding to the confusion by using unnecessarily complex sentence structures and complicated wording. Thus a clear, understandable writing style—commonly referred to as "plain English"—is essential to a legal writer's credibility as an intelligent, articulate advocate.

### 1.   Substantive Means of Establishing that One Is Articulate

It should be readily obvious that the most effective way for a legal writer to convince a reader that he or she is articulate is by writing in a clear and grammatically correct way. In particular, writers show that they are articulate in the following ways:

   a.   By using proper grammar;

   b.   By using correct punctuation;

   c.   By writing in a clear, understandable, uncomplicated style.

A legal advocate who writes in this way benefits both in terms of logos and ethos. In terms of logos, the advocate is more persuasive because an articulate writing style allows readers to understand more easily the substance of the arguments. Moreover, errors in punctuation and grammar can distract readers from the substance. A distracted audience is much more difficult to persuade than an attentive one. In terms of ethos, effective grammar and a clear writing style indicate to readers that the writer is articulate and intelligent. Thus, these aspects of a document enhance the writer's credibility in the eyes of the reader.

## 2.   Highlighting Strategies for Establishing that One Is Articulate

Highlighting strategies for evincing that one is articulate are relatively rare in legal writing because a reader can readily tell from the document at hand if the advocate is articulate. This is not to say, however, that such highlighting strategies do not exist. In fact, they are used with some regularity in another form of writing: journalism. The most common strategy involves the writer's intentional use of grammatically incorrect or awkward language and an immediate acknowledgment of that use. Consider the following examples:

*Example 8.33*

From John Bierman, *View from Abroad: U.S. Finds Mideast Diplomacy a Profitable Path*, The Financial Post, October 5, 1992, at 6 (a satiric piece regarding the United States' sale of weapons to foreign countries) (emphasis added):

> American ships, tanks, planes and guns don't just provide more bang for the buck. They also contribute to world peace, by virtue of the fact that they are **(if you'll excuse the double negative)** non-destabilizing.

*Example 8.34*

From Maggie Campbell, *Private Lives: Your Son Still Harbours Dreams of an Acting Career at Your Expense. Should He be Cut Loose?*, The Guardian (London), January 26, 1998 (providing advice to a reader whose thirty-plus-year-old son still lives at home) (emphasis added):

> Get real, lady! Stop giving this feckless waster any more of your hard-earned cash and let him sink or swim. You will have to wean him first, though, as you seem to have failed to do this until now. Remember, doormats get walked on—**I make no excuses for ending with a preposition** as I am incensed by the behaviour of this work-shy parasite.

*Example 8.35*

From Denise Tom, *Jerry Rice: Hard-Working, Hard-Playing Receiver*

*Dazzles with his Dedication and Dramatic Catches*, USA Today, January 8, 1988, NFL Playoffs Bonus Section, Playoff review, at 2 (emphasis added):

> **Pardon the double negatives**, but [professional football player] Jerry Lee Rice has never not known hard work.
>
> Whether picking cotton and corn as a youngster on the family farm in Crawford, Miss., or repeatedly running pass routes to get his timing down as a third-year pro football player, Rice is a shining example of the work ethic.

*Example 8.36*

From Lou Hudson, *Texas Beat: All Pay No Work*, The Fort Worth Star-Telegram, May 17, 1991 (emphasis added):

> Texas Trivia: The Fort Griffin State Historical Park in Albany . . . is a historical attraction in its own right.
>
> But it's also the home to the Texas State Longhorn Herd. . . .
>
> Is there any other state [that] has its own official herd of cattle? Can't be very many of 'em anyway. Strange thing to have an official state collection of, **you should pardon the dangling preposition (a grammatical situation up with which we should not put)**.

In the foregoing examples, the journalists writing these excerpts expressly acknowledge their use of grammatically awkward phrasing. This writing technique serves two rhetorical functions. First, it draws the readers' attention to and thus emphasizes the point being made. Its second function, and the one relevant to our discussion in this chapter, is to enhance the writer's credibility as an intelligent and articulate writer by highlighting his or her knowledge of the (here intentionally violated) rules of grammar.

Although highlighting strategies like these are not uncommon in journalism, they are rarely appropriate in legal writing. For one thing, they are a bit too informal for the serious and formal nature of persuasive legal writing. Second, they often come across to readers as attempts at humor, as we can see in Examples 8.34 and 8.36 above. Humor is rarely appropriate in legal writing.

## I.    The Eloquent Writer

The ninth trait of an intelligent legal writer is *eloquence*. In the preceding discussion, we saw that legal writers should establish that they are articulate by writing in a clear and grammatically correct way. Eloquence, on the other hand, refers to the dramatic or rhetorical flair of one's writing. Those writers who effectively incorporate rhetorical stylistic devices into their writing—such as metaphor, personification, and alliteration, to name a few—are generally viewed as intelligent. In fact, many of the most respected legal minds in history have gained this respect, at least in part, because of their ability to write with poetic flair. Benjamin Cardozo, Oliver Wendell Holmes, Learned Hand, Robert Jackson, Louis Brandeis—their reputations for being brilliant jurists are due in large part to their eloquence in writing. Even ancient classical rhetoricians recognized rhetorical eloquence as a sign of genius. As classical rhetorician Quintilian stated: "[B]y the employment of skillful ornament [an advocate] commends himself at the same time [as he commends his argument]."[22]

### 1.    Substantive Means of Establishing that One Is Eloquent

Just as one establishes that one is articulate by writing articulately, one establishes that one is eloquent by writing eloquently. In particular, a writer can convey eloquence by effectively using stylistic rhetorical devices in a document.

In Chapters 9 and 10, we explore many of the devices that writers traditionally use to give their writing rhetorical flair. We will also explore the rhetorical functions that such stylistic devices serve. We will see that, as we have discussed here, one of the functions served by these devices is that they enhance a writer's credibility as an intelligent source of information.

### 2.    Highlighting Strategies for Establishing that One Is Eloquent

The most common technique legal writers use to highlight their eloquence is to draw attention to their use of specific stylistic devices. Consider the following examples:

*Example 8.37*

From *Department of Revenue of Mont. v. Kurth Ranch*, 511 U.S. 767, 803 (1994) (Scalia, J., dissenting) (citation omitted) (emphasis added):

> We dodged the bullet in [the] *Halper* [case]—**or perhaps a more precise metaphor would be that** we thrust our lower-court colleagues between us and the bullet—by leaving it to the lower courts to determine at what particular dollar level the civil fine exceeded the Government's "legitimate nonpunitive governmental objectives" and thus became a penalty.

*Example 8.38*

From *State v. Ranson*, 488 S.E.2d 5, 13 (W. Va. 1997) (Maynard, J., dissenting) (emphasis added):

> I believe the majority has created a "Fishing Expedition Exception" to the First Amendment guarantee of a free press. **To continue the aquatic life metaphor**, the majority is swimming in the jaws of a crocodile.

In these examples, the writers not only use metaphor as a stylistic device, they highlight this use by expressly calling attention to their metaphors. The language in

---

[22] Marius Fabius Quintilianus, *Institutio Oratoria* 213 (H.E. Butler, trans. 1954), *quoted in* Michael Frost, *Greco-Roman Analysis of Metaphoric Reasoning*, 2 Legal Writing 113, 127 (1996).

bold in both of these examples adds nothing substantive to the discussions. The writers could have presented their metaphors without specifically identifying their language as being metaphoric. But such highlighting devices serves two rhetorical functions. First, they emphasize the writer's point by encouraging readers to slow down and take note of *how* the writer is writing. Second, they draw the reader's attention to the writer's intelligence. Because eloquence is a sign of intelligence, highlighting language such as this is designed to enhance a writer's credibility as an eloquent and intelligent source of information. Such language essentially says to a reader, "Look how clever I am to use this stylistic device in my writing."

Sometimes highlighting one's eloquence can come across to readers as pretentious and self-congratulatory. If a writer says to a reader, "Look how clever I am," the writer must be sure the reader will agree. If used ineffectively, such highlighting can turn readers off and thus undermine a writer's credibility. Consider, for example, the following excerpt from *Potts v. Smith*.[23]

> [O]ur late beloved brother, Judge Eberhardt, with his **aptness for appropriate apothegms** [FN1] expressed the situation in this aphorism: "If the parties to a transaction do not create binding agreements, the courts are powerless to do it for them or to afford a remedy for a breach."

> FN1. **In addition to an alliteration addiction, the writer has been accused of being lexiphanic (using pretentious words).**

In this example, the writer not only uses alliteration and big words but, in a footnote, expressly takes credit for his alliterative efforts and extensive vocabulary. In highlighting his intelligence in this way, the writer may have gone too far. The writer's efforts to draw attention to his writing style come across as immodest and pretentious (admittedly!?). Thus, this language undermines the writer's credibility more than it enhances it. (Moreover, the alliteration is a bit too obvious and forced to be effective, and the use of the words "apothegm" and "lexiphanic" ill-advisedly complicated.) While such language may be acceptable for Judge H. Sol Clark of the Georgia Court of Appeals (who is "former Dean of the International Academy of Trial Lawyers, former President of SCRIBES, and is acknowledged as 'one of Georgia's great judges'"[24]), it is not advisable for advocates whose success depends as much on their credibility as on their lawyering skills.

## J.     The Detail-Oriented Writer

The tenth trait of intelligence that a legal advocate should project through his or her writing is that he or she is *detail-oriented*. In this context, a "detail-oriented" writer is one who prepares written documents with careful attention to the details of presentation. In our discussion of intelligence trait #4—analytical—we discussed that

---

[23] 215 S.E.2d 697, 698 & n.1 (Ga. Ct. App. 1975) (citations omitted) (emphasis added).

[24] *Russell v. State*, 372 S.E.2d 445, 447 (Ga. Ct. App. 1988).

advocates should evince "analytical precision" in their writing. There, precision referred to sharpness of analysis in interpreting and applying legal authorities. Our focus here is different and more basic. Here we are referring to "crossing *t*'s" and "dotting *i*'s," that is, to being precise in the editing of a final written work.

Readers tend to have more trust and confidence in writers who pay attention to the minute details in a written product. A document that contains misspelled words and typographical errors sends readers the message that the writer is not detail-oriented. Such errors cause readers to lose confidence in the writer, for if the writer is not precise enough to catch basic errors such as these, who knows what other details might be missing from the document. Consequently, it is important for writers to establish that they are precise and detailed-oriented.

### 1.  Substantive Means of Establishing that One Is Detail-Oriented

A legal writer establishes that he or she is detail-oriented by paying attention to details in the preparation of a document. More specifically, a legal writer evinces that he or she is detail-oriented in the following ways:

   a.  By eliminating misspelled words;

   b.  By eliminating typographical errors;

   c.  By presenting a neat and professional-looking product;

   d.  By carefully and fully complying with court rules regarding the format of a document submitted to that court, including rules regulating cover color, page length, type size, and so on; and

   e.  By carefully and fully complying with applicable citation rules in the citation of authorities.

A writer who complies with these guidelines in preparing a persuasive document will be a more persuasive advocate in terms of both logos and ethos. In terms of logos, misspellings and typographical errors hinder effective communication. Thus, such errors can prevent a reader from comprehending the persuasive substance of an advocate's document. Moreover, errors of this nature distract a reader from the substance of a document. It is very difficult to persuade a reader through logic and reasoning if the reader is distracted. Second, in terms of ethos, errors of this nature send a message to a reader that the writer is not careful, precise, and detail-oriented. Consequently, such errors cause a reader to lose confidence in the writer as an intelligent and capable source of information.

### 2.  Highlighting Strategies for Establishing that One Is Detail-Oriented

As discussed in the prior section, a writer establishes that he or she is detail-oriented through the *substance* of a document by paying attention to minute details in the completion of the document. There are no highlighting strategies for evincing editorial precision.

## K.    *The Innovative Writer*

The eleventh trait of intelligence that a legal advocate should project through his or her writing is that he or she is *innovative*. For this last trait, you will provide the analysis.

---

**Exercise 8.6    Analyzing the Intelligence Trait of Being Innovative**

At the beginning of this chapter, we listed eleven traits that indicate intelligence in a legal writer. The preceding discussions analyze ten of these traits. The last trait is "innovativeness." For this exercise, you are to write an essay analyzing this final trait. More specifically, you are to write an essay (1) analyzing what you think it means for a legal writer to be "innovative," (2) analyzing how you think legal writers establish that they are innovative through the *substance* of their documents, and (3) exploring how a legal writer may emphasize his or her innovative skills through *highlighting strategies*. Use the discussions of the previous ten traits as guidelines for your essay.

---

# IV.    SUMMARY AND CONCLUSION

## A.    *A Summary of the Traits Indicating Intelligence*

As we discussed at the beginning of the chapter, intelligence is an important component of an advocate's credibility. In this chapter, we have specifically identified eleven traits of an intelligent legal writer and the means by which a legal writer evinces these traits to readers. This information appears in the table below, which summarizes for each of the eleven traits (1) what the trait means, (2) how a writer establishes that trait through the substance of a persuasive document, and (3) examples of language used to highlight that trait.

| Intelligence Trait | What It Means | How Established Through Substance | Typical Highlighting Language |
|---|---|---|---|
| Informed | Having a full understanding of the *facts*, *law*, and *non-legal sources* relevant to the matter | - By demonstrating mastery of the facts<br>- By demonstrating mastery of the law and non-legal sources | "Based on a thorough review of the record"<br>"Exhaustive research reveals" |

| | | | |
|---|---|---|---|
| **Adept at Legal Research** | Having strong skills in legal research | - By including mandatory legal authority<br>- By including persuasive legal authority<br>- By including persuasive secondary sources<br>- By including non-legal sources | [language indicating *how* the cited authority was found] |
| **Organized** | Having strong organizational skills | - By organizing complicated law and/or facts<br>- By presenting an organized Statement of Facts<br>- By effectively organizing the Argument<br>- By using effective presentational techniques | [language indicating that the writer's document reflects an effort to organize complicated information] |
| **Analytical** | Having strong skills in legal analysis | - By demonstrating strong skills in reading, synthesizing, interpreting and applying legal authority | [language emphasizing the issue under discussion is complex]<br>"a close reading reveals"<br>"a subtle point" |
| **Deliberate** | Carefully considering competing arguments | - By addressing adverse authority<br>- By addressing opposing arguments | "after careful deliberation"<br>"reasonable arguments exist on both sides"<br>"this is a close question" |
| **Empathetic to the Reader** | Having the ability to put oneself in the position of the reader | - By "signposting"<br>- By omitting vague references<br>- By setting out foundational information<br>- By explaining the application fully | "in order to appreciate" |
| **Practical** | Considering the practical and policy implications of position advocated | - By incorporating the practical and policy implications of the relief sought | "from a practical / public policy standpoint" |
| **Articulate** | Writing in a clear and grammatically correct style | - By using proper grammar and punctuation<br>- By using "plain English" writing style | [language acknowledging the intentional use of awkward wording] |
| **Eloquent** | Adding rhetorical flair | - By effectively using rhetorical stylistic devices | [language acknowledging the use of rhetorical style] |
| **Detail-Oriented** | Editing with precision | - By eliminating typos<br>- By following format and citation rules<br>- By presenting a neat final product | None |
| **Innovative** | | | |

**Exercise 8.7     Analyzing How a Legal Writer Evinces Intelligence
in a Legal Document**

Find and read the case *Cheney v. Village 2 at New Hope, Inc.*, 241 A.2d 81 (Pa.
1968). The opinion in this case was written by Pennsylvania Supreme Court
Justice (later Chief Justice) Samuel J. Roberts. Write an essay analyzing how
Justice Roberts establishes credibility as an intelligent writer through his writing.
In particular, analyze how he establishes any or all of the traits of intelligence
discussed in this chapter through either the opinion's substance or through
highlighting strategies. To the extent that the writer evinces a lack of a trait of
intelligence, analyze this aspect of the opinion as well.

**Exercise 8.8     Analyzing How a Legal Writer Evinces Intelligence
in a Legal Document**

Choose a judicial opinion (a majority, concurring, or dissenting opinion in any
case), and write an essay analyzing how the writer establishes credibility with the
reader as an intelligent source of information. In particular, analyze how the writer
establishes any or all of the traits of intelligence discussed in this chapter through
either the opinion's substance or through highlighting strategies. To the extent that
the writer evinces a lack of a trait of intelligence, analyze this aspect of the
opinion as well.

### B.     Putting It All Together: An Outline of the Components of Logos, Pathos, and Ethos

Over the last three chapters we have analyzed the three primary processes of
persuasion recognized by classical rhetoricians—logos, pathos, and
ethos—discussing the last in considerable detail. The following outline extends the
outline presented in Chapter 6, by incorporating the information on ethos covered in
Chapters 7 and 8.

**An Outline of the Three Fundamental Processes of Persuasion Recognized by Classical Rhetoricians**

- **Logos:** Persuading through logic and rational argument.

- **Pathos:** Persuading through emotion. The two aspects of pathos are:

  - *Emotional Substance:* refers to persuading by arousing an emotional reaction in the audience as to the substance of the matter under consideration.

  - *Medium Mood Control:* refers to generating a positive emotional reaction in the audience through the medium of the message.

- **Ethos:** Persuading by establishing credibility in the eyes of the audience. The three components of ethos are:

  - *Character:* refers to the general moral character of an advocate. The five traits that an advocate should evince to establish good moral character are:

    1. Truthfulness
    2. Candor
    3. Zeal
    4. Respect
    5. Professionalism

  - *Good Will:* refers to how an advocate is disposed toward the audience, an adversary, or someone who will be affected by the position advocated.

  - *Intelligence:* refers to the intelligence and ability of an advocate. The eleven traits that an advocate should evince to establish himself or herself as an intelligent source of information are:

    1. Informed
    2. Adept at legal research
    3. Organized
    4. Analytical
    5. Deliberate
    6. Empathetic to the reader
    7. Practical
    8. Articulate
    9. Eloquent
    10. Detail-oriented
    11. Innovative

# PART III

## PERSUASIVE WRITING STRATEGIES BASED ON CLASSICAL RHETORIC THEORY: RHETORICAL STYLE

In Part II we analyzed the three fundamental *processes* of persuasion recognized by classical rhetoricians: logos, pathos, and ethos. That discussion involved an analysis of the *substantive means* by which advocates persuade audiences. We saw that, according to classical rhetoric theory, the substance of a document can persuade through logic and emotion and by establishing credibility. The substance of a document, however, must be communicated through words; that is, advocates must use words to convey their logical and emotional arguments and to establish credibility. Thus, classical rhetoricians have also recognized that writing *style*—the way in which substance is communicated through words—is also important in persuasive discourse. As Aristotle said so eloquently more than twenty-three hundred years ago, "[I]t is not enough to know what to say—one must also know how to say it."[1]

In keeping with their recognition of the importance of effective writing style, classical rhetoricians have produced countless books, treatises, and articles on the subject. These materials provide comprehensive guidance on how advocates can most effectively communicate their substantive arguments through writing. Among the topics covered are large-scale organization, paragraph structure, sentence structure, grammar and syntax, word choice, punctuation, and presentational strategies.

Many of these lessons have found their way into modern texts on effective legal writing style. The following list includes a few of the modern texts that provide comprehensive instruction on effective legal writing style:

> Anne Enquist and Laurel Currie Oates, *Just Writing: Grammar, Punctuation, and Style for the Legal Writer* (2001)
> Bryan A. Garner, *Legal Writing in Plain English* (2001)
> Bryan A. Garner, *The Elements of Legal Style* (1991)
> Terri LeClercq, *Guide to Legal Writing Style* (2d ed. 2000)
> Richard C. Wydick, *Plain English for Lawyers* (4th ed. 1998)
> William Strunk, Jr., and E. B. White, *The Elements of Style* (3d ed. 1979)*
> Joseph M. Williams, *Style: Ten Lessons in Clarity and Grace* (6th ed. 2000)*

> \* Although these last two books were not specifically written as "legal style" books, legal writers frequently refer to them for guidance.

Texts such as these focus exclusively on writing *style*. They borrow from and build on the lessons provided by classical rhetoricians to provide legal writers with essential information on how to convey thoughts clearly and accurately in writing.

In addition to these texts that focus exclusively on legal writing style, most of the more general introductory legal writing texts provide condensed instruction on effective writing style. This book, therefore, designed to build on introductory legal writing instruction, will not cover the general principles of legal style, already so thoroughly covered elsewhere. Instead, we will focus our discussion on a single aspect of advanced legal writing style: rhetorical figures of speech.

Rhetorical figures of speech are stylistic devices that help give writing eloquence

---

[1] Aristotle, *The Rhetoric of Aristotle* 182 (Lane Cooper trans. 1932) (emphasis in original).

and dramatic flair. As we will see, eloquence in writing, no matter how impressive, is neither inexplicable nor mysterious. On the contrary, classical rhetoricians have analyzed and dissected eloquence with scientific precision and have identified, labeled, and categorized the many stylistic devices used by eloquent writers to give their writing a near-poetic quality. Part III explores these figures of speech in significant detail. First, in Chapter 9, we will explore one of the most common—and one of the most powerful—rhetorical figures: the metaphor. Following our discussion of metaphors, we will cover in Chapter 10 many of the other figures of speech that legal advocates can use to add force to their writing.

# Chapter 9

# *The Power of Metaphor and Simile in Persuasive Writing*

> Let us begin [our analysis of figures of speech] . . . with the commonest and by far most beautiful of [figures], namely, metaphor.
>
> — Quintilian

As the ancient Roman rhetorician Quintilian did in his famous treatise on rhetoric, *Institutio Oratoria*, we will begin our discussion of rhetorical figures of speech with an analysis of metaphor. Metaphor is regarded by many classical rhetoricians as the "most beautiful" rhetorical figure, the "supreme ornament" of prose.[1] In this chapter we will examine what metaphor is and why it is held in such high regard by rhetoricians. In this discussion, we will see that metaphor is more than mere stylistic adornment. In fact, we will find that there are many forms of metaphor useful in persuasive writing and that they serve a number of very important rhetorical functions. We will also examine guidelines and suggestions regarding the use of metaphors so that you will be able to use them to empower and enrich your own writing.

## I.     DEFINING METAPHOR

### A.     *The Basic Definition of Metaphor*

Because of its versatile nature, metaphor is difficult to define with much specificity. In our discussion of metaphoric literary references in Chapter 2, we briefly defined a metaphor as "an implied comparison between two things of unlike nature that yet have something in common."[2] Most other books on writing and rhetoric define metaphor with a similar amount of generality. Aristotle, for example, defines metaphors as devices "by which we give names to nameless things."[3] Writing expert Theodore M. Bernstein defines metaphor as "a figure of speech in which a word or

---

[1] 3 Marius Fabius Quintilianus, *Institutio Oratoria* 199 (H. E. Butler trans. 1954).

[2] *See* Chapter 2, Section I.A. (quoting Edward P. J. Corbett and Robert J. Conners, *Classical Rhetoric for the Modern Student* 396 (4th ed. 1999)).

[3] Aristotle, *The Rhetoric of Aristotle* 188 (Lane Cooper trans. 1932).

phrase implies a comparison or identity."[4] Poet Robert Frost defines it as "saying one thing and meaning another."[5]

Despite the generality of these definitions, metaphors are commonly regarded as having three characteristics. First, they involve language that makes a *comparison* between two things. Second, while the language involves a comparison, it *does not include explicit words of comparison*. That is, the comparison does not involve words such as "like" or "as" that would make the comparison explicit. Instead, one thing is simply equated to another thing or discussed in close proximity to another thing in a context that suggests that the two things are being compared. (This aspect of metaphor is what distinguishes it from *simile*, which involves explicit comparison. We will discuss simile in more detail below.) The third characteristic of metaphor is that the comparison is *figurative* or *symbolic*, not literal. That is, the two things being compared are not literally alike, but are alike in some symbolic or figurative way.

Consider the following example; the **bold** sentence contains the metaphor.

*Example 9.1*

Equitable estoppel is a doctrine that is simply stated, yet its principles apply across a wide variety of factual and legal situations. The sheer variety of circumstances argues strongly that we should not lightly substitute our judgment for that of the trial courts. That does not, however, mean that we will always defer. **There are times when we must expand or contract or more closely define the pasture within which the trial courts may roam in the exercise of that discretion: this is one such situation.**

Zimmerman, C. J., in *State Dep't of Human Servs. v. Irizarry*, 945 P.2d 676, 685 (Utah 1997) (Zimmerman, C. J. dissenting) (citation omitted).

In the above excerpt, the writer employs a metaphor, *comparing* the lower courts' discretion in the area of equitable estoppel to a "pasture." The passage, however, does not include explicit words of comparison. The writer does not explicitly state that discretion of the lower courts is "like" a pasture. The writer, in discussing judicial discretion, simply refers to a pasture and to trial courts "roaming" therein. We know by the context, however, that a comparison is being made between these concepts. Moreover, the comparison is *figurative*, not literal. The writer is not saying that judicial discretion is literally like a pasture. Rather, the writer is saying that judicial discretion, like a pasture, allows some freedom, but that, also like a pasture (which is enclosed by a perimeter fence), such freedom has limits. Restated in literal terms, the writer's meaning is that, while lower courts must have the authority to consider the facts of individual cases in deciding if equitable estoppel is applicable, the higher court must be able to establish and adjust the outer limits of that authority. By employing a metaphor, however, the writer expressed this idea more creatively, and,

---

[4] Theodore M. Bernstein, *The Careful Writer: A Modern Guide to English Usage* 275 (1982).

[5] James Boyd White, *The Legal Imagination: Studies in the Nature of Legal Thought and Expression* 57 (1973) (quoting Robert Frost).

interestingly enough, more simply, more succinctly, and more vividly.[6]

Below are several additional examples of metaphors. In those cases where the quoted language contains multiple sentences, the sentence or sentences containing metaphor have been set out in **bold**.

*Example 9.2*

**[A] civil RICO suit may be maintained, not only in mail fraud cases where the deceitful mailing is the blade rushing down toward the guillotine victim, but also in cases involving more grandiose schemes to cheat, where the mailing is but part of the frame that holds the blade.**

Hall, J., in Chisolm v. Transouth Fin. Corp., 95 F.3d 331, 337 (4th Cir. 1996).

*Example 9.3*

**[T]he work of the Alabama Legislature in the area of medical liability is a mule—the bastard offspring of intercourse among lawyers, legislators, and lobbyists, having no pride of ancestry and no hope of posterity.**

Smith, J., in Hayes v. Luckey, 33 F. Supp. 2d 987, 995 n.16 (N.D. Ala. 1997).

*Example 9.4*

If deference to a military judge is to mean anything at all, it should mean that we may disagree with a ruling without reversing it. . . . **[W]e should not stand behind the home plate umpire and decide that he missed a call because he called a strike when, to our eyes, it was low and away. If the pitch sails over the backstop, then we can say that a called strike is a "clear abuse of discretion." This one caught the corner of the plate.**

Morgan, J., in United States v. Wiley, No. ACM 31379, 1996 WL 399966, at *8 (A. F. Ct. Crim. App., July 8, 1996) (Morgan, J., concurring in part and dissenting in part).

*Example 9.5*

**[C]onspiracy . . . [is the] darling of the modern prosecutor's nursery.**

Hand, J., in Harrison v. United States, 7 F.2d 259, 263 (2d Cir. 1925).

*Example 9.6*

If the small claims court is to be the "People's Court," it must not be

---

[6] Some readers may also see this metaphor as humorously comparing trial court judges to cows. While Judge Zimmerman, the writer here, may be able to get away with this potentially insulting metaphor, practitioners should be more cautious. Later in this chapter we will discuss the dangers of humorous and potentially insulting metaphors.

encumbered with rules and restrictions which can only frustrate and hinder the litigant who resorts to that court in response to its promise of speedy and economical justice. **In the case of inexperienced pro se litigants, it is better to err on the side of admitting an ore-heap of evidence in the belief that nuggets of truth may be found amidst the dross, rather than to confine the parties to presenting assayed and refined matter which qualifies as pure gold under the rules of evidence.**

> Dabney, J., in *Houghtaling v. Superior Court*, 21 Cal. Rptr. 2d 855, 860 (Cal. Ct. App. 1993).

*Example 9.7*

[P]arties to a preliminary agreement may . . . provide that they do not intend to be bound until the transaction is buttoned up by a more detailed and formal agreement. **There is commercial utility to allowing persons to hug before they marry.**

> Kass, J., in *Goren v. Royal Invs. Inc.*, 516 N.E.2d 173, 176 (Mass. App. Ct. 1987).

*Example 9.8*

**[Evidence] should not be admitted . . . where the minute peg of relevancy will be entirely obscured by the dirty linen hung upon it.**

> Hill, J., in *State v. Goebel*, 218 P.2d 300, 306 (Wash. 1950).

*Example 9.9*

**[E]scape hatches let off steam that otherwise might rupture a rigid rule.**

> James G. Wilson, *Surveying the Forms of Doctrine on the Bright Line-Balancing Test Continuum*, 27 Ariz. St. L.J. 773, 788 (1995).

*Example 9.10*

**[I]nternational law is an edifice built on a volcano—state sovereignty**.

> Antonio Cassese, *On the Current Trends Towards Criminal Prosecution and Punishment of Breaches of International Humanitarian Law*, 9 Eur. J. Int'l L. 2, 4 (1998), *quoted in* Mary Margaret Penrose, *Lest We Fail: The Importance of Enforcement in International Criminal Law*, 15 Am. U. Int'l L. Rev. 321, 394 n.261 (2000).

*Example 9.11*

**[E]ach [oppressive] practice is one wire in a birdcage; while no one wire could prevent the bird's escape, the wires woven together make a thoroughly effective prison.**

> Louise M. Antony, *Back to Androgyny: What Bathrooms Can Teach Us About Equality*, 9 J. Contemp. Legal Issues 1, 4 (1998). The author attributes the origin of this metaphor to Marilyn Frye, *Oppression*, in *The Politics of Reality* 1 (1983).

*Example 9.12*

**Congress builds a ship and charts its initial course, but the ship's ports-of-call, safe harbors and ultimate destination may be a product of the ship's captain, the weather, and other factors not identified at the time the ship sets sail. . . . The dimensions and structure of the craft determine where it is capable of going, but the current course is set primarily by the crew on board.**

> T. Alexander Aleinikoff, *Updating Statutory Interpretation*, 87 Mich. L. Rev. 20, 21 (1988).

*Example 9.13*

**[T]he Wagner Act has been reduced to a shell that once protected but now threatens to strangle the living form of the labor movement within.**

> James Gray Pope, *Labor-Community Coalitions and Boycotts: The Old Labor Law, the New Unionism, and the Living Constitution*, 69 Tex. L. Rev. 889, 919 (1991). The author attributes the origin of this metaphor to Charles Heckscher, *The New Unionism* 80 (1988).

---

**Exercise 9.1     Analyzing a Metaphor**

For one of the metaphors in Examples 9.2 through 9.13 above, write a few paragraphs explaining why it is a metaphor and how the writer has used it. In particular, explain (1) how the excerpt involves a *comparison*; (2) why the comparison is implicit rather than explicit; and (3) why the comparison is *figurative* rather than literal. Also explain in literal terms what the writer has conveyed through metaphor. Use the discussion of Example 9.1 as a guide. If necessary or helpful to your understanding of the selected quote, look up the full document from which it was taken.

---

## B.     *Distinguishing Simile*

Similes, as briefly mentioned above, resemble metaphors in that they make *figurative comparisons* between two things. Similes differ from metaphor, however, in that they include explicit words of comparison, such as when one thing is said to be "like" another thing. Consider the following examples. In each example, the simile is in **bold**; the language that makes the comparison explicit is in ***bold italics***.

*Example 9.14*

**Being free to engage in unlimited political expression subject to a ceiling on expenditures is *like* being free to drive an automobile as far and as often as one desires on a single tank of gasoline.**

> *Buckley v. Valeo*, 424 U.S. 1, 19 n.18 (1976) (per curiam).

*Example 9.15*

**The reason for my concern is that the instant decision, overruling that announced about nine years ago, tends to *bring* adjudications of this tribunal *into the same class as* a restricted railroad ticket, good for this day and train only.** I have no assurance, in view of current decisions, that the opinion announced today may not shortly be repudiated and overruled by justices who deem they have new light on the subject.

Roberts, J. in Smith v. Allwright, 321 U.S. 649, 669 (1944) (Roberts, J., dissenting).

*Example 9.16*

[T]he defendants' efforts to obtain dismissal of this lawsuit in the superior court and the plaintiff's efforts here for reinstatement have been much ado about nothing. **The proceedings below were *the legal equivalent of* burning a dock after the ship has sailed. *Like* the dock, the complaint will be of significance only if the parties choose to return to a judicial port to litigate the dispute on the merits.**

Crosby, J., in Byerly v. Sale, 251 Cal. Rptr. 749, 751 (Cal. Ct. App. 1988).

*Example 9.17*

**[A] conspiracy is *like* a train. When a party knowingly steps aboard, he is part of the crew, and assumes conspirator's responsibility for the existing freight—or conduct—regardless of whether he is aware of just what it is composed.**

Aldrich, J., in United States v. Baines, 812 F.2d 41, 42 (1st Cir. 1987).

*Example 9.18*

**Unless this Court is willing to say that citizenship of the United States means at least this much to the citizen, then our heritage of constitutional privileges and immunities is only a promise to the ear to be broken to the hope, a teasing illusion *like* a munificent bequest in a pauper's will.**

Jackson, J., in Edwards v. California, 314 U.S. 160, 186 (1941) (Jackson, J., concurring).

*Example 9.19*

***As* nightfall does not come all at once, neither does oppression. *In both instances*, there is a twilight when everything remains seemingly unchanged. And it is in such twilight that we all must be most aware of change in the air—however slight—lest we become unwitting victims of the darkness.**

Justice William O. Douglas, The Douglas Letters: Selections from the Private Papers of Justice William O. Douglas 162 (Melvin I. Urofsky ed. 1987) quoted in State v. Valentine, 935 P.2d 1294, 1317 (Wash. 1997) (Sanders, J., dissenting).

These similes, like the metaphors in Examples 9.2 to 9.13, make figurative comparisons between two things that are literally different yet are similar in some symbolic way. The similes differ from metaphors only in that they contain explicit language of comparison. In Example 9.14, the comparison between political expression and driving an automobile is made explicit by the word "like." The other examples also contain explicit comparisons: Example 9.15 ("bring . . . into the same class as"); Example 9.16 ("the legal equivalent of" and "Like"); Example 9.17 ("like"); Example 9.18 ("like"); and Example 9.19 ("As" and "In both instances").

The words "like" and "as" are the most common words of comparison used in similes. However, as indicated by the above examples, similes are not limited to these words. Similes can involve any language that makes the comparison explicit. The following common words and phrases are used in connection with similes:

> like, as, similar to, akin to, the same as, analogous to, comparable to, equivalent to, identical to, tantamount to, in the manner of, a la, reminiscent of, remindful of, suggestive of, conjures up, resembles, evokes

While this is not a complete list of the possibilities, it gives you an idea of the types of language writers use in similes.

### Exercise 9.2    Analyzing a Simile

For one of the similes in Examples 9.14 through 9.19, write a few paragraphs explaining why it is a simile and how the writer uses it. In particular, explain (1) how the excerpt involves a *comparison*; (2) what makes the comparison *explicit*; and (3) why the comparison is *figurative* rather than literal. Also explain in literal terms what the writer has conveyed through simile. If necessary or helpful to your understanding of the selected quote, look up the full document from which it was taken.

As we have seen, similes are similar to metaphors. They are so similar, in fact, that figurative comparisons often contain aspects of both simile and metaphor. Consider the following examples:

*Example 9.20*

> **Like the mythical Hydra, [Defendant] seeks to grow two figurative heads in place of each one of its heads of legal argument that gets lopped off from time to time in the course of this lawsuit. It is time to cauterize, and thus to kill permanently, [Defendant]'s most recent attempted renewal—its currently tendered "Renewed Motion to Narrow the Issues."**
>
> Shadur, J., in *Zip Dee, Inc. v. Dometic Corp.*, 905 F. Supp. 535, 536 (N.D. Ill. 1995).

*Example 9.21*

**[T]he use of legislative history [to interpret a statute is]** *the equivalent of* **entering a crowded cocktail party and looking over the heads of the guests for one's friends. . . . The legislative history of Section 205 of the Soldiers' and Sailors' Civil Relief Act contains a variety of diverse personages, a selected few of whom—its "friends"—the Court has introduced to us in support of its result. But there are many other faces in the crowd, most of which, I think, are set against today's result.**

Scalia, J., in Conroy v. Aniskoff, 507 U.S. 511, 519 (1993) (Scalia, J., concurring).<br>Justice Scalia attributes the origin of this metaphor to Judge Harold Leventhal.

These two examples use both simile and metaphor. The first sentence of Example 9.20 uses "like" to form a simile explicitly comparing the Defendant's new arguments to the Hydra of Greek mythology. The second sentence, which builds on the first, uses the metaphoric words "cauterize" and "kill." Similarly, the phrase "the legal equivalent of" in Example 9.21 creates a simile that explicitly compares the use of legislative history to a search for one's friends in a crowd. The subsequent sentences contain various metaphoric references such as "diverse personages," "introduced to us," "other faces in the crowd," and "set against." Thus, as these examples demonstrate, metaphor and simile can be, and often are, used in connection with one another.

Because of their closeness in form and use, we will not further distinguish simile and metaphor in this chapter. In the remaining sections of this chapter, we will focus our discussion on metaphors. Most of the concepts that we will discuss apply with equal force to similes.

## II.   FOCUSING ON ORIGINAL CREATIVE METAPHORS

Metaphor abounds in legal writing. In fact, metaphor abounds in language in general. Metaphor is indispensable to the way humans make sense of and describe the world around them. Much of our general, everyday language is actually metaphoric in nature, even though we do not think of it as such. Moreover, new metaphors are continually being created and incorporated into our language as idioms, becoming forever part of our lexicon.

In view of the prevalence of metaphor in language generally, we must narrow the focus of our discussion of metaphor in this chapter. Here, we will focus primarily on one specific type of metaphor: *original creative metaphor*. That is, we will focus on those metaphors—like the ones illustrated in Examples 9.1 through 9.13—that are artistic and imaginative and that are created originally by a writer to add power and grace to a persuasive argument.

By narrowing our focus in this way, we are eliminating two rather large categories of metaphor: "inherent metaphors" and "pre-existing creative metaphors." To understand the category of metaphor with which we are most concerned—that is, to understand what is meant by "original creative metaphors"—we must describe and distinguish these two other categories of metaphors.

## A.   *Distinguishing Original Creative Metaphors from Inherent Metaphors*

Much has been written in recent years about the "inherent" nature of metaphor. Linguists, philosophers, and cognitive psychologists have established that metaphors are not merely stylistic writing devices; rather, metaphors permeate our everyday language and are inherent to the way we view, experience and describe our world.

One does not have to look far to find words that, although used regularly and unthinkingly, are actually metaphoric in nature. Consider for example the words "up" and "down," which in literal terms describe the spatial orientation of a thing as being away from or close to the center of the earth. As Professor George Lakoff (linguistics) and Professor Mark Johnson (philosophy) demonstrate in their well-regarded book, *Metaphors We Live By*,[7] the concepts of "up" and "down" have many metaphoric uses in our everyday language:

> HAPPY IS UP; SAD IS DOWN
>> I'm feeling *up*. That *boosted* my spirits. My spirits *rose*. You're in *high* spirits. Thinking about her always gives me a *lift*. I'm *depressed*. He's really *low* these days. I *fell* into a depression. My spirits *sank*. . . .
>
> CONSCIOUS IS UP; UNCONSCIOUS IS DOWN
>> Get *up*. Wake *up*. I'm *up* already. He *rises* early in the morning. He *fell* asleep. He *dropped* off to sleep. He's *under* hypnosis. He *sank* into a coma. . . .
>
> HEALTH AND LIFE ARE UP; SICKNESS AND DEATH ARE DOWN
>> He's at the *peak* of health. Lazarus *rose* from the dead. He's in *top* shape. As to his health, he's way *up* there. He *fell* ill. He's *sinking* fast. He came *down* with the flu. His health is *declining*. He *dropped* dead. . . .
>
> HAVING CONTROL OR FORCE IS UP; BEING SUBJECT TO CONTROL OR FORCE IS DOWN
>> I have control *over* her. I am *on top of* the situation. He's in a *superior* position. He's at the *height* of his power. He's in the *high* command. He's in the *upper* echelon. His power *rose*. He ranks *above* me in strength. He is *under* my control. He *fell* from power. His power is on the *decline*. He is my social *inferior*. He is *low man* on the totem pole.[8]

As these examples illustrate, our language contains many words and concepts that are fundamental to our way of communicating, yet when examined closely, are actually metaphoric in nature. We will refer to these types of metaphors as "inherent" metaphors because they are natural to our language and are intrinsic to the way we

----

[7] George Lakoff and Mark Johnson, *Metaphors We Live By* (1980).

[8] *Id.* at 15. These are just samples of the metaphoric uses of the concepts of "up" and "down." Professors Lakoff and Johnson discuss a number of others. *Id.* at 15-17.

communicate about certain things. In some senses, the word "inherent" is used here to mean the opposite of "creative." Inherent metaphors are not intentionally crafted or used for artistic or stylistic purposes. Rather, they are intrinsic to the way we view and describe our world.

Professor Steven L. Winter explains the process by which humans inherently construct fundamental metaphors to make sense of and describe the world around us:

> [T]he human mind constructs meaning "from the ground up," bootstrapping from its own basic experience in the world and imaginatively elaborating those thought structures or *schemata* in its further interactions with its physical and social environment.
>
> The human mind employs basic, embodied experiences to construct more elaborate and abstract social meanings. As embodied organisms, we achieve upright posture and balance in the world. We experience our bodies as structured wholes with identifiable parts. We individuate objects outside ourselves. Our visual field appears to have a foreground or center in which objects are in sharpest focus and a periphery, both at the horizon and at the sides, in which things are relatively less clear. We propel ourselves through space to obtain desired objects. Sometimes, our way is blocked by an obstacle and we must exert additional force in order to overcome or avoid it. Some objects are so configured as to contain other objects. Some objects are connected to other objects, even as we link ourselves to others by handholding and other physical means.
>
> Each of these quite basic interactions with the world is generalizable, and each is in fact generalized across a series of other domains. Each of these generalizations is a mental construct by which the human mind creates meaning, a "recurring structure" or "repeatable pattern" that is "a chief means for achieving order in our experience so that we can comprehend and reason about it." These basic image-schemata—like *up-down*, *balance*, *part-whole*, *object*, *center-periphery*, *source-path-goal*, *force-barrier*, *container*, and *link* —are indispensable to human rationality. They provide structure to human thought, although they are neither objective nor determinate aspects of the world itself. These schemata are, nevertheless, powerful aspects of human rationality because their operation is automatic and unreflexive—that is, without conscious awareness, reflection, or control.
>
> The unreflexive use of these schemata to structure our understandings of more complex, abstract domains is everywhere apparent. For example, the use of the *balance* schema to structure legal reasoning as a process of "weighing" the evidence, "weighing" competing interests, applying multi-part "balancing" tests, and the like all attest to the centrality of our direct embodied experiences to the elaboration and understanding of our abstract intellectual endeavors. Similarly, the *source-path-goal* schema is the basic structure by means of which we elaborate many diverse concepts metaphorically, as in:
>
> > LIFE IS A JOURNEY—One "makes one's way" in life; a successful person is one who "goes far in life"; a person may be unsuccessful because he or she has no "direction."

PURPOSES ARE DESTINATIONS, IMPEDIMENTS TO PURPOSES ARE OBSTACLES TO MOTION—What's the "point" of your project? How "far along" is it? The project is growing by "leaps and bounds"; the project has hit a "snag"; it is at an "impasse."

ADJUDICATION IS MOVEMENT ALONG A PATH—Litigation is a judicial "proceeding"; the plaintiff must "carry the burden" of proof; a presumption may "shift" the burden of "going forward"; the parties cite supporting "grounds" for their "motions"; alternatively, parties may decide to "forego" their procedural rights.[9]

Professor James Boyd White examines the prevalence of inherent metaphors in legal writing specifically:

Here are some phrases for your consideration: the good judicial opinion "considers all relevant factors"; "takes everything into account"; "balances (or weighs) the real interests"; "reconciles apparent inconsistencies"; and so on. Are those metaphorical or direct statements? . . .

Implicit in some of the foregoing and other such phrases are a series of metaphors such as these: a problem has *parts* which *fit together* to make a *whole*; arguments have *strengths* and *weaknesses*; interests have *bulk* or *weight*, which permit them to be *measured*, *weighed*, and *balanced*; general rules, like boxes, have lots of specific rules *inside* them; every rule has a reason (or a policy) which determines its *proper course*, like a tractor driver; conflicts between rules can be *harmonized* (is that music in the law?); every case presents a *problem* with a *solution*; and so on.[10]

As these excerpts illustrate, many words and phrases commonly used in legal discourse are actually metaphoric in nature. The following list offers a small, randomly compiled sample of other inherent metaphors common in legal writing. Many of these words and phrases are generally thought of as literal terms. However, when they are examined more closely, one realizes that they are actually metaphoric.

| | |
|---|---|
| *advance* an argument | going *forward* with an action or |
| *attack* a *position* | claim |
| *bind* by a contract | *grounds* for an argument |
| *broad* rule | *higher* court |
| *carry* the *burden* of proof | looking *deeper* into an argument |
| *cast light* on a subject | *lower* court |
| *chain* of title | *merging* of claims |
| *depart* from precedent | *narrow* exception to a rule |
| *gain ground* in an argument | on its *face* |

---

[9] Steven L. Winter, *The Cognitive Dimension of the Agon Between Legal Power and Narrative Meaning*, 87 Mich. L. Rev. 2225, 2231-32 (1989) (quoting M. Johnson, *The Bodily Basics of Meaning, Imagination, and Reason* 28 (1987)).

[10] White, *supra* note 5, at 695 (emphasis added).

| | |
|---|---|
| on the *surface* of an argument | *set up* a *defense* to an argument |
| party's *new line of attack* | *sliding scale* test or formula |
| *running* of a statute of | *spectrum* of considerations |
| limitations | *sphere* of influence |
| send a case *back down* | *standing* to sue |

Such inherent metaphors do not do much to advance persuasive writing, and for this reason we will discuss them no farther here. Our focus will be on imaginative metaphors intentionally created by a writer to communicate as forcefully as possible a specific point in a legal argument. That is, we will focus on the types of metaphors reflected in Examples 9.1 through 9.13—metaphors that are not inherent, but are intentionally and imaginatively crafted to empower and enrich a persuasive argument.

## B.    *Distinguishing Original Creative Metaphors from Pre-existing Creative Metaphors*

As discussed above, we will not be focusing on "inherent" metaphors in this chapter; we will be focusing on "creative" metaphors. However, our focus is actually even narrower than that. We will not be focusing on *all* metaphors that can be characterized as creative and imaginative. We will be focusing only on "original" creative metaphors. That is, we will focus only on creative metaphors that are originally crafted by a writer. We will not focus on "pre-existing" creative metaphors—that is, creative metaphors that are already established (such as cliche metaphors) or that are borrowed from another writer.

The English language in general is laden with cliche creative metaphors. Consider the following examples:

| | |
|---|---|
| bend over backwards | pull strings |
| bite the dust | put one's ear to the ground |
| bury the hatchet | shoot the breeze |
| cat is out of the bag | slap on the wrist |
| face the music | smell a rat |
| foot in the door | spill the beans |
| get the ball rolling | spread oneself too thin |
| go to bat for someone | stick out one's neck |
| keep under one's hat | stick to one's guns |
| kick the bucket | straddle the fence |
| lose one's shirt | straight from the horse's mouth |
| make ends meet | throw in the towel |
| one's hands are tied | throw one's hat into the ring |
| out of the woods | turn the other cheek |
| out on a limb | up one's sleeve |
| pull one's leg | |

In addition to cliche metaphors such as these that exist in language in general, there are many cliche metaphors that are unique to (or at least particularly prevalent in) legal discourse. Consider these examples:

| | |
|---|---|
| ambulance chaser | marketplace of ideas |
| arm's length transaction | meeting of the minds |
| bright-line rule | open the floodgates |
| bundle of property rights | parade of horribles |
| chilling effect | parent corporation |
| clean hands | penumbra of rights |
| [a] cloud on one's title | piercing the corporate veil |
| deep pocket | slippery slope |
| fishing expedition | smoking gun |
| forum-shopping | stand in the shoes of |
| fruit of the poisonous tree | straw man |
| hired gun | wall of separation between |
| long-arm statute | church and state |

All of the above are "creative" metaphors in the sense that they were, at the time of their original creation, imaginative and artistic. These metaphors do not qualify as "inherent" metaphors because they are not intrinsic to the language; rather they were imaginatively created by some writer or speaker. Nevertheless, these types of metaphors are beyond our focus because they are not *original*. As stated earlier, we are concerned only with metaphors originally crafted by a writer in a specific instance or situation. We are not focusing on situations in which a writer employs a "pre-existing" metaphor such as those listed above. Nor are we focusing on situations in which a writer quotes or otherwise borrows a creative metaphor from another writer. Our focus is on how writers can craft their own imaginative metaphors and the rhetorical benefits that such metaphors provide in persuasive writing.

## III.   THE BASIC FORMS OF CREATIVE METAPHORS

Creative metaphors can come in many different grammatical forms. They can be complete sentences or even complete paragraphs. They can also be smaller parts within sentences, such as phrases, clauses, or individual words such as nouns, verbs, adjectives, and adverbs. Because of the versatile nature of metaphors, it is helpful to categorize them into the general grammatical structures in which they can appear. While these categories are somewhat artificial, and while the dividing line between some of these categories can be blurry, a discussion of these categories will nevertheless help you in analyzing metaphors in the writing of others and in creating your own. In this section we will explore the following basic forms of metaphor:

- Metaphoric Sentences (which comprise two types):
  - "Pure" Metaphoric Sentences
  - "Interwoven" Metaphoric Sentences
- Metaphoric Clauses
- Single-Word Metaphors
- Extended Metaphors (which comprise two types):
  - "Single-Comparison" Extended Metaphors
  - "Single-Theme/Multiple-Comparison" Extended Metaphors

## A.    *Metaphoric Sentences*

One of the most common grammatical structures of metaphors is the "metaphoric sentence." A metaphoric sentence is a sentence that communicates its main point through the use of a metaphor. Stated another way, a metaphoric sentence is a sentence that (1) contains metaphoric language, and (2) uses the metaphoric language to communicate the primary concept for which the sentence stands.

To understand more clearly what qualifies as a metaphoric sentence we must first review the definition of a "sentence" in grammatical terms. A "sentence" is a group of words, punctuated as an independent unit, that "expresses an assertion, a question, a command, a wish or an exclamation."[11] That is, a sentence is an independent grammatical unit that expresses or stands for an identifiable concept. Every sentence has a primary substantive concept that it expresses. Consequently, a "metaphoric sentence" is a sentence that communicates its main point through the use of metaphoric language. For an illustration, let's look again at Example 9.1:

> There are times when we must expand or contract or more closely define the pasture within which the trial courts may roam in the exercise of that discretion: this is one such situation.

The main point of this sentence—that is, the substantive concept it expresses— is that the higher court must from time to time adjust the limits the trial courts' discretion (in the area of equitable estoppel, referred to in preceding sentences). Because this sentence communicates its main point through metaphoric language ("pasture," "roam"), it is a metaphoric sentence.

The metaphoric sentence is a very common form of metaphor. In fact, metaphoric sentences are what most people think of when they hear the word metaphor. They also are the most powerful type of metaphor. All of the examples of metaphor set out in Examples 9.1 through 9.13 are metaphoric sentences.

We will explore two different types of metaphoric sentences: "pure" metaphoric sentences and "interwoven" metaphoric sentences.

### 1.   "Pure" Metaphoric Sentences

Pure metaphoric sentences are sentences that are entirely metaphoric; they contain no literal language. That is, they contain no references to the literal point that is being addressed in the discussion surrounding the metaphoric sentence. The substantive point of a pure metaphoric sentence can be understood only by considering the context that surrounds it. Consider the following example. The pure metaphoric sentence is set out in **bold**.

---

[11] *Webster's New Collegiate Dictionary* 1048 (1981).

*Example 9.22*

This is a petition by Polaroid Corporation, hereinafter called taxpayer, to review a decision of the Tax Court holding that certain income received during the years 1951, 1952 and 1953 did not constitute "abnormal income" within the meaning of Sec. 456(a)(2), Internal Revenue Code of 1939. . . .

. . . In argument before this court [taxpayer] described itself as "a discovery company," exclusively engaged in exploiting its own discoveries. [Taxpayer] . . . is internationally known for inventions in the optical and photographic fields, perhaps the most notable of which is the Polaroid Land Camera and film, income from the manufacture and sale of which constitutes the principal matter herein involved. The camera and film together (they cannot be used separately) are termed by taxpayer the Polaroid Land process. This process is unique in that it enables any user to develop his own pictures and obtain positive prints anywhere, sixty seconds after exposure. . . .

Under the provisions of Sec. 456 . . . , income is regarded as "abnormal income" . . . if it falls into certain specified "classes." . . . The principal issue here is whether the income falls within that class described in Sec. 456(a)(2)(B): "Income resulting from exploration, discovery or prospecting, or any combination of the foregoing, extending over a period of more than 12 months." Taxpayer asserts that the word "discovery" is broad enough to encompass its process. The government contends that in the context of the Act it relates only to discovery of coal, oil, gas and other natural resources. . . .

[T]here is [a] . . . serious difficulty if "discovery" is to include all processes and patented inventions. What, then, is the purpose of subparagraph (C), "Income from the sale of patents, formulae, or processes," of Sec. 456(a)(2)? True, that subparagraph relates only to income from the *sale* of the patent or process. But subparagraph (B) relates to *all* income. If "discovery" in subparagraph (B) includes inventions, what is the role of subparagraph (C)? **If there is a big hole in the fence for the big cat, need there be a small hole for the small one?**

> Aldrich, J., in *Polaroid Corp. v. Commissioner of Internal Revenue*, 278 F.2d 148, 150-53 (1st Cir. 1960).

In the above excerpt, the court addresses the issue of whether the wording "income resulting from . . . discovery" in Section (B) of the applicable tax statute includes income from inventions. The court points out that a different section—Section (C)—specifically addresses income from the "sale" of inventions. The court also points out that if the broader section, Section (B), includes *all income* from inventions then there would be no need for the narrow provisions of Section (C) regarding income from the *sale* of inventions. To make this point, the opinion writer sets out a metaphoric rhetorical question: "If there is a big hole in the fence for the big cat, need there be a small hole for the small one?" With this, the court concludes that the word "discovery" in Section (B) should not be interpreted to include inventions, for such an interpretation would render Section (C) superfluous.

The opinion writer's metaphor in this excerpt is an example of a "pure" metaphoric sentence. The sentence contains no literal language; the wording of the sentence is entirely metaphoric. The sentence refers to "fences," "holes," and "cats," but makes no reference to the statute or any other literal concept. It is only by the placement of this sentence within the paragraph analyzing Sections (B) and (C) of the tax statute that we know and understand the metaphoric comparison being made.

Pure metaphoric sentences often sound like proverbs. In fact, many well-known proverbs are pure metaphoric sentences. Consider these examples:

> The early bird catches the worm.
> People who live in glass houses shouldn't throw stones.
> Every cloud has a silver lining.
> Too many cooks spoil the broth.
> A bird in the hand is worth two in the bush.

Each of these proverbs is a sentence unto itself. Moreover, the entire sentence is metaphoric. Thus, these proverbs, and ones like them, can be classified as pure metaphoric sentences. However, as we discussed earlier, our focus is on the creation of "original" metaphors, not the use of established or cliche metaphors. Thus, while proverbs such as these are examples of pure metaphoric sentences, they are not the type with which we are concerned.

The following are additional examples of original pure metaphoric sentences:

*Example 9.23*

**A house divided against itself cannot stand.**

> Abraham Lincoln, Acceptance Speech for Republican Nomination for the U.S. Senate (June 1858), in *Created Equal? The Complete Lincoln-Douglas Debates of 1858* 2 (Paul M. Angle ed. 1958).

*Example 9.24*

**A rising tide lifts all boats.**

> President John F. Kennedy (advocating his free market trade proposals).

Pure metaphoric sentences are not used as frequently as the second category of metaphoric sentences we will address, interwoven metaphoric sentences. In fact, none of the metaphors set out in Examples 9.1 through 9.13 involve pure metaphoric sentences. A couple of them come close, however. Consider Example 9.4 again:

> [W]e should not stand behind the home plate umpire and decide that he missed a call because he called a strike when, to our eyes, it was low and away. If the pitch sails over the backstop, then we can say that a called strike is a "clear abuse of discretion." This one caught the corner of the plate.

This quote comes very close to being a series of pure metaphoric sentences. The sentences are worded primarily in terms of baseball jargon. However, this quoted language is not purely metaphoric because several references to literal concepts are included. First, the words "we" and "our" are included in the first sentence, which are literal references to the court deciding the case. Second, the phrase "clear abuse of discretion" is included in the second sentence, which is a literal reference to the court's standard of review in the case. Finally, the third sentence contains the words "this one," which is a literal reference to the lower court judge's decision in this matter.

## Exercise 9.3    Understanding Pure Metaphoric Sentences

Reread Examples 9.7 and 9.9:

> There is commercial utility to allowing persons to hug before they marry.

> [E]scape hatches let off steam that otherwise might rupture a rigid rule.

Like Example 9.4 discussed above, these two examples come close to being pure metaphoric sentences, but are not. Write a few paragraphs explaining why these two quotes are **not** pure metaphoric sentences. Use the above discussion of Example 9.4 as a guide for your essay.

### 2.   "Interwoven" Metaphoric Sentences

The second category of metaphoric sentences is the interwoven metaphoric sentence. In an interwoven metaphoric sentence, metaphoric language is interwoven with literal language to help communicate the main point of the sentence. Interwoven metaphoric sentences are, by far, the most common type of metaphoric sentences.

While interwoven metaphoric sentences can be structured in many ways, the most basic and common structure is illustrated in Examples 9.3, 9.5, 9.10, 9.11, and 9.13: The writers simply state in single sentences that a literal concept "is" a figurative concept.

> [T]he work of the Alabama Legislature in the area of medical liability *is* a mule—the bastard offspring of intercourse among lawyers, legislators, and lobbyists, having no pride of ancestry and no hope of posterity.

> [C]onspiracy [*is* the] darling of the modern prosecutor's nursery.

> [I]nternational law *is* an edifice built on a volcano—state sovereignty.

> [E]ach [oppressive] practice *is* one wire in a birdcage; while no one wire could prevent the bird's escape, the wires woven together make a thoroughly effective prison.
> [T]he Wagner Act *has been reduced to* a shell that once protected but now threatens to strangle the living form of the labor movement within.

In each of these examples, the sentence contains both literal language and figurative language. Moreover, the sentence structures are all the same in that they each contain three standard components: (1) a literal concept; (2) a figurative concept; and (3) a form of the verb "to be" or its equivalent connecting these two concepts. In the first quote, for example, the writer states that "The work of the Alabama Legislature" (literal concept) "is" "a mule" (figurative concept). The others follow the same pattern, with the writer of the final quote using as a variant of "to be," the phrase "has been reduced to."

Although this structure of interwoven metaphoric sentences is very common, it is not the only structure. In fact, as the remaining excerpts from Examples 9.1 through 9.13 reflect, interwoven metaphoric sentences can come in a wide variety of structures. Examples 9.1 and 9.6 are good illustrations:

> There are times when we must expand or contract or more closely define the **pasture** within which the trial courts may **roam** in the exercise of that discretion: this is one such situation.

> In the case of inexperienced pro se litigants, it is better to err on the side of admitting an **ore-heap** of evidence in the belief that **nuggets** of truth may be found amidst the **dross**, rather than to confine the parties to presenting **assayed and refined matter** which qualifies as **pure gold** under the rules of evidence.

In these examples, the metaphoric concepts are set out in bold and are thoroughly interwoven with the literal aspects of the sentences. As these examples illustrate, there is no limit on the number of ways in which a metaphor can be woven into a sentence. Metaphoric words can operate as nouns, verbs, adjectives, adverbs, and prepositional phrases and can be arranged in innumerable ways. The only limitation on the construction of interwoven metaphoric sentences is the imagination of the writer.

When choosing between "pure" metaphoric sentences and "interwoven" metaphoric sentences, writers often find that one form works better than the other for specific points. For some points, however, either form will work just as well and the choice between the two is merely a matter of the writer's preference. Consider the following example:

*Example 9.25*

**A minor participant in the orchestra of a conspiracy is as much a part of it as is the concert master.**

Van Graafeiland, J., in *United States v. Armedo-Sarmiento*, 545 F.2d 785, 794 (2d Cir. 1976).

This statement was made by a court analyzing whether minor participants in a criminal conspiracy are as culpable as major conspirators; the court found that they were. In making this point, the opinion writer crafted an interwoven metaphoric sentence comparing conspirators to orchestra musicians. The writer stated this point in the form of an "interwoven" metaphoric sentence: the literal concept of "conspiracy" was woven into the primarily metaphoric sentence about orchestra members. The writer, however, might just as easily have expressed this idea in a "pure" metaphoric sentence by leaving out the "conspiracy" reference:

> A minor participant in an orchestra is as much a part of it as is the concert master.

Readers, using the context of the discussion, would interpret this pure metaphoric sentence in exactly the same way as the writer's interwoven metaphoric sentence.

## B.     *Metaphoric Clauses*

In the preceding section, we saw that metaphors can come in the form of complete sentences or series of sentences. In these types of metaphors, the metaphoric language helps to communicate the sentence's main substantive point. At times, however, sentences may contain metaphoric language and yet not be metaphoric sentences, because the metaphor relates only to part of the sentence, not to the sentence as a whole. That is, sometimes a metaphoric clause will be used in a sentence to help communicate a point incidental to the main point of the sentence. Such a use is termed a "metaphoric clause."

Consider the following example:

*Example 9.26*

> **After you have brushed the foam off the beer,** the plaintiffs' argument concerns only one item—money.

> Loiselle, J., in *Horton v. Meskill*, 376 A.2d 359, 378 (Conn. 1977) (Loiselle, J., dissenting).

This sentence communicates two separate ideas: first, that one must look beyond the surface of the plaintiff's argument to see the underlying concern, and second, that the plaintiff's true concern is "money." The latter point—the true concern of the plaintiff—is the main point communicated by the sentence. The first point is incidental to this primary point. The metaphor in the sentence, however, is used to communicate the sentence's incidental point, not its main point. Thus, this is not a metaphoric sentence; rather, it is a metaphoric clause.

Consider another example of a metaphoric clause:

*Example 9.27*

> [The] reasoning process [of the lower court] merely disguises, **we think with a rather thin veil**, the inconsistency of the court's results with our decisions in *Schlesinger* and *Richardson*.

> Rehnquist, J., in *Valley Forge Christian College v. Americans United for Separation of Church and State, Inc.*, 454 U.S. 464, 483 (1982).

In this sentence, Justice Rehnquist communicates two separate substantive concepts using two separate clauses. First, he states that the reasoning of the Court of Appeals is an attempt to conceal the inconsistency between that court's conclusion and the Supreme Court's prior cases of *Schlesinger* and *Richardson*. Second, in a separate clause, Justice Rehnquist states that this effort to conceal is not a very effective one. The first point is the main point of the sentence; the second point is incidental to the primary meaning of the sentence. However, the metaphoric language—the reference to a "veil"—is used with the incidental point, making this a metaphoric "clause" as opposed to a metaphoric "sentence." Had Justice Rehnquist structured the sentence as follows, it would have qualified as a metaphoric sentence:

> The reasoning process of the lower court **is but a thin veil** disguising the inconsistency of the court's results with our decisions in *Schlesinger* and *Richardson*.

In this structure, the two substantive concepts are combined into one, and the metaphoric language communicates the sentence's main point.

## C.    *Single-Word Metaphors*

The third basic type of metaphoric structure is the single-word metaphor. Writers use single-word metaphors when they use a metaphoric word in place of a noun or a verb or an adjective or an adverb in a sentence simply to enrich the sentence with powerful and vivid language. With a single-word metaphor, the writer uses a metaphoric word primarily for stylistic purposes rather than to make a substantive metaphoric comparison. Consider the following examples:

*Example 9.28*

> Crimes committed because of the perpetrator's hatred of the race, color, religion or national origin of the victim have the obvious tendency to **ignite** further violence by provoking retaliatory crimes and inciting community unrest.
>
> Price, J., in *State v. Vanatter*, 869 S.W.2d 754, 755 (Mo. 1994).

*Example 9.29*

> To permit the present sense impression exception to apply to overheard conversations, such as in the instant case, would in effect permit this exception to substantially **devour** the entire hearsay rule of exclusion.
>
> Gordon, J., in *Estate of Parks v. O'Young*, 682 N.E.2d 466, 471 (Ill. App. Ct. 1997).

*Example 9.30*

> At the other end of the spectrum of constitutional errors lie "structural defects in the constitution of the trial mechanism, which defy analysis by 'harmless-error' standards." The existence of such defects—deprivation of the right to counsel, for example—requires automatic reversal of the

conviction because they **infect** the entire trial process.

Rehnquist, C. J., in *Brecht v. Abrahamson*, 507 U.S. 619, 629-30 (1993) (citation omitted).

*Example 9.31*

Drug dealing is particularly **corrosive** to the well-being of Idaho communities.

Schwartzman, J., in *State v. Devore*, 2 P.3d 153, 158 (Idaho Ct. App. 2000).

*Example 9.32*

Where substantially necessary to present to the jury the complete story of the crime, . . . evidence or testimony may be given even though it may reveal or suggest other crimes. These holdings are made necessary by the danger that, otherwise, testimony by the witnesses for the prosecution too carefully **manicured** might lead alert jurors to the thought that something of importance was being withheld. Such suspicions on the part of jurors could lead to a mischievous miscarriage of justice.

Robertson, J., in *McFee v. State*, 511 So.2d 130, 139 (Miss. 1987) (Robertson, J., concurring in part and dissenting in part) (citation omitted).

*Example 9.33*

[Plaintiff] takes issue with the defendants' use of the *McDonnell Douglas* test and cites a **ragbag** of cases in apparent support of the proposition that the test is inapplicable here. Because her argument is so poorly developed, however, we are entitled to disregard it.

Zagel, J., in *Emerson v. E.I. Du Pont de Nemours and Co.*, 707 F. Supp. 336, 338 n.1 (N.D. Ill. 1989).

In the above sentences, the following words are in bold: ignite, devour, infect, corrosive, manicured, ragbag. These words (which include three verbs, two adjectives and a noun) operate as metaphors in their respective sentences because they are used figuratively rather than literally. In Example 9.28, for instance, the verb "ignite" is used not in its literal sense—to set afire—but as a vivid and powerful alternative to the word "cause." Similarly, in Example 9.29, the word "devour"—which in literal terms means to eat or consume greedily—is used as a dramatic alternative to the word "destroy" or "cancel." The other words—infect, corrosive, manicured, ragbag—are used in similar metaphoric fashion in the other examples.

Despite the fact that these sentences contain individual words that are metaphoric in nature, these metaphors cannot be classified as metaphoric sentences or even metaphoric clauses. The metaphoric language in these sentences is very different than the metaphoric language we saw in the prior examples of metaphoric sentences and metaphoric clauses. In each of those examples, the metaphoric language was used to help communicate a substantive point in the discussion. That is, the nature of metaphoric sentences and metaphoric clauses is such that they force a reader to compare substantive concepts within the writers' discussions to symbolically similar concepts. These comparisons help to communicate substantive points to the reader by providing the reader with helpful figurative analogies. In the examples above, the metaphoric language serves a much more limited purpose. The metaphoric words in these examples are used by the writers simply to add flair and vividness to their statements. Single-word metaphors such as these function more as stylistic adornment than as symbolic analogies that help communicate substantive points.

For the remainder of this chapter, we will not focus on single-word metaphors. While it is important for you to recognize individual words such as these as metaphors, and while the use of metaphoric words to enrich one's writing style has many advantages, this use of metaphoric language falls more under the topic of general writing style than under our limited topic of rhetorical figures of speech. Many of the general legal style books and many of the introductory legal writing texts provide substantial instruction for using vivid and concrete language to enrich one's prose. Thus, we will not focus further attention on that use of metaphoric language. Instead, we will turn to the more sophisticated uses of metaphor: the metaphoric sentence, the metaphoric clause, and our next topic, the extended metaphor.

## D.    *Extended Metaphors*

The fourth and final form of metaphor is the extended metaphor. Extended metaphors "extend" over several successive sentences. Not limited to one or two sentences, they can encompass a number of sentences or even paragraphs. There are two types of extended metaphors: (1) "single-comparison" extended metaphors, and (2) "single-theme/multiple-comparison" extended metaphors.

### 1.   "Single-Comparison" Extended Metaphors

A "single-comparison" extended metaphor is simply a metaphor that requires several sentences to communicate it. It involves a single metaphoric comparison but is "extended" in the sense that it is longer than the typical metaphoric sentence. Consider the following example:

*Example 9.34*

> A metaphor may better illuminate the distinction between contending evidence is irrelevant to prove a claim as opposed to asserting that sufficient evidence was not adduced to prove such claim. **Assume that the pieces of two jigsaw puzzles, one of a horse and the other of a ship, were inadvertently commingled. Assume further that we are concerned only with putting together the horse puzzle. By raising a relevancy contention, the objector is effectively claiming that the puzzle builder is using a piece from the ship puzzle to build the horse puzzle. The ship piece does not belong there. A sufficiency of the evidence contention, on the other hand, effectively states that, while the puzzle builder has used only horse pieces to assemble the horse puzzle, the picture is not yet complete.**

> Harrell, J., in *Anderson v. Litzenberg*, 694 A.2d 150, 161 n.11 (Md. Ct. Spec. App. 1997).

In this example, the opinion writer explains the difference between "irrelevant" evidence and "insufficient" evidence using a lengthy metaphor involving jigsaw puzzles of a horse and a ship. This metaphor, like a metaphoric sentence, uses a symbolic analogy to help communicate the writer's point. The only difference is that, in this instance, several sentences are needed to complete the metaphor.

Extended metaphors such as this resemble another rhetorical figure of speech: allegory. An allegory is a symbolic story or narrative designed to communicate an identifiable principle or point. Although relatively rare in legal writing, allegories are sometimes used to persuade. Consider, for example, Justice Sparling's concurring opinion in *Coyle v. Texas*.[12] In *Coyle*, the Texas Court of Appeals addressed an issue regarding the propriety of certain statements made by a prosecutor about a criminal defendant during the punishment phase of a trial.[13] The majority found that the prosecutor's statements violated the defendant's Fifth Amendment right against self-incrimination.[14] In a concurrence, Justice Sparling questioned the dramatic evolution of the relevant law from the original constitutional provision to the latest case on the issue.[15] According to Justice Sparling, the law in the area had changed incrementally, first from the original constitutional provision to Texas' statutory version of the right and then from the Texas statute to the case law interpreting the statute. Justice Sparling stated that the latest case on the issue—on which the majority relied—bore little resemblance to the original constitutional pronouncement.[16] To communicate this point, Justice Sparling offered the following:

> I liken this area of law to the allegory of the woodcutter who attempted to cut firewood in uniform lengths. Instead of measuring each successive log to the original, he measured it to the log cut immediately before. At the end of the cord, he discovered that the last log bore no resemblance in length to the first.[17]

## 2.   "Single-Theme/Multiple-Comparison" Extended Metaphors

The second type of extended metaphor is the "single-theme/multiple-comparison" extended metaphor. This type of extended metaphor uses several metaphoric comparisons, all revolving around the same theme or symbolic concept. The single-comparison extended metaphor, discussed above, is "extended" only in the sense that it communicates a comparison over several sentences. A single-theme/multiple-

---

[12] 693 S.W.2d 743 (Tex. App. 1985).

[13] *Id.* at 743-45.

[14] *Id.* at 744-45.

[15] *Id.* at 745-46.

[16] *Id.*

[17] *Id.* at 745 (Sparling, J., concurring). Granted, Justice Sparling does not craft an "original" allegory. Nevertheless, this excerpt effectively illustrates what an allegory is.

comparison extended metaphor, on the other hand, is "extended" in the sense that an initial metaphor is extended into several related, yet separate, metaphoric comparisons.

One of the best examples in legal writing of a single-theme/ multiple-comparison extended metaphor appears in the Fifth Circuit case of *Shanley v. Northeast Indiana School District*.[18] In *Shanley*, the court held that, under the First Amendment, a school board did not have the right to prevent high school students from distributing an underground newspaper near a school.[19] In the case, the court had to balance the rights of school boards to establish school disciplinary policies with the students' First Amendment rights of freedom of expression. The court relied on a previous Supreme Court case, *Tinker v. Des Moines Independent Community School District*,[20] which established guidelines for balancing constitutional rights against the rights and duties of school officials. Writing for the majority in *Shanley*, Judge Goldberg compared *Tinker* to a "dam":

*Example 9.35*

*Tinker's* dam to school board absolutism does not leave dry the fields of school discipline. This court has gone a considerable distance with the school boards to uphold its disciplinary fiats where reasonable. *Tinker* simply irrigates, rather than floods, the fields of school discipline. It sets canals and channels through which school discipline might flow with the least possible damage to the nation's priceless topsoil of the First Amendment.[21]

This excerpt from *Shanley* is a single-theme/multiple-comparison extended metaphor because Judge Goldberg's initial metaphor of a "dam" is extended into several related metaphors: "irrigates," "floods," "fields of school discipline," "canals and channels," and "topsoil of the First Amendment." Rather than making one metaphoric comparison, Judge Goldberg makes several, all revolving around a single theme: farm irrigation.

Consider the following additional examples:

*Example 9.36*

The [parties to this bankruptcy proceeding] are both in the same boat faced with a serious and common problem that may well sink all who are aboard, including the equity holders and lenders. . . . The response needed is for all

---

[18] 462 F.2d 960 (5th Cir. 1972). The extended metaphor in *Shanley* has been discussed in at least two works on the use of metaphor in judicial opinions. *See* Haig Bosmajian, *Metaphor and Reason in Judicial Opinions* 181-82 (1992); Michael Frost, *Greco-Roman Analysis of Metaphoric Reasoning*, 2 Legal Writing 113, 128-30 (1996).

[19] *Shanley*, 462 F.2d at 975.

[20] 393 U.S. 503 (1969).

[21] *Shanley*, 462 F.2d at 978 (citations omitted).

to bail water, pull together, throw overboard that portion of the heavy cargo that can be sacrificed, head for safe ground and try to weather the storm with the hope that all will not be lost.

> Mencer, J., in *In re Wheeling-Pittsburgh Steel Corp.*, 52 B.R. 997, 1004 (W.D. Pa. 1985).

*Example 9.37*

[T]he State fumbled the ball when it filed an indecipherable petition and brief with this Court. But rather than ordering rebriefing, the majority removes their robes, dons the uniforms of the State, picks up the fumbled ball and articulates an argument for the State. The majority then returns to its referee position and declares their argument a winner. Such result oriented, judicial activism is truly unforgivable.

> Baird, J., in *Barrera v. State*, 982 S.W.2d 415, 418 (Tex. 1998) (Baird, J., dissenting) (citation omitted).

In each of these examples, the writer begins with one metaphor and then builds on it by making additional, yet related, metaphoric comparisons. In Example 9.36, the writer begins with a metaphor describing the parties to the proceeding as being in the "same boat." Building on this same theme, the writer then makes several other metaphoric comparisons: "bail water," "throw overboard," "cargo," "head for safe ground," and "weather the storm." Similarly, in Example 9.37, the writer extends an initial reference to a "fumbled ball" to a number of other football-related metaphors: "dons the uniforms," "picks up the fumbled ball," "referee position," and "winner."

It should be noted that not all groups of metaphors discussed in close proximity can be characterized as single-theme/multiple-comparison extended metaphors. To qualify for this designation, the metaphors must all revolve around a single theme.

## E.     *The Difficulty in Categorizing Different Metaphoric Structures*

In the foregoing discussion, we identified four basic metaphoric structures: metaphoric sentences, metaphoric clauses, single-word metaphors, and extended metaphors. The fact that these are "basic" metaphoric structures must be emphasized. Frequently, one will come across a metaphor that doesn't fit neatly into any of these categories, or, alternatively, fits into more than one category. Metaphoric language is very versatile. Moreover, these different types of metaphors can be used in combination with one another. Thus, this categorization will not help in identifying and analyzing all metaphors. Nevertheless, these categories will help you to organize your approach to metaphors. By appreciating that metaphors can come in many different forms and structures, you will be more effective at evaluating the metaphors of others and at creating your own.

**Exercise 9. 4    Understanding the Basic Forms of Metaphor**

Find examples of the following basic metaphoric structures in judicial opinions:

> One pure metaphoric sentence
> One interwoven metaphoric sentence
> One metaphoric clause
> Three single-word metaphors (one verb; one adjective or adverb; and one noun)
> One single comparison extended metaphor
> One single-theme/multiple-comparison extended metaphor
> One simile

Choose original creative metaphors (not "inherent" or "pre-existing" metaphors, as defined earlier in this chapter). Once you have chosen your metaphors, write an essay explaining why each illustrates its particular category of metaphor. Attach copies of the cases in which you found the metaphors to your essay.

## IV.    THE FUNCTIONS OF ORIGINAL CREATIVE METAPHORS

Some people think of metaphor as mere stylistic adornment. As we discussed earlier in this chapter, however, classical rhetoricians have long considered metaphor to be the most powerful rhetorical figure of speech, an admiration based on more than ornamental usefulness. According to classical rhetoricians (as well as modern linguists and cognitive psychologists[22]), metaphors serve a number of very important rhetorical functions in persuasive discourse.

### A.    *The Logos Function*

In Chapter 6, we identified *logos* as one of the fundamental processes of persuasion recognized by classical rhetoricians. Logos refers to the process of persuading through logical substance. Logos, as we discussed in Chapter 6, is integral to legal advocacy because argumentation based on logical reasoning and the application of legal authorities plays a dominant role in persuasive legal writing.

    According to classical rhetoric theory, metaphors serve important logos functions by helping to communicate an argument's substance through relevant analogies. When writers use metaphors, they provide their readers with symbolic analogies that can help clarify and communicate the writer's substantive point.

    In fact, some substantive points are *easier* to communicate using metaphors than

---

[22] *See* Frost, *supra* note 18, at 135-40 (discussing the analysis of metaphors by modern cognitive psychologists); *see also* Bosmajian, *supra* note 18, at 35-48.

using literal terms. Aristotle expressed this when he said that metaphors are devices by which "we give names to nameless things."[23] Some substantive points can be difficult to explain in abstract, literal terms. The figurative, yet concrete, comparisons of metaphor can make them easier to grasp. As Michael Frost explains:

> [Metaphors] function by means of "reciprocal representations" in which "both subjects of comparison [are placed] before our very eyes, displaying them side by side." The comparison allows the audience to gain cognitive insights not usually achievable by linear or syllogistic reasoning. . . . [Classical rhetorician] Cicero observed that "when something that can *scarcely be conveyed* by the proper (literal) term is expressed metaphorically, the meaning we desire to convey is made clear by the resemblance of the thing that we have expressed by the word that does not belong." That is, a metaphor may be the only way to make or emphasize a particular point.[24]

Earlier in this chapter, we saw that metaphor is inherent to the way humans make sense of abstract concepts. In view of our natural tendency toward metaphoric constructs, it is not difficult to appreciate how well-crafted metaphors can contribute significantly to the communication of an argument's substance.

## B.   The Pathos Functions

In addition to contributing to the logical substance of an argument, metaphors play a significant role in emotional arguments, or *pathos*. In Chapter 6, we saw that pathos—that is, the process of persuading through emotion—constitutes the second basic persuasive process recognized by classical rhetoricians. We also saw that pathos involves two separate components: "emotional substance" and "medium mood control." "Emotional substance" refers to persuading by arousing an emotional reaction in a reader regarding the substance of the matter under discussion. "Medium mood control" refers to the process of arousing a positive emotional reaction in a reader through the form in which a document is written as opposed to its substance. Both emotional substance and medium mood control are relevant to the analysis of the persuasive force of metaphors.

In terms of emotional substance, a well-crafted, apt metaphor can greatly enhance the emotion generated in readers by a substantive emotional argument. By way of illustration, let's reconsider Example 9.11:

> [E]ach [oppressive] practice is one wire in a birdcage; while no one wire could prevent the bird's escape, the wires woven together make a thoroughly effective prison.

---

[23] *See supra* note 3.

[24] Frost, *supra* note 18, at 118 (quoting Quintilian, *supra* note 1, at 255 (alterations in original), and Cicero, *De Oratore* 123 (E. Sutton trans. 1942) (emphasis and alterations in original)).

In the document from which this excerpt was taken, the writer advances a highly emotional argument: the devastating cumulative effect that results from numerous individual acts of oppression. The writer's use of the "birdcage" metaphor contributes greatly to the feelings of dread and sorrow the argument is designed to evoke in the reader.

In terms of medium mood control, metaphors can contribute significantly to a reader's positive reaction to the way in which a document is written. As we saw in connection with our discussion of literary metaphors in Chapter 2, the use of a metaphoric comparison as a stylistic writing device can help put a reader in a positive, receptive mood. As noted in that discussion, readers find metaphors pleasing because, first, their logos effect helps make penetration of the writer's argument easier; scond, the symbolic or figurative comparisons made in metaphors are like "riddles" that readers often find pleasant to solve; and third, metaphors, particularly clever ones, create unexpected, often entertaining juxtapositions.

## C.     The Ethos Function

*Ethos*, the third general process of persuasion recognized by classical rhetoricians, refers to persuading by establishing credibility in the eyes of the reader. Classical rhetoricians have long recognized that the effective use of metaphors can enhance a writer's credibility as an eloquent and intelligent source of information.

As we saw in our discussion of ethos in Chapter 8, the perceived intelligence of a writer plays a significant role in the degree of confidence a reader will place in the writer's arguments and advice. We also saw that the use of eloquent language, including metaphors, can enhance a reader's impression of a writer's intelligence. As Aristotle said, the skill of constructing effective metaphors "is, in itself, a sign of genius."[25] Consequently, the effective use of metaphor contributes to an advocate's persuasiveness by indicating to readers that he or she is an intelligent, and therefore credible, source of information.

## D.     The Rhetorical Style Function

While metaphors are more than stylistic adornment, they nevertheless do serve rhetorical stylistic functions in addition to their other functions. Specifically, metaphors are a means for writers to present their ideas and arguments in clever and unexpected ways. Thus, as stylistic devices, they draw attention to certain points and render them more memorable to readers.

---

[25] Aristotle, *Aristotle's Poetics: A Translation and Commentary for Students of Literature* 41 (Leon Golden trans., 1968), *quoted in* Frost, *supra* note 18, at 127.

**Exercise 9.5     Evaluating the Functions of a Metaphor**

From the examples of metaphor set out at the beginning of this chapter (Examples 9.2 through 9.13), choose one and write an essay explaining the communicative and persuasive functions the metaphor serves in the document from which it was taken. If you did Exercise 9.1, choose a *different* metaphor for this exercise. If necessary or helpful, look up the full document from which the quote was taken.

# V.   CAUTIONS AND SUGGESTIONS REGARDING THE USE OF METAPHORS

With the understanding gained in the preceding sections of the general characteristics and functions of metaphors, we will now turn our attention to the process of drafting our own. In this section, we will examine specific cautions and guidelines that persuasive writers should consider when drafting metaphors. In the final section, we will discuss the specific steps involved in creating and drafting an original metaphor.

## A.     *Overuse of Metaphors*

Metaphors, like all rhetorical figures of speech, are most effective when they are unexpected. They must be used strategically and infrequently.

Overuse of metaphors is a serious, yet common problem in persuasive writing. Considering themselves supreme stylists because they have mastered the craft of composing metaphors, many writers undermine their documents' overall effectiveness by using metaphors indiscriminately. The truly effective stylist uses metaphor selectively to emphasize particular points within a discussion.

The overuse of metaphors undermines an argument in several ways. First, and most obviously, it dilutes the rhetorical effectiveness of each individual metaphor. The presentation of an idea through metaphor is hardly "unexpected" if a discussion is laden with metaphors. Second, overuse of metaphors interferes with the persuasive process of "logos" by complicating the presentation of the argument's substance. As Quintilian stated, "While a temperate and timely use of metaphor is a real adornment to style, . . . its frequent use serves merely to obscure our language."[26] Third, overuse of metaphors negatively affects their "ethos" function by undermining a writer's appearance of intelligence. The unrestrained use of metaphor suggests to the reader that the writer lacks discernment and judgment in the strategic use of rhetorical figures. Finally, overuse of metaphors negatively affects the "medium mood control" aspect of "pathos." Readers often find the use of numerous metaphors tiresome, irritating and distracting. Moreover, it suggests that the writer is less interested in the reader and more interested in amusing himself or herself. This self-indulgence—this manifested lack of interest in the reader—can frustrate and irritate the reader. Thus,

---

[26] Quintilian, *supra* note 1, at 307-09.

when using metaphor, one should remember these words from Thomas Haggard: "[Metaphors] are like strong seasoning; a dash will enhance the flavor enormously, but too much will ruin the dish."[27]

## B.     Mixed Metaphors

Writers should also avoid composing "mixed metaphors," that is, metaphors containing incompatible references. Consider the following:

> A careful reading of the contract reveals a loophole that we can hang our hat on.

This sentence employs two incompatible metaphoric references: "loophole" and "hang our hat on." One does not "hang a hat" on a "loophole."[28] In literal terms, this sentence is nonsensical.

As we discussed previously, one important function of an effective metaphor is to evoke a concrete image in readers' minds that serves as a helpful analogy to the substantive point being made. Mixed metaphors evoke no clear picture in readers' minds, and what jumbled mental pictures they do create confuse more than they clarify.

Writers tend to create mixed metaphors when they lose sight of the literal sense of the language they are employing and think only of its metaphoric sense. In the example above, the writer equated "loophole" with its metaphoric meaning ("a favorable textual ambiguity") and equated "that we can hang our hat on" with its metaphoric meaning ("that we can rely on"). In a pure metaphoric sense, the sentence is understandable—*A careful reading of the contract reveals a favorable textual ambiguity that we can rely on*—and this is what the writer meant to convey by the sentence. By losing sight of the literal meaning of the words used, however, the writer inadvertently created an absurd sentence.

This phenomenon of a writer losing sight of the literal meaning of metaphoric language occurs most frequently in connection with "inherent" metaphors and metaphors that are cliched and idiomatic. Because such metaphors are so familiar, writers automatically equate the words with their metaphoric meaning and forget their original, literal meaning. Thus, mixed metaphors often result from the use of two or more idiomatic metaphors in a single sentence or when a writer incorporates an idiomatic metaphor in the same sentence as an original creative metaphor. To guard against inadvertently mixing incompatible metaphors, writers must be sensitive to both the literal and metaphoric meanings of the words they choose.

Consider these additional examples of ineffective mixed metaphors:

> The defendant's argument is nothing more than a *red herring* that will not *fly*.

---

[27] Thomas R. Haggard, *Rhetoric in Legal Writing, Part I*, 8-Jun S. C. Law. 13, 13 (1997).

[28] Literally, a "loophole" is a small opening in a wall through which one can shoot a weapon or light can enter.

The contract in question bears the *earmarks* of an *arm's-length* transaction.

The exception created by the court establishes a *slippery slope* that will eventually *swallow* the general rule.

---

**Exercise 9.6      Understanding Mixed Metaphors**

Write a few paragraphs analyzing one of the above mixed metaphors. In particular, (1) explain how the metaphors in the sentence are incompatible in a literal sense, (2) explain what the writer meant to communicate by the sentence, and (3) rewrite the sentence in literal terms.

---

**Exercise 9.7      Understanding Mixed Metaphors**

1.      Draft three ineffective mixed metaphors similar to the ones above.

2.      Write a few paragraphs analyzing your metaphors. In particular, (1) explain how the metaphors in your sentences are incompatible in a literal sense, (2) explain what you meant to communicate by the sentences, and (3) rewrite the sentences in literal terms.

This exercise is designed to make you more aware of and sensitive to mixed metaphors. It is my hope that the last time you draft a mixed metaphor will be in the completion of this exercise.

---

## C.    *Insulting or Offensive Metaphors*

Writers, needless to say, should avoid composing metaphors that may insult or offend their readers. There are two general types of offensive metaphors. The first type occurs when a writer loses sight of the literal meaning of the metaphoric language he or she is using, and this literal meaning is potentially insulting to the reader. Consider, for example, the following statement made to a judge by an attorney:

> [These allegations are] a "dog's breakfast," an effort by the plaintiff to "offer up a bowl of mixed leftovers to a mutt" as an appetizing meal.[29]

In this statement, the attorney uses metaphoric language to argue that the

---

[29] *In re Fuqua Indus. Shareholder Litig.*, No. CIV.A. 11974, 1997 WL 257460, at *3 n.10 (Del. Ch. May 13, 1997) (quoting plaintiff's oral argument).

plaintiff's allegations, despite the forceful tone with which they are made, are actually insignificant and groundless. However, if the word "leftovers" in this sentence refers to the plaintiff's allegations, then it follows that the "mutt" to which the leftovers were offered would be the judge. The attorney, caught up in the metaphoric meaning of the statement, lost sight of its literal meaning and inadvertently called the presiding judge a "mutt"—a point not lost on the judge. Fortunately for the attorney, the judge responded to this mistake with humor and humility. Referring to the attorney's statement, the judge called it a "colorful metaphor, with perhaps an apt reference to my role in this matter."[30]

While the judge in this case responded well to the attorney's use of a potentially offensive metaphor, legal writers cannot expect all judges (or other readers) to be so forgiving and understanding. Thus, as we discussed above in connection with mixed metaphors, writers must be cognizant of both the literal and figurative meanings of their words so as to avoid inadvertently incorporating insulting metaphors in their arguments.

The second common type of offensive metaphor is one which is, by its nature or content, insulting or insensitive to a specific class of people. Racist or sexist metaphors fall under this category. Consider, for example, the response by the court to a sexist metaphor employed by the attorney for the plaintiffs in *Spahl v. Raymark Industries*.[31] Although the court does not divulge the offending reference, its reaction is quite forceful:

> The court feels compelled to address another unrelated matter. The plaintiffs' brief in opposition to these motions to dismiss contains in footnote 8 a simile which is highly inappropriate and offensive. The court assumes that plaintiffs' counsel will be more circumspect and sensitive in the future and avoid gender-biased metaphor.[32]

The lesson to be learned from *Spahl* is that persuasive writers must make sure that the metaphors they choose cannot be interpreted by the reader as racist, sexist, or otherwise offensive to a specific class of people.

## D.    *Arcane Metaphors*

Legal writers should also avoid using arcane or esoteric metaphoric references. For a metaphor to be effective, it must be based on well-known concepts easily evoked in the mind of the reader. Consider the following example:

> The Bill of Rights was but a tub to a whale, designed to distract anti-federalists from the text of the Constitution that gave immense power to the

---

[30] *Id.*

[31] No. CV 9550359, 1996 WL 798746 (Conn. Super. Ct. Sept. 9, 1996).

[32] *Id.* at *2.

federal government.[33]

In this sentence, the phrase "tub to a whale" is a metaphoric reference to the practice by early whalers of throwing a wooden tub or barrel toward a whale to distract it until the whalers could harpoon it. The metaphor in the above statement is intended to convey that the Bill of Rights was offered merely to distract anti-federalists from other portions of the Constitution that empowered the federal government, at least until the Constitution was adopted (that is, until the harpoon was secure). If one knows the meaning of "throwing a tub to a whale," one can see that this metaphor is actually rather clever and apt. However, few readers (at least since the 1900s) would know what this phrase means. In modern writing, this metaphor would be too arcane to be effective.

### E.    *Forced Metaphors*

Related to arcane metaphors are forced metaphors. A forced metaphor occurs when the symbolic similarity between two things is not readily apparent to readers. That is, it occurs when a writer tries to "force" a metaphoric comparison in a situation where no real resemblance exists. "Forced" metaphors differ from "arcane" metaphors in a significant way. With arcane metaphors, the metaphoric referent is unknown to the reader. With forced metaphors, the referent is known to the reader, but its symbolic similarity with the writer's substantive point is unclear. That is, with "arcane" metaphors, it is the *referent* that is obscure. With "forced" metaphors, it is the *similarity* between the referent and the writer's substantive point that is obscure.

When a writer forces a metaphoric comparison, the metaphor comes across as harsh and artificial. Thus, writers should only use a metaphor if readers will easily appreciate the symbolic similarity. As Aristotle said, "[M]etaphors . . . must not be far-fetched; rather we must draw them from kindred and similar things; the kinship must be seen the moment the words are uttered."[34]

### F.    *Overly Grand and Trivializing Metaphors*

Legal writers should tailor the level of "grandeur" of a metaphor to the significance or seriousness of the point with which it is used. For example, a writer should not use an overly grand or dramatic metaphor to communicate a rather minor or insignificant point. Likewise, a writer should not "trivialize" a major point in an argument by using a trite or simplistic metaphor. As Quintilian advised, "A metaphor must not be too great for its subject or, as is more frequently the case, too little."[35]

---

[33] This statement and the ensuing explanation is based on David A. Anderson's discussion of the adoption of the Constitution and Bill of Rights in David A. Anderson, *The Origins of the Press Clause*, 30 U.C.L.A. L. Rev. 455, 497 & n.251 (1983).

[34] Aristotle, *supra* note 3, at 188.

[35] Quintilian, *supra* note 1, at 309.

### G.    Thematically Inconsistent Metaphors and the Art of "Internal Allusion"

Experts on metaphor advise that the theme of a metaphor should not be inconsistent with the theme of the general discussion in which the metaphor appears. That is, the literal meaning of metaphoric language should not contradict or be inharmonious with the substance of the discussion in which it is placed. Bryan Garner, for example, has warned that "[a] writer would be ill advised . . . to use rustic metaphors in a discussion of the problems of air pollution, which is essentially a problem of the bigger cities and outlying areas."[36] Thus, in drafting metaphors, legal writers should not only consider the more obvious question of whether the symbolic meaning of the metaphor accurately communicates the intended point, but should also consider the more subtle question of whether the literal meaning of the metaphoric words is thematically consistent with the overall discussion.

This fairly advanced consideration in the creation of metaphors can even be taken one step further: Metaphors can be crafted so as to involve *internal allusion*. "Internal allusion" occurs when the literal meaning of the metaphoric language alludes to a substantive concept within the surrounding discussion. Let's consider an example.

In the case of *United States v. Brooke*, the defendant, Susan Brooke, was charged with several crimes stemming from the manufacture of a pipe bomb and its use against the girlfriend of the defendant's ex-lover.[37] During the trial, the prosecution introduced extensive testimony that the defendant had falsely told her friends and acquaintances that she suffered from cancer. This evidence was designed to discredit the defendant and to project the defendant as manipulative.[38] After the defendant was convicted, she appealed, alleging, among other things, that the evidence regarding her lies to her friends about cancer was impermissibly prejudicial. The appellate court decided for the defendant and reversed the conviction. In connection with its finding that the evidence of the defendant's feigned illness had a wide-spread negative impact on the fairness of the defendant's trial, the court stated the following:

> Like an evidentiary cancer, the erroneously-admitted evidence infected the testimony of nearly every witness. Brooke is entitled to a trial cured of such a pervasive defect.[39]

The court's use of the "cancer" metaphor is not merely thematically consistent with the overall discussion in the opinion; it is an internal allusion. The literal meaning of the metaphoric word "cancer" in this passage is an obvious allusion—that is, an obvious internal reference—to the illness the defendant was alleged to have feigned. Thus, although it is somewhat facile, this excerpt provides us with a clear

---

[36] Bryan A. Garner, *A Dictionary of Modern Legal Usage* 558 (2d ed. 1995).

[37] 4 F.3d 1480, 1481-82 (9th Cir. 1993).

[38] *Id.* at 1482.

[39] *Id.* at 1488.

example of a metaphor that involves internal allusion.

Judge Benjamin Cardozo provides us with a more subtle and graceful example of internal allusion in *Hynes v. New York Central Railroad*.[40] *Hynes* dealt with the death of a sixteen-year-old boy killed when electrical wires belonging to a railroad fell from overhead poles and landed on him.[41] At the time of the accident, the boy was standing on a make-shift diving board protruding from the railroad's land along the Harlem River out over the public waterway. The boy was preparing to dive when the wires fell on him, sending him to his death in the water below.[42] The boy's family sued the railroad for damages.

The issue addressed by the court in *Hynes* was whether, at the time of the accident, the decedent was in the public waterway (and, therefore, entitled to recover) or a trespasser on the defendant's land (and, therefore, barred from recovery). The defendant railroad argued that, because the diving board was affixed to the defendant's land, it was a part of the land, making the decedent a trespasser at the time of his death. The plaintiff argued that, because the decedent was in the air space of the public waterway running beneath the diving board, he was on public land at the time of the accident.[43]

The New York Court of Appeals found for the plaintiff. In writing the opinion for the court, Judge Cardozo offered the following:

> We assume, without deciding, that the springboard was a fixture, a permanent improvement of the defendant's right of way. Much might be said in favor of another view. We do not press the inquiry for we are persuaded that the rights of bathers do not depend upon these nice distinctions. Liability would not be doubtful, we are told, had the boy been diving from a pole, if the pole had been vertical. The diver in such a situation would have been separated from the defendant's freehold. Liability, it is said has been escaped because the pole was horizontal. The plank when projected lengthwise was an extension of the soil. We are to concentrate our gaze on the private ownership of the board. We are to ignore the public ownership of the circumambient spaces of water and of air. Jumping from a boat or a barrel, the boy would have been a bather in the river. Jumping from the end of a springboard, he was no longer, it is said, a bather, but a trespasser on a right of way.
>
> Rights and duties in systems of living law are not built upon such quicksands.[44]

---

[40] 131 N.E. 898 (N.Y. 1921).

[41] *Id.* at 898-99.

[42] *Id.* at 899.

[43] *Id.*

[44] *Id.*

Judge Cardozo's "quicksand" metaphor at the end of this excerpt is a classic example of an internal allusion. In figurative terms, Judge Cardozo's metaphor is saying that a legal system cannot be founded on unstable technicalities and distinctions that ignore commonsense and equity. In literal terms, however, the "quicksand" metaphor is an allusion to the decedent's tragic death in the waters of the Harlem River. Richard Weisberg explains:

> These lines, a paragraph unto themselves, cast our imaginations into a spatial sphere deliberately evocative of Hynes' last moments on earth. The railroad's arguments, based on the "quicksands" of ancient property-law concepts, are equated imagistically with the sad end of the lad's life on the sands adjacent to the Harlem River.[45]

Internal allusion is a sophisticated skill (at least when it is employed effectively). The difference between the "cancer" reference in *Brooke* and the "quicksand" reference in *Hynes* highlights the difference between the merely fair and the truly elegant. Few writers will ever attain the skill of Cardozo. Yet, this illustration of internal allusion in *Hynes* shows us what can be accomplished by one trained in the subtleties of persuasive writing.

## H.     *Inappropriate Tone in Metaphors (Humorous Metaphors)*

Related to both the guidelines regarding the "level of grandeur" of a metaphor and the guidelines regarding the "thematic consistency" of a metaphor is a caution regarding the "tone" of a metaphor. Specifically, the tone or mood created by a metaphor must be consistent with the tone or mood of the discussion in which it is used. The use of a humorous or whimsical metaphor, for example, would not be appropriate in a serious or solemn discussion. (And considering that legal matters are invariably serious to the parties involved, humorous metaphors are rarely, if ever, appropriate in legal writing.)

Consider, by way of illustration, Justice Musmanno's use of metaphor in the case of *Pavlicic v. Vogtsberger*.[46] In this case, George Pavlicic sued Sara Jane Vogtsberger to recover certain gifts he had given to Ms. Vogtsberger in anticipation of a marriage between the two. After receiving the gifts, Ms. Vogtsberger refused to marry the plaintiff and, instead, married another man.[47] The Pennsylvania Supreme Court held for the plaintiff, finding that the case involved "conditional gifts," not an unenforceable "contract to marry." In writing the opinion for the court, Justice Musmanno stated the following:

> A gift given by a man to a woman on condition that she embark on the sea of

---

[45] Richard Weisberg, *Poethics, and Other Strategies of Law and Literature* 20 (1992).

[46] 136 A.2d 127 (Pa. 1957).

[47] *Id.* at 128.

matrimony with him is no different from a gift based on the condition that the donee sail on any other sea. If, after receiving the provisional gift, the donee refuses to leave the harbor,— if the anchor of contractual performance sticks in the sands of irresolution and procrastination—the gift must be restored to the donor. *A fortiori* would this be true when the donee not only refuses to sail with the donor, but, on the contrary, walks up the gangplank of another ship arm in arm with the donor's rival.[48]

While the nautical "theme" of Musmanno's metaphor is not necessarily inconsistent with a case involving conditional gifts and a breach of contract to marry, the humorous "tone" of the metaphor is arguably inappropriate. In fact, Michael Frost has criticized the tone of Justice Musmanno's metaphor in *Pavlicic*, advising legal writers to be wary of projecting such a tone in their own documents:

> In selecting and then using the "sea of matrimony" metaphor in this jocular fashion, Justice Musmanno reveals a very distinctive judicial *ethos*. He seems to be amusing himself as he interweaves abstract contractual principles into his nautical business metaphor. Moreover, this metaphor is similar in tone to others in the same opinion. . . . The "sea of matrimony" metaphor, especially when combined with several other mock-serious metaphors in the opinion, projects a self-indulgent judicial *ethos* that a careful and resourceful advocate should be aware of when preparing written and oral arguments.[49]

## I.   *Extended Metaphors*

Earlier in this chapter we discussed two type of extended metaphors: (1) single-comparison extended metaphors, those involving single metaphoric comparisons that take several sentences to explain, and (2) single-theme/multiple-comparison extended metaphors, those involving several metaphoric comparisons centered on a single theme or concept. Writing experts disagree on whether either of these types of extended metaphors are effective in persuasive writing.

Some legal writing experts argue that lengthy single-comparison metaphors, by being unduly obtrusive and conspicuous, impede persuasive arguments. Most experts, however, believe that lengthy metaphors can be effective if they offer readers symbolic analogies that help communicate the writers' points. Like allegories, lengthy metaphors often provide insight into discussions that would not be possible with purely literal language.

More disagreement exists over the usefulness of single-theme/multiple-comparison extended metaphors. While some writers find them effective, many experts believe that extending an initial metaphor into several related metaphors

---

[48] *Id.* at 130.

[49] Frost, *supra* note 18, at 131.

strikes readers as facile and contrived.[50] In the end, it's a judgment call. However, when drafting metaphors, legal writers should be aware that many readers view multipart metaphors less as graceful devices and more as awkward and forced contrivances.

## J.     *Labeling Metaphors*

Some writers introduce their metaphors with phrases such as "to use a metaphor . . ." or "stated as a metaphor . . .". Such "labeling" of metaphors is generally not effective, for two reasons. First, metaphors, like all figures of speech, are most effective when they are unexpected. Announcing one's metaphors in advance thus dilutes their impact. Second, phrases such as those above sound as if the writer is apologizing for or is unsure of his or her decision to use a metaphor. Writers should choose the placement and content of their metaphors carefully. Once they have done so, however, they should use them with confidence and enthusiasm and let the metaphor "speak" for itself.

## K.     *Metaphors as "Enslaving Thought"*

A discussion of cautions regarding the use of metaphor in legal writing would not be complete without recalling the most famous criticism of metaphor ever uttered by a member of the legal profession: "Metaphors in law are to be narrowly watched, for starting as devices to liberate thought, they end often by enslaving it."[51]

This statement was made in the case of *Berkey v. Third Avenue Railroad* by Judge Benjamin Cardozo—that's right, the same Benjamin Cardozo that we saw employ metaphor so skillfully in *Hynes v. New York Central Railroad*.[52] Judge Cardozo made this statement (interestingly enough, itself phrased as a metaphor) in an analysis of corporate law, particularly the metaphoric concepts of "parent corporation" and "subsidiary." In the discussion from which this quote was taken, Judge Cardozo reasoned that courts must look beyond established metaphoric labels in determining the relationships between entities and in deciding the consequences of those relationships.[53]

Cardozo's warning to look beyond metaphoric constructs when analyzing legal issues has been applied in numerous other contexts over the years. Supreme Court Justice William Rehnquist, for example, used this concept to advocate reevaluating the "wall of separation" metaphor traditionally used to characterize the relationship

---

[50] *See, e.g.,* Garner, *supra* note 36, at 559-60 (discussing "overwrought" metaphors); Bosmajian, *supra* note 18, at 181 (criticizing the "*Tinker* dam" extended metaphor discussed earlier in this chapter as "[bringing] too much attention to itself"). *But see, e.g.*, Frost, *supra* note 18, at 130 n.85 (questioning Bosmajian's criticism).

[51] *Berkey v. Third Ave. R.R.*, 155 N.E. 58, 61 (N.Y. 1926).

[52] *See supra* Section V.G.

[53] *Berkey*, 155 N.E. at 61.

between church and state under the Constitution.[54] According to Cardozo and those following his advice, legal professionals must be wary of legal concepts that are commonly understood in the form of metaphoric constructs. Such metaphors often restrict analysis because they lead lawyers and judges to evaluate the issues exclusively in terms of the metaphoric representations of the ideas rather than in terms of their true, literal nature. While metaphors can help put abstract concepts into concrete terms, the figurative constructs cannot possibly account for all of the dimensions and nuances associated with the concepts. Thus, to rephrase Cardozo's statement, while metaphors can help us to understand abstract concepts by giving them concrete faces, legal professionals must guard against equating figurative representations of concepts with the concepts themselves. Analyzing issues exclusively in terms of established metaphoric constructs prevents a broader, more open approach to the issues and inhibits development and growth.

Cardozo's statement in this regard has little relevance to our discussion, however. In this chapter we focus on creating "original" metaphors, not on analyzing legal issues that are expressed through established metaphoric constructs. Cardozo's warning applies only to legal professionals who blindly follow *established* metaphoric constructs in analyzing legal issues. Thus, while Cardozo's statement reflects great insight into the nature and shortcomings of metaphor, it has minimal application to legal writers who are crafting their own original metaphors.

## VI.   GUIDELINES FOR DRAFTING METAPHORS

In Chapter 2, we learned that drafting effective "literary" metaphors requires more "premeditation" than "inspiration."[55] The same is true for nonliterary metaphors. Devising and drafting an effective metaphor is a deliberate process involving identifiable and learnable steps. Granted, some writers may have a natural gift for crafting metaphors. But all writers—even writers for whom metaphors do not come naturally—can learn to employ them to enrich and empower their persuasive documents. In this section, we will explore with specificity the basic steps involved in creating and drafting effective metaphors in legal writing.

The process of drafting a metaphor can be broken down into four basic steps:

Step 1:   *The writer must identify the point in the discussion that he or she wants to express through metaphor.*

Step 2:   *The writer must back away from a narrow, specific conception*

---

[54] *See Wallace v. Jaffree*, 472 U.S. 38, 107 (1985) (Rehnquist, J., dissenting) ("[The] "wall" [metaphor] has proved all but useless as a guide to sound constitutional adjudication. It illustrates only too well the wisdom of Benjamin Cardozo's observation that '[m]etaphors in law are to be narrowly watched.'"); *see also, e.g.*, Chad M. Oldfather, *The Hidden Ball: A Substantive Critique of Baseball Metaphors in Judicial Opinions*, 27 Conn. L. Rev. 17, 29 (1994) ("The 'marketplace of ideas' [metaphor] makes it easy to emphasize the damaging effects that metaphors can have, and to imagine them running amok, taking control of legal doctrines whenever they are used.").

[55] *See supra* Chapter 2, Section I.C.7 (*quoting* Frost *supra* note 18, at 126).

*of the point and think of it in broad, generalized terms.*

Step 3:     *The writer must think of a concrete, tangible image that also meets the broad conception of the point.*

Step 4:     *The writer must draft a metaphor that expresses this figurative analogy, observing the cautions and guidelines covered earlier in this chapter. The following is a summary of these guidelines:*
  - *Avoid the overuse of metaphors*
  - *Avoid mixed metaphors*
  - *Avoid insulting or offensive metaphors*
  - *Avoid arcane metaphors*
  - *Avoid forced metaphors*
  - *Avoid overly grand or trivializing metaphors*
  - *Avoid thematically inconsistent metaphors*
  - *Avoid an inappropriate tone in your metaphors*
  - *Reconsider extended metaphors*
  - *Reconsider labeling your metaphors*

Let's walk through these four steps, using as an example the metaphor composed by Justice Dabney of the Fourth District, California Court of Appeal already introduced above as Example 9.6.

> If the small claims court is to be the "People's Court," it must not be encumbered with rules and restrictions which can only frustrate and hinder the litigant who resorts to that court in response to its promise of speedy and economical justice. **In the case of inexperienced pro se litigants, it is better to err on the side of admitting an ore-heap of evidence in the belief that nuggets of truth may be found amidst the dross, rather than to confine the parties to presenting assayed and refined matter which qualifies as pure gold under the rules of evidence.**

Justice Dabney wrote this metaphor in the majority opinion of the case of *Houghtaling v. Superior Court.*[56] *Houghtaling* involved the issue of whether the rules of evidence (and, in particular, the rule regarding the exclusion of hearsay evidence) should be applicable to pro se parties in small claims court. The majority in *Houghtaling* reversed the exclusion of hearsay evidence by a small claims judge and held that such rules of evidence do not apply in small claims proceedings.[57]

Writing for the majority, Justice Dabney analyzed two main points in reaching this conclusion. First, Justice Dabney examined the issue in terms of California's Evidence Code and precedent cases interpreting those rules.[58] Second, Justice Dabney examined the practical and public policy considerations regarding the goals behind

---

[56] 21 Cal. Rptr. 2d 855 (Cal. Ct. App. 1993).

[57] *Id.* at 861.

[58] *Id.* at 857-59.

small claims proceedings.[59] In connection with this second point, Justice Dabney explained that small claims proceedings were originally created to provide an inexpensive and speedy method of recourse for unsophisticated citizens in petty matters. Justice Dabney reasoned that applying technical rules of evidence to small claims matters would subvert these goals. It was in connection with this last point that Justice Dabney offered the above metaphor.[60]

Although we cannot know the actual steps undertaken by Justice Dabney in crafting this metaphor, we can imagine the process and use it to illustrate our four basic steps.

Step 1. *The writer must identify the point in the discussion that he or she wants to express through metaphor.* As we discussed earlier, metaphor should be used infrequently and strategically in an argument. Thus, when planning to use a metaphor, a writer should think carefully about what point in the discussion will most benefit from its use. To do this, the writer should, first, consider whether any point in the discussion could be better communicated through metaphor. As we discussed in connection with the functions of metaphor, a metaphor is sometimes the *best way* to explain a concept that is difficult to explain in abstract literal terms. Thus, the first consideration in deciding whether and where to use a metaphor is whether any particular point in the argument could benefit substantively from a figurative analogy.

The second consideration in the placement of a metaphor is whether the writer wishes to emphasize any particular point in the argument. As we discussed earlier, one of the primary functions of metaphor is to draw attention to a specific point. Thus, the placement of a metaphor also depends on the strategic decision of which point in an argument should be highlighted for the reader through the use of this rhetorical device.

In terms of the *Houghtaling* example, we will assume that Justice Dabney gave serious thought to the questions of whether and where to place a metaphor in the opinion. We will also assume that the placement of the metaphor—that is, its position in the discussion of the policy rationales behind small claims proceedings—was a strategic one based on the considerations described above. Justice Dabney may, of course, have placed this metaphor by instinct rather than design. The result is nonetheless effective according to our criteria. First, the metaphor is substantively effective because it helps explain a rather complicated point in concrete terms. Thus, the placement of the metaphor is supported by the fact that it is used to provide a figurative analogy for a point that otherwise would be difficult to explain. Second, the point with which the metaphor is used is one of two main points in the majority opinion. Thus, in terms of the strategic use of metaphor to emphasize crucial points in an argument, the metaphor again appears to be well placed.

Step 2: *The writer must back away from a narrow, specific conception of the point and think of it in broad, generalized terms.* Once a writer has chosen a point to express through metaphor, the writer must revise his or her conceptions of the point from the narrow to the general. We can see this process best using our example.

In the *Houghtaling* opinion, Justice Dabney wanted to explain that it is better to

---

[59] *Id.* at 859-61.

[60] *Id.* at 860.

err on the side of allowing too much evidence into small claims proceedings, leaving it to the presiding judge to evaluate its reliability, rather than to increase the expense and duration of such proceedings by holding pro se parties to the rigors of the technical rules of evidence. Under the second step of drafting metaphors, Justice Dabney had to generalize this specific point and reconceptualize it in broad terms. Thus, the specific, narrow point became the following generalized concept in Justice Dabney's mind:

When

> (1) one desires to obtain "good" material, and
> (2) "good" material is mixed in with "bad" material, and
> (3) the process of separating the "good" from the "bad" requires expertise not possessed by the person submitting the material, and
> (4) one desires to minimize the cost of presenting the material to an expert,

then it is better to allow the non-expert to submit mixed material to the expert for consideration rather than requiring the non-expert to present only good material.

Step 3: *The writer must think of a concrete, tangible image that also meets the broad conception of the point.* After mentally recharacterizing the concept in broad terms, the next step is for the writer to devise a tangible image that also reflects this broad concept. In terms of our *Houghtaling* illustration, Justice Dabney had to think of a concrete image that reflected the generalized concept expressed above under step two. The image he came up with was the process of presenting mine ore to an assayer with the hope of finding gold. Justice Dabney mentally recognized that, just as a pro se litigant presents a judge with a mass of evidence, both reliable and not, a miner presents a gold assayer with ore containing both gold and dross. He also recognized that, just as minimizing the cost of assaying gold ore requires the assayer to accept raw ore for consideration rather than asking miners to submit only refined matter, minimizing the cost of pro se litigation requires allowing submission of both questionable and reliable evidence rather than asking parties to present only evidence that satisfies the technical rules of evidence. Thus, Justice Dabney thought of a tangible construct that satisfied his broad conception of his point.

Step 4: *The writer must draft a metaphor that expresses this figurative analogy, observing the cautions and guidelines covered earlier in this chapter.* The writer must now take the final step and draft the planned metaphor while staying alert to the cautions and guidelines outlined in this chapter. Justice Dabney's success at this can be seen in his result: a clever and helpful metaphor that supports and enriches his argument.

The following table offers hypotheses for how the writers quoted in Examples 9.1, 9.11, and 9.13 might have followed these four steps in crafting their metaphors.

| Example # | Step 1 Substantive point to be expressed through metaphor | Step 2 Generalized conception of point | Step 3 Concrete, tangible image that meets broad conception | Step 4 Resulting metaphor |
|---|---|---|---|---|
| 9.1 | While lower courts must have the authority to consider the facts of individual cases in deciding if equitable estoppel is applicable, the higher court must be able to establish and adjust the outer limits of that authority. | While a thing must have some freedom, there must be an outer limit or restriction on that freedom. | While an animal in a pasture (such as a cow or horse) has the freedom to roam and maneuver, the pasture must be enclosed by a perimeter fence that puts an outer limit on the animal's freedom. | "There are times when [the higher court] must expand or contract or more closely define the pasture within which the trial courts may roam in the exercise of discretion [in determining equitable estoppel]." |
| 9.11 | Numerous acts of discrimination against an individual operate together and have the cumulative effect of completely repressing the individual. | The accumulation of several instances or items has the effect of dominating, subduing, or restraining something. | While no one wire could prevent a bird's escape, the cumulative effect of many wires woven together is the creation of cage that imprisons the bird. | "[E]ach [oppressive] practice is one wire in a birdcage; while no one wire could prevent the bird's escape, the wires woven together make a thoroughly effective prison." |
| 9.13 | While the Wagner Act was originally created to protect and empower labor unions, its antiquated provisions now hinder the labor movement by prohibiting many modern effective labor practices. | A thing that once protected and empowered another thing, now serves to restrict it and impede its development. | A small shell that once protected a young hermit crab early in its life now threatens to impede the mature crab's future development. | "[T]he Wagner Act has been reduced to a shell that once protected but now threatens to strangle the living form of the labor movement within." |

## Exercise 9.8     Drafting and Analyzing an Original Creative Metaphor

1.  For a judicial opinion of your choice, select a discussion of a specific point within the opinion and rewrite that portion of the opinion incorporating an original creative metaphor. In creating your metaphor, follow the four basic steps for drafting a metaphor discussed above. Attach a copy of the opinion's original discussion to your revised version of it.

2.  Write an essay analyzing your metaphor. In particular, (1) explain how you applied each of the four steps for drafting a metaphor; (2) analyze the communicative and persuasive functions that your metaphor serves in the revised opinion; and (3) analyze the effectiveness of your metaphor in terms of the cautions and guidelines for using metaphors discussed in this chapter.

# Chapter 10

# Beyond Metaphor and Simile: Using Other Figures of Speech in Persuasive Writing

Writing is an art and no art can be taught by recipe.
— Samuel Butler

. . . all a rhetorician's rules
Teach nothing but to name his tools.
— Burges Johnson

[T]hough each of us is a prisoner of his personality, though few of us have the ultimate talent for expression, any of us, by intelligent study and practice of the principles of rhetoric, can develop all the power of expression possible to him. This is a large consolation, for, as writers, most of us function far below our potentialities.
— Arthur Zeiger

[L]et us seek wholeheartedly that true majesty of expression, the fairest gift of God to man, without which all things are struck dumb and robbed both of present glory and the immortal acclaim of posterity; and let us press on to whatever is best, because, if we do this, we shall either reach the summit or at least see many others far beneath us.
— Quintilian

Various opinions are held on the question of whether eloquence can be taught or learned. The quotations above from Samuel Butler and Burges Johnson represent the more skeptical end of the spectrum of opinion: They both hold that eloquence in writing is a natural gift; some people have it, and others do not. According to them, efforts to dissect eloquent language are futile, the mere "naming of an artist's tools." Just as an untalented painter cannot become a skilled artist by dissecting the techniques and strategies of a master painter, a writer who does not naturally possess the skill of eloquence in writing cannot become an effective stylist by dissecting and labeling the techniques instinctively employed by gifted writers. Fortunately for our enterprise here, however, this is the minority position.

Most rhetoricians firmly believe that eloquence can be learned. According to these experts, all writers can become more eloquent through careful study and practice. While it may be true that eloquence comes more naturally to some than to others, and while it may be true that few of us will ever become supreme stylists, all of us can empower our writing with artistic flair by studying the principles of classical rhetoric. As Arthur Zeiger noted in the quotation set out above, most of us "function far below our potentialities" when it comes to writing eloquently. By studying the principles of eloquent style developed by classical rhetoricians, each of us can write with a higher level of eloquence and learn to "develop all the power of expression possible" to us.

Three basic steps can help writers become more eloquent. First, they should become more familiar with the stylistic devices at their disposal. As stated earlier, eloquence comes naturally to some gifted writers. For these writers, eloquence does not involve a conscious process of choosing among available stylistic tools. Rather, it involves "intuitive inspiration" by which eloquent and artistic phrasing comes naturally to the writer. Most writers, however, must take a more calculated and conscious approach to achieving eloquence, and their first step must be to become acquainted with the stylistic devices available to them.

Many of us recognize eloquent language when we read it. From time to time, many of us even create eloquent phrasing in our own writing (more often by accident than by design). Despite our ability to appreciate the eloquence of others and despite our own occasional flashes of eloquence, few of us have ever given much thought to what makes an eloquent passage effective. Without this understanding, we will remain unable to draft eloquent language at will and, more importantly, unable to use eloquence strategically to empower our persuasive arguments. Thus, the first crucial step in becoming a more eloquent writer is to become more knowledgeable about what makes language eloquent.

Classical rhetoricians have devoted much thought and many pages to the tools of eloquence. In fact, they have identified, labeled, and defined more than two hundred figures of speech.[1] In this chapter, we will explore a number of these figures, focusing on those most useful in persuasive legal writing. Our goal here is to establish an inventory of the stylistic tools available to us as persuasive writers. This step alone is very empowering. By having a list of the more effective stylistic devices and by understanding their nature and functions, you will immediately be able to use eloquence more deliberately and strategically in your persuasive documents.

The second step in improving one's eloquence is to develop judgment and discernment in using figures of speech. Merely knowing about stylistic devices will not lead to their effective use. One must also know when and how to use the devices at one's disposal. Thus, the discussions below of the various tools of eloquence cover not only their essential attributes, but also strategies for using them most effectively.

The third step in becoming a more eloquent writer is to practice. One cannot become proficient at employing an eloquent style merely by reading about it. One must practice the art. Exercises at the end of this chapter will allow you to use what you have learned.

## I.    DEFINING "FIGURES OF SPEECH": TROPES AND SCHEMES

Quintilian defined a figure of speech as "a form of speech artfully varied from

---

[1] Edward P. J. Corbett and Robert J. Conners, *Classical Rhetoric for the Modern Student* 378 (4th ed. 1999).

common usage."[2] Stated another way, figures of speech involve the use of language in an atypical way for the purposes of adding grace and emphasis to writing. Classical rhetoricians have traditionally divided figures of speech into two main groups: *tropes* and *schemes*. Tropes involve deviation in the *meaning or signification of words*. That is, a trope involves a writer using a word to mean something other than its traditional, ordinary meaning. A metaphor is a classic example of a trope. As we saw in Chapter 9, metaphors use words for their figurative or symbolic meanings, as opposed to their literal meanings. Other common tropes include simile (an explicit figurative comparison), hyperbole (a dramatic exaggeration), and personification (the attribution of human characteristics to animals or inanimate objects).

The term "schemes" refers to deviations in the *grammatical structure or arrangement of words*. In deploying a scheme, a writer arranges the words of a sentence in a way that differs from the ordinary or customary order of words. The figure of speech called *anastrophe* serves as a good example of a scheme. Anastrophe involves a writer inverting the customary order of words in a sentence for the purpose of achieving a rhetorical effect Consider, for example, the following line by poet Ogden Nash:

> How Sunday into Monday melts![3]

If the words of this sentence were arranged in typical grammatical fashion, the sentence would read: How Sunday melts into Monday! However, by employing anastrophe, that is, by intentionally inverting the verb "melts" and the prepositional phrase "into Monday," the poet was able to add flair and grace to his statement. Other common examples of schemes include alliteration (using words in close conjunction that begin with the same letter or sound) and parallelism (using similar grammatical structures in successive phrases or clauses).

Despite the efforts of classical rhetoricians to carefully subdivide figures of speech into tropes and schemes, we will not pursue those subclassifications in this chapter. Rather, we will combine them into one general discussion. While it is important that we explore the types of stylistic devices that are available to us as persuasive writers, it is not necessary for our purposes that we categorize the various figures of speech as either tropes or schemes.[4]

The reference to "anastrophe" in the foregoing discussion raises another topic that we should address from the outset. As this reference suggests, many of the figures of speech that we will be exploring have rather bizarre names (for the most part derived from Greek). In this chapter we will be exploring figures of speech that have names like *antonomasia*, *polysyndeton*, and *paralepsis*.

You need not memorize these names, nor even learn to pronounce them correctly.

---

[2] *Id.* at 379 (quoting Marius Fabius Quintilianus, *Institutio Oratoria* IX, i. II. (H. E. Butler trans. 1954)).

[3] Ogden Nash, Time Marches On, in *I'm a Stranger Here Myself* (1938).

[4] For an in-depth discussion of the differences between tropes and schemes, *see* Corbett and Conners, *supra* note 1, at 377-411.

These names are merely titles given to specific, identifiable stylistic devices. The titles themselves are not important. What is important is that the devices have titles, for these titles allow us to separate the devices and explore them more systematically. Thus, you should not be intimidated by the strange names given to the figures of speech discussed in this chapter. The names are merely reference labels. You should concentrate your efforts simply on understanding the nature and characteristics of the various devices to which these names refer.

## II.   FIGURES OF SPEECH EFFECTIVE IN PERSUASIVE LEGAL WRITING

### A.   *The Functions of Figures of Speech in Persuasive Legal Writing*

#### 1.   The Pathos Functions

In Chapter 6, we saw that one of the fundamental processes of persuasion recognized by classical rhetoricians is persuading through emotion. Classical rhetoricians call this process "pathos." We also saw that pathos actually involves two separate components: (1) persuading by arousing emotions in the reader as to the substance of the matter, called "emotional substance"; and (2) persuading by arousing a positive emotional reaction in the reader as to the way in which the document is written, called "medium mood control." Figures of speech are relevant to both of these aspects of pathos.

With regard to emotional substance, figures of speech can assist a writer in eliciting a strong emotional response from the reader. Figures of speech are primarily designed to add drama and emphasis to a discussion. While drama can be effective in connection with the discussion of arguments based on legal reasoning, drama is most effective in connection with the discussion of arguments based on emotional facts and policy—the essence of "emotional substance."

Eloquent language also helps to put a reader in a contented and receptive mood. As we discussed in Chapter 6, the concept of "medium mood control" refers to how a reader's emotions are affected by the medium of a message—that is, how the style with which a message is conveyed, as opposed to its substantive content, affects the reader. In that discussion, we saw that writers whose writing style can charm and captivate their readers have an advantage over writers whose style irritates or bores theirs. We also saw that one of the most effective ways that legal writers can positively affect their readers' moods is by writing with rhetorical flair. As Quintilian stated, "[R]hetorical ornament contributes not a little to the furtherance of our case . . . . For when our audience finds it a pleasure to listen, their attention and their readiness to believe what they hear are both alike increased, while they are generally filled with delight, and sometimes even transported by admiration."[5]

---

[5] III Marius Fabius Quintilianus, *Institutio Oratoria* 213 (H. E. Butler trans, 1954).

## 2.   The Ethos Function

In the quotation above, the great rhetorician Quintilian points out that eloquence has the ability to "delight" an audience and, perhaps, even to inspire "admiration" for the advocate. While the concept of arousing delight in an audience refers to the medium mood control function of eloquent language, the concept of inspiring admiration actually refers to a separate function: the ethos function.

In Chapters 6 though 8, we saw that ethos refers to the process of persuading by establishing credibility in the eyes of the audience. We also discussed briefly how eloquence in writing helps to improve the writer's credibility because it is a sign of intelligence, and decision-makers tend to put more trust in advocates they perceive to be intelligent. Thus, when Quintilian stated that eloquent language can inspire admiration, he was referring to its credibility-establishing function—its ethos function. Quintilian elaborated by offering the following insight into how eloquent language benefits not only the argument but also the arguer: "[B]y the employment of skillful ornament the [advocate] commends himself at the same time [that he commends his argument]."[6]

## 3.   Emphasis

One of the most fundamental functions of eloquent language is achieving emphasis. Because figures of speech involve unusual or atypical uses of language, they tend to draw readers' attention. Thus, as we will see below, many of the figures of speech are used when persuasive writers wish to emphasize and render more memorable specific important points in their discussions. An idea expressed with eloquence is more indelible than one expressed with lifeless language.

## 4.   Euphony and Rhythm

The effective use of figures of speech also helps writers control the rhythm of their writing. Although legal prose is more often meant to be read silently rather than aloud, rhythm is nevertheless important for legal writers.

"Euphony" is the term used to describe discussions that are pleasing to the ear; its opposite, "cacophony," describes harsh and discordant discussions. Classical rhetoricians have long recognized that the concepts of euphony, cacophony, and rhythm are not limited to verse and creative writing. They also influence the success of functional and serious prose, such as legal writing. A smooth rhythmic writing style allows readers to glide through discussions with less effort. A lack of rhythm, on the other hand, causes even silent readers to stumble and falter as they read.

Euphony and rhythm are achieved primarily though effective word choice and sentence structures and by varying sentence patterns. Figures of speech, however, also influence a discussion's rhythm. In this chapter, we will explore a number of stylistic devices that, in addition to their other rhetorical functions, can contribute significantly to the euphony and rhythm of legal prose.

---

[6] *Id.* at 211-13.

### 5.  Increasing Drama

Figures of speech also can help add drama to an argument or discussion. Drama can be effective in legal arguments if it is used selectively and strategically. As we will see, many figures of speech are specifically designed to increase the suspense and drama of a discussion.

## B.    *Caution: Do Not Overuse Figures of Speech in Persuasive Legal Writing*

In discussing individual figures of speech, we will explore relevant cautions and guidelines for their effective use in legal writing. However, one overriding caution must be stressed from the outset: Legal writers should not overuse figures of speech!

Having armed themselves with the arsenal of rhetorical devices set out in this chapter, some legal writers may be tempted to use them excessively. This temptation must be resisted. While the strategic use of stylistic devices can add grace and emphasis to specific points in a persuasive argument, the use of too many figures of speech undermines a writer's overall effectiveness in several ways. First, overuse of figures of speech undermines the writer's credibility as an intelligent source of information (that is, the process of ethos) by suggesting to readers that the writer lacks judgment in the strategic use of figurative language. Second, excessive use of flowery or melodramatic language is distracting and irritating to readers. At best, the reader will find such language laughable. At worst, the reader will see it as an effort to manipulate the reader. Either way, the excessive use of figures of speech negatively affects the "mood" of the reader and thereby undermines the process of pathos. Third, overuse of figures of speech undermines the logos process of persuasion by obscuring the argument's substance. Finally, excessive use of figures of speech undermines their function of drawing emphasis. Figures of speech are most effective in their function of creating emphasis when they are used surprisingly and unexpectedly. The use of numerous figures of speech dilutes the impact of each.

Remember that legal writing is not poetry, but serious, relatively conservative prose. Figurative language should be used selectively in legal writing, and always to achieve a specific, justifiable rhetorical effect.

## C.    *Exploring Specific Figures of Speech*

### 1.  Alliteration

*Alliteration* is most commonly defined as the use of two or more words in close proximity to each other that begin with (or prominently contain) the same letter sound. Alliteration contributes to the euphony of writing. Because of the sound repetition, alliterative writing flows smoothly and melodically. As a consequence, an idea written with alliteration often stands out in the mind of a reader. It is not surprising then that alliteration is very popular in verse—and in advertising—as indicated by the following examples.

> *First fight.* Then *fiddle.*

Gwendolyn Brooks, "First Fight. Then Fiddle"

Nature's first *green* is *gold*,
*Her hardest hue* to *hold*.

Robert Frost, "Nothing Gold Can Stay"

Nothing *comforts* your *cold* like *Kleenex ColdCare.*

Print advertisement for Kleenex tissues

Must "*B*" *Brummel* & *Brown.*

Print advertisement for Brummel & Brown dairy spread

Despite its popularity in verse and advertising, alliteration is often discouraged in prose. Many writing experts feel that alliteration is inappropriate in serious writing because of its conspicuously artistic nature. Nonetheless, alliteration can be used effectively in legal writing if it is used sparingly and strategically. The key to the effective use of alliteration in serious writing is to be sure it serves a purpose. Random or forced alliteration is not effective. The selective use of alliterative language to emphasize important points, however, can be appropriate and effective. Consider the following examples:

I have a dream my four little children will one day live in a nation where they will not be judged by the *color* of their skin but by the *content* of their *character.*

Martin Luther King, Jr., "I Have a Dream" (1963)

*So* let u*s* begin anew, remembering on both *sides* that *civility* is not a *sign* of weakne*ss*, and *sincerity* is alway*s* *subject* to proof.

John F. Kennedy, "Inaugural Address" (1961)

In these examples, Dr. King and President Kennedy used subtle alliteration to add force and emphasis to their points. Legal writers, too, can do the same. Consider this powerful, subtly alliterative statement by Judge Ann Williams:

It takes no great *leap* of *logic* to see that within the *cluster* of *constitutionally* protected *choices* that includes the right to have *access* to *contraceptives*, there must be *included* within that *cluster* the right to submit to a medical procedure that may *bring about*, rather than *prevent*, *pregnancy.*

Williams, J., in *Lifchez v. Hartigan*, 735 F. Supp. 1361, 1377 (N.D. Ill. 1990).

Alliteration in legal writing, however, need not be so subtle. More conspicuous alliteration can be used effectively in legal writing as long as (1) it is used sparingly, and (2) it is used strategically to emphasize an important point. Consider the following more obvious uses of alliteration by legal writers:

[E]very *bequest* is *but* a *bounty*, and a *bounty* must be taken as it is given.

> Johnson, J., in *Hunter v. Bryant*, 15 U.S. 32, 37 (1817).

*Crime* is *contagious*.

> Brandeis, J., in *Olmstead v. United States*, 277 U.S. 438, 485 (1928).

*Courts* do not weary of *cautioning counsel* to *distinguish dictum* from *decision*.

> Cardozo, J., in *Smith v. Hedges*, 223 N.Y. 176, 184 (1918).

The *life* of the *law* has not been *logic*; it has been experience.

> Oliver Wendell Holmes, *The Common Law* 5 (1881).

The case before us . . . is so unique that it is without *precedent* and it is likely to be without *progeny*.

> Jackson, J., in *Western Pac. R.R. Corp. v. Western Pac. R.R. Corp.*, 345 U.S. 247, 275 (1953).

*Proof* implies *persuasion*.

> Brandeis, J., in *St. Louis & O'Fallon Ry. Co. v. United States*, 279 U.S. 461, 492 (1929).

When *suspicion* is *suggested*, it is *easily entertained*.

> Holmes, J., in *United States v. Clark,*, 200 U.S. 601, 609 (1906).

Moral *turpitude* is not a *touchstone* of *taxability*.

> Murphy, J., in *Commissioner of Int. Rev. v. Wilcox*, 327 U.S. 404, 408 (1946).

In the foregoing examples, the writers' use of alliteration is more obvious than in the previous examples. Nevertheless, the alliteration is effective because it is used intentionally and strategically to emphasize important ideas in the writers' discussions. Compare these examples to the following alliterative passages by Judge H. Sol Clark, Georgia Court of Appeals, a self-confessed "alliteration addict."[7]

> Having received from my colleagues freedom of expression, a *privilege* cherished because of a *personal penchant* for *prolix prose*, I add these views to my concurrence.
>
> > *Cunningham v. State*, 205 S.E.2d 899, 899 (Ga. Ct. App. 1974) (Clark, J., concurring).

> We have *scrupulously scrutinized, scanned*, and *searched*, followed by additional efforts in which we *relentlessly reviewed, retrospected, re-examined* and *recapitulated* the 121 pages of *record*. All our efforts were

---

[7] *Brown v. Hilton Hotels Corp.*, 211 S.E.2d 125, 126 n.1 (Ga. Ct. App. 1974).

to no avail.

*Lowe v. Payne*, 203 S.E.2d 309, 311 (Ga. Ct. App. 1973).

*Personal prefatory pensive ponderings*, such as the foregoing, recognizably *play partial part* in this court's eventual decision.

*Kingston Dev. Co. v. Kenerly*, 208 S.E.2d 118, 119 (Ga. Ct. App. 1974).

"No Room At The Inn." *Titled thusly, this tristful tale takes this tribunal* into deciding if the alleged failure of the Hilton Hotels Corp. to provide plaintiffs with a hotel room pursuant to a guaranteed reservation constitutes a breach of contract or a tort arising out of a contract.

*Brown v. Hilton Hotels Corp.*, 211 S.E.2d 125, 126 (Ga. Ct. App. 1974).

Judge Clark's light-hearted use of alliteration in these passages is not recommended for legal advocates. For one thing, such overly conspicuous alliterative passages can strike readers as forced and contrived. Moreover, the alliteration in these passages serves minimal rhetorical functions because it is used randomly in connection with nonessential ideas rather than to draw attention to central concepts in the discussions. While Judge Clark—with a guaranteed audience—may be able to get away with such mock-serious uses of alliteration, lawyers must be more selective and strategic in their use of this device.

### 2.  Allusion

In broad terms, "allusion" is any casual, subtle, or indirect reference to a person, idea, or event "which, it is assumed, is 'embalmed in the deepest memory of all educated minds.'"[8] As a stylistic device, however, allusion refers to any such casual or subtle reference that can be considered clever or innovative.

The most common type of allusion in legal writing is *literary allusion*, discussed in detail in Chapters 2 through 5. We also examined the concept of *internal allusion* in connection with our discussion of metaphors in Chapter 9. Here is another example of clever allusion in persuasive writing:

> Fivescore years ago, a great American, in whose symbolic shadow we stand today, signed the Emancipation Proclamation.

Martin Luther King, Jr., "I Have a Dream" (1963)

While Reverend King makes direct reference to Abraham Lincoln as the signer of the Emancipation Proclamation, he also includes a clever allusion to President Lincoln by his words "fivescore years ago." This archaic phrasing is an allusion to President Lincoln's Gettysburg Address, which begins with the famous words, "Fourscore and seven years ago . . . ".

Obviously, for an allusion in persuasive writing to be effective, it must be clear

---

[8] *Encyclopedia of English* 351 (Arthur Zeiger ed. 1959).

to the reader. Vague or arcane allusions will only confuse readers; overly subtle allusions serve no function at all.

### 3.   Anastrophe

Anastrophe, also called inversion, occurs when the words of a sentence are deliberately inverted and placed out of their natural or usual order. Arthur Zeiger offers the following examples of anastrophe in everyday speech: "Right you are," "The house beautiful," and "Gone are the days."[9] The following are more formal examples, first from poetry and then from legal writing.

> How Sunday into Monday melts!
>
> > Ogden Nash, "Time Marches On," in *I'm a Stranger Here Myself* (1938).

> Forgiveness to the injured does belong.
>
> > John Dryden, "The Conquest of Granada"

> Unblemished let me live, or die unknown.
>
> > Alexander Pope, *The Temple of Fame*

> How the Court arrived at that conclusion I know not, am unable to discern, and will never understand.
>
> > Bistline, J., in *Hudson v. Cobbs*, 797 P.2d 1322, 1362 (Idaho 1990) (Bistline, J., dissenting).

> [T]here appears to be only one conspirator, and one conspirator does not a conspiracy make.
>
> > Duff, J., in *Bertoncini v. Schrimpf*, 712 F. Supp. 1336, 1342 (N.D. Ill. 1989).

> Ungenerous and unwise such discrimination may be. It is not for that reason unlawful.
>
> > Cardozo, J., in *People v. Crane*, 214 N.Y. 154, 161 (1915).

> Not lightly vacated is the verdict of quiescent years.
>
> > Cardozo, J., in *Coler v. Corn Exchange Bank*, 250 N.Y. 136, 141 (1928).

Anastrophe is a classic example of rhetorical style. Here the customary rules of grammar are intentionally broken to achieve emphasis. Anastrophe only works, of course, if the writer has otherwise used good grammar in his or her work. If a writer has not established credibility as to his or her general grammatical skills, an attempt at anastrophe will come off simply as shoddy writing. As with many stylistic devices, the power of anastrophe comes from mastering the customary rules of grammar and

---

[9] *Id.* at 345.

consciously (and infrequently!) breaking them for effect.

### 4.   Antithesis

Stated broadly, antithesis is achieved when two contrasting ideas are juxtaposed in a discussion. However, while the juxtaposition of any two contrasting ideas would technically be antithesis, we are concerned most with those incidences where the two contrasting ideas are set out side-by-side in parallel structure. It is this form of antithesis that has been long recognized as a powerful stylistic device.

> We know what we are, but know not what we may be.
>
> William Shakespeare, *Hamlet* act 4, sc. 5.

> That's one small step for man, one giant leap for mankind.
>
> Neil Armstrong, taking his first step as the first man to walk on the moon

> If a free society cannot help the many who are poor, it cannot save the few that are rich.
>
> John F. Kennedy, "Inaugural Address" (1961)

> The right to be heard does not automatically include the right to be taken seriously.
>
> Hubert H. Humphrey, speech to the National Student Association, Madison, Wisconsin, August 23, 1965

> Yesterday is not ours to recover, but tomorrow is ours to win or to lose.
>
> Lyndon B. Johnson, "Address to the Nation," November 28, 1963

> The law is not the place for the artist or the poet. The law is the calling of thinkers.
>
> Oliver Wendell Holmes, *Speeches* 22-23 (1934).

> He read to learn, and not to quote; to digest and master, and not to merely display.
>
> Joseph Story, *Story's Miscellaneous Writings* 206 (1835).

> [T]he law does all that is needed when it does all that it can.
>
> Holmes, J., in *Buck v. Bell*, 274 U.S. 200, 208 (1927).

> The act of hanging a criminal is executive; but to say when and where and how he shall be hanged is clearly legislative.
>
> McReynolds, J., in *Myers v. United States*, 272 U.S. 52, 186 (1926) (McReynolds, J., dissenting).

> Whenever equality is the theme, men live together in peace. Whenever inequality is the practice, grievances and complaints fester.
>
> William O. Douglas, *We the Judges* 425 (1956).

> To those who practice economy, a given sum will afford comfort, while to those of contrary habit the same sum will be wholly inadequate.
>
> Sutherland, J., in *Adkins v. Children's Hospital*, 261 U.S. 525, 555 (1923).

> Renunciation of one home is not sufficient without the acquisition of another.
>
> Cardozo, J., in *In re Blankford*, 241 N.Y. 180, 183 (1925).

As these examples show, antithesis provides a powerful tool for achieving emphasis. Many of the above quotations even attain an aphoristic quality. The power of these statements comes from antithesis' three main characteristics: (1) the presentation of contrasting ideas; (2) the presentation of these ideas side-by-side (either in one sentence or in successive sentences); and (3) the use of similar wording and parallel grammatical structure in the presentation of the two ideas.

### 5.  Antonomasia

Antonomasia occurs when a proper name is used in place of a common word to represent a quality associated with the name. Examples of antonomasia in everyday speech include using the name "Benedict Arnold" for "traitor" or "Einstein" for "genius." The following are more formal examples.

> A defendant is not entitled to representation by a "modern-day *Clarence Darrow*"—mere competence will suffice.
>
> Mordue, J., in *United States v. Barbour*, No. 00-CR-267, 2001 WL 636937, at *10 (N.D.N.Y. June 6, 2001).

> Unless [the suspect] were either an acrobat or a *Houdini*, . . . we cannot conceive how the closet could have fallen within the area of her immediate control.
>
> Kaufman, J. in *United States v. Mapp*, 476 F.2d 67, 80 (2d Cir. 1973).

### 6.  Aporia

Aporia occurs when a writer states that it is difficult to determine where to begin or what to do in light of the magnitude of a task. Aporia is intended to attract the reader's attention and establish a dramatic tone for the ensuing discussion.

> *It is difficult to know where to begin* to analyze such a truly extraordinary assertion respecting the operation of the judicial process.
>
> Harlan, J., in *United States v. White*, 401 U.S. 745, 793 (1971) (Harlan, J., dissenting).

There are so many weaknesses in this argument that *it is difficult to know where to begin.*

> Shabaz, J., in *Voie v. Flood*, 589 F. Supp. 746, 749 (W.D. Wis. 1984).

*All that can be said is that the Court is at a loss for words* to describe the profound foolishness of this argument.

> Batts, J., in *T.B.I. Indust. Corp. v. Emery Worldwide*, No. 94-CIV-1505, 1995 WL 753896, at *1 (S.D.N.Y. Dec. 18, 1995).

Because of its overly obvious, dramatic, and—often—critical nature, aporia should be used only rarely, if at all, in legal writing. If aporia is employed, the ensuing discussion should be of such a magnitude of complexity as to justify the writer's hesitation. Feigned or unworthy aporia can irreparably damage a writer's credibility.

## 7.  Apostrophe

Apostrophe is employed when a writer turns away from the regular course of the discussion to address an "absent person or a personified abstraction."[10]

Ah Fortune, what god is more cruel to us than thou! How thou delightest ever to make sport of human life!

> Horace, *Satires*

Equity, oh Equity, the fairest flower in the judicial garden, where art thou?

> Steffen, J., in *Elliott v. Denton & Denton*, 860 P.2d 725, 728 (Nev. 1993) (Steffen, J., dissenting).

Send well to this Court, in all good time, the courage and the wisdom with which to confess the error of today's myopic majority.

> Black, J., in *Fritts v. Krugh*, 92 N.W.2d 604, 618 (Mich. 1958) (Black, J., dissenting) (presumably speaking to some omniscient force or power).

As these examples show, apostrophe is extremely dramatic. In fact, it is probably too dramatic for legal writing. Even Justice Steffen, in the example from *Elliott v. Denton* above, felt obliged to apologize for his use of apostrophe. After making this plea to Equity, Justice Steffen stated, "Hopefully, my colleagues and others who may stumble across this dissent, will overlook my inability to resist a brief sojourn into the world of drama."[11] Lawyers, therefore, would probably be better off leaving apostrophe to the worlds of drama and poetry.

---

[10] Corbett and Conners, *supra* note 1, at 402.

[11] *Elliot*, 860 P.2d at 728 (Steffen, J., dissenting).

### 8.  Bulk

Bulk involves matching one's composition style with the substantive idea being expressed. Most commonly, a writer employs the device of bulk when he or she matches the size or importance of a substantive concept with a "commensurate use of words."[12] For example, in connection with stating that something is small or insignificant, a writer may use small words and short sentences and paragraphs. Contrastingly, in connection with stating that something is large or awkward, a writer may use long paragraphs, large words, and perhaps even somewhat clumsy sentence structures. The matching of word length and sentence structure with the substantive idea that the words convey can be a subtle yet effective stylistic device.

### 9.  Conjunction Deviation

Classical rhetoricians have long recognized that writers can achieve emphasis, drama, and rhythm by altering the traditional use of conjunctions. Conjunction deviations fall into two general categories: *asyndeton* and *polysyndeton*.

**a. Asyndeton.** Asyndeton is the deliberate *omission* of conjunctions between words or phrases in a series.

> *The energy, the faith, the devotion* which we bring to this endeavor will light our country and all who serve it, and the glow from that fire can truly light the world.
>
> John F. Kennedy, "Inaugural Address" (1961)

> *The book, the speech, the pamphlet* open new horizons for people.
>
> William O. Douglas, *We the Judges* 321 (1956).

> We are today one people, with *one flag, one political creed, one loyalty.*
>
> William O. Douglas, *We the Judges* 17 (1956).

> *Private citizens, private clubs, private groups* may make such deductions and reach such conclusions as they choose from the failure of a citizen to disclose *his beliefs, his philosophy, his associates.* But government has no business penalizing a citizen merely for his beliefs or associations.
>
> Douglas, J., in *Lerner v. Casey*, 357 U.S. 399, 414 (1958) (Douglas, J., dissenting).

> By means of food preserved in a compact and nutritious form, protected from its natural tendency to decay, *deserts are traversed, seas navigated, distant regions explored.* It is less brilliant, but more useful, than all the inventions for the destruction of the human race that have ever been known.
>
> Hunt, J., in *Sewall v. Jones*, 91 U.S. 171, 187 (1875).

---

[12] *Encyclopedia of English*, *supra* note 8, at 353.

**b. Polysyndeton.** The opposite of asyndeton, polysyndeton involves an excessive use of conjunctions.

> *And* God said, "Let there be light," *and* there was light. *And* God saw that the light was good, *and* he separated the light from the darkness. God called the light "day," *and* the darkness he called "night." *And* there was evening, *and* there was morning—the first day.
>
> *Genesis* I:3-5.

> All this will not be finished in the first one hundred days. *Nor* will it be finished in the first one thousand days, *nor* in the life of this Administration, *nor* even perhaps in our lifetime on this planet. But let us begin.
>
> John F. Kennedy, "Inaugural Address" (1961)

> Neither snow, *nor* rain, *nor* heat, *nor* gloom of night stays these couriers from the swift completion of their appointed rounds.
>
> Postal Pledge

> Logic, *and* history, *and* custom, *and* utility, *and* the accepted standards of right conduct, are the forces which singly or in combination shape the progress of the law.
>
> Benjamin N. Cardozo, *The Nature of the Judicial Process* 112 (1921).

Asyndeton and polysyndeton are employed primarily to control rhythm of prose. Asyndeton produces a somewhat hurried rhythm. In fact, asyndenton is often used to quicken the rhythm of a dramatic passage that is building toward a crescendo. Polysyndeton, on the other hand, produces a slower rhythm. Moreover, when the items in a series are separated by conjunctions as with polysyndeton, the reader is forced to focus more attention on each separate item in the series. This is less true with the hurried rhythm created by the omission of conjunctions.

## 10. Correction

The device of correction emphasizes by calling a statement back and replacing it with another.

> Racist, sexist, and homophobic thoughts cannot, alas, be abolished by fiat but only by the time-honored methods of persuasion, education and *exposure to the other guy's—or excuse me, woman's*—point of view.
>
> Barbara Ehrenreich, "Teach Diversity with a Smile," *Time,* April 8, 1991.

> No man is allowed to be a judge in his own cause, because his interest would certainly bias his judgment, and, not improbably, corrupt his integrity. *With equal, nay with greater reason,* a body of men are unfit to be both judges and parties at the same time.
>
>             Ginsburg, J., in *Gutierrez de Martinez v. Lamagno*, 515 U.S. 417, 428 (1995) (quoting The Federalist No. 10, p. 79 (C. Rossiter ed. 1961)).

> *I view with dismay the action—or should I say the inaction—*of my respected colleagues in the matter before us.
>
>             Corbin, J., in *Simpson v. Pulaski County Circuit Court*, 899 S.W.2d 50, 52 (Ark. 1995) (Corbin, J., dissenting).

> I assume that a state could not forbid divorce . . . , or limit married couples to two children, or forbid such couples to have sexual intercourse more than twice a month, or, coming a bit closer to the present case, require parents to live apart, or to send their children to boarding school. Such regulations would be held to violate equal protection or due process or both. But that is far from saying that *every state rule—more, every interpretation, every application, of every such rule—*that could be thought to interfere *with the family, or rather with a particular family*, is subject to fish-eyed scrutiny by federal judges applying a vague norm of reasonableness.
>
>             Posner, J., in *Crane v. Indiana High School Athletic Ass'n*, 975 F.2d 1315, 1327 (7th Cir. 1992) (Posner, J., dissenting) (citation omitted) (employing correction twice in one sentence!).

As these illustrations indicate, writers using correction make a statement only to quickly amend it—usually by restating it more forcefully. When correction has been used by a writer we know it has been used intentionally because the writer, in the editing process, could have simply deleted the imprecise expression and substituted the more correct phrasing. By intentionally keeping (or calculatingly inserting!) the imprecise phrase and displaying the correction, writers show the reader not only what they mean, but also what they do not mean. It also demonstrates that the writer chose his or her words carefully and feels strongly about their precision of meaning. As a consequence, the corrected expression receives greater emphasis and is highlighted for the reader.

## 11. Ellipsis

Ellipsis occurs when words otherwise necessary for the complete grammatical construction of a sentence are intentionally omitted, without undermining the sentence's coherence. Consider the following example by Benjamin Franklin:

> Laws too gentle are seldom obeyed; too severe, seldom executed.
>
>         Benjamin Franklin, *Poor Richard's Almanac*

If this sentence had been written without ellipsis, it would have read "Laws too gentle are seldom obeyed; laws too severe are seldom executed." The original as written by

Benjamin Franklin, however, omitted the words *laws* and *are* from the second clause. Nevertheless, the meaning of the statement is not lost because these omitted words are implied by the first clause.

As suggested by this illustration, ellipsis is most commonly achieved by creating a sentence with two parallel clauses and then omitting language from the second clause. The structure of the first clause supplies a context for the second and, as such, implies the omitted words. Here are a few more examples:

> To err is human, *to forgive divine.*
>
> Alexander Pope, "An Essay on Criticism"

> Fire is the test of gold; *adversity, of strong men.*
>
> Seneca, *On Providence*

> Mystery magnifies danger as *the fog the sun.*
>
> Charles Caleb Colton, *Lacon* (This statement includes both ellipsis and simile.)

> While such evidence may indicate that the Plaintiff himself was the victim of some form of discrimination, one thread does not a pattern make, nor *one incident a custom.*
>
> Van Antwerpen, J., in *Wentling v. Honey Brook Township*, No. Civ.A. 96-8569, 1998 WL 103184, at *9 (E.D. Pa. Feb. 27, 1998). (This statement includes not only ellipsis, but also metaphor and anastrophe.)

> [T]he drink characterizes the name as much as *the name the drink.*
>
> Holmes, J., in *Coca-Cola Co. v. Koke Co. of Am.*, 254 U.S. 143, 146 (1920).

Ellipsis is designed to add emphasis and drama. Ellipsis is similar to *anastrophe* (the deliberate inversion of words in a sentence) in that they both intentionally break grammatical rules to achieve emphasis. It follows then that ellipsis also resembles anastrophe in that it must be used sparingly, and only by writers who otherwise demonstrate a mastery of grammar.

## 12. Hyperbole

Hyperbole—the deliberate use of exaggeration—is so common in everyday communication that it hardly needs an elaborate explanation here. In fact, most people engage in, or at least encounter, hyperbole on a daily basis. When we say, "I gain 100 pounds over the holidays" or "I'm so hungry I could eat a horse," we are engaging in hyperbole. Here are a few more formal examples:

> I was the senior associate in an office led by former Judge Frank S. Righeimer, who made General Patton appear to be a pastry cook.
>
> Thomas A. Foran, Eulogy at Memorial Service for Judge Robert E. Wiss (October 30, 1995) reported at 45 M.J. 29 (1995).

The air was so damp that fish could have come in through the doors and swum out the windows, floating through the atmosphere in the rooms.

Gabriel Garcia Marquez, *One Hundred Years of Solitude*

If his IQ slips any lower, we'll have to water him twice a day.

Molly Ivans, *Molly Ivans Can't Say That, Can She?*

Although hyperbole is commonly used in everyday speech, it is not recommended in persuasive legal writing. Lawyers are required to be precise, credible, and professional. The exaggeration of hyperbole is inconsistent with these traits. In fact, countless examples exist of courts specifically criticizing lawyers or other judges for engaging in hyperbole. Legal writers would be well advised to avoid hyperbole and to use other methods to add emphasis to their writing.

### 13. Irony

Irony occurs when the intended meaning of a statement is the opposite of its literal meaning. Like hyperbole, irony is very common in everyday conversation. Consider, for example, a person who steps inside from a blizzard and remarks, "Nice weather." This person's statement is irony because, by saying "Nice weather," the person is actually saying that the weather is anything but "nice." The same would be true of a hungry diner who stares at a minuscule portion of food on a plate in a fancy restaurant and says, "I couldn't possibly eat all that." Both of these statements are examples of irony because the people uttering them are communicating ideas that are the complete opposite of a literal translation of the words stated.

Irony, although common, is a fairly sophisticated communication device. Only with a full understanding of the context in which the ironic statement is made can we know that an opposite, rather than a literal, meaning is intended. And the complications only increase with *written* irony. In the above examples of verbal irony, hearers of these statements would have at their disposal the physical context of the statements, the history of the events leading up to the statements, as well as the speakers' facial expressions and voice intonations. All of these provide a context that allows the hearers to appreciate the ironic nature of the statements. It is much more difficult, however, to provide an accurate context with written irony.

For this reason, irony is not recommended for legal writing. Legal writing should be precise and direct. Irony is too oblique and leaves too much room for miscommunication and misunderstanding. Furthermore, irony typically has a sardonic or sarcastic tone, which is inconsistent with the professional tone required of legal writers. Accordingly, while legal writers should be familiar with irony, they should not attempt to employ it in their professional writing.

### 14. Litotes

Litotes is similar to hyperbole, which we discussed earlier. Whereas hyperbole is a deliberate exaggeration, litotes is deliberate *understatement*.[13] Also like hyperbole, litotes has worked its way into everyday conversation:

He is no rocket scientist.

> Referring to someone of questionable intelligence.

Michael Jordan he's not.

> Referring to someone with questionable athletic skills (and also using anastrophe (inversion)).

She is no dummy.

> Referring to someone who is quite bright or, more narrowly, to someone who recently made an intelligent choice.

I believe we made a little money on that deal.

> Referring to a business transaction that was quite lucrative.

The understatement of litotes is used, not to deceive, but to draw emphasis to what is said. When we say "she is no dummy," for example, we are actually emphasizing that the subject of our statement is quite smart. And while the exaggeration of hyperbole is disfavored in legal writing, litotes is less risky. Whereas exaggeration and overstatement could be viewed by a reader as efforts to deceive or manipulate, the understatement of litotes is not as controversial or as prone to abuse. Nevertheless, litotes is arguably inconsistent with the direct and precise nature of legal writing. Thus, if a legal writer uses litotes, it should be used selectively and with careful consideration of how it will be received by the reader.

## 15. Metonymy

Metonymy involves referring to a thing, not by its literal name, but by a word suggestive of or associated with it.[14] Many examples of metonymy exist in everyday speech: "the pen" for "writing," "the bottle" for "alcoholic drinks," "the cloth" for "the clergy," "bread" for "food in general," "mouths" for "people to feed," "roofs" for "houses," and so on. Consider the following formal illustrations:

---

[13] Some rhetoricians limit litotes to those incidences in which understatement is achieved by the use of negatives (e.g., "He is no rocket scientist."). These rhetoricians call understatement not achieved by negatives **meiosis** (e.g., "I believe we made a little money on that deal."). This distinction, however, is losing its significance. Thus, referring to litotes as "[u]nderstatement, whether or not effected by negatives . . . is probably the more widely accepted sense of the word." *Encyclopedia of English, supra* note 8, at 357.

[14] Some rhetoricians distinguish between metonymy and the related figure of speech **synechdoche**. The difference between the two is minor, however, and distinguishing the two and discussing them separately can confuse. Thus, the concepts represented by these two figures are here combined and discussed together under the single heading "metonymy."

The *pen* is mightier than the *sword*.

Edward George Bulwer-Lytton, *Richelieu*, act II, sc. ii

Over the *bottle* many a friend is found.

Yiddish Proverb

Those that live by *bread* alone will submit, for the sake of it, to the vilest abuse, like a hungry dog.

Jami, "The Dog and the Loaf of Bread," in *Baharistan*

[T]he First Amendment . . . presupposes that right conclusions are more likely to be gathered out of a multitude of *tongues*, than through any kind of authoritative selection.

Hand, J., in *United States v. Associated Press*, 52 F. Supp. 362, 372 (S.D.N.Y. 1943).

The corporation was but a passive purchaser of goods emanating from the Orient, and the totality of its contacts with and within Hong Kong were purely ancillary to that role. Its brushes with the colony were not of a "continuous and systematic nature." There was no rational basis upon which [the corporation] could have expected to be haled into court on those *distant shores*.

Selya, J., in *Oman Int'l Fin. Ltd. v. Hoiyong Gems Corp.*, 616 F. Supp. 351, 359 (D.R.I. 1985) (citations omitted).

It can hardly be argued that either students or teachers shed their constitutional rights to freedom of speech or expression *at the schoolhouse gate*.

Fortas, J., in *Tinker v. Des Moines Indep. Community School Dist.*, 393 U.S. 503, 506 (1969).

In the example above by Judge Hand, he uses the word "tongues" to represent the more general concept of "people talking." Similarly, Judge Selya uses the words "distant shores" to mean "foreign countries," and Justice Fortas uses "schoolhouse gate" to represent "school property." As these examples illustrate, metonymy is an effective yet relatively simple device for adding artistic flair to one's writing.

### 16. Paralepsis

Paralepsis involves emphasizing something by pretending to pass it over. As Arthur Zeiger explains, paralepsis is a "pretended suppression that really emphasizes what it pretends to pass by."[15] Consider this example:

---

[15] *Encyclopedia of English*, *supra* note 8, at 359.

> [H]is testimony is frequently contradictory and whimsical, *to say nothing of his outright admission of perjury.*
>
> Downey, J., in Vlacich v. State, 536 So.2d 1173, 1175 (Fla. Dist. Ct. App. 1989).

In this excerpt, the writer emphasizes that the defendant in the case, in addition to giving contradictory and whimsical evidence, expressly admitted to committing perjury. The writer emphasizes this point by falsely and calculatingly stating that he is going "to say nothing" of the admission of perjury. This is the essence of paralepsis. Writers draw attention to a concept by stating their intention not to discuss it. Consider these additional examples:

> In sum, there simply is very little showing, *to say nothing of* the "clearest proof" required by *Ward,* that OCC money penalties and debarment sanctions are criminal.
>
> Rehnquist, J., in Hudson v. United States, 522 U.S. 93, 105 (1997).

> [W]here the applicability—*not to mention* the validity—of that theory is far from clear, the temptation to make order out of chaos at any cost should be resisted.
>
> O'Connor, J., in Commissioner of Int. Rev. v. Estate of Hubert, 520 U.S. 93, 112 (1997) (O'Connor, J., concurring).

> Needless to say, such a rule would place considerable constraint upon religious speech, *not to mention* that it would be ridiculous.
>
> Scalia, J., in Capitol Square Review and Advisory Bd. v. Pinette, 515 U.S. 753, 769 (1995).

> Today, four years and countless millions in damages and attorney's fees later (*not to mention* prison sentences under the criminal provisions of RICO), the Court does little more than repromulgate . . . hints as to what RICO means.
>
> Scalia, J., in H.J. Inc. v. Northwestern Bell Telephone Co., 492 U.S. 229, 251 (1989) (Scalia, J., concurring).

As these examples show, paralepsis is a fairly limited and narrow stylistic device. Furthermore, the phrases typically associated with paralepsis —"not to mention" and "to say nothing of"—have become so common in everyday speech that they retain very little emphatic power.

## 17. Personification

Personification involves ascribing human qualities to animals, inanimate objects, or abstractions.

> April
> Comes like an idiot, babbling and strewing flowers.
>
> Edna St. Vincent Millay, "Spring," in Second April

Wisdom, I know is social. She seeks her fellows, but Beauty is jealous, and illy bears the presence of a rival.

> Thomas Jefferson, "Letter to Abigail Adams" (September 25, 1785)

Truth always lags last, limping along on the arm of Time.

> Baltasar Gracian, *The Art of Worldly Wisdom* 146 (Joseph Jacobs, trans.)

Truth looks tawdry when she is overdressed.

> Rabindranath Tagore, *The Cycle of Spring* (1915)

Justice should remove the bandage from her eyes long enough to distinguish between the vicious and the unfortunate.

> Robert G. Ingersoll, *Prose-Poems and Selections* (1884)

[J]ustice is not to be taken by storm. She is to be wooed by slow advances.

> Benjamin Cardozo, *The Growth of the Law* 133 (1924).

Our Constitution is color-blind.

> Harlan, J., in *Plessy v. Ferguson*, 163 U.S. 537, 559 (1896).

As these illustrations demonstrate, personification is often very dramatic. Thus, it should be used sparingly in legal writing, and only when the writer wants to elicit an emotional reaction in the reader.

## 18. Puns

Puns are witty plays on words. Consider the following examples from advertising:

Why should you get her book? Simple. She has an incredibly *fertile* mind.

> Print advertisement for *Jane Pepper's Garden*, a book on gardening

Here's *Eye-Opening* News.

> Print advertisement for Centrum multivitamin for healthy eyes

Good things come in *Giant* packages.

> Print advertisement for Green Giant frozen vegetables

Dinner's *in the bag*.

> Print advertisement for Reynolds Oven Bags

Rhetoricians have identified and labeled a number of different types of puns.[16] We, however, will not take the time to explore them, for puns of any kind are inappropriate in persuasive legal writing. When a lawyer writes a persuasive document on behalf of a client, serious matters are at stake. A professional legal advocate should not mock or make light of the situation by employing puns, no matter how witty. In Chapter 9, we discussed how humorous metaphors can undermine a legal writer's credibility (ethos). The same is true of puns. Legal writers who use puns in persuasive writing unwisely project self-indulgence and insensitivity.[17]

### 19. Repetition

Repetition is of inestimable value when seeking to emphasize key points in an argument. Rhetoricians have identified a number of forms of this popular strategy, four of which we will explore here.

**a. Anadiplosis.** Anadiplosis is the use of the same word or phrase at the end of one clause and at the beginning of the subsequent clause.

Still he sought for *fame—fame*, that last infirmity of a noble mind.

> John Milton, "Lycidas"

Those who won our independence . . . valued liberty both as an end and as a means. They believed liberty to be the secret of happiness and courage to be the secret of liberty. They believed that freedom to think as you will and to speak as you think are means indispensable to the discovery and spread of political truth; that without free speech and assembly discussion would be futile; that with them, discussion affords ordinarily adequate protection against the dissemination of noxious doctrine; that the greatest menace to freedom is an inert people; that public discussion is a political duty; and that this should be a fundamental principle of the American government. They recognized the risks to which all human institutions are subject. But they knew that order cannot be secured merely through fear of punishment for its infraction; that it is hazardous to discourage thought, hope and imagination; *that fear breeds repression; that repression breeds hate; that hate menaces stable government;* that the path of safety lies in the opportunity to discuss freely supposed grievances and proposed remedies; and that the fitting remedy for evil counsels is good ones.

> Brandeis, J., in *Whitney v. California*, 274 U.S. 357, 375 (1927) (Brandeis, J., concurring).

---

[16] *See, e.g.,* Corbett and Conners, *supra* note 1, at 398-400.

[17] As Bryan A. Garner points out, puns are more acceptable in law-review articles and other *scholarly* legal writing. *See* Bryan A. Garner, *The Elements of Legal Style* 155-57 (1991). Here, however, we focus on persuasive writing done in the context of representing a client. When writing on behalf of a client, legal practitioners should not use puns or other devices that evoke a humorous tone.

**b. Anaphora.** In anaphora, writers use the same word or group of words at the beginning of successive clauses.

A young man is *so* strong, *so* mad, *so* certain, and *so* lost. He has everything and he is able to use nothing.

Thomas Wolfe, *Of Time and the River* 51 (1935).

*Now is the time* to make real the promises of democracy; *now is the time* to rise from the dark and desolate valley of segregation to the sunlit path of racial justice; *now is the time* to lift our nation from the quicksands of racial injustice to the solid rock of brotherhood; *now is the time* to make justice a reality for all God's children.

Martin Luther King, Jr., "I Have a Dream" (1963)

We are today *one* people, with *one* flag, *one* political creed, *one* loyalty.

William O. Douglas, *We the Judges* 17 (1956).

There is a tide in the affairs *of* nations, *of* parties, and *of* individuals.

John Marshall, quoted in II Albert J. Beveridge, *The Life of John Marshall* 515 (1916).

**c. Antimetibole.** Antimetibole involves the immediate repetition of a clause but in reverse or inverted order.

And so, my fellow Americans, ask not what your country can do for you; ask what you can do for your country.

John F. Kennedy, "Inaugural Address" (1961)

Let us never negotiate out of fear, but let us never fear to negotiate.

John F. Kennedy, "Inaugural Address" (1961)

Government can easily exist without law, but law cannot exist without government.

Bertrand Russell, "Ideas That Have Helped Mankind" in *Unpopular Essays* (1950).

Suit the action to the word, the word to the action.

William Shakespeare, *Hamlet* act III, sc 2. (This quote also employs ellipsis.)

Man is not the creature of circumstances. Circumstances are the creatures of men.

Benjamin Disraeli, *Vivian Grey* 6.7 (1826).

We are not final because we are infallible, but we are infallible only because we are final.

Jackson, J., in *Brown v. Allen*, 344 U.S. 443, 540 (1953) (Jackson, J., concurring).

**d. Epistrophe.** In epistrophe, the writer uses the same word or group of words at the end of successive clauses.

... and that government of *the people*, by *the people*, for *the people*, shall not perish from the earth.

Abraham Lincoln, "The Gettysburg Address" (1863)

The old believe *everything*, the middle-aged suspect *everything*, the young know *everything*.

Oscar Wilde, "Phrases and Philosophies for the Use of the Young" (1891)

With this faith we will be able to work *together,* to pray *together,* to struggle *together,* to go to jail *together,* to stand up for freedom *together*, knowing that we will be free one day.

Martin Luther King, Jr., "I Have a Dream" (1963)

## 20. Rhetorical Question

A rhetorical question is a question asked by a writer with regard to which there is no hope or expectation of an answer from the reader. It is a question asked for effect, not to elicit an answer from the reader. There are actually two types of rhetorical questions: transitional rhetorical questions and substantive rhetorical questions.

**a. Transitional Rhetorical Questions.** A transitional rhetorical question occurs when a writer uses a self-posed question to set up an immediate answer or to transition to a new point of discussion. That is, the writer asks a question simply to set up an ensuing discussion.

What are the great objects of all free governments? They are, the protection and preservation of the personal rights, the private property, and the public liberties of the whole people.

Joseph Story, *Miscellaneous Writings* 151 (1835).

Why may not these powers be exercised by the respective states? The answer is, because they have parted with them, expressly for the general good. Why may not a state coin money, issue bills of credit, enter into a treaty of alliance or confederation, or regulate commerce with foreign nations? Because these powers have been expressly and exclusively given to the federal government.

Marshall, J., in *Worcester v. Georgia*, 31 U.S. 515, 592 (1832).

And what is the decision of reason on the merits of these conflicting pretensions? Her first and favorite answer would be, that where the scales equally suspended between the parties the decision ought to be given in favor of humanity.

> Johnson, J., in *The Nereide*, 13 U.S. 388, 434 (1815). (This statement also employs personification.)

[W]hat is a monopoly, as understood in law? It is an exclusive right granted to a few of something which was before of common right.

> Story, J., in *Charles River Bridge v. Proprietors of The Warren Bridge*, 36 U.S. 420, 607 (1837) (Story, J., dissenting).

Transitional rhetorical questions are rather modest style devices. Their primary function is to serve as transitions to the ensuing discussions. They do, however, have a slight emphasizing function. Transitional rhetorical questions draw a reader's attention by announcing that a question that has become apparent by the preceding discussion (and which may be in the reader's mind) is about to be answered.

**b. Substantive Rhetorical Questions.** A substantive rhetorical question occurs when a writer makes a substantive point by stating it in the form of a self-answering question rather than as an assertive statement. With such rhetorical questions, the context suggests an answer that the writer intends, so the writer's point is made—albeit obliquely rather than directly.

> Of what use would it be to attempt to bring bodies of men to agreement and compromise of controversies if you put out of view the influences which move them or the fellowship which binds them . . . to make the cause of one the cause of all?

> McKenna, J., in *Adair v. United States*, 208 U.S. 161, 185 (1908) (McKenna, J., dissenting).

> Of what avail are written constitutions whose bills of right, for the security of individual liberty, have been written too often with the blood of martyrs shed upon the battle-field and the scaffold, if their limitations and restraints upon power may be overpassed with impunity by the very agencies created and appointed to guard, defend, and enforce them?

> Matthews, J., in *Poindexter v. Greenhow*, 114 U.S. 270, 291 (1885).

> Has skill in the use of language ever been so universal, or will it ever be so universal, as to make indubitably clear the meaning of legislation?

> McKenna, J., in *Citizens' Bank of Louisiana v. Parker*, 192 U.S. 73, 86 (1904).

> Is it worse for the creditor to lose a little by depreciation than everything by the bankruptcy of his debtor?

> Bradley, J., in *Legal Tender Cases*, 79 U.S. 457, 564 (1870) (Bradley, J., concurring).

Where is there a more enduring monument of political wisdom than the separation of the judicial from the legislative power?

Joseph Story, *Miscellaneous Writings* 39 (1835).

In substantive rhetorical questions, the writer does not directly assert a specific point; rather, the point is made by posing a question that elicits an answer made "obvious" from the context. While such rhetorical questions do add emphasis and drama to a discussion, legal writers should use them with care. A legal advocate's job is to answer questions, not pose them. Moreover, presenting ideas as questions rather than assertions leaves room for misunderstanding and miscommunication. In most situations, a legal writer is better off stating his or her point directly and assertively. If you nevertheless decide to use a substantive rhetorical question in your legal writing, be sure that the context makes your intended answer obvious to your readers.

## Summary of Figures of Speech

**1. Alliteration** — The use of two or more words in close proximity that begin with (or prominently contain) the same letter sound.

**2. Allusion** — A clever or innovative casual, subtle, or indirect reference to a person, idea, or event.

**3. Anastrophe** — The deliberate inversion of expected order of words in a sentence.

**4. Antithesis** — The juxtaposition of contrasting ideas in a parallel structure.

**5. Antonomasia** — The use of a representative proper name in place of a common name for an object or concept.

**6. Aporia** — The use of a statement expressing the difficulty of beginning the writing task at hand.

**7. Apostrophe** — A remark addressed to an absent person or personified abstraction.

**8. Bulk** — The matching of one's word length and sentence structure to the substantive idea the words convey.

**9. Conjunction Deviation**

   **a. Asyndeton** — The deliberate omission of conjunctions between items in a series.

   **b. Polysyndeton** — The excessive use of conjunctions.

**10. Correction** — The recall of a word or statement and its replacement with another generally stronger one.

**11. Ellipsis** — The intentional omission from a sentence of grammatically necessary words that are then implied by the context.

**12. Hyperbole** — A deliberate exaggeration.

**13. Irony** — A statement in which the intended meaning is the opposite of the literal meaning.

**14. Litotes** — A deliberate understatement.

**15. Metonymy** — A reference to an object using a word suggestive of or associated with the thing or some aspect of it.

**16. Paralepsis** — The emphasis of an idea by pretending to pass it over.

**17. Personification** — The ascription of human qualities to animals, inanimate objects, or abstractions.

**18. Puns** — Witty plays on words.

**19. Repetition**

   **a. Anadiplosis** — The use of the same word at the end of one clause and the beginning of the next.

   **b. Anaphora** — The use of the same word or group of words at the beginning of successive clauses.

   **c. Antimetibole** — The immediate repetition of a clause in reverse or inverted order.

   **d. Epistrophe** — The use of the same word or group of words at the ends of successive clauses.

**20. Rhetorical Question**

   **a. Transitional** — The use of a self-posed question to set up an answer or to transition to a new idea.

   **b. Substantive** — Making a point by stating it in the form of a self-answering question.

## Exercise 10.1   Understanding and Analyzing Figures of Speech

In Appendix A of this text you will find the published dissenting opinion of Justice Michael J. Musmanno of the Pennsylvania Supreme Court in the case of *Dapra v. Pennsylvania Liquor Control Board*, 227 A.2d 491 (Pa. 1967). Justice Musmanno was well known for using many figures of speech in his judicial opinions. Write an essay identifying and analyzing the various figures of speech Justice Musmanno used in this opinion. (Your analysis should include metaphors and similes, which were discussed in Chapter 9.) The lines of the opinion have been numbered to make it easier for you to refer to specific wording. For each figure of speech you identify, (1) explain why it is the figure you believe it to be, and (2) analyze its effectiveness.

**Note:** In *Dapra*, as in much of his other writing, Justice Musmanno uses many figures of speech. Earlier in this chapter, we discussed that legal advocates should avoid the excessive use of figures of speech in a single document. Thus, you should keep in mind that this assignment is designed merely to give you an opportunity to *identify* figures of speech in a legal discussion. This opinion by Justice Musmanno was chosen over others because its extensive use of rhetorical devices gives you an opportunity to identify many figures of speech in a relatively short document. However, you should not view Justice Musmanno's opinion as a model for how you as a practitioner should write. Justice Musmanno, as a Pennsylvania Supreme Court justice, had more poetic license than you do as a lawyer writing on behalf of a client.

## Exercise 10.2   Understanding and Analyzing Figures of Speech

Locate an example of each figure of speech discussed in this chapter in a judicial opinion and write an essay analyzing the figure's effectiveness. For each figure of speech, your essay should (1) quote the example and cite the case in which it appears, (2) explain why the quoted language illustrates the figure you assert that it does, and (3) analyze the effectiveness of the quoted language, in and of itself and in the context of the surrounding discussion. Attach copies of the relevant pages of the opinions to your essay.

**Exercise 10.3   Drafting and Analyzing Figures of Speech**

| | |
|---|---|
| 1. Alliteration | 11. Ellipsis |
| 3. Anastrophe | 15. Metonymy |
| 4. Antithesis | 17. Personification |
| 9. Conjunction Deviation | 19. Repetition |
| 10. Correction | |

1.      For each of the figures of speech listed above, revise a passage from an existing legal opinion of your choice to incorporate it. While you are not required to use a different legal opinion for each figure of speech, do not incorporate all of them into a single opinion. For conjunction deviation and repetition, choose *one* of their subcategories. Attach copies of the original versions of the passages to your revised versions.

2.      Write an essay analyzing your use of these figures of speech in your revisions. For each figure of speech, (1) explain how your use of the figure meets the definition of the figure set out in this chapter, and (2) analyze the effectiveness of your use of the figure, in and of itself and in the context of the surrounding discussion.

# PART IV

## PERSUASIVE WRITING STRATEGIES BASED ON PSYCHOLOGY THEORY

# Chapter 11

# The Cognitive Dimensions of Illustrative Narratives in the Communication of Rule-Based Analysis

> Without the concrete instances the general proposition is baggage, impedimenta, stuff about the feet.
> — Karl Llewellyn, *Bramble Bush*

Consider the following excerpts from two hypothetical appellate briefs:

*Example 11.1*

**Under California law of statutory construction, "[w]here a statute referring to one subject contains a critical word or phrase, omission of that word or phrase from a similar statute on the same subject generally shows a different legislative intent."** *Craven v. Crout*, 163 Cal. App. 3d 779, 783, 209 Cal. Rptr. 649, 652 (1985); *accord, e.g., Hennigan v. United Pac. Ins. Co.*, 53 Cal. App. 3d 1, 8, 125 Cal. Rptr. 408, 412 (1975). *In* Craven, *for example, the plaintiff in a medical malpractice suit was awarded a lump-sum judgment of more than one million dollars by the superior court.* 163 Cal. App. 3d at 781, 209 Cal Rptr. at 650. *Two months after the judgment was entered, the defendants filed a request with the superior court to have the damages paid by periodic payments pursuant to California Civil Procedure Code section 667.7 (West 1985), which allows a trial court to order periodic payments of awards issued in medical malpractice actions.* Craven, *163 Cal. App. 3d at 781, 209 Cal Rptr. at 650-51. The trial court granted the defendants' request, and the plaintiff appealed, claiming that the superior court lacked the power to modify the original judgment of a lump-sum payment after it was entered.* Id. *at 781-82, 209 Cal Rptr. at 650-51.*

*In resolving this issue, the court noted that, while section 667.7 was silent on the issue of whether a superior court has the authority under that section to amend an award after final judgement has been entered, a separate provision, California Civil Procedure Code section 85 (West 1985), expressly authorizes "municipal courts" to amend their money judgments at any time, even after final judgement.* Craven, *163 Cal. App. 3d at 783, 209 Cal Rptr. at 652. Applying the rule of statutory construction quoted above, the court concluded that the fact that section 85 expressly allows for the modification of a money award by a municipal court after final judgment and "section 667.7 contains no similar language is an unmistakable indication that the Legislature did not intend that section to authorize modification of an entered judgment."* Id. *at 783-84, 209 Cal Rptr. at 652. Thus, the court reversed the order of the superior court that provided for periodic payments by the defendants.* Id. *at 785, 209 Cal Rptr. at 653.*

The issue in the present case is whether California's criminal statute on vandalism requires the state to prove "lack of permission" as an element of the offense. The vandalism statute, California Penal Code section 594 (West 1999), does not expressly state that "lack of permission" is an element of the offense. However, the defendant in this case argues that this element should be read into the statute and that, because the prosecution did not prove this element at trial, his conviction should be reversed.

A review of California's Penal Code reveals that "lack of permission" has expressly been made an element of other crimes. Robbery, for example, is defined as "the felonious taking of personal property in the possession of another, from his person or immediate presence, and *against his will,* accomplished by means of force or fear." Cal. Penal Code sec. 211 (West 1999) (emphasis added). Similarly, rape is defined as "an act of sexual intercourse accomplished with a person not the spouse of the perpetrator . . . [w]here it is accomplished *against a person's will* by means of force, violence, duress, menace, or fear." Cal. Penal Code sec. 261(a)(2) (West 1999) (emphasis added). And, regarding the poisoning of animals, California Penal Code sec. 596 (West 1999) (emphasis added) provides, "Every person who, *without the consent of the owner,* wilfully administers poison to any animal . . . is guilty of a misdemeanor." The omission of language in section 594 making lack of permission an element of vandalism, when such language has been inserted in other criminal statutes to make lack of permission or consent an element of the offenses, is indicative of a legislative intent not to make lack of permission an element of vandalism.[1]

*Example 11.2*

Another factor this Court considers in determining whether the prolonged pretrial detention of a criminal defendant violates his due process rights is the complexity of the case. **This Court has held that if the delay in bringing a defendant to trial is attributable to the complexity of the case, as opposed to the misconduct or inaction of the prosecution, this factor will support a finding that the extended pretrial detention of the defendant is not a violation of due process.** *See, e.g., United States v. Gonzales Claudio,* 806 F.2d 334, 341 (2d Cir. 1986) *(finding that, because of the complex nature of the case, which involved 20 defendants, events that occurred in numerous locations, and hundreds of audio cassettes, video cassettes, and documents that had to be translated from Spanish to English,*

---

[1] This illustration was developed from *In re Rudy L.*, 29 Cal. App. 4th 1007, 34 Cal. Rptr. 864 (1994). Some language from *Rudy* has been quoted without indication.

*this factor supported a finding that the prolonged pretrial detention of the defendant did not violate his due process rights); United States v. El-Hage,* 213 F.3d 74, 80 (2d Cir. 2000).

In the present case, much of the delay in bringing this case to trial is attributable to its inherent complexity. The defendant is charged along with seven co-defendants with numerous counts of embezzlement and transporting stolen vehicles across state lines. Coordinating the proceedings on this many charges with this many defendants has been a laborious process. Moreover, witnesses and evidence relevant to the case are scattered over four states. Finally, as to the embezzlement charges, the process of reviewing the volumes of financial documents relevant to these charges has been unavoidably time consuming. Thus, much of the delay in this case is attributable, not to misconduct on the part of the prosecution, but to the complex nature of the case itself and these facts support a finding that the defendant's due process rights will not be violated by his continued pretrial detention.

The foregoing excerpts demonstrate a writing technique employed by some legal writers in the communication of rule-based analysis: setting out not only the relevant rule, but also an illustration of how the rule was applied in a precedent case, prior to applying the rule to the facts of the present matter. In each of these excerpts, the rule is indicated in **bold** type and the illustration in *italics*. In Example 11.1, the rule involves a canon of statutory construction. An illustration of the rule is set out in the text of the discussion before the rule is applied to the facts of the present case. In Example 11.2, the rule involves one factor of a weighing test that federal courts consider in determining whether pretrial detention violates a defendant's due process rights. An illustration of the rule is set out as a parenthetical in the citation of an applicable case before the rule is applied to the facts of the case before the court.

This technique of providing a narrative illustration of a rule before applying the rule is fairly common in persuasive legal writing. Despite its popularity, however, it has not been analyzed in much depth. In this chapter, we will analyze in detail the communicative and persuasive functions of illustrative narratives in rule-based analysis. To this end, we will turn to the field of cognitive psychology. We will see that cognitive psychology theory indicates that the human brain processes "stories" and "narratives" more effectively than abstract propositions and rules. We will also see that this discovery by cognitive psychologists has great significance to us as legal writers, for illustrative narratives are not merely stylistic devices; they are important communicative devices that facilitate a reader's understanding of abstract rules. Thus, we will see that communicating rule-based analysis using narrative illustrations is effective (if not essential) because it allows us to tap into the fundamental way that the human brain processes information. In the end, with a fuller appreciation of the cognitive dimensions of illustrative narratives, we will discuss how we as legal writers can use this technique even more effectively to communicate the analysis in our persuasive documents.

# I.   COMMUNICATING RULE-BASED ANALYSIS IN LEGAL WRITING: THE PROBLEM, THE ANSWER, AND THE IMPACT

## A.    *The Problem: The Paradox of Rule-Based Analysis*

The analysis of legal issues involves a number of different types of legal reasoning. Linda H. Edwards, in fact, has identified four basic modes of legal reasoning: (1) rule-based reasoning, (2) analogical reasoning, (3) policy-based reasoning, and (4) narrative reasoning.[2] In this chapter, we are most interested in rule-based reasoning. However, to fully understand what rule-based reasoning is, we must differentiate it from the other forms of reasoning.

Rule-based analysis involves the mental process of applying a general proposition or rule to the facts of the case at hand. That is, it involves applying a legal principle, stated in the form of an abstract rule, to the facts of a specific case. Consider this simple example:

> A person under the age of twenty-one who purchases an alcoholic beverage is guilty of a misdemeanor. In the present case, the defendant was nineteen when she purchased beer from a liquor store. Thus, the defendant is guilty of a misdemeanor.

In this example, a general proposition regarding the purchase of alcohol by a minor is applied to the facts of the present case to reach a conclusion on the issue addressed by the rule. This is rule-based analysis.

Analogical reasoning (also called "case comparison reasoning") involves the mental process of comparing the facts of a precedent case to the facts of the present case for the purposes of determining how the cases are similar and different and the legal significance of those similarities and differences.[3] Whenever, in the analysis of a legal issue, a writer explains how the present case is similar to or distinguishable from a precedent case, the writer is engaging in analogical analysis.[4]

---

[2] Linda Holdeman Edwards, *Legal Writing: Process, Analysis and Organization* 4-8 (2d ed. 1999) [hereinafter Edwards, *Legal Writing*]; *see also* Linda H. Edwards, *The Convergence of Analogical and Dialectic Imaginations in Legal Discourse*, 20 Legal Stud. F. 7, 9-17 (1996).

[3] Professor Edwards differentiates between analyzing the "similarities" between cases (called "analogical reasoning") and analyzing the "differences" between cases (called "counter-analogical reasoning"). *See* Edwards, *Legal Writing*, *supra* note 2, at 5-6. For our purposes, these forms can be combined and treated as one, which we will term "analogical reasoning."

[4] Some legal writers may argue that setting out a precedent case in detail, as in Example 11.1, constitutes analogical reasoning, not rule-based reasoning. However, the difference between "rule-based analysis with a narrative illustration" and "analogical analysis" lies in the application step. With analogical analysis, a precedent case is explained to set up

Policy-based reasoning occurs when a legal writer explains how broad public policy considerations impact the resolution of an issue. It asserts that $X$ is the answer, not because some rule of law dictates it, but because "that answer will encourage desirable results for our society and discourage undesirable results."[5] Finally, narrative reasoning is reasoning that is based on the facts of the present case and the moral values that those facts implicate. It asserts that $X$ is the answer because the emotional facts of the case and societal values require it, regardless of what the legal rules or applicable precedent may say.

These four modes of reasoning often work together in the resolution of a legal issue. However, rule-based analysis is the dominant form of reasoning. Our legal system for resolving legal disputes is based on the idea of applying established legal rules to the facts of a specific dispute. Thus, rule-based analysis plays the primary role in resolving legal issues; the other forms of reasoning play secondary roles.[6]

Despite its preeminence in legal reasoning, rule-based analysis suffers from a major shortcoming: It is inconsistent with the fundamental way the human brain processes information. Recent developments in cognitive psychology suggest that humans do not think effectively in terms of abstract general propositions.[7] This presents quite a paradox for legal writers. On the one hand, our system for resolving legal disputes relies heavily on the application of general rules to the facts of a specific case (that is, rule-based analysis). On the other hand, our brains (in particular, the brains of our readers) do not easily understand and process ideas expressed in the form of general propositions. Thus, legal advocates constantly face a dilemma inherent in the system. We are forced to reason based on general rules, yet rules as concepts are cognitively flawed.

## B. The Answer: The Cognitive Dimensions of Illustrative Narratives

As we just discussed, cognitive theory indicates that the human brain does not effectively process abstract rules. According to cognitive psychologists, humans understand concepts expressed in the form of "stories" or "narratives" better than they understand concepts explained as abstract principles. That is, narrative as a mode

---

a "comparison" discussion between the precedent case and the present case. The application step involves a comparison analysis. With rule-based analysis, a precedent case is set out merely to illustrate and explicate the general rule. The application step of rule-based analysis does not involve a comparison between the cases; it involves application of the general rule.

[5] *See* Edwards, *Legal Writing*, *supra* note 2, at 6.

[6] The rules employed in rule-based analysis can come from a variety of sources. They can be statutory rules enacted by a legislative body, administrative rules issued by an executive department, or common law rules announced by or generated from a judicial opinion written by a court.

[7] *See generally* Steven L. Winter, *The Cognitive Dimension of the Agon Between Legal Power and Narrative Meaning*, 87 Mich. L. Rev. 2225 (1989) [hereinafter Winter, *The Cognitive Dimension*]; Steven L. Winter, *Transcendental Nonsense, Metaphoric Reasoning, and the Cognitive Stakes for Law*, 137 U. Pa. L. Rev. 1105 (1989).

of communication is more effective than general propositions. As Steven L. Winters has stated, "[N]arrative . . . corresponds more closely to the manner in which the human mind makes sense of experience than does the conventional, abstracted rhetoric of the law."[8]

A short answer to the question of why narrative has such communicative power is that a person learns through story in the same way that he or she learns through experience. Starting at infancy, human beings learn by interacting with and experiencing the world around them. And because life is continual and occurs over the passage of time, much of learning by experience happens as events, ideas, and concepts build on each other. A person is basically the protagonist in the story that is his or her own life. And much of what we learn is learned by chronologically experiencing related events that build on each other.

Story as a mode of communication functions in the same way. Just as life involves experiencing the chronological passing of related events, stories too, by definition, involve a chronological telling of related events. When we hear a story, we place ourselves in the role of the protagonist. "We imagine ourselves as the protagonist and picture ourselves in the protagonist's shoes as we proceed from introduction to conclusion."[9] And we learn from this experience in the same way we learn from our participation in our own lives. As Winter states,

> [narrative] engage[s] the audience in the cognitive process by which it regularly makes meaning in its day-to-day world. . . . [T]he process of making sense of the projected experience of the story [is] mimetic of the process by which humans always make meaning. The audience "lives" the story-experience, and is brought personally to engage in the process of constructing meaning out of another's experience.[10]

Thus, "narrative's communicative capacity is rooted in the way that the mind interprets, processes, and understands information."[11] The most fundamental way that we learn and process information is through living the experience. Stories communicate the same way and thus take advantage of the most fundamental way that humans process and understand information. For this reason, narrative has a communicative advantage over general propositions. As Winter puts it,

> The grounding of all human cognition in experience means that there is a greater cognitive "clout" to images from lived experience as compared to propositional formulations that attempt to "literalize" their meaning. The

---

[8] Winter, *The Cognitive Dimension*, *supra* note 7, at 2228. It is beyond the scope of this chapter to delve in-depth into how cognitive theory explains the effectiveness of narrative as a mode of communication. If you are interested in these cognitive principles, read Winter's fascinating works and the numerous sources referenced therein.

[9] *Id.* at 2272.

[10] *Id.* at 2277.

[11] *Id.* at 2271.

dramatic image of [narrative] has a communicative power that is unmatched by the "equivalent" propositional statement.[12]

What does all of this mean for the legal writer who must communicate rule-based reasoning? As we have seen, rule-based reasoning is indispensable to legal discourse. Yet, as we have also seen, the human mind does not effectively process general principles. Consequently, legal writers should heed this information from cognitive theory and combine illustrative narratives with rules when communicating rule-based analysis. When a legal writer must communicate rule-based analysis, the writer, knowing the cognitive limitations of the human mind, should consider supplementing a statement of the general rule with a narrative that illustrates how the rule operated in a precedent case.

We see this strategy of combining a general proposition with an illustrative narrative in everyday conversations. Frequently, a person trying to explain a point will supplement an abstract statement with an illustration or example. Similarly, "how to" books on all subjects (including this one) frequently supplement their abstract descriptions with illustrations. This general tendency to supplement propositions with illustrations is a manifestation of an innate sense held by all humans that general propositions alone lack communicative force and precision.

It is not surprising then that, as we saw in the beginning of this chapter, some legal writers already employ the strategy of combining rules with illustrative narratives when communicating rule-based analysis. Again, the existence of this writing strategy is a manifestation of an instinctive sense on the part of some legal writers that many concepts cannot be adequately explained by a rule alone. Thanks to cognitive theory, however, we now know why this is true. Consequently, with this knowledge from cognitive psychology, we as legal writers can now approach the communication of rule-based analysis more consciously and strategically. The use of illustrative narratives should no longer be a result of accident or intuition; the use of illustrative narratives should be the result of conscious choice in view of our knowledge of the cognitive limitations of rules and the cognitive benefits of narrative.

## C.    *The Impact: In-Text and Parenthetical Illustrations*

The answer to the inherent communicative problems with rules is to supplement them with illustrative narratives. Traditionally in legal writing this has been accomplished by incorporating illustrative narratives with rules in one of two ways: (1) through in-text illustrations, or (2) through parenthetical illustrations.

Consider the following two examples of legal discussions analyzing the same substantive point using rule-based analysis. In Example 11.3, narrative illustrations of the applicable rule appear in the *text* of the discussion, immediately following the statement of the rule. In Example 11.4, the illustrations of the rule appear as *parentheticals* within the citations of the applicable cases. (In both examples, the rule is set out in **bold** type and the illustrations are set out in *italic* type.)

---

[12] *Id.* at 2276-77.

*Example 11.3*

The first factor Georgia courts consider in deciding whether to bar a tort suit between married parties is whether allowing the suit will foster marital disharmony and disunity between the parties. The Georgia Supreme Court has recognized that, "[a] truly adversary tort lawsuit between husband and wife, by its very nature, would have an upsetting and embittering effect upon domestic tranquility." *Robeson v. International Indemnity Co.*, 282 S.E.2d 896, 898 (Ga. 1981). Consequently, most tort suits between spouses will be barred for this reason. *See id.* **However, the Georgia Supreme Court has also held that, if the facts of the case indicate that marital harmony will not be disrupted by an interspousal suit, this consideration will not require that the suit be barred.** *See Harris v. Harris*, 313 S.E.2d 88, 90 (Ga. 1984); *Jones v. Jones*, 376 S.E.2d 674, 675 (Ga. 1989).

*In* Harris, *for example, the case involved a personal injury suit between parties who were legally married, but who had been living in a state of separation for ten years. 313 S.E.2d at 89-90. The Supreme Court held that the "marital disharmony" factor did not require that the suit be barred because "there was, realistically speaking, no 'marital harmony' to be protected by application of the interspousal immunity rule."* Id. *at 90. Similarly, in* Jones, *the Georgia Supreme Court held that a tort suit between the estate of a deceased spouse and a surviving spouse was not barred under the doctrine of interspousal immunity. 376 S.E.2d at 676. In analyzing the "marital disharmony" factor, the court stated, "First, and most obviously, there can be no marital harmony to foster when one spouse has died."* Id. *at 675.*

*Example 11.4*

The first factor Georgia courts consider in deciding whether to bar a tort suit between married parties is whether allowing the suit will foster marital disharmony and disunity between the parties. The Georgia Supreme Court has recognized that, "[a] truly adversary tort lawsuit between husband and wife, by its very nature, would have an upsetting and embittering effect upon domestic tranquility." *Robeson v. International Indemnity Co.*, 282 S.E.2d 896, 898 (Ga. 1981). Consequently, most tort suits between spouses will be barred for this reason. *See id.* **However, the Georgia Supreme Court has also held that, if the facts of the case indicate that marital harmony will not be disrupted by an interspousal suit, this consideration will not require that the suit be barred.** *See Harris v. Harris*, 313 S.E.2d 88, 90 (Ga. 1984) *(holding that a suit between spouses who had been separated for ten years was not barred under the "marital disharmony" factor because there was no marital harmony to be protected)*; *Jones v. Jones*, 376 S.E.2d 674, 675 (Ga. 1989) *(holding that a suit between the estate of a deceased spouse and a surviving spouse was not barred under the "marital disharmony" factor because "there can be no marital harmony to foster when one spouse has died")*.

As the above examples illustrate, narrative illustrations of rules can be inserted into the text of a discussion or into citation parentheticals. Later in this chapter we will discuss some guidelines for writers to consider when deciding between these two approaches.

## II.   THE COMMUNICATIVE FUNCTIONS OF ILLUSTRATIVE NARRATIVES

In the preceding discussion, we saw that illustrative narratives facilitate the communication of abstract rules because they are more consistent with the way the human brain processes information. A closer look at illustrative narratives, however, indicates that they can actually serve several specific communicative functions. Below is a summary of the functions they can serve, followed by a more in-depth discussion of each.

- Illustration for Elucidation
- Illustration for Elimination
- Illustration for Affiliation
- Illustration for Accentuation

### A.   *Illustration for Elucidation*

The most important function served by illustrative narratives is explaining the substance of a rule. As we previously discussed, many legal concepts are too nebulous or complex to be fully understood in the form of an abstract rule. Thus, the primary function of an illustrative narrative is to elucidate the meaning of a rule by providing an example of how the rule operated in a precedent case. The narrative puts the rule in concrete terms and thereby makes it more understandable. Consider the following example:

> *Example 11.5*
>
> Another factor federal courts consider in determining whether the unauthorized use of copyrighted material is permissible under the "fair use" doctrine is whether the alleged infringer's use of the copyrighted material is "transformative." If the use is transformative, this will support a finding that the use is fair. To constitute a "transformative use" the alleged infringer's use must add something new to the original material and thereby alter its purpose, meaning, or character. *See, e.g., Campbell v. Acuff-Rose Music, Inc.*, 510 U.S. 569, 579 (1994); *Religious Tech. Ctr. v. Netcom On-Line Communication Servs., Inc.*, 923 F. Supp. 1231, 1243 (N.D. Cal. 1995); *Belmore v. City Pages, Inc.*, 880 F. Supp. 673, 677-78 (D. Minn. 1995).
>
> The *Belmore* case provides a good illustration of what is meant by "transformativeness." In that case, the plaintiff, a policeman, wrote an article entitled "Tale of Two Islands" and published it in the local police federation newspaper. *Belmore*, 880 F. Supp. at 675. The article was written in the form of a fable and portrayed a dispute between the inhabitants of two fictitious

neighboring islands—one populated by clean, considerate, industrious people and the other populated by lazy, dirty, dishonest people. *Id.* at 675, 681 app. Subsequently, the local Minneapolis newspaper, City Pages, without the permission of the plaintiff, reprinted the entire fable in an article criticizing it as evidence of racism in the local police department. *Id.* at 675. The author of the fable then sued City Pages for copyright infringement. *Id.* In analyzing whether City Pages' verbatim copying of the plaintiff's fable was fair use, the court considered, among other things, whether the defendant's use was transformative. *Id.* at 677-78. The court noted that City Pages added new expression to the fable by incorporating the fable into a longer article that criticized it and the local police department. *Id.* at 675, 678. The court also noted that City Pages altered the character and purpose of the fable. City Pages' purpose in using the fable was to set it out for criticism and to offer it as evidence of racism in the police department, a purpose quite different than that of the original author. *Id.* at 678. Thus, the court found that the use was transformative and that this factor supported a finding that the copying by City Pages was fair use. *Id.*

The above example involves the "fair use" defense to copyright infringement. As the example indicates, one factor federal courts consider in determining fair use is whether the use of the copyrighted material by the alleged infringer was "transformative." The example begins by setting out the definition of "transformativeness" as a general proposition. This general definition, however, is vague and ambiguous. The concept of "transformativeness" is difficult to understand as an abstract rule. Consequently, the example supplements the rule with an illustration from the *Belmore* case. It is only through this illustration that one gains an appreciation of what is meant by a "transformative use of copyrighted material."

Such is often the case with abstract rules. They are frequently incapable of clearly and accurately conveying complicated legal concepts. Thus, the first and primary function of illustrative narratives is to help communicate the substance of abstract rules.

## B.    *Illustration for Elimination*

Illustrative narratives can also serve to eliminate possible misinterpretations of general rules. Because general rules are limited in their capacity to communicate precisely, they can sometimes be susceptible to multiple interpretations. A writer can eliminate interpretations other than the one he or she intends by supplementing the rule with an illustration. Consider this example:

*Example 11.6*

In order for a criminal victim to recover restitution under Florida Statutes section 775.089(1)(a), the victim must show that the expenses in question are sufficiently connected to the crimes of which the defendant was convicted. *See, e.g., State v. Williams*, 520 So. 2d 276, 277-78 (Fla. 1988); *Faulkner v. State*, 582 So. 2d 783, 784 (Fla. 5th Dist. Ct. App. 1991); *Jones v. State*, 480 So. 2d 163, 164 (Fla. 1st Dist. Ct. App. 1985). In *Faulkner*, the court reversed a restitution order that required the defendant to reimburse two burglary victims for items taken during a burglary of their home and not recovered. 582 So. 2d at 784. Although there was evidence in the record that the defendant was involved in the burglary, he was not convicted of that crime. The defendant was convicted only of dealing in stolen property. The court concluded that the missing items were related to the burglary itself, not the offense of which the defendant was actually convicted—dealing in stolen property. Thus, restitution was inappropriate. *Id.*; *see also Jones*, 480 So. 2d at 164 (finding that a defendant could not be held responsible for the cost of repairing a window broken during a burglary committed by the defendant when the defendant was convicted only of dealing in stolen property and not the burglary itself).

In the foregoing example, the general rule states that restitution under the relevant statute is appropriate only where the expenses in question are connected to the crimes of which the defendant was "convicted." Without the illustrations from the *Faulkner* case and the *Jones* case, a reader may not appreciate the significance of the word "convicted" in this rule. A reader might interpret this rule as merely requiring that the expenses be related to the crimes the defendant *committed* or the crimes with which the defendant was *charged*. Only by the inclusion of the illustrations does the reader appreciate the significance and importance of the word "convicted." To a less-than-careful reader, the general rule is susceptible to multiple interpretations. Thus, the illustrations serve to eliminate the inaccurate interpretations of the general rule.[13]

The function of *eliminating* erroneous alternative interpretations of a rule is slightly different from the first function of *elucidating* a vague rule. The elucidation function applies when a rule is too complex or vague to conjure up *any* clear meaning in readers' minds. The rule is understandable in general only through a narrative illustration. The elimination function, on the other hand, applies when the rule appears to make sense on its face, but is actually susceptible to erroneous interpretations. In such cases, the illustrations eliminate the possible erroneous interpretations and highlight the correct one. Consider the following additional example of Illustration for Elimination:

*Example 11.7*

Another factor federal courts consider in determining whether the unauthorized use of copyrighted material is permissible under the "fair use" doctrine is whether the alleged infringer's use of the copyrighted material had a negative impact on the potential market of the original work. Federal

---

[13] I have created hypothetical problems using this rule in a number of my introductory legal writing classes. I have found that many, many students do not at first appreciate the significance of the word "convicted" in the rule. It is only by reading a number of cases in which the result turned on this word that the students come to appreciate its significance. This anecdotal evidence supports the idea that some general rules are susceptible to misinterpretation and that this misinterpretation can be eliminated upon seeing how the rule works in actual cases.

courts generally hold that, if the copying of copyrighted work by an alleged infringer has an adverse impact on the commercial market for the original work, this factor will strongly support a finding that the alleged infringer's use of the material is not fair use. *See, e.g., Campbell v. Acuff-Rose Music, Inc.*, 510 U.S. 569, 590 (1994); *Consumer Union of United States, Inc. v. General Signal Corp.*, 724 F.2d 1044, 1050-51 (2d Cir. 1983); *Religious Tech. Ctr. v. Netcom On-Line Communication Servs., Inc.*, 923 F. Supp. 1231, 1248 (N.D. Cal. 1995).

   In *Religious Tech. Ctr.*, the defendant copied and posted on the Internet a number of copyrighted works owned by the Church of Scientology for the purpose of criticizing the works and the Church in general. 923 F. Supp. at 1238-39. The Church then sued the defendant for copyright infringement. *Id.* at 1239. In analyzing whether the defendant's copying of the Church's works was permissible under the fair use doctrine, the court considered, among other things, whether the copying by the defendant had a negative effect on the marketability of the original works. *Id.* at 1248-49. The court noted that the only relevant inquiry under this factor was whether the posting of the works on the Internet usurped the demand for the original works—that is, whether the posting diminished the public's need to purchase these works from the Church. *Id.* at 1248. The court specifically held that, if the defendant's criticism of the materials and the Church caused a reduction in the sale of the works, this was beyond the focus of this factor. The court stressed that this factor is only concerned with whether the *copying* affected the market, not whether the defendant's criticism affected the market. *Id.* at 1248 n.19.

In the above example, the general rule is as follows: If the copying of copyrighted work by an alleged infringer has an adverse impact of the commercial market for the original work, this factor will strongly support a finding that the alleged infringer's use of the material is not fair use. This rule is relatively straightforward and appears to make sense on its face. However, based on a simple reading of the rule, a reader may not appreciate that it is not enough that the market of the original work was negatively affected by the infringer's use; it must also be shown that the negative impact was caused by the *copying*. A quick reading of the rule may suggest that any negative impact on the market of the original work is sufficient under this factor. It is only by reading the illustration from the *Religious Tech. Ctr.* case that the reader can appreciate the significance of the wording "If the *copying* . . . has an adverse impact. . . ." Again, the illustration has the function of eliminating an erroneous interpretation of the general rule.

## C.   *Illustration for Affiliation*

The third function that narrative illustrations can serve in rule-based analysis is to make a rule more meaningful to a reader by explaining it in familiar terms. Rules are often sterile abstractions of general legal concepts, personally meaningless to a reader. Because of the abstract nature of rules, a reader can often feel removed and detached from a rule. Illustrative narratives can help a reader to appreciate a rule more fully by putting the rule in a familiar context, thereby creating a closer connection between the reader and the general rule. Consider this example:

*Example 11.8*

Another factor federal courts consider in determining whether the unauthorized use of copyrighted material is permissible under the "fair use" doctrine is whether the copyrighted work is primarily informational or creative. The courts generally "broaden the protection of those works that are creative, fictional, or highly original and lessen the protection for those works that are factual, informational, or functional." *Religious Tech. Ctr. v. Netcom On-Line Communication Servs., Inc.*, 923 F. Supp. 1231, 1246 (N.D. Cal. 1995); *accord, e.g., Campbell v. Acuff-Rose Music, Inc.*, 510 U.S. 569, 586 (1994); *Harper & Row, Publishers, Inc. v. Nation Enters.*, 471 U.S. 539, 563 (1985). From a policy standpoint, federal courts have reasoned that there is less of a need to disseminate works of fiction than factual works. Consequently, less copying will be allowed for fictional works than for factual works. *See, e.g., Harper & Row*, 471 U.S. at 563. In terms of this factor then, if the work copied by an alleged infringer is a creative, highly original work, this consideration will weigh against a finding of fair use. Conversely, if the original work is primarily informational, this factor will weigh in favor of fair use. *See, e.g., id.; Campbell*, 510 U.S. at 586; *Consumers Union of United States, Inc. v. General Signal Corp.*, 724 F.2d 1044, 1049-50 (2d Cir. 1983) (finding that, because the material in the magazine *Consumer Reports* is primarily informational rather than creative, this consideration supported a finding of fair use by an alleged infringer).

In the above example, the general rules by themselves are probably understandable to a reader. Thus, an illustration is not required to communicate the substance of the rules. However, the illustration regarding *Consumer Reports,* a magazine with which many people are familiar, puts the rule in a familiar context. Consequently the rule seems less abstract and gains personal significance for the reader. Consider these additional examples of Illustration for Affiliation:

*Example 11.9*

To establish duress as a defense to a contract under Florida law, the party alleging duress must show that he or she acted "involuntarily" in entering into the contract. *See, e.g., McLaughlin v. State Dep't of Natural Resources*, 526 So. 2d 934, 936 (Fla. 1st Dist. Ct. App. 1988); *City of Miami v. Kory*, 394 So. 2d 494, 497 (Fla. 3d Dist. Ct. App. 1981). One factor Florida courts consider in determining whether a person involuntarily entered into a contract is the fairness of the contract itself. If the resulting contract is grossly unfair to the person claiming duress, this will support a finding that the person acted involuntarily in signing the contract. *See Berger v. Berger*, 466 So. 2d 1149, 1151 (Fla. 4th Dist. Ct. App. 1985) (finding that, because a property settlement agreement between divorcing spouses gave the wife nothing, this factor supported a finding that the wife signed the agreement involuntarily).

*Example 11.10*

From *Johnson v. Automotive Ventures, Inc.*, 890 F. Supp. 507, 511 (W.D. Va. 1995) (some citations omitted):

> In the spirit of protecting expression without stifling ideas, courts have refused to extend [copyright] protection to short phrases. *See Takeall*, 1993 WL 509876, at 509878 (holding that the slogan "You've got the right one, uh-huh" "fails to evince the requisite degree of originality to entitle it to copyright protection and is a short expression of the sort that courts have uniformly held uncopyrightable").

In the above examples, illustrative narratives are not essential to understand the general propositions. Yet the illustrations are helpful to readers because they put the rules into a familiar context. In Example 11.9, the general rule regarding the fairness of a contract allegedly made under duress is made more meaningful to a reader by the inclusion of the illustration from the *Berger* case. The fact scenario of the *Berger* case—a husband pressuring his wife to sign an unfair separation agreement—is more vivid and real for the reader than is the abstract, impersonal rule. Similarly, the reference to Diet Pepsi's famous slogan "You've got the right one, uh-huh" in Example 11.10 provides the reader with a concrete illustration of the types of short phrases deemed unworthy of copyright protection. These examples demonstrate how illustrative narratives can serve an "affiliation" function by which they make general rules more vivid and meaningful to a reader.

## D.      *Illustration for Accentuation*

Illustrative narratives can also serve to emphasize the operative effect of a general rule. Consider the following examples:

*Example 11.11*

Under Rule 9(B) of the Local Rules of Appellate Procedure, an appellant's brief may not exceed 30 pages. *See* Loc. R. 9(B); *see also State v. Untied*, No. 00-CA-32, 2001 WL 698024, at *8 (Ohio Ct. App. June 5, 2001) (refusing to address "appellant's Ninth, Tenth, Eleventh or Twelfth Assignments of Error as these assignments of error are contained in the portion of appellant's brief that exceeds the page limit under Loc. R. 9(B)").

*Example 11.12*

The statute of limitations of 28 U.S.C. 2401(b) relevant to tort actions filed against the United States is strictly enforced. *See, e.g., McDuffee v. United States*, 769 F.2d 492, 493-94 (8th Cir. 1985) (dismissing under 28 U.S.C. 2401(b) a complaint that was filed one day late and reversing the holding by the lower court that barring the suit offended "notions of fair play").

In Example 11.11, the general rule regarding the limit on the length of appellate briefs is emphasized with a dramatic illustration from the *Untied* case. The court in that case completely disregarded the portions of the appellant's brief that exceeded the 30-page limit. Similarly, the illustration from the *McDuffee* case in Example 11.12 highlights in dramatic fashion the rigidity of the statute of limitations under 28 U.S.C. 2401(b). These examples demonstrate how narrative illustrations of general rules can serve to accentuate and emphasize the operative effect of a rule.

As we discussed previously, narratives communicate effectively because readers of narratives tend to project themselves into the stories as protagonists. As the reader learns of the circumstances that befall the person in the narrative, the reader empathizes with the person and imaginatively experiences the circumstances himself or herself. Thus, as we can see from reading Examples 11.11 and 11.12, narratives can provide unparalleled emphasis. Imaginatively experiencing a dramatic or startling event indicative of the operation of a legal rule can indelibly imprint that legal concept in the mind of a reader.

---

**Exercise 11.1   Understanding the Functions of Illustrative Narratives**

- Illustration for Elucidation
- Illustration for Elimination
- Illustration for Affiliation
- Illustration for Accentuation

1.  Above is a summary of the functions illustrative narratives can serve in rule-based analysis. Find an example of each type in a judicial opinion. Because a single illustrative narrative can serve more than one function simultaneously, your choice for each type should have that specific function as its *dominant function*. The examples you choose can be either in-text illustrations or parenthetical illustrations.

2.  Write an essay analyzing your examples. For each example, your essay should (1) explain why the relevant discussion in the judicial opinion involves "rule-based analysis," (2) explain why the example is an illustration of the category you believe it represents, and (3) to the extent that the example serves more than one function, explain its other functions. Attach copies of the relevant judicial opinions to your essay.

---

## III.   CHOOSING BETWEEN IN-TEXT ILLUSTRATIONS AND PARENTHETICAL ILLUSTRATIONS

As we saw above in Section I.C., illustrative narratives can be placed either in the text of a discussion or in a parenthetical within the cites to relevant authority. How as a legal writer do you decide where to put your narrative illustrations? Answering this question involves several considerations.

First, as a threshold question, the writer must ask himself or herself whether an illustration of the relevant rule should be included at all. Sometimes a rule is so vague as a general proposition that it cannot be understood by the reader without an illustration. In these situations, an illustrative narrative of the rule is imperative. However, even where the rule is understandable by itself without an illustration, the writer should consider whether an illustration would nevertheless benefit the reader in any of the ways discussed in Section II above. Some rules are plain and simple enough not to require an illustration. However, considering the cognitive problems with rules and the cognitive advantages of narrative illustrations, a writer would be better off in most cases erring on the side that affords better communication: the inclusion of an illustration of the rule.

The second consideration is the importance of the rule to the issue under discussion. If the rule is dispositive of or otherwise plays a major role in resolving the entire issue being addressed, then the writer should most definitely include an illustration of the rule from a precedent case and should place that illustration in the text of the discussion. If a single rule from a precedent case answers the entire issue, the reader generally expects (and is entitled to) a full explanation of that rule, and this includes a textual explanation of how the rule was applied in a precedent case.

If a writer has decided to include an illustration of a rule and the rule is not dispositive of the whole issue (but merely relevant to one aspect of the issue, like a single element or factor), the writer must next consider whether the illustration can be explained effectively in a single sentence. If so, the writer can include the illustration as a parenthetical. If not, the illustration should be placed in the text of the discussion. As we will see below in connection with the discussion of guidelines in drafting parenthetical illustrations, parentheticals are limited to one sentence. Thus, if an illustration cannot be explained in a single, relatively short and understandable sentence, then it must be explained in the text.

Finally, a writer must consider the overall length of the document. All courts have rules limiting the page length of submitted briefs. Furthermore, the prevailing standard for modern legal writing requires that writers be concise and to the point. Lengthy illustrative narratives can be inconsistent with both of these requirements. Consequently, a brief writer often faces a dilemma. On the one hand, a premium is placed on brevity; on the other, communication principles derived from cognitive psychology suggest that merely stating rules may not be enough. A legal writer must balance these competing considerations when drafting a brief. In many cases, the compromise will be to use parenthetical illustrations, which can provide the reader with an illustrative narrative without adding significant length.

The following exercises—Exercises 11.2(a), (b) and (c)—are designed to give you practice in evaluating whether an illustrative narrative should be included in the discussion of a point governed by a rule in a case and, if so, whether the illustration should be explained in the text or in a parenthetical. These exercises are designed to be completed together. The full effect of the assignment is only achieved by completing (a), (b) and (c).

## Exercise 11.2(a) Choosing Among Rule-Based Analysis Techniques

Write a short essay analyzing which of the following versions of this point is most effective in terms of the concepts we have discussed in this chapter.

### Version 1: Rule Only

Another factor Florida courts consider in determining whether a worker is an "employee" or an "independent contractor" is who supplies the worker's tools. If the worker supplies his or her own tools, this factor will support a finding that the worker is an independent contractor, as opposed to an employee. *See, e.g., Kane Furniture Corp. v. Miranda*, 506 So. 2d 1061, 1065 (Fla. 2d Dist. Ct. App. 1987); *T & T Communications, Inc. v. Department of Labor and Employment Sec.*, 460 So. 2d 996, 998 (Fla. 2d Dist. Ct. App. 1984). In the instant case, Ms. Green provided her own musical instrument when playing with the Miami Symphony Orchestra. This fact supports a finding that Ms. Green is an independent contractor, rather than an employee, of the orchestra.

### Version 2: Rule with Parenthetical Illustration

Another factor Florida courts consider in determining whether a worker is an "employee" or an "independent contractor" is who supplies the worker's tools. If the worker supplies his or her own tools, this factor will support a finding that the worker is an independent contractor, as opposed to an employee. *See, e.g., Kane Furniture Corp. v. Miranda*, 506 So. 2d 1061, 1065 (Fla. 2d Dist. Ct. App. 1987) (finding that, because a carpet installer supplied his own installation equipment in performing his work, this factor supported a finding that he was an independent contractor); *T & T Communications, Inc. v. Department of Labor and Employment Sec.*, 460 So. 2d 996, 998 (Fla. 2d Dist. Ct. App. 1984). In the instant case, Ms. Green provided her own musical instrument when playing with the Miami Symphony Orchestra. This fact supports a finding that Ms. Green is an independent contractor, rather than an employee, of the orchestra.

### Version 3: Rule with In-Text Illustration

Another factor Florida courts consider in determining whether a worker is an "employee" or an "independent contractor" is who supplies the worker's tools. If the worker supplies his or her own tools, this factor will support a finding that the worker is an independent contractor, as opposed to an employee. *See, e.g., Kane Furniture Corp. v. Miranda*, 506 So. 2d 1061, 1065 (Fla. 2d Dist. Ct. App. 1987); *T & T Communications, Inc. v. Department of Labor and Employment Sec.*, 460 So. 2d 996, 998 (Fla. 2d Dist. Ct. App. 1984).

In *Kane*, the plaintiff brought a wrongful death action against Kane Furniture Corporation after the plaintiff's wife was killed in a collision with a vehicle owned and operated by a carpet installer that worked for Kane Furniture. 506 So. 2d at 1063. Because an employer can be held responsible only for the torts of an employee, and not for the torts of an independent contractor, the court had to determine whether the installer was an employee of Kane or an independent contractor. *Id.* at 1063-67. In analyzing this issue, the court considered, among other factors, whether the employer or the worker supplied the worker's tools. *Id.* at 1065. The court reasoned that, because the worker supplied his own installation equipment, this factor supported a finding that the worker was an independent contractor. *Id.*

In the instant case, Ms. Green provided her own musical instrument when playing with the Miami Symphony Orchestra. This fact supports a finding that Ms. Green is an independent contractor, rather than an employee, of the orchestra.

## Exercise 11.2(b) Choosing Among Rule-Based Analysis Techniques

Write a short essay analyzing which of the following versions of this point is most effective in terms of the concepts we have discussed in this chapter.

### Version 1: Rule Only

Estoppel will not be applied against a state agency for misrepresentations of "law," as opposed to misrepresentations of "fact." *See, e.g., Dolphin Outdoor Advertising v. Department of Transp.*, 582 So. 2d 709, 710 (Fla. 1st Dist. Ct. App. 1991); *Austin v. Austin*, 350 So. 2d 102, 105 (Fla. 1st Dist. Ct. App. 1977); *Brown v. Richardson*, 395 F. Supp. 185, 190 (W.D. Pa. 1975).

In the instant case, a representative of the Florida Department of General Services addressed a group of applicants for certification as state contractors and misrepresented the statutory requirements for certification. Because this misrepresentation was a misrepresentation of law, as opposed to a misrepresentation of fact, the Department of General Services cannot be bound by estoppel to these erroneous statements.

### Version 2: Rule with Parenthetical Illustration

Estoppel will not be applied against a state agency for misrepresentations of "law," as opposed to misrepresentations of "fact." *See, e.g., Dolphin Outdoor Advertising v. Department of Transp.*, 582 So. 2d 709, 710 (Fla. 1st Dist. Ct. App. 1991); *Austin v. Austin*, 350 So. 2d 102, 105 (Fla. 1st Dist. Ct. App. 1977) (holding that the Florida Division of Retirement was not bound by estoppel to an erroneous statement of law made in a pamphlet distributed by the Division that explained the features of the new Florida retirement statute); *Brown v. Richardson*, 395 F. Supp. 185, 190 (W.D. Pa. 1975).

In the instant case, a representative of the Florida Department of General Services addressed a group of applicants for certification as state contractors and misrepresented the statutory requirements for certification. Because this misrepresentation was a misrepresentation of law, as opposed to a misrepresentation of fact, the Department of General Services cannot be bound by estoppel to these erroneous statements.

### Version 3: Rule with In-Text Illustration

Estoppel will not be applied against a state agency for misrepresentations of "law," as opposed to misrepresentations of "fact." *See, e.g., Dolphin Outdoor Advertising v. Department of Transp.*, 582 So. 2d 709, 710 (Fla. 1st Dist. Ct. App. 1991); *Austin v. Austin*, 350 So. 2d 102, 105 (Fla. 1st Dist. Ct. App. 1977); *Brown v. Richardson*, 395 F. Supp. 185, 190 (W.D. Pa. 1975). In *Austin*, for example, the wife of a deceased state employee challenged the distribution of the decedent's retirement benefits by the Florida Department of Administration. 350 So. 2d at 103-04. The department decided that the benefits should be distributed to the beneficiaries designated by the decedent before his death. *Id.* In support of her claim of entitlement to the benefits, the plaintiff pointed out that a pamphlet published by the Department of Administration explaining the features of the new Florida retirement statute specifically stated that a surviving spouse would receive benefits even if the surviving spouse was not a designated beneficiary. *Id.* at 105. Although this statement in the pamphlet was erroneous, the plaintiff claimed that the Department was bound by the statement and was estopped from denying her benefits. *Id.*

*continued*

In analyzing this claim, the court held that the statement in the pamphlet was not a misrepresentation of "fact" as required for estoppel; it was a misstatement of the law. *Id.* The court further held that the state cannot be estopped through mistaken statements of "law" as opposed to misstatements of "fact." *Id.* Thus, the court concluded that the plaintiff's estoppel claim was invalid. *Id.*

In the instant case, a representative of the Florida Department of General Services addressed a group of applicants for certification as state contractors and misrepresented the statutory requirements for certification. Because this misrepresentation was a misrepresentation of law, as opposed to a misrepresentation of fact, the Department of General Services cannot be bound by estoppel to these erroneous statements.

## Exercise 11.2(c) Choosing Among Rule-Based Analysis Techniques

Write a short essay analyzing which of the following versions of this point is most effective in terms of the concepts we have discussed in this chapter.

### Version 1: Rule Only

The second element of the absolute immunity afforded to defamatory statements made during the course of a judicial proceeding requires that the statements have some relevance to the proceeding. *See, e.g., Wright v. Yurko*, 446 So. 2d 1162, 1164 (Fla. 5th Dist. Ct. App. 1984); *Sussman v. Damian*, 355 So. 2d 809, 811 (Fla. 3d Dist. Ct. App. 1977).

In the instant case, Mr. Black's defamation suit stems from statements made by Mr. Carreson during a settlement conference regarding Mr. Carreson's negligence suit against Mr. Black. Mr. Carreson's suit alleges that Mr. Black negligently caused an automobile accident between the parties. At the settlement conference between the parties and their respective attorneys, Mr. Carreson accused Mr. Black of being intoxicated at the time of the accident. As this statement is related to the negligence suit, the second element of the absolute immunity is established.

### Version 2: Rule with Parenthetical Illustration

The second element of the absolute immunity afforded to defamatory statements made during the course of a judicial proceeding requires that the statements have some relevance to the proceeding. *See, e.g., Wright v. Yurko*, 446 So. 2d 1162, 1164 (Fla. 5th Dist. Ct. App. 1984); *Sussman v. Damian*, 355 So. 2d 809, 811-12 (Fla. 3d Dist. Ct. App. 1977) (finding that a statement by an attorney (Sussman) to another attorney (Damian) during a deposition that Damian was a "damned liar" was relevant to a legal proceeding as required for immunity because the statement was made during the deposition and concerned whether Damian's client had produced documents subject to discovery in the case, whereas, Damian's statements to Sussman after the deposition accusing Sussman of mishandling client funds were not privileged because they were in no way relevant to the pending lawsuit).

*continued*

In the instant case, Mr. Black's defamation suit stems from statements made by Mr. Carreson during a settlement conference regarding Mr. Carreson's negligence suit against Mr. Black. Mr. Carreson's suit alleges that Mr. Black negligently caused an automobile accident between the parties. At the settlement conference between the parties and their respective attorneys, Mr. Carreson accused Mr. Black of being intoxicated at the time of the accident. As this statement is related to the negligence suit, the second element of the absolute immunity is established.

### Version 3: Rule with In-Text Illustration

The second element of the absolute immunity afforded to defamatory statements made during the course of a judicial proceeding requires that the statements have some relevance to the proceeding. *See, e.g., Wright v. Yurko*, 446 So. 2d 1162, 1164 (Fla. 5th Dist. Ct. App. 1984); *Sussman v. Damian*, 355 So. 2d 809, 811 (Fla. 3d Dist. Ct. App. 1977). In *Sussman*, two attorneys, Robert Sussman and Vincent Damian, sued each other for defamation for statements made by the attorneys while representing adverse parties in a civil suit. In a deposition on the civil suit, the attorneys began to argue over whether Mr. Sussman's client had produced certain relevant documents. After Mr. Damian insisted that the documents had not been produced, Mr. Sussman called Mr. Damian a "damned liar." The deposition then terminated. *Sussman*, 355 So. 2d at 810.

Sometime later, after attending a hearing related to the suit, the attorneys got into another argument in the hallway and elevator of the courthouse. At that point, Mr. Damian attacked Mr. Sussman's professional integrity and accused him of improperly handling client monies and trust funds in matters unrelated to the pending lawsuit. Subsequent to this, Mr. Sussman filed his defamation action against Mr. Damian. Mr. Damian then filed a counter-claim for defamation based on the statement made at the deposition. *Id.* at 810-11.

In analyzing the respective defamation claims by the attorneys and whether the statements were protected by the absolute immunity for statements made during a judicial proceeding, the appellate court addressed whether the statements were "relevant to the judicial proceeding" as required by the immunity doctrine. *Id.* at 811-12. Regarding Mr. Sussman's statement made during the deposition, the court concluded that it was relevant to the lawsuit because it concerned whether Mr. Sussman's client had produced documents subject to discovery in the case. *Id.* at 811. The court concluded that, although Mr. Sussman's statement was "intemperate and unprofessional," it was nevertheless absolutely privileged in a defamation action. *Id.*

Regarding Mr. Damian's statements made in the hallway and elevator of the courthouse, the court reasoned that the statement was in no way relevant to the pending lawsuit. Accordingly, it was not absolutely privileged. *Id.* at 812.

In the instant case, Mr. Black's defamation suit stems from statements made by Mr. Carreson during a settlement conference regarding Mr. Carreson's negligence suit against Mr. Black. Mr. Carreson's suit alleges that Mr. Black negligently caused an automobile accident between the parties. At the settlement conference between the parties and their respective attorneys, Mr. Carreson accused Mr. Black of being intoxicated at the time of the accident. As this statement is related to the negligence suit, the second element of the absolute immunity is established.

## IV.   GUIDELINES FOR DRAFTING PARENTHETICAL ILLUSTRATIVE NARRATIVES

Drafting an in-text illustration is relatively straightforward, but drafting an effective parenthetical illustration involves meeting a number of technical requirements. In this section, we will review guidelines for drafting effective parenthetical illustrations of legal rules.

### A.   *Specific Guidelines for Drafting Parenthetical Illustrations*

#### 1.   The Location of Parenthetical Illustrations

Parenthetical illustrations should be inserted into the citation of the case to which it applies. In the citation, the parenthetical statement should follow the parenthetical that contains the date of the opinion (with a space but no punctuation between the parentheticals).[14] In a basic case citation, for example, the parenthetical statement should be located as follows:

> *Case Name*, Vol. Rptr. Page (Ct. Date) (Parenthetical Illustration).

If the case citation includes subsequent history, the parenthetical statement should precede the reference to the subsequent history.[15]

> *Case Name*, Vol. Rptr. Page (Ct. Date) (Parenthetical Illustration), Subsequent History.

In short citation form, the parenthetical comes at the end of the cite.

> *Short Case Name*, Vol. Rptr. at Page (Parenthetical Illustration).

> *Id.* at Page (Parenthetical Illustration).

In a citation sentence that includes more than one case, the parenthetical should be included in the citation of the case to which it applies. Thus:

> *Case #1 Name*, Vol. Rptr. Page (Ct. Date) (Parenthetical Illustration for Case #1); *Case #2 Name*, Vol. Rptr. Page (Ct. Date).

---

[14] *See The Bluebook: A Uniform System of Citation* Rule 1.5 (16th ed. 1996); *see also* Darby Dickerson, Association of Legal Writing Directors, *ALWD Citation Manual: A Professional System of Citation* Rule 47.2 (2000) [hereinafter "*ALWD*"].

[15] *See The Bluebook, supra* note 14, at Rule 10.6 & 10.7; *ALWD, supra* note 14, at Rule 12.10(e).

## 2.   Start with a Present Participle

A parenthetical illustration ordinarily begins with a *present participle*—a verb ending in "ing"—that modifies the cited case by explaining some action by the court in the case.[16] Common present participles used to begin parenthetical illustrations are "finding," "holding," "reasoning," "ruling," "stating," "concluding," and the like.

Two exceptions exist to this rule. First, parenthetical illustrations need not begin with present participles when they enumerate a series of related illustrations set up by the text sentence. The *Bluebook* offers this example.

> *Example 11.13*
>
> Such standards have been adopted to address a variety of environmental problems. *See, e.g.,* H.B. Jacobini, *The New International Sanitary Regulations*, 46 Am. J. Int'l L. 727, 727-28 (1952) (health-related water quality); Robert L. Meyer, *Travaux Preparatoires for the Unesco World Heritage Convention*, 2 Earth L.J. 45, 45-81 (1976) (conservation of protected areas).[17]

In this example, a text sentence sets up the list of illustrations that are included in parentheticals with the cites. When listing a series of illustrations like this, writers need not begin each parenthetical illustration with a present participle.

The second exception occurs when the parenthetical illustration consists of a full-sentence quote from the applicable case.[18] Consider the following example:

> *Example 11.14*
>
> Another factor federal courts consider in deciding whether to grant a motion for change of venue is the convenience of the alternative forums to the parties. Federal courts have held, however, that this factor supports rejecting the motion for transfer if the effect of the transfer is simply to shift the inconvenience from the defendant to the plaintiff. *See, e.g., Graff v. Qwest Communications Corp.*, 33 F. Supp. 2d 1117, 1121 (D. Minn. 1999); *K-TEL Int'l, Inc. v. Tristar Products, Inc.*, No. CIV 00-902, 2001 WL 392405, at *8 (D. Minn. March 28, 2001) ("Based on the fact that a transfer to New Jersey would only serve to shift the inconvenience between the parties, this court concludes that this factor weighs in favor of maintaining this action in Minnesota.").

In this example, the parenthetical illustration was generated from a quote from the case itself. In such instances, it is not necessary to begin the illustration with a

---

[16] *See The Bluebook, supra* note 14, at Rule 1.5; *ALWD, supra* note 14, at Rule 47.3.

[17] *See The Bluebook, supra* note 14, at Rule 1.5.

[18] *See id.* at Rule 1.5; *see also ALWD, supra* note 14, at Rule 47.3.

present participle. Be forewarned, however; only rarely is a court so kind as to provide a ready-made sentence that can be used as a parenthetical illustration. In the large majority of cases, writers must construct the illustration themselves. It follows then that in the large majority of cases writers must begin any parenthetical illustration with a present participle.

### 3.   Provide a Factually Specific Illustration

Because the parenthetical should provide the reader with a "narrative illustration" of how the stated rule was applied in a specific factual context, it should refer to specific facts of the cited case. However, because the reader will not necessarily have read the cited case, factual references should be stated in somewhat general terms. This means, for example, using indefinite articles "a" and "an" instead of the definite article "the" when referring initially to specific facts of the cited case, referring to the parties of the case by descriptive titles rather than by proper names, and so on. These two considerations appear to be contradictory: be specific, but be general at the same time. With practice, however, it will make more sense. The parenthetical illustration should not be so general that it merely restates the general rule. By the same token, however, the illustration should not include references to facts that require reading the case to be understood. The examples in this chapter will help you develop a feel for how parenthetical illustrations can be drafted to satisfy these two considerations.

### 4.   Explain the Illustration in the Context of the Rule Being Discussed

The substance of the parenthetical illustration should be given a specific context. That is, the illustration should explain what the court decided in the *context* of the general legal proposition being discussed. The example below under "Common Mistakes" will help to clarify this point.

### 5.   Begin the Parenthetical Statement with a Lower Case Letter

Because the parenthetical statement is part of the overall citation sentence, it should begin with a lower case letter, not a capital letter.[19] An exception to this rule is when the parenthetical illustration consists of a full-sentence quote from the applicable case.[20] Look again at Example 11.14 above, in which the quotation in the parenthetical illustration begins with a capital letter.

### 6.   Limit the Parenthetical Illustration to One Sentence

A parenthetical illustration should not include more than one sentence. (In fact, because it begins with a present participle, the parenthetical illustration is actually a

---

[19] *See The Bluebook*, *supra* note 14, at Rule 1.5; *see also ALWD*, *supra* note 14, at Rule 47.3.

[20] *Id.*

sentence fragment.) If it is not possible to effectively explain an illustration using a single understandable sentence, the illustration should be placed in the text of the discussion rather than in a parenthetical.

### 7.  Do Not Include Ending Punctuation

The parenthetical statement should not end with any punctuation mark inside the closing parenthesis.[21] Again, parenthetical illustrations consisting of full-sentence quotations are an exception to this rule. Example 11.14 demonstrates the use of ending punctuation in a parenthetical quotation.

### 8.  The Number of Illustrations

It is not necessary to give parenthetical statements for each case cited for the general proposition. If you feel that the reader would benefit from more than one illustration, however, it is permissible to include parentheticals for more than one of the cited cases.

## B.    *Common Mistakes in Drafting Parenthetical Illustrations*

### 1.  Common Mistake #1: Putting the Rule in a Parenthetical

One common mistake made by legal writers in using parenthetical illustrations is putting the statement of the applicable rule in the parenthetical rather than in the text of the discussion. This happens most frequently when the writer provides a transition to the point, but fails to state the actual rule in the text. Let's look at a revised version of Example 11.2 as an illustration:

> *Not Effective:*    Another factor this Court considers in determining whether the prolonged pretrial detention of a criminal defendant violates his due process rights is the complexity of the case. *See, e.g., United States v. Gonzales Claudio*, 806 F.2d 334, 341 (2d Cir. 1986) (holding that, if the delay in bringing a defendant to trial is attributable to the complexity of the case, as opposed to the misconduct or inaction of the prosecution, this factor will support a finding that the extended pretrial detention of the defendant is not a violation of due process); *United States v. El-Hage*, 213 F.3d 74, 80 (2d Cir. 2000).

Because the first sentence merely serves as a transition, this discussion is not effective. The actual rule is never stated in the text of the discussion; it has been relegated to a parenthetical. As discussed before, the rule should be stated in the text; the parenthetical should supplement the rule by illustrating how the rule was applied in a specific factual context. Compare the foregoing example to Example 11.2.

---

[21] *Id.*

### 2. Common Mistake #2: Restating the Rule in a Parenthetical

Another common mistake is merely restating the general rule in the parenthetical. Consider the following example:

> *Not Effective:* Another factor this Court considers in determining whether the prolonged pretrial detention of a criminal defendant violates his due process rights is the complexity of the case. This Court has held that if the delay in bringing a defendant to trial is attributable to the complexity of the case, as opposed to the misconduct or inaction of the prosecution, this factor will support a finding that the extended pretrial detention of the defendant is not a violation of due process. *See, e.g., United States v. Gonzales Claudio*, 806 F.2d 334, 341 (2d Cir. 1986) (holding that if the delay in bringing a defendant to trial is attributable to the complexity of the case, this factor will support a finding that the extended pretrial detention of the defendant is not a violation of due process); *United States v. El-Hage*, 213 F.3d 74, 80 (2d Cir. 2000).

This example is not effective because the parenthetical merely restates the rule already stated in the text; it adds nothing new. This parenthetical comment should be either deleted or redrafted to supplement the rule by illustrating how it was applied to the facts of the cited case. Again, compare this to Example 11.2.

### 3. Common Mistake #3: Stating the Parenthetical Illustration in Overly Broad Terms

The third common mistake is stating the parenthetical in terms so general that it constitutes merely a restatement of the general rule already stated in the text. Consider this example:

> *Not Effective:* Another factor this Court considers in determining whether the prolonged pretrial detention of a criminal defendant violates his due process rights is the complexity of the case. This Court has held that if the delay in bringing a defendant to trial is attributable to the complexity of the case, as opposed to the misconduct or inaction of the prosecution, this factor will support a finding that the extended pretrial detention of the defendant is not a violation of due process. *See, e.g., United States v. Gonzales Claudio*, 806 F.2d 334, 341 (2d Cir. 1986) (finding that, because the case was of a complex nature, this factor supported a finding that the prolonged pretrial detention of the defendant did not violate his due process rights); *United States v. El-Hage*, 213 F.3d 74, 80 (2d Cir. 2000).

This example is ineffective because the parenthetical is so general that it adds little to the rule itself. Such broad statements do not constitute a "narrative illustration" and serve little function.

### 4.  Common Mistake #4: Stating the Parenthetical Illustration in Overly Specific Terms

A fourth common mistake is stating the parenthetical in terms so factually specific that it is difficult to understand without reading the referenced case. Most often this mistake involves a writer referring to the parties of the precedent case by their proper names rather than using descriptive titles. When writing a parenthetical, keep in mind that it must make sense to someone who has not read the referenced case.

### 5.  Common Mistake #5: Failing to Place the Parenthetical Illustration in Context

The fifth common mistake writers make when composing parenthetical illustrations is to fail to indicate the relevant context in the parenthetical. This occurs when a writer summarizes what the court decided too narrowly, without making it clear how this finding fit into the court's analysis of the general rule being discussed. Consider the following example:

> *Not Effective:*    Another factor this Court considers in determining whether the prolonged pretrial detention of a criminal defendant violates his due process rights is the complexity of the case. This Court has held that if the delay in bringing a defendant to trial is attributable to the complexity of the case, as opposed to the misconduct or inaction of the prosecution, this factor will support a finding that the extended pretrial detention of the defendant is not a violation of due process. *See, e.g., United States v. Gonzales Claudio*, 806 F.2d 334, 341 (2d Cir. 1986) (finding that the case was of a complex nature because it involved 20 defendants, events that occurred in numerous locations, and hundreds of audio cassettes, video cassettes, and documents that had to be translated from Spanish to English); *United States v. El-Hage*, 213 F.3d 74, 80 (2d Cir. 2000).

This parenthetical regarding the *Gonzales Claudio* case is ineffective because, while it tells the reader that the court found the case to be of a complex nature, it does not explain how this finding affected the court's decision on the due process issue. This finding of the court has not been put into the context of the general legal proposition being discussed. The reader has no idea whether the *Gonzales Claudio* case is even a "due process" case, or whether it has been taken completely out of context. The parenthetical illustration should not only tell the reader that the court found the case to be complex; it should also explain that this fact weighed in favor of a finding that the defendant's due process rights had not been violated. Compare the above example to Example 11.2.

### 6.  Common Mistake #6: Drafting Overly Long Parenthetical Illustrations

The sixth common mistake involves drafting parenthetical comments that are too long. As stated in the drafting guidelines above, a parenthetical illustration should consist of only one sentence. If more than one sentence is required to explain the illustration, the illustration should be placed in the text of the discussion, not in a parenthetical. Furthermore, forcing an illustration into an extremely long, convoluted sentence is not the solution.

### 7.  Common Mistake #7: Omitting Articles in Parentheticals

Another common mistake committed by legal writers in drafting parentheticals is omitting the articles "a," "an," and "the." Consider this example from *Jet, Inc. v. Sewage Aeration Systems*, 165 F.3d 419, 422 (6th Cir. 1999):

> *Not Effective:*  It was correct [for the magistrate judge] to classify the parties' devices as "related" under the broad standard used to decide whether two trademarks are competing in the same market. *See, e.g., Wynn*, 839 F.2d at 1187 (finding that car wash service and seller of car care products "fundamentally are selling the same thing—a clean car"); *Little Caesar Enters., Inc. v. Pizza Caesar, Inc.*, 834 F.2d 568, 571 (6th Cir. 1987) (finding that sit-down restaurant and carry-out operation sold "quite closely related" goods and services).

The writer of the parentheticals in the above example has omitted the article "a" before the nouns "car wash service," "seller of car care products," "sit-down restaurant," and "carry-out operation." Some legal writers consistently omit such articles from parentheticals, presumably to save space. However, this writing style is not effective. Failure to follow standard grammatical rules distracts readers. The small amount of space saved by omitting articles does not justify the distraction such omissions cause to readers.

### 8.  Common Mistake #8: Starting the Parenthetical with a Gerund

The final common mistake in drafting parenthetical illustrations is starting a parenthetical with a gerund rather than a present participle. As we saw in the drafting guidelines above, the parenthetical illustration should generally begin with an "ing" word—that is, a present participle—related to an action by the court deciding the case. Present participles commonly used include "finding," "holding," "reasoning," "stating," "deciding," and the like.

Some legal writers, however, insert an "ing" word that relates to the parties, not to the court. This makes the "ing" word a *gerund* (an "ing" word operating as a noun) as opposed to a *present participle* (an "ing" word operating as an adjective). Consider this example, revised from Exercise 11.2(a):

> *Not Effective:*  Another factor Florida courts consider in determining

whether a worker is an "employee" or an "independent contractor" is who supplies the worker's tools. If the worker supplies his or her own tools, this factor will support a finding that the worker is an independent contractor, as opposed to an employee. *See, e.g., Kane Furniture Corp. v. Miranda*, 506 So. 2d 1061, 1065 (Fla. 2d Dist. Ct. App. 1987) (supplying his own installation equipment in performing his work supported a finding that a carpet installer was an independent contractor); *T & T Communications, Inc. v. Department of Labor and Employment Sec.*, 460 So. 2d 996, 998 (Fla. 2d Dist. Ct. App. 1984). In the instant case, Ms. Green provided her own musical instrument when playing with the Miami Symphony Orchestra. This fact supports a finding that Ms. Green is an independent contractor, rather than an employee, of the orchestra.

In this example, the use of the word "supplying" at the beginning of the parenthetical is inaccurate because it refers to one of the parties, not the court. The word "supplying" is a noun (a gerund) serving as the subject of the verb "supported." This parenthetical should read as it appeared in Example 11.2(a): (finding that, because a carpet installer supplied his own installation equipment in performing his work, this factor supported a finding that he was an independent contractor). Here, the word "finding" acts as a present participle referring to an action by the court that decided the cited case.

## Exercise 11.3 Drafting and Analyzing Illustrative Narratives

**Hypothetical Fact Pattern:**\* As authorized by the Florida Constitution and Florida Rules of Judicial Administration, the Chief Judge of the Dade County Circuit in Miami, Florida appointed county court judge Edward H. Fleeting to serve temporarily in the circuit court. The administrative order appointed Judge Fleeting

> to temporarily serve as an Acting and Temporary Judge of the FAMILY CIVIL DEPARTMENT of the Circuit Court, to hear, try, conduct, determine and dispose of those cases assigned to him by the Associate Administrative Judge of the Family Division of the Circuit Court, effective from December 1, 1999, to December 31, 2000.

In January 1999, Michael Foster and Sarah Gates executed a surrogate parenting agreement under which Ms. Gates agreed to bear Mr. Foster's child and then give it to Mr. Foster and his wife. Ms. Gates gave birth in March 2000 and turned the child over to the Fosters. In May 2000, the Fosters filed a petition for adoption with the Dade County Circuit Court. The matter was assigned to Judge Fleeting by the clerk of the court. However, the matter was not assigned to Judge Fleeting by the "Associate Administrative Judge of the Family Division of the Circuit Court" as specified in the administrative order. Despite this procedural defect, Judge Fleeting presided over the matter and, in June 2000, he granted the Fosters' petition to adopt the child. Neither the Fosters nor Ms. Gates raised, or even knew of, the issue of the procedural error in the assignment of the case to Judge Fleeting prior to Judge Fleeting's final order in the matter.

In January 2001, Ms. Gates petitioned the circuit court for relief from the judgment of adoption, alleging that the administrative order assigning Judge Fleeting to the circuit court did not authorize him to enter a final judgment of adoption. Ms. Gates argued that, because the "Associate Administrative Judge of the Family Division of the Circuit Court" did not assign the case to Judge Fleeting specifically as required by the original administrative order, Judge Fleeting had no authority to hear it. A different judge—a full-time circuit court judge—upheld Ms. Gates' petition and invalidated Judge Fleeting's adoption order. The judge held that Judge Fleeting lacked authority over the matter because the case was not assigned to him in accordance with the specific provisions of the administrative order. The Fosters have appealed the case to the Florida District Court of Appeal.

**Issue:** Should the adoption order issued by Judge Fleeting be upheld under the "de facto judge doctrine"?

**Authority:** *Card v. State*, 497 So. 2d 1169 (Fla. 1986)
        *McNealy v. State*, 549 So. 2d 248 (Fla. Dist. Ct. App. 1989)

*continued*

---

\* This hypothetical problem was developed from the facts of *Stein v. Foster*, 557 So. 2d 861 (Fla. 1990).

**Assignment:**

1.       Look up and read the above-referenced cases on Florida's de facto judge
         doctrine. Writing as if you were the attorney for the Fosters, draft three versions
         of the argument that Judge Fleeting's adoption order should be upheld under the
         de facto judge doctrine. Your three versions should fulfill these criteria:

>        Version 1: Rule Only. Explain the rules of the de facto judge doctrine in
>        general terms and cite to the referenced cases. Then apply the general rules
>        to the facts of your client's case.
>        Version 2: Rule with Parenthetical Illustration(s). Repeat version 1, but draft
>        parenthetical illustrations for one or both cites.
>        Version 3: Rule with In-Text Illustration(s). Repeat version 1, but draft in-
>        text illustrations for one or both of the cases cited.

         [Your three versions of this argument should look similar to the three versions of
         the arguments set out in Exercises 11.2(a), (b), and (c).]

2.       Write an essay analyzing which of your three versions of this argument is most

---

### Exercise 11.4   Drafting and Analyzing Illustrative Narratives

1.       Find a "rule-based" discussion in a judicial opinion of your choice in which the
         court (1) sets out a general rule, (2) cites authority for the rule, and (3) applies the
         rule to the facts of the case. Rewrite the discussion in two ways:

>        Version 1: Rule with Parenthetical Illustration. Insert a parenthetical
>        illustration of the rule into the discussion that summarizes one of the cited
>        cases.
>        Version 2: Rule with In-Text Illustration. Insert an in-text illustration of the
>        rule into the discussion that summarizes one of the cited cases.

         Attach to your assignment (1) a copy of the original discussion, and (2) a copy
         of the case you used as the basis for your illustration.

2.       Write an essay analyzing which of the three versions of this argument is most
         effective in terms of concepts we have discussed in this chapter.

# Chapter 12

# The Quest for Coherence and the Creation of Factor Tests in Persuasive Legal Writing

> We are predisposed to see order, pattern, and meaning in the world, and we find randomness, chaos, and meaninglessness unsatisfying. Human nature abhors a lack of predictability and the absence of meaning.
> —T. Gilovich

Many legal issues are governed by "factor tests"—that is, legal rules that enumerate various factors or criteria that courts must consider and weigh in resolving the issues. Very often, the factors of a factor test have been made explicit by either a legislative body or a court. In such situations, the analysis of the issue involves merely applying the listed factors to the facts of the present case and weighing the results of the individual factors against each other to reach an overall conclusion.

Sometimes, however, the law on an issue is still in the early stages of development and neither the legislature nor a court has yet articulated the factors relevant to the resolution of the issue. In these situations, the case law on the issue appears to consist merely of random opinions decided based on the facts of the individual cases and the discretionary judgment of the courts, with no overriding rule to govern the analysis. Such situations present important opportunities for the persuasive legal writer. In these situations, an advocate has the opportunity to actively participate in the development of the law by synthesizing the existing (and apparently random) cases into a newly created factor test.

In this chapter, we will explore in detail this analytical strategy of formulating new factor tests for legal issues. We will begin by analyzing the specific nature of factor tests and differentiating them from other common rule structures. We will then discuss how factor tests are created and the opportunities that exist for legal writers to create their own factor tests. In connection with this discussion, we will examine the specific types of legal issues for which this strategy is relevant. Next, we will consider guidelines for how an advocate can most effectively communicate the analysis of a factor test in writing. Finally, we will examine the *persuasive dimensions* of creating new factor tests. Here we will turn to the fields of cognitive, behavioral, and social psychology.

According to psychology theory, the human mind abhors chaos and randomness. Human beings have an innate need to make sense of arbitrary information by organizing it into coherent patterns. In the legal context, the existence of seemingly random cases on an issue can be highly disturbing to the human mind. It follows then that formulating a new factor test on an issue can be a powerful analytical and persuasive strategy because it taps into the human need for coherence and clarity. By formulating a new factor test, an advocate offers to convert the random and chaotic into the meaningful and predictable. Such an offer is often irresistible to a decision-maker. And, as we will see, an advocate using this strategy can gain numerous advantages over an opposing party.

# I.   DEFINING A FACTOR TEST

The analysis of a legal issue is almost always governed by a relevant rule of law. Legal rules, however, can come in a variety of structures. Perhaps the most common rule structure is the "element test." An element test rule identifies a number of requirements, or "elements," that must be satisfied for the rule to be operative. Linda H. Edwards offers this example of a rule that sets out an element test.

> [I]magine that you are working on a course outline for a course in criminal law. You are about to outline the rule that defines burglary. Assume that you have learned that the rule is this:
>
>> Burglary is the breaking and entering of the dwelling of another in the nighttime with the intent to commit a felony therein.
>
> Now, how might you "outline" this rule—that is, write it out in a way that makes its structure visible? As you can see, this rule contains a number of elements, and *each* must be established before a set of facts can constitute burglary. Here is an outline of this rule:
>
>> To establish a burglary, the state must prove *all* of the following elements:
>>
>> A.  breaking
>> B.  entering
>> C.  dwelling
>> D.  of another
>> E.  in the nighttime
>> F.  intent to commit felony therein
>
> . . . The burglary rule above is an example of [a] "mandatory elements" structure.[1]

     In contrast to the element test rule structure is another common rule structure—the "factor test." A factor test rule sets out a flexible legal standard that must be applied, together with a list of criteria, or "factors," that must be considered in determining if the standard is met. As this definition indicates, there are two crucial

---

[1] Linda Holdeman Edwards, *Legal Writing: Process, Analysis, and Organization* 18-19 (2d ed. 1999).

aspects of a factor test rule. First, the rule sets out a flexible legal standard to be applied to the facts of a given case. Second, in order to guide the determination of whether the standard has been met, the rule lists a number of categories of factual inquiry that must be considered. The individual categories of factual inquiry are called "factors." No single factor is dispositive of the issue, and the ultimate determination under a factor test rule is made by "weighing" or "balancing" the conclusions on the individual factors against one another. A factor test functions as a type of pro/con list. Some factors may favor one conclusion, while other factors favor a different conclusion. The final determination depends on which conclusion has the strongest support when all of the factors are considered together. Professor Edwards offers this example of a factor test:

> Child custody shall be decided in accordance with the best interests of the child. Factors to be considered in deciding the best interests of the child are:
>
> A.  the fitness of each possible custodian;
> B.  the appropriateness for parenting of the lifestyle of each possible custodian;
> C.  the relationship between the child and each possible custodian;
> D.  the placement of the child's siblings, if any;
> E.  living accommodations;
> F.  the district lines of the child's school;
> G.  the proximity of extended family and friends;
> H.  religious issues;
> I.  any other factors relevant to the child's best interests.[2]

In this example, we can clearly see the two aspects of factor tests discussed above. First, the rule sets out a flexible standard for determining which possible custodian of a child should get custody of the child. The standard established by the rule is the "best interest of the child" standard. Second, the rule sets out a number of factors a court must consider in determining what is in the best interest of the child in terms of custody. These factors represent relevant categories of factual inquiry. Factor A, for example, instructs the court to consider the facts relevant to the "fitness" of each possible custodian. No single factor is determinative of the issue. The ultimate determination of custody under this rule involves a "balancing" of the factors. Some factors may favor one custodian, while other factors favor a different custodian. The final conclusion is reached by determining which of the possible custodians has the strongest support when all the factors are considered together.

At this point, it is important that we reiterate the difference between elements and factors. As we previously discussed, elements are mandatory. Under an element test, all of the elements must be established for the rule to be met. Factors, on the other hand, function quite differently. It is not necessary that all the factors of a factor test support the same result. Some factors may support one result, and other factors the opposite result. To draw a conclusion under a factor test, the decision-maker must mentally balance the conflicting factors to determine which conclusion has the most

---

[2] *Id.* at 20.

support.

In this chapter, we are most interested in factor tests. Such tests abound in the law. As the following examples demonstrate, factor test rules are created frequently by both legislatures and courts.

(1) From 33 U.S.C. Sec. 2006 (2001) (Inland Navigational Rules):

> Every [shipping] vessel shall at all times proceed at a safe speed so that she can take proper and effective action to avoid collision and be stopped within a distance appropriate to the prevailing circumstances and conditions.
>
> In determining a safe speed the following factors shall be among those taken into account:
> (a) By all vessels:
>     (i) the state of visibility;
>     (ii) the traffic density including concentration of fishing vessels or any other vessels;
>     (iii) the maneuverability of the vessel with special reference to stopping distance and turning ability in the prevailing conditions;
>     (iv) at night the presence of background light such as from shore lights or from back scatter of her own lights;
>     (v) the state of wind, sea, and current, and the proximity of navigational hazards;
>     (vi) the draft in relation to the available depth of water.
> (b) Additionally, by vessels with operational radar:
>     (i) the characteristics, efficiency and limitations of the radar equipment;
>     (ii) any constraints imposed by the radar range scale in use;
>     (iii) the effect on radar detection of the sea state, weather, and other sources of interference;
>     (iv) the possibility that small vessels, ice and other floating objects may not be detected by radar at an adequate range;
>     (v) the number, location, and movement of vessels detected by radar; and
>     (vi) the more exact assessment of the visibility that may be possible when radar is used to determine the range of vessels or other objects in the vicinity.

(2) From California Rules of Court 45.5 (Rules on Appeal):

> Rule 45.5. Standards for time extensions.
>
> (a) When good cause appears, an extension of time [for the filing of an appellate brief] shall . . . be granted. . . .
> (b) . . . An application to extend time shall be made by a declaration containing specific facts, not mere conclusions, and shall be served on all parties to the appellate proceeding. The application shall state

when the document is due, how long an extension is requested, and whether any prior extensions have been granted and, if so, their length, and whether granted by stipulation or by the court.

(c) . . . In determining good cause, the court shall consider the following factors, if applicable:

(1) The degree of prejudice, if any, to any party. . . .

(2) In civil cases, the position of the client and any opponent concerning the extension being sought.

(3) The number and complexity of the issues raised. . . .

(4) Settlement negotiations, including how far they have progressed and when they will be completed.

(5) Whether the case in which the application is made involves litigation entitled to priority.

(6) Whether counsel handling the appeal is new to the case, or the necessity for other counsel or the client to review the document to be filed.

(7) Whether the counsel responsible for preparing the document has other time-limited commitments during the affected period.

. . .

(8) Illness of counsel, a personal emergency, or a planned vacation which cannot reasonably be rearranged and which was not reasonably expected to conflict with the due date.

(9) Any other factor which in the context of a particular case constitutes good cause.

(3) From *Community for Creative Non-Violence v. Reid*, 490 U.S. 730, 751-52 (1989) (footnotes omitted).

In determining whether a hired party is an employee [as opposed to an independent contractor] under the general common law of agency, we consider the hiring party's right to control the manner and means by which the product is accomplished. Among the other factors relevant to this inquiry are the skill required; the source of the instrumentalities and tools; the location of the work; the duration of the relationship between the parties; whether the hiring party has the right to assign additional projects to the hired party; the extent of the hired party's discretion over when and how long to work; the method of payment; the hired party's role in hiring and paying assistants; whether the work is part of the regular business of the hiring party; whether the hiring party is in business; the provision of employee benefits; and the tax treatment of the hired party.

**Exercise 12.1   Understanding the Factor Test Rule Structure**

Write a few paragraphs explaining why the above three rules meet the definition of a factor test as described in preceding section.

## II.   CREATING A FACTOR TEST: THE PROCESS OF INDUCTION

### A.     *Defining Induction*

Before we can specifically discuss how factor tests are created, we must explore the primary mental process at work in the creation of these tests: the process of induction. Induction is a mental process by which a person forms a general proposition from a specific instance or a series of specific instances. That is, it is the process by which we mentally explain an event or a group of related events by creating a general proposition that would explain what happened in the event or events.

Dan Hunter has written a comprehensive article on the process of induction in the law in which he offers this introductory explanation of induction:[3]

> Induction is, generally, the process of taking a number of specific cases or instances, classifying them into categories according to relevant attributes and outcomes, and deriving a broadly applicable rule from them. That is, we take a number of isolated experiences and attempt to explain them by a general rule that covers all the instances examined. For example, prior to any theory about the movements of the heavens, early humans noticed that on day one the sun rose in the east and set in the west. The same thing, they saw, happened on day two, day three, and so on. From many observational instances they were able to induce the rule: "The sun always rises in the east and sets in the west."[4]

Induction in its simplest form occurs when one induces a general proposition from a single instance. Assume, for example, that a friend takes a new job as a car salesman at a new car dealership. Assume further that you notice one day shortly after your friend begins his new job that he drove home in a new car with a "dealer" licence plate. From this single observance, you might induce the general rule that sales people at the dealership are allowed to take new cars home as part of their jobs.

Induction from a single event, however, is frequently unreliable. A number of reasons could explain why your friend drove a dealer car home on that one particular

---

[3] Dan Hunter, *No Wilderness of Single Instances: Inductive Inference in Law*, 48 J. Legal Educ. 365 (1998).

[4] *Id.* at 369.

occasion. Thus, when logicians talk about induction they are usually referring to induction from multiple related incidences. Professor Hunter's illustration above regarding the rising and setting of the sun is an example of induction from multiple incidences. The general rule that the sun always rises in the east and sets in the west was induced from numerous observational instances.

The process of induction plays a very significant role in the analysis of legal issues. Often an attorney will come across an area of the law that is still in the early stages of development. This area could involve a fairly broad issue or, more likely, a narrower sub-issue within a broader issue. The attorney might discover that no general rule or proposition has yet been announced by a court or legislative body that dictates the analysis of the issue. Rather, there are simply a number of cases addressing the issue and reaching their conclusions based on the specific facts of the individual cases. In such situations, the process of induction becomes relevant. The individual cases reflect different fact patterns and various conclusions, all relevant to the same legal issue. In terms of induction, the individual cases are multiple related "instances." Applying induction, the attorney in this situation can attempt to organize and categorize the various cases and fashion an encompassing legal proposition that explains the conclusions in all of them. Sometimes the induced rule is a fairly simple one, with only one operative concept. More frequently, however, the induced rule is a more sophisticated, multi-part rule. Once the induced rule has been created, it can serve as a guideline for the analysis of the issue in future cases.

Some legal writers term the process of inducing a general rule from a group of related cases "synthesizing."[5] Helene S. Shapo, Marilyn R. Walter, and Elizabeth Fajans offer this example of induction, or synthesis, in the context of legal writing:

> Suppose you are analyzing some cases on the question of whether parents are immune from tort suits brought by their children. In this situation you know part of the rule, that parents may be immune from suit. Read the four case summaries to synthesize the rest of the rule. All suits are in the jurisdiction where the age of majority is 18. (Full citations are omitted.)

> Case 1:
> Jack Abbott sued his father Joseph for negligently pouring hot liquids in the Abbott kitchen so that he burned Jack in the process. Jack is twelve years old. Held: Mr. Abbott is immune from suit. Abbott v. Abbott (1985).

> Case 2:
> James White sued his father Walter for battery, an intentional tort. Walter knocked James's baseball cap off his head because James struck out in the last inning of a Little League game. James is ten years old. Held: Mr. White is not immune from suit. White v. White (1990).

> Case 3:
> Joan Brown sued her father Matt for assault, an intentional tort, for brandishing

---

[5] *See, e.g.*, Edwards, *supra* note 1, at 64-65, 68-70; Richard K. Neuman, Jr., *Legal Reasoning and Legal Writing: Structure, Strategy, and Style* 139-41 (4th ed. 2001); Helene S. Shapo et al., *Writing and Analysis in the Law* 49-54 (4th ed. 1999).

a tennis racket at her after she lost her serve in the final set of the women's 25 and under local tennis tournament. Joan is twenty-four years old and lives at home. Held: Mr. Brown is not immune from suit. <u>Brown v. Brown</u> (1991).

Case 4:
George Black sued his father for negligently burning him in Mr. Black's kitchen by handing him a large hot pot. George is a twenty-four-year-old business man and is married. Held: Paul Black is not immune from suit. <u>Black v. Black</u> (1992).

These cases involve two requirements of whether the parent is immune from suit. To analyze the topic, you should identify them and consider how they determine immunity. Look at the facts that evidently have led the courts to decide that the parent is immune, and at the facts that evidently have led the courts to decide that the parent is not immune.

In each case, the court mentions the child's age. In Case 1, the child was a minor and the parent was immune from the suit. In Case 2, however, the child was a minor but the parent was not immune from the suit. In seeking an explanation for this difference, you notice that the second requirement is involved, the type of tort, whether an intentional tort or negligence. In Case 4, the parent was negligent, but the child was not a minor and the parent was not immune from the suit. These two requirements now become part of the rule: (1) the child must be a minor, and (2) the child must sue for negligence.
. . .

[Thus the resulting synthesized rule:] Parents are immune from a tort suit brought by their children if the suit is for negligence and the child is a minor.[6]

The above example reflects the induction of a general rule from a group of related cases. More specifically, it reflects the induction of an "element test" rule. The four cases summarized in the example reflect the body of cases addressing parental immunity in the particular jurisdiction. When these cases were decided, no express general rule existed regarding the applicability of parental immunity. Thus, the courts reached their conclusions simply by reasoning from the specific facts of the cases and deciding what seemed appropriate under those facts. As the example shows, however, a lawyer coming to this issue after these cases have been decided can attempt, through the process of induction, to fashion a general rule from them. The lawyer can review the cases and look for common patterns or concepts that might explain and reconcile the various conclusions. In the example, the common pattern that emerges has two separate requirements: (1) that the suit involve a minor, and (2) that the suit involve negligence as opposed to an intentional tort. Thus, through the process of induction, a two-element rule can be created to explain the different conclusions in the four parental immunity cases: Parents are immune from a tort suit brought by their children if the suit is for negligence and the child is a minor. This rule can tbe used to guide the analysis of parental immunity issues in this jurisdiction in the future.

This is the essence of induction in the law. Through the process of induction, a lawyer develops a general rule from the fact-specific conclusions in a series of related cases and by so doing actively participates in the development of the law.

---

[6] Shapo et al., *supra* note 5, at 50-51.

## B.     *Induction of a Factor Test*

In the parental immunity example above, the rule created through induction involved a definitive two-element test. Sometimes, however, the cases on an issue cannot be synthesized into a definitive rule. Rather, the most that can be accomplished is to synthesize the cases into a more flexible factor test. It is this type of induction with which we are most concerned in this chapter.

The types of legal issues that give rise to the inductive creation of a factor test have two general characteristics. First, the law on an issue must set out some kind of flexible legal standard designed to control the outcome on the issue. Second, a number of cases must exist in which the courts of the jurisdiction endeavored to apply the flexible legal standard to the facts of specific cases. In situations where these two requirements are met, the opportunity exists to synthesize the law by creating a factor test. This process is best explained through an illustration.

———————

Assume that you are practicing law in the fictitious state of Lincoln. Assume further that, under the law of Lincoln, a person can invalidate a contract to which he or she is a party by proving that the contract was entered into under duress. Duress under Lincoln law is defined as follows:

> Duress exists when a person enters into a contract involuntarily as the result of an illegal threat by the opposite contracting party.

Case law in Lincoln has broken this definition of duress into a two-element test:

> (1) The party claiming duress must have been subjected to an illegal threat by the other party; and
> (2) The threat must have caused the party claiming duress to act involuntarily.

Regarding the second element—that the party claiming duress acted "involuntarily"—the following five cases have been decided by the courts of Lincoln.

> Case 1: *Kory v. City of Maintown*[7] (Lincoln intermediate appellate court, 1981).
>
> *Facts:* Ms. Kory, a temporary employee for the City of Maintown, claimed that she signed a resignation agreement under duress. Regarding the "involuntary act" element, the court held:
>
>> On the facts of this case, it is clear that Ms. Kory did not act "involuntarily" in signing the resignation agreement. The idea of resigning was initiated by her. When she was told that she was going to be fired, she asked if she could resign instead. Under such circumstances, one could hardly say that the resignation

———————

[7] Adapted from *City of Miami v. Kory*, 394 So. 2d 494 (Fla. Dist. Ct. App. 1981).

agreement was forced on her. Moreover, Ms. Kory was given 24 hours to reach her decision. This time to deliberate further supports our conclusion that her act of executing the resignation agreement was a voluntary one.

Case 2: *Paris v. Paris*[8] (Lincoln's highest appellate court, 1982).

*Facts:* Ms. Paris sued to invalidate a property settlement agreement that she executed with her ex-husband in connection with their divorce. Ms. Paris claimed that she executed the agreement under duress because her ex-husband threatened to tell their minor children damaging things about her if she did not sign the agreement. Specifically, the husband threatened to tell their minor children that another minor child who was thought to be a cousin was actually the child of Ms. Paris from a previous relationship and that Ms. Paris had had numerous extramarital affairs. Both of these things were true but unknown to the parties' children. Regarding the "involuntary act" element, the court held:

> We find that Ms. Paris did act involuntarily. First, if she did not sign the agreement, she ran the risk of severely damaging her reputation in the eyes of her own children. It is not difficult to conclude that one faced with such a prospect is not acting of her own volition. Moreover, unlike in the *Kory* case, Ms. Paris had mere minutes to make her decision. The pressing nature of the decision further suggests its involuntary nature.

Case 3: *Berger v. Berger*[9] (Lincoln's highest appellate court, 1985).

*Facts:* Ms. Berger sued to invalidate a property settlement agreement executed between her and her ex-husband. Regarding the "involuntary act" element, the court held:

> Any doubt that Ms. Berger signed the agreement involuntarily is resolved by the fact that the agreement gave her nothing. Under the terms of the agreement, Ms. Berger gave up her interest in the family home, the household furnishings, the primary family vehicle, and the joint owned savings account. She even gave up primary custody of the couple's two minor children. The only thing Ms. Berger got under the settlement agreement was ownership of the secondary vehicle (which is barely operational and has minimal commercial value) and sole ownership of the beauty salon (which has little worth other than Ms. Berger's skills as a beautician).

Case 4: *Collins v. King* (Lincoln intermediate appellate court, 1990).

*Facts:* Mr. King is the president of Shady Oaks Country Club, where Mr. Collins is a long-time member. Mr. Collins sued Mr. King to invalidate a lease agreement between the two claiming he executed it under duress. In the

---

[8] Adapted from *Paris v. Paris*, 412 So. 2d 952 (Fla. Dist. Ct. App. 1982).

[9] Adapted from *Berger v. Berger*, 466 So. 2d 1149 (Fla. Dist. Ct. App. 1985).

suit, Mr. Collins claimed that in order to pressure him into leasing some property he owned to Mr. King at below market value, Mr. King threatened to cancel Mr. Collins' reserved parking space at the Club. Regarding the "involuntary act" element, the court held:

> While we are sure that losing the parking space would have caused an inconvenience to Mr. Collins, we can not say that such a threat caused him to act involuntarily. The severity of the consequences for not complying with Mr. King's demands was not of the level such that we can conclude that one faced with such consequences acts involuntarily. This threat was not severe enough to cause Mr. Collins to lease his property at a rate significantly below market value. There must be some other explanation for his conduct. Nevertheless, the "involuntary act" element is not met in this case.

Case 5: *Mullan v. School Board*[10] (Lincoln's highest appellate court, 1985).

*Facts:* Mr. Mullan, a teacher at a public high school, was accused of hitting a student while disciplining the student. The school's principle, Mr. Wise, told Mr. Mullan that he was fired. After Mr. Mullan protested, Mr. Wise announced that Mr. Mullan could resign with compensation or be fired without pay. Mr. Mullan signed a resignation agreement prepared by Mr. Wise. Mr. Mullan later sued to have the agreement invalidated under duress. Regarding the "involuntary act" element, the court held:

> Unlike in *Kory*, it was Mr. Wise who first proposed the resignation agreement. Furthermore, Mr. Wise presented to Mr. Mullan a typed resignation agreement within minutes of their altercation, and Mr. Mullan was pressured to sign it immediately. In view of these facts, we conclude that Mr. Mullan acted involuntarily in signing the resignation.

A close review of the above hypothetical situation reveals several important things. First, we see that the definition of duress under Lincoln law involves two required elements. We also see that the second element requires the party claiming duress to prove that he or she acted "involuntarily." "Involuntariness," however, is a rather nebulous concept. Whether a person has acted involuntarily is not subject to a definitive test; it is more of a judgment call. Thus, the second element of duress establishes what amounts to a "flexible legal standard."

Perhaps the easiest way to see how the second element establishes a flexible standard is to compare it to the first element. The first element of duress requires that the party claiming duress prove that he or she was the target of an "illegal threat." According to this element, a person has not engaged in duress if he or she threatens something he or she has a legal right to threaten. Applying pressure with a legitimate and legal threat is not duress.

The determination of element one, compared to element two, is relatively straightforward. Whether a person has a legal right to make a threat is a concrete

---

[10] Adapted from *Mullan v. Bishop of the Diocese of Orlando*, 540 So. 2d 174 (Fla. Dist. Ct. App. 1989).

concept subject to definitive analysis. A person either does or does not have a legal right. Involuntariness, on the other hand, is more amorphous. Thus, where element one sets out a concrete requirement relatively easy to ascertain, element two requires more discretionary judgment.

Because the "involuntary" requirement of element two sets out a flexible legal standard, the hypothetical situation also includes a number of judicial opinions in which the courts of the state applied this standard to the facts of specific cases. None of the five hypothetical case opinions sets out a general rule for determining involuntariness. Each opinion simply reasons from the specific facts of the case (or, in some instances, distinguishes the facts of the case from the facts of other cases). In this situation, a lawyer can review the precedent cases to see if, through the process of induction, he or she can identify general categories of facts that the courts have found relevant in determining involuntariness. To the extent that the reasoning in these cases can be generalized and categories of factual inquiries relevant to the issue identified, a list of factors can be devised to help guide the analysis of this issue in future cases.

A review of Case 1, Case 2, and Case 5 reveals what is perhaps the most obvious concept the Lincoln courts have considered in determining involuntariness: the amount of time the party claiming duress had to deliberate over the decision to enter into the contract. In Case 1, Ms. Kory was given ample time in the eyes of the court, and this supported the court's conclusion that she did not act involuntarily in signing the resignation agreement. In Cases 2 and 5, on the other hand, the courts found that the immediacy of the decisions supported the conclusions that the parties in question did act involuntarily. Thus, from these cases we can induce that one factor Lincoln courts consider in determining if a person claiming duress acted involuntarily is the amount of time he or she had to deliberate over the situation.

A review of Cases 1 and 5 reveals a second factor: which of the two parties initiated the contract in question. In Case 1, Ms. Kory herself first proposed the idea of resigning, and the court in Case 1 specifically mentioned this fact as a reason for its conclusion that Ms. Kory acted voluntarily. Case 2 reflects the converse of this idea. In that case, the "duressor" initially proposed the contract in question. This fact supported the court's conclusion that Mr. Mullan acted involuntarily.

A third factor can be induced from Cases 2 and 4: the severity of the consequences for not entering into the contract in question. In Case 2, the court expressly mentioned that the fear of having one's reputation damaged in the eyes of one's children is strong enough to compel a person to act involuntarily. Contrastingly, the court in Case 4 found that the fear of losing a reserved parking space could not compel someone to act involuntarily. These two cases indicate that another factor Lincoln courts will consider in determining whether a person alleging duress acted involuntarily is the severity of the threat that he or she was facing.

A fourth and final factor is suggested in Case 3. In this case, the property settlement agreement was unfair to Ms. Berger. The court concluded that this was evidence that she signed the agreement involuntarily. Thus, Case 3 indicates that the fairness of the agreement to the party alleging duress is another factor Lincoln courts will consider in determining involuntariness.

The following table summarizes the results of this inductive process. The summary also indicates the case or cases from which a particular factor was induced.

**Table 12.1**

In determining whether a person claiming duress acted "involuntarily," Lincoln courts consider the following factors:

  A.  The amount of time the party claiming duress had to deliberate over the decision to enter into the contract.
  Case 1: *Kory v. City of Maintown*
  Case 2: *Paris v. Paris*
  Case 5: *Mullan v. School Board*
  B. Which party initiated the contract in question.
  Case 1: *Kory v. City of Maintown*
  Case 5: *Mullan v. School Board*
  C. The severity of the consequences for not entering into the contract.
  Case 2: *Paris v. Paris*
  Case 4: *Collins v. King*
  D. The fairness of the contract in question to the party claiming duress.
  Case 3: *Berger v. Berger*

Most factor tests that exist in law were created through this same inductive process. A legislature or court establishing a factor test for the resolution of an issue typically generates the factors by reviewing cases addressing the issue just as we have done here. Such factor tests synthesize the apparently random cases on an issue and provide a structure for analyzing the issue in future cases.

This technique is available to legal writers as well.[11] By using induction and creating factor tests, we can contribute directly to the development of the law. If, for example, we were practicing in Lincoln and representing a client in a duress case, we could offer the above test to the court as an analytical framework for evaluating involuntariness. This test synthesizes the apparently random cases on involuntariness and provides the court with a mechanism by which it can analyze the issue more systematically. Later in this chapter we will examine why this technique is effective for legal writers and the circumstances under which it can be used most strategically.

---

[11] In fact, most courts and legislatures create their factor tests with the help of legal advocates.

**Exercise 12.2    Creating a Factor Test Through the Process of Induction**

You are an attorney practicing law in the fictitious state of Lincoln. Lincoln courts follow the United States Supreme Court case of *Miranda v. Arizona*, which requires a police officer to inform a suspect who is in custody of his or her constitutional rights prior to interrogating the suspect (i.e., "You have the right to remain silent . . .").

Any statements made by a suspect in custody who was not informed of his or her Miranda rights cannot be used against the suspect. Under Lincoln law, however, Miranda warnings are required only when a defendant is in "custody." Statements made by an individual to a police officer when the individual is not in "custody" can be used against the individual even if no Miranda warning was given prior to the statements.

The concept of "custody" is a fairly ambiguous one. Lincoln courts have not set out a rule defining custody. Whether or not a suspect is in custody is a judgment call. In terms of the concepts we have discussed in this chapter, "custody" is a "flexible legal standard."

In **Appendix B** of this text, you will find six cases decided by the courts of Lincoln on the issue of custody. Review these cases and, using the process of induction, identify the "factors" that Lincoln courts consider in determining if a person is in "custody" for the purposes of Miranda warnings. Prepare a list of the factors and the cases from which each factor has been induced. Your final product should resemble Table 12.1.

# III.  THE COMMUNICATION OF FACTOR TEST ANALYSIS

In your introductory legal writing courses you learned how to communicate the analysis of a legal issue effectively. That general instruction also applies to communicating the analysis under a factor test. A few additional guidelines will nonetheless be useful when writing an argument based on a factor test.

## A.    *Large-Scale Organization*

The overall organization of an argument based on a factor test is fairly obvious: the argument should be structured around an analysis of each factor, one at a time, followed by a conclusion in which the factors are weighed together to reach the bottom line. More specifically, the large-scale organization of a factor analysis should contain the following components:

- **An "Umbrella" Section** (which should include an explanation of the general rule that establishes the legal standard on the issue, together with a summary of the factors to be analyzed).

- **An Analysis of Each Factor Separately** (which should include an explanation of the law on each factor and an application of the factor to the facts of the present case).
- **A Bottom Line Conclusion** (in which the writer should weigh together the "mini-conclusions" on each individual factor to reach an overall conclusion on the issue).

Each of these components will be discussed in more detail below. The following is a sample organizational outline of an argument based on the duress hypothetical discussed earlier in this chapter. As we saw in that previous discussion, duress under the law of Lincoln involves a two-element test. However, the "factor test" concept is only relevant to element two. Thus, while the outline below sets out both elements, it is the second element with which we are most concerned. The portion of the outline dealing with element two and its factor test has been set out in **bold**.

Outline of the Duress Issue

I.   UMBRELLA SECTION.
  A.   SET OUT GENERAL DEFINITION OF DURESS.
  B.   EXPLAIN HOW THE DEFINITION OF DURESS IS BROKEN DOWN INTO TWO SEPARATE ELEMENTS.
II.   ANALYSIS OF ELEMENT 1: THE PARTY CLAIMING DURESS MUST HAVE BEEN SUBJECTED TO AN ILLEGAL THREAT.
      [Because element one has not been the focus of our discussion, a detailed breakdown of the analysis of this element has been omitted.]
III.  **ANALYSIS OF ELEMENT 2: THE PARTY CLAIMING DURESS ACTED "INVOLUNTARILY."**
  A.   **MINI-UMBRELLA SECTION.**
    1.   **SET OUT THE GENERAL RULE THAT THE THREAT BY THE OTHER PARTY MUST HAVE CAUSED THE PARTY CLAIMING DURESS TO ACT "INVOLUNTARILY."**
    2.   **SET OUT A LIST OF THE FACTORS LINCOLN COURTS CONSIDER IN DETERMINING IF A PARTY CLAIMING DURESS ACTED INVOLUNTARILY.**
  B.   **FACTOR 1: THE AMOUNT OF TIME THE PARTY CLAIMING DURESS HAD TO DELIBERATE OVER THE DECISION TO ENTER INTO THE CONTRACT.**
    1.   **EXPLAIN THE LAW ON THIS FACTOR.**
    2.   **APPLY THIS FACTOR TO THE FACTS OF THE PRESENT CASE AND STATE A MINI-CONCLUSION OF THIS FACTOR.**
  C.   **FACTOR 2 : WHICH PARTY INITIATED THE CONTRACT IN QUESTION.**
    1.   **EXPLAIN THE LAW ON THIS FACTOR.**
    2.   **APPLY THIS FACTOR TO THE FACTS OF THE PRESENT CASE AND STATE A MINI-CONCLUSION OF THIS FACTOR.**
  D.   **FACTOR 3: THE SEVERITY OF THE CONSEQUENCES FOR NOT ENTERING INTO THE CONTRACT.**
    1.   **EXPLAIN THE LAW ON THIS FACTOR.**
    2.   **APPLY THIS FACTOR TO THE FACTS OF THE PRESENT CASE AND STATE A MINI-CONCLUSION OF THIS FACTOR.**
  E.   **FACTOR 4 : THE FAIRNESS OF THE CONTRACT IN QUESTION TO THE**

PARTY CLAIMING DURESS.
1.   EXPLAIN THE LAW ON THIS FACTOR.
2.   APPLY THIS FACTOR TO THE FACTS OF THE PRESENT CASE AND
     STATE A MINI-CONCLUSION OF THIS FACTOR.
F.   CONCLUSION ON ELEMENT 2: WEIGH ALL THE FACTORS TOGETHER
     AND REACH A BOTTOM LINE ON THE INVOLUNTARY ELEMENT.
IV.  OVERALL CONCLUSION CONSIDERING BOTH ELEMENT 1 AND ELEMENT 2.

## B.    The "Umbrella" Section

An argument based on a factor test, like most legal arguments, should begin with a general discussion that sets out the broad rule governing the analysis of the issue. Some legal writing texts call this an introductory paragraph, but, like Edwards, we will call it the "umbrella section,"[12] because in it the writer sets out the general "umbrella" rule that, broken into subparts, will form the structure of the remainder of the argument.

In the context of an argument based on a factor test, the umbrella discussion should, at a minimum, set out (1) the general rule that establishes the flexible legal standard relevant to the issue, and (2) a summary of the factors courts in the jurisdiction consider when determining if the legal standard is met.[13] The following is a sample umbrella section for element two of the duress hypothetical.[14]

> The second element of duress requires that the party claiming duress prove that he or she acted "involuntarily" in entering into the contract. Lincoln courts consider the following factors in determining whether a party claiming duress acted involuntarily: (1) the amount of time the party claiming duress had to deliberate over the decision to enter into the contract; (2) which party initiated the contract in question; (3) the severity of the consequences for not entering into the contract; and (4) the fairness of the contract in question to the party claiming duress.

## C.    The Analysis of Each Separate Factor

In analyzing each separate factor, employ the general paradigm you learned in your introductory legal writing course for communicating the analysis of an issue. Some legal writing materials refer to this as the IRAC paradigm. Others refer to it as the Rule Explanation / Rule Application paradigm. Whatever you call it, the paradigm

---

[12] *See* Edwards, *supra* note 1, at 138.

[13] The introduction, or "umbrella" section, can also set out a *thesis statement,* as recommended by most introductory persuasive writing texts.

[14] As the outline above indicates, this sample discussion actually reflects a "mini-umbrella." The general umbrella section at the beginning of the argument would set out the broad two-element test for duress. The sample discussion sets out the umbrella rule for a subpart of that discussion—that is, element two—which itself is broken down into subparts comprised of the factors of our test.

for communicating the analysis of a specific factor involves two general steps:

Step 1:  Explain the law on the factor and cite to relevant authority.[15]

Step 2:  Apply the factor to the facts of the present case and state a mini-conclusion[16] on the factor.

The following is an example of the analysis of the first factor of the "involuntary" element of the duress hypothetical:

| | |
|---|---|
| Step 1: Explanation of the law | The first factor Lincoln courts consider in determining if a party claiming duress acted involuntarily is the amount of time that party had to deliberate over the decision to enter into the contract. Lincoln courts have held that if the party claiming duress had time to carefully consider whether to enter into the contract in question, this factor will support a finding that the party acted voluntarily. *See Kory v. City of Maintown.* Conversely, if the party claiming duress was forced to make a decision immediately, without time to deliberate, this factor will support a finding that the decision was an involuntary one. *See Paris v. Paris; Mullan v. School Board* (reasoning that the fact that an employee was pressured to sign a resignation agreement "immediately" supported a finding that the employee acted involuntarily in signing the agreement). |
| Step 2: Application and mini-conclusion | In the present case, the plaintiff was given more than two weeks to decide whether to enter into the licensing agreement. Consequently, the plaintiff had ample time to deliberate over the contract and its terms. These facts support a finding that the plaintiff acted voluntarily when he executed the licensing agreement. |

The presentation of the remaining three factors of the "involuntary" element would follow this same basic structure. For each factor, the writer would explain the law on the factor and then apply the law to the facts of the present case.

## D.     *Language Indicating the Operative Effect of a Single Factor*

The foregoing example suggests another important feature of communicating the

---

[15] It may not be necessary to apply this two-step paradigm for each factor in an *established* factor test expressly set out by a court or statute. In that case, listing the factors at the beginning of the discussion and then applying them one by one to the facts of the present case may be enough. When a legal writer has created a *new factor test*, however, it is important that the writer show the reader from which case or cases each factor was induced. Thus, when employing a new factor test, a writer should scrupulously apply both steps for each factor.

[16] The word "mini-conclusion" is used because the overall "conclusion" is not reached until the end of the argument, when all the factors are weighed against each other.

analysis on a particular factor. Notice that in the statement of the rule from the *Kory* case and in the statement of the rule from the *Paris* and *Mullan* cases the rules contain the phrasing "*supports* a finding." Notice further that the concluding sentence in the application step contains the phrasing, "These facts *support* a finding . . . ". The use of the wording "supports a finding" in these contexts is very important. Recall from our introductory discussion of factor tests that no single factor of a factor test is dispositive. The conclusion on an issue governed by a factor test is reached only after the factors are all weighed together. Thus, when analyzing a single factor, the most that one can say about that factor is that it "supports" or "weighs toward" a particular conclusion. Consider the following revised version of the application step from the previous example:

> *Not Effective:*   In the present case, the plaintiff was given more than two weeks to decide whether to enter into the licensing agreement. Consequently, the plaintiff had ample time to deliberate over the contract and its terms. *Based on these facts, the plaintiff acted voluntarily when he executed the licensing agreement.*

This wording is inaccurate. The final sentence states that, based on the factor, the plaintiff "acted voluntarily." This wording suggests that the factor is dispositive of the issue of "voluntariness." However, as we know from our basic discussion of how factor tests operate, no single factor is determinative of an issue. Thus, when stating the general rule of a factor and when applying a factor to the facts of the present case, a writer must avoid using wording that suggests that the factor is dispositive. The most common phrases used by legal writers in stating the operative effect of a single factor are "supports a finding," "weighs in favor of," and "weighs against." Phrases such as this accurately indicate to the reader that the conclusion on a single factor is only one consideration among a number that must be analyzed to determine the bottom line conclusion on the issue.

## E.   *The Bottom Line Conclusion*

After each factor has been analyzed, the writer must conduct an overall weighing or balancing of the various mini-conclusions under the individual factors. Some factors may support one conclusion while other factors support the opposite conclusion. Such is the nature of factor tests. In the end, the writer must explain the bottom line conclusion based on a complete weighing of all the factors.

Sometimes the bottom line conclusion is based on "quantitative" analysis. In these situations, the *number* of factors supporting one conclusion exceeds the *number* of factors supporting the opposite conclusion. Sometime the bottom line conclusion involves more of a "qualitative" analysis. In these situations, the factors the courts have identified as being the most important, or as having the most weight, tend to dictate the conclusion. Frequently, the final determination involves a combination of both quantitative and qualitative analyses. Whatever the case, the writer must reach a bottom line conclusion and explain how it was reached.

## Exercise 12.3   Drafting an Argument Based on a Factor Test

Writing as if you were the attorney for the defendant in the hypothetical below, draft the argument that the defendant was in "custody" for the purposes of Miranda warnings. Organize your argument around the factor test you created in Exercise 12.2 and the cases in **Appendix B**. In your argument, cite to the cases by case name only.

**Hypothetical Fact Pattern:** Cole Lutter is the owner of a hardware store in Maintown, Lincoln. On a recent Sunday, Maintown police found an abandoned stolen car containing a number of receipts from Mr. Lutter's store. Upon further investigation, the police determined that Mr. Lutter's store had been burglarized early that Sunday morning while it was closed. The police hypothesized that the burglar took the contents of the store's safe—the money and receipts—and left the scene in the stolen car. The culprit then abandoned the car and the store receipts.

Later that day, the police asked Mr. Lutter to come down to the police department to confirm that the receipts came from Mr. Lutter's store and to discuss any possible leads that Mr. Lutter could provide in the case. Mr. Lutter went down to the police station, where he was questioned for four hours.

The questioning was conducted by two detectives and took place in a small conference room in the police station. Initially, the questioning involved any information that Mr. Lutter may have regarding the burglary. At about the one-hour mark of the interview, however, separate detectives brought a suspect in the burglary case into the police station. While being interviewed in a separate room, the suspect stated that the burglary was part of an insurance scam concocted by Mr. Lutter. The detectives interviewing Mr. Lutter were immediately told of the burglary suspect's allegation. Mr. Lutter, however, was not told of the allegation nor did he know that a suspect had been captured.

At no time during the interview was Mr. Lutter advised of his Miranda rights. Furthermore, the detectives' demeanor towards Mr. Lutter did not change during the interview. They did not question Mr. Lutter about the burglary suspect's allegation, nor were they at any time confrontational or aggressive toward Mr. Lutter.

At one point during the interview, while Mr. Lutter was alone, he attempted to leave the interview room to use the restroom. He discovered that the door to the interview room was locked. When the police returned they escorted Mr. Lutter to the restroom and back to the interview room. Mr. Lutter, however, never questioned the police about the locked interview room door.

At the end of the four-hour interview, Mr. Lutter was arrested for conspiracy to commit insurance fraud. At a trial on the charge, the prosecutor has attempted to introduce into evidence a number of the statements that Mr. Lutter made during the four-hour interview. You, as Mr. Luttor's attorney, have made a motion to have the statements excluded on the theory that the statements were made without Mr. Lutter being informed of his Miranda rights. Write the argument section of a brief in support of this motion arguing that Mr. Lutter was in custody at the time of his incriminating statements and that the statements should thus be excluded.

# IV.   FACTOR TESTS AS PERSUASIVE STRATEGIES

So far in this chapter we have discussed the fundamental nature of factor tests in legal analysis and the process by which new factor tests are created. We have also discussed general guidelines for how to effectively communicate factor analysis in writing. Here we will discuss the *persuasive dimensions* of creating factor tests.

## A.   *The Threshold Question: Should An Advocate Create a Factor Test for a Particular Issue?*

Just because an issue is ripe for the creation of a factor test does not mean that an advocate must or should create such a test. The decision of whether to create a factor test on a particular issue is a strategic one.[17] In fact, the creation of a factor test will sometimes undermine an advocate's argument rather than help it.

As we discussed earlier in this chapter, the opportunity to create a new factor test arises when the law on an issue manifests two characteristics: First, it has established a "flexible legal standard" designed to control the outcome of the issue; and second, it contains a number of case opinions in which the courts of the jurisdiction endeavored to apply the flexible legal standard to the facts of specific cases. When an advocate comes across such an issue, the advocate can apply the techniques discussed in this chapter to create a new factor test for the issue. If the advocate chooses this approach, the advocate will present the newly created factor test to the court as a structural framework for analyzing the issue. The advocate will then present his or her argument on the issue in the context of the factor test, arguing that the client should prevail under the test.

Sometimes, however, upon undertaking the task of inducing a factor test, an advocate will realize that the test as a whole actually hurts his or her argument. That is, an advocate may realize that the factor test, if applied, is likely to lead to a conclusion contrary to the advocate's position. Such a conclusion may become evident because more factors favor the opposing side (i.e., a quantitative analysis) or because the more important factors favor the other side (i.e., a qualitative analysis), or a combination of the two. In such situations, the prudent strategy may be to forgo creating a factor test and to choose another approach instead.

There is nothing ethically wrong with considering and then rejecting the creation of a new factor test as a persuasive writing strategy. An advocate does not have to create a factor test just because the opportunity exists. As the existing precedent cases on the issue reflect, less encompassing approaches to the issue (such as arguing the favorable facts in terms of the general legal standard or analogizing to specific favorable cases) are legitimate. From a persuasive strategy standpoint, an advocate should only offer a new factor test if the advocate knows his or her client will fare well under the new test.

Consider our duress hypothetical as an illustration. Assume that you are

---

[17] In this section, we are discussing only whether an advocate should *create a new factor test* for an issue. If an issue is governed by an existing factor test that has been made explicit by a court or a statute, an advocate has no choice but to present his or her arguments in the context of the established test.

practicing law in the fictitious state of Lincoln and that you have a client that would like to invalidate a contract under the theory of duress. Assume further that, regarding the second duress element of "involuntariness," you have reviewed the relevant cases and have induced the factors reflected in Table 12.1. Finally, assume that, after you have created this factor test in your mind, you realize that you are likely to be unsuccessful at proving involuntariness" under this four-factor test. In this situation, you would be better off approaching the issue using a different strategy rather than offering a newly created factor test that you know you cannot meet.

## B.     The Persuasive Functions of a Newly Created Factor Test: The Human Quest for Coherence

In the preceding section, we saw that an advocate's decision on whether to create a new factor test on a particular issue is a strategic one. If, however, an advocate does decide to employ a new factor test, the advocate will be the beneficiary of a number of persuasive forces that are inherently linked to this strategy. Offering a new factor test for the analysis of an issue can have dramatic impact on a decision-maker and, thus, can be a powerful persuasive writing device. The source of this power can best be explained through psychology theory.

According to psychologists, humans have an innate tendency to try to make sense of the world, a fundamental "need to know." This need to know has been explained in a variety of ways by a number of subdisciplines of psychology. We will consider three here: attribution theory, curiosity theory, and gestalt psychology theory.

According to *attribution theory,* first devised by the philosopher John Stuart Mill in the nineteenth century, the theoretical basis for the process of induction lies in the innate human tendency to attribute causation to events. Humans have a natural desire to determine the causes of things and events they observe. One way in which this need manifests itself is induction.[18] As we discussed earlier in this chapter, induction involves the mental process of forming a general proposition based on a specific instance or group of instances. The tendency of the human mind to think inductively stems from the basic need to *attribute* a general cause sufficient to explain the specific instances.

Psychological literature would later support Mill's theory of an innate human need to attribute a cause to observed events.[19] Psychologists have suggested that the source of this need lies in our desire to see the world as controllable. "[B]ecause people want to see the world as controllable, they seek explanations that help them form a coherent picture of the world. Making attributions helps them to predict how

---

[18] III John Stuart Mill, *A System of Logic* 318-20, 323-27 (J. M. Robson ed. 1973).

[19] *See generally, e.g.*, Peter A. White, *Toward a Causal Realist Account of Causal Understanding*, 112 Am. J. Psychol. 605 (1999); Alan M. Leslie and Stephanie Keeble, *Do Six-Month-Old Infants Perceive Causality?*, 25 Cognition 265 (1987).

others will behave, so personal behaviors can be planned accordingly."[20]

*Curiosity theory* (related to attribution theory) describes human curiosity as a byproduct of the basic human urge to resolve uncertainty.[21] According to psychologist J. Kagan, humans have a "motive for cognitive harmony, consonance, equilibrium, or simply the motive to know."[22] According to Kagan, "incompatibility between ideas" is one of the main sources of uncertainty.[23] Thus, humans are strongly motivated by an innate drive to resolve inconsistencies and to seek harmony, coherence, and predictability.

*Gestalt psychology* ("Gestalt" is German for "whole") is a school of psychological thought that studies human behavior by viewing the human experience as a whole, rather than breaking down human behavior into elements or isolated parts.[24] Psychologist George Loewenstein offers this explanation of the Gestalt perspective on the human need for coherence:

> [The] notion that there is a natural human need for sense making has received broad support from diverse areas of research. . . . As Gilovich wrote, "We are predisposed to see order, pattern, and meaning in the world, and we find randomness, chaos, and meaninglessness unsatisfying. Human nature abhors a lack of predictability and the absence of meaning."
>
> Gestalt psychologists have been some of the most persistent advocates of the view that there is a human need for sense making. Indeed, the very notion of a gestalt reflects the fundamental human tendency to make sense of information by organizing it into coherent "wholes." More important, Gestalt psychologists have argued that the drive toward gestalt creation has motivational force. As H. Kreitler and Kreitler wrote in their book on aesthetics, the "pressure to straighten out, to improve, or to perfect . . . perceived figures may be so potent that it can be neither disregarded nor withstood by the spectator and is accompanied by tension and discomfort until it is resolved by a proper perceptual act." An analogous observation . . . was made by Reiser, who noted that "a problem presents itself as an open Gestalt which 'yearns' for a solution, and it is the function of thought to find

---

[20] 1 Encyclopedia of Human Emotions *Attribution* 93 (David Levinson, et al., eds. 1999) (discussing psychologist Fritz Heider who "is credited with the original ideas about attribution").

[21] *See* George Loewenstein, *The Psychology of Curiosity: A Review and Reinterpretation*, 116 Psychol. Bull. 75, 82-83 (1994).

[22] J. Kagan, *Motives and Development*, 22 J. Personality and Social Psychol. 51, 54 (1972), *quoted in* Loewenstein, *supra* note 21, at 82.

[23] Loewenstein, *supra* note 21, at 82 (discussing the theories of J. Kagan).

[24] B.R. Hergenhahn, *An Introduction to the History of Psychology* 397 (2d ed. 1992).

the solution by transforming the open Gestalt into a closed one."[25]

In view of the strong human need to seek coherence, it is not difficult to see how the creation of a new factor test for a legal issue can be a powerful persuasive device. On those issues where the creation of a factor test is possible, the law is made up of seemingly random cases endeavoring to apply an ambiguous legal standard to the facts of specific cases. Before the creation of the factor test, no general rule exists that explains or harmonizes the various opinions or guides the analysis of the issue in future cases to assure consistency and predictability. Judges, at a basic human level, find such randomness and chaos disturbing. Thus, when an advocate comes along and offers to provide order and coherence to this chaos, the impact can be dramatic. Through a newly created factor test, an advocate offers to convert a disorderly body of cases into a coherent pattern of cases and to convert seemingly random decision-making into consistent and predictable decision-making. Such an offer can be irresistible and highly appreciated by a judge, for it taps into the judge's basic human need for certainty, order, and coherence.

The impact of creating a new factor test can be explained more specifically in terms of the basic persuasive processes recognized by classical rhetoricians. The following is a detailed discussion of these specific persuasive functions.

### 1.  The Logos Function

In Chapter 6, we learned that logos refers to the process of persuading through logic and rational argument. The legal writing strategy of creating a new factor test gets much of its persuasive force through logos. By developing a factor test, an advocate organizes and systematizes the analysis of an issue that, up to that point, was devoid of organization. As a consequence, the substance of the advocate's legal argument is communicated more clearly and can be appreciated more thoroughly. The primary reason behind inducing a factor test out of seemingly random cases is to provide a coherent analytical framework within which to examine the issue. It follows, then, that one of the basic persuasive functions of a newly created factor test is its function of communicating the substance of an argument more clearly and efficiently.

### 2.  The Ethos Functions

*Ethos* refers to the process of persuading by establishing credibility in the eyes of the reader. In Chapter 8, we learned that one of the fundamental components of ethos is *intelligence*. In that discussion, we saw that readers will have more confidence in—and, therefore, will be more persuaded by—a writer they find to be intelligent. The more capable and intelligent an advocate is perceived to be, the more confidence and trust the advocate will inspire in readers.

The concept of ethos also helps explain the persuasive force behind the creation

---

[25] Loewenstein, *supra* note 21, at 83 (citations omitted) (quoting T. Gilovich, *How We Know What Isn't So: The Fallibility of Human Reason in Everyday Life* 9 (1991); Hans Kreitler and Shulamith Kreitler, *Psychology of the Arts* 87 (1972) (alteration in original); O. L. Reiser, *The Logic of Gestalt Psychology*, 38 Psychol. Rev. 359, 361 (1931)).

of new factor tests. In fact, the creation of a new factor test enhances the perceived intelligence of a writer in two ways. First, the creation of a factor test is, in and of itself, a sign of intelligence. The inductive process of creating a factor test out of seemingly random cases requires highly developed organizational and analytical skills. Thus, a writer improves his or her appearance of being an intelligent source of information, generally, by demonstrating the ability to synthesize the law on an issue into a coherent whole.

The second way that the creation of a new factor test enhances a writer's perceived intelligence is by suggesting that the writer is a person who is prone to careful deliberation. In Chapter 8, we saw that one characteristic of an intelligent writer that tends to inspire confidence in a reader is that of being *deliberate*. A deliberate person is not rash, impulsive, or quick to come to a decision. Rather, a deliberate person thoughtfully considers the competing arguments on both sides of an issue. Readers tend to have more confidence in the advice of a deliberate person than they do in the advice of a rash and impulsive person.

By their very nature, factor tests call for careful deliberation of an issue. As we saw in our original discussion of how factor tests operate, all the factors of a factor test rarely, if ever, point to the same conclusion. For most issues, some factors of the factor test will support one conclusion, while other factors of the test will support the opposite conclusion. It follows then that, when a writer proposes a new factor test for the resolution of an issue, the writer is, by necessity, offering up arguments that both support and contradict the writer's position. By doing so, the writer presents himself or herself as a deliberate and contemplative person. Granted, we know based on our prior discussion that the writer would not have offered the new factor test if the writer did not know in advance that the bottom line under the test favors the writer's position. Nevertheless, a factor test has the appearance of careful deliberation, and an advocate who creates a new factor test has the appearance of being a person committed to the deliberative process. This somewhat subtle aspect of factor tests becomes more apparent when you compare the factor test approach of arguing an issue to alternative approaches that only argue the favorable facts and ignore weaknesses in the case. These alternative approaches can strike readers as more biased and rash than an argument based on a factor test. Thus, creating a new factor test on an issue can subtly enhance a writer's credibility as a deliberate and intelligent person.

Finally, presenting one's analysis in the form of a newly created factor test enhances an advocate's credibility by indicting that the advocate is *candid* and *honest*. In Chapter 7, we saw that the perceived *moral character* of an advocate is crucial to the perception of an advocate's credibility. We also saw that candor and honesty are important components of character. In that discussion, we saw that advocates who are candid about adverse authority are able to gain the respect and trust of their readers and are, as a consequence, more persuasive.

Factor tests, by their nature, indicate candor. As we discussed above, some factors of a factor test will support the advocate's position, while others will support the opponent's position. Although the test as a whole will favor the advocate (otherwise the advocate would not have offered it), the advocate nevertheless enhances his or her credibility by offering up a test that openly analyzes both the strengths and weaknesses of the advocate's position. Rather than arguing favorable authority and disregarding damaging authority, an advocate who structures the analysis of an issue around a newly formulated factor test has the ability to show the court that a conclusion in his or her favor is warranted, even if the adverse authority is legitimately considered. Such a candid approach undoubtedly enhances the advocate's credibility.

### 3.   The Pathos Function

As we saw in Chapter 6, *pathos* refers to the process of persuading by appealing to the emotions of a reader. We also saw that one component of pathos is *medium mood control*. Medium mood control refers to the emotional response, or mood, that a writer generates in a reader through the way an argument is written rather than through its substance. We saw that writers who can use an effective writing style to generate a positive reaction in their readers will gain a distinct persuasive advantage over those who cannot.

The concept of medium mood control offers further insight into the persuasive force of a newly created factor test. As we discussed earlier, through a newly created factor test, an advocate converts a disorderly body of cases into a coherent framework. The factor test has the ability to both harmonize the past cases and assure consistency for future cases. Both of these consequences are highly pleasing to decision-makers. Thus, newly created factor tests can generate positive emotions in a reader and, by so doing, can take advantage of the medium mood control aspect of pathos.

### 4.   Practical Consequences

In addition to the foregoing more formal persuasive functions, newly created factor tests also serve some practical persuasive functions. First, by creating a new factor test for an issue, a writer dictates the analytical framework to be followed in deciding the issue. This undoubtedly gives the writer a distinct advantage over the opposing party.

Second, because the test created by the advocate is a new one that only appears in the advocate's brief, a judge is likely to rely heavily on that brief. The new test establishes a new paradigm for the analysis of the issue, and the judge is likely to keep the source of that new paradigm—the advocate's brief—close at hand. This provides a clear practical advantage to the advocate who created the new test.

### Exercise 12.4    Understanding the Strategic Dimensions of Creating a New Factor Test

You are an attorney practicing in the fictitious state of Lincoln, and you are representing the defendant in the hypothetical case described below. In connection with writing a brief on behalf of your client, you contemplate presenting the factor test you created in Exercise 12.2 to the court and using it to structure your argument. Your assignment is to write an essay analyzing whether this strategy is a good one and, if not, describing what alternative strategy would be preferable. Your essay should also analyze how the strategy under this hypothetical situation differs from the strategy in the hypothetical situation presented in Exercise 12.3.

**Hypothetical Fact Pattern:** Ina Frey was recently downtown in the city of Maintown, Lincoln, when a riot broke out between the fans of two rival baseball teams. The two teams were playing each other in the Maintown Stadium at the time. As the riot escalated, the rioters began to smash cars, throw bottles, and loot stores. Ms. Frey was hit by a flying piece of glass and was slightly injured. Concerned for Ms. Frey's well-being, a police officer at the scene put Ms. Frey in the back of a squad car with another officer so that her injury could be treated. Because Ms. Frey believed that the injury was minor, she resisted being put in the squad car. Once she was in the car, she immediately attempted to get out, but found that the doors were locked. While being treated in the car, Ms. Frey had a conversation with the police officer, which lasted approximately five minutes. During this conversation, Ms. Frey made some incriminating statements about her involvement in the looting of a store and the stashing of numerous items taken in the looting. After these statements, the officer exited the car and located the hiding place of Ms. Frey's stolen goods. During this time Ms. Frey was still locked inside the squad car. Upon his return to the car, the officer placed Ms. Frey under arrest and took her to the police station for booking.

   At Ms. Frey's criminal trial, the prosecutor introduced into evidence over your objection the statements made by Ms. Frey in the back of the squad car. On appeal, you would like to argue that the statements are inadmissible because Ms. Frey was not given her Miranda rights before the statements. To succeed you must prove that Ms. Frey was in "custody" under Lincoln law at the time the statements were made.

# PART V

## THE ETHICS AND MORALITY OF PERSUASION

# Chapter 13

# The Ethics and Morality of Persuasion: Justifying the Life of a Professional Advocate

In this book, we have looked closely at strategies and techniques lawyers can use to make their writing more persuasive. The strategies we have covered are based on aspects of human nature that have been identified in other disciplines and that are relevant to the process of persuasion. These strategies are designed to make legal writers more effective by allowing them to write in ways that take advantage of human behavioral tendencies. This text merely scratches the surface of the topic, however. As we discussed in the introduction to Part I, underlying effective persuasive writing is a whole world of persuasive forces that we as a profession are just beginning to explore. As we learn more about how the human mind works, as we increase our efforts to borrow and learn from other disciplines, we as a profession will continue to expand our arsenal of persuasive writing strategies. This book is but one step in a new and exciting field of exploration. Before we end our discussion, however, we must back up and consider a more fundamental topic relevant to such a course of study; we must consider the ethical and moral implications of systematically studying how to be a "professional persuader."

## I.   THE CRITICISM: THE LAWYER-AS-ADVOCATE IS NOTHING MORE THAN A LEGAL PROSTITUTE WHO DOES DISSERVICE TO CLIENT, SOCIETY, AND SELF

Upon seeing the word "ethics" in this chapter's title, most readers will automatically think of the rules and canons of professional responsibility that regulate lawyers in their roles as advocates. As most introductory persuasive writing books indicate, several ethical guidelines exist that are relevant to the lawyer-as-persuasive-writer. These guidelines forbid lawyers from such practices as making false statements of law or fact to a court[1] or failing to disclose to a court adverse controlling authority not disclosed by opposing counsel.[2] In short, the guidelines forbid lawyers from going

---

[1] *See* Model Rules of Professional Conduct Rule 3.3(a)(1) (2000).

[2] *See* Model Rules of Professional Conduct Rule 3.3(a)(3) (2000).

beyond the bounds of persuasion into the realm of deception.[3]

However, these formal guidelines regulating the "strategies" that lawyers can employ in advocating for their clients are not what I mean by "ethics and morality" in the context of this chapter. Our focus here is the ethics and morality of persuasion in a more general, more philosophical sense. In short, our focus here is whether the life of a professional advocate in general is morally justifiable (or "morally worthy" to use the phrase of ethics expert Professor David Luban[4]).

A lawyer, in the role of an advocate by definition, seeks to persuade an audience (be it a judge, a jury, an administrative official, or opposing counsel) to make a decision favoring a client's interests. As some would argue, the lawyer-as-advocate is concerned not with "justice," but with achieving the most favorable results possible for his or her client. A legal advocate, so the argument goes, is indifferent

> to the client's ends—. . . helping the client facilitate whatever transaction the client desires to have effectuated, even if what the client desires to have happen is morally criticizable. Provided only that what the client desires to do is not illegal, . . . it is no part of the lawyer's role to determine whether what the client desires is morally criticizable; instead, the role of the lawyer qua lawyer is to help the client bring about the desired transaction.[5]

Viewed this way, then, the fundamental essence of being a lawyer—of being an advocate for hire who pursues victory with indifference to justice—is subject to moral impeachment.

Steven L. Pepper calls this dilemma "the gap between law and justice":

> The fact that you have a legal right to do x does not mean it is morally right for you to do x; a right to do x does not entail that x is the right thing to do. A great deal of speech protected by the First Amendment, for example, is unjustifiably harmful to other people. . . . As patient or client you may have a legal right to file a malpractice suit against a doctor or lawyer. Under the facts and the law you might have a sufficiently colorable claim that a complaint would not be considered frivolous and subject to dismissal or sanction. Under those same facts, however, the likelihood of success might be so low and the absence of truly wrongful or negligent conduct on the part of the doctor or lawyer so clear that it would be a moral wrong for you to file the suit. . . .

---

[3] For a good introductory discussion of the formal ethical guidelines that regulate lawyers in their roles as persuasive writers, see Beverly J. Blair, *Ethical Considerations in Advocacy: What First-Year Legal Writing Students Need to Know*, 4 Legal Writing 109 (1998).

[4] David Luban, *Introduction*, in *The Good Lawyer: Lawyers' Roles and Lawyers' Ethics* 1, 1 (David Luban ed. 1983).

[5] Richard Wasserstrom, *Roles and Morality*, in *The Good Lawyer*, *supra* note 4, at 25, 27.

Rights as law mark off an area of individual autonomy; how the individual uses that autonomy may or may not be morally justifiable. . . . A lawyer who enables a client to achieve or actualize her rights—to act within that area of autonomy—does not necessarily enable a morally justifiable result. . . . The fact that a person has a right to behave in a particular way therefore does not mean that person may not be subject to justifiable moral criticism for so behaving. This gap between what a client has the right to do and what it is right for the client to do is an unavoidable problem for lawyers.[6]

In the foregoing excerpt, Pepper illustrates this moral dilemma facing legal advocates with two examples: (1) defending unjustifiably harmful speech on First Amendment grounds; and (2) pursuing a specious malpractice claim. Other ethics experts have offered other examples of this moral dilemma: representing a client who is guilty of a crime and who refuses to plead guilty;[7] defending a notorious pornographer by challenging on constitutional grounds the statute prohibiting distribution of child pornography;[8] defending, either under a statute of limitations or statute of frauds, a "client threatened with suit on what she admits is a just debt";[9] "assisting a wealthy, spiteful landlord to evict a needy tenant on a 'technicality'";[10] "representing the bank Credit Suisse in claims brought by survivors of Holocaust victims whose property was looted by Nazis and laundered through the bank";[11] representing a college, as an alternative beneficiary, in its effort to invalidate a

---

[6] Stephen L. Pepper, *Lawyer's Ethics in the Gap Between Law and Justice*, 40 S. Tex. L. Rev. 181, 185-86 (1999).

[7] *See, e.g.*, Robert P. George, *Reflections on the Ethics of Representing Clients Whose Aims Are Unjust*, 40 S. Tex. L. Rev. 55, 55-56 (1999) ("There is . . . a sense in which a lawyer who represents a criminal who refuses to confess is facilitating or 'cooperating' with his client's unjust efforts to evade just punishment."). This, by far, is the most common scenario thought of when discussing the moral implications of representing a client whose goals are unjust. Voluminous literature exists discussing the many ethical implications involved in the representation of a guilty client. Most of these concepts are beyond the scope of this chapter. Interested readers should see generally Monroe H. Freedman, *Professional Responsibility of the Criminal Defense Lawyer: The Three Hardest Questions*, 64 Mich. L. Rev. 1469 (1969); Monroe H. Freedman, *Lawyers' Ethics in an Adversary System* (1975); Gerard V. Bradley, *Plea Bargaining and the Criminal Defendant's Obligation to Plead Guilty*, 40 S. Tex. L. Rev. 65 (1999); Catherine Greene Burnett, *Of Crime, Punishment, Community and an Accused's Responsibility to Plead Guilty: A Response to Gerard Bradley*, 40 S. Tex. L. Rev. 281(1999).

[8] This example is adapted from George, *supra* note 7, at 58.

[9] Pepper, *supra* note 6, at 189.

[10] Wasserstrom, *supra* note 5, at 27.

[11] Terry Carter, *Sins of the Client: Disdain Over Unpopular Causes Often Brands Law Firms, Lawyers*, 87 A.B.A. J. 20, 22 (2001).

decedent's bequest to his devoted sister;[12] or defending the operations of an environmental polluter.[13] In each of these situations, a professional advocate is hired to achieve a morally questionable result: The client's aims may be legal, but they are also immoral. The lawyers in these examples have been hired to their skills as advocates, their powers of persuasion, to "facilitate" injustice. Such is often the case with professional advocates. Consequently, the question we face is whether such a way of life—a way of life that often requires a lawyer to facilitate injustice—is morally justifiable.

Perhaps the best explanation of this moral dilemma is set out in the following passage by James Boyd White, from his essay, "A Dialog on the Ethics of Argument."[14] In this essay, White examines the morality of advocacy through a fictitious dialog between Socrates and two modern lawyers. Viewing the issue on several levels, White analyzes the moral legitimacy of a life as a modern advocate in terms of *client*, *society*, and *self*. Speaking as Socrates addressing the "modern lawyer," White writes:[15]

> [B]y reason of your training and natural capacities you have what is commonly called a great power, the power of persuading those who have power of a different kind, political and economic power, to do what you wish them to do. . . . Your professional aim is to present your case, whatever its merits, so that those with control over economic and political forces will decide for your client, and you most succeed when you most prevail. You use your mind, as we used to say of the Sophists, to make the weaker argument appear the stronger. Your goal in all of this is to get the most, first for your client, but ultimately for yourself, for what you do with your "power" of persuasion is to sell it, getting in exchange another "power," that of money. Of course neither the power of money nor the power of persuasion is a good thing of itself: that depends upon whether it is used to advance or injure one's interests, and that is no concern of yours, with respect to your client or apparently to yourself.
>
> You say you are your client's friend, but you do not serve his interests; in truth you are not his friend, but his flatterer, which is to be his enemy. For your concern is not with his real interests, but with assisting him to attain whatever it is he may desire. ["[Y]ou are in this respect no different from the keeper of one of those Pleasure Ranches they have out West, who sells his

---

[12] John J. Worley, *Foreword: Neutralism, Perfectionism, and the Lawyer's Duty to Promote the Common Good*, 40 S. Tex. L. Rev. 1, 1-2 (1999) (discussing the plot of the novel *The Just and the Unjust*, by James Gould Cozzens).

[13] *See generally, e.g.*, Richard N. Morrison, *The Evolution of Environmental Ethics*, 2 U. Denv. Water L. Rev. 99 (1998).

[14] James Boyd White, *Plato's Gorgias and the Modern Lawyer: A Dialogue on the Ethics of Argument*, in *Heracles' Bow: Essays on the Rhetoric and Poetics of the Law* 215 (1985).

[15] *Id.* at 218-19.

customers whatever they desire, however bad for them it might be: too much food and liquor and drugs, and every kind of sex. In both cases it is not the client's interests that are catered to but his desires, and in the case of law the desire in question is more dangerous than any other, for it is the desire for power."[16]] If it should happen that what you do does advance his true interests and thus tends to make him happy rather than unhappy, that still does not make you his friend, because for you that result is accidental, of no interest or consequence. Not having been your object, it can be no ground for your satisfaction. Likewise, you are no friend to the law, for you will always say that justice requires whatever it is that your client wishes, and you use all your skill and art to make it seem that this is so.

In all of this you are least of all friend to yourself, for in return for money that you cannot take the time to learn how to spend, or not to spend, you give yourself the mind and character of one who does these things. You never ask yourself in a serious way what fairness and justice require in a particular case, for to do that would not leave time for what you do. In fact you incapacitate yourself for the pursuit of such a question by giving yourself the mind of the case-maker and brief-writer, the mind of one who looks ceaselessly for the characterization, the turn of phrase, or the line of argument that will make your client's case, however weak, seem the stronger. To persuade those whom you must persuade, you devote yourself with the attention of a lover to the ways in which they can be pleased, to the tricks of voice and manner and tone, to the kinds of argument, that will persuade this jury or that judge, this tax official or that fellow lawyer.

The art of rhetoric is in fact the art of ministration to the pleasures of another, really a species of prostitution. As the sexual responses and energies of a prostitute are debased and debasing by the way they are employed, so also are your intellectual energies and responses, your ways of seeing things and describing them, your ways of making appeals and claims and arguments, the very workings of your mind and the feelings of your heart. When you represent an unjust client, you are in the position of actually wanting an unjust result. And what do you get in return? A prostitute's pay. Like other flatterers you tend to become like the object of your flattery, but since you have so many and various objects of attention, what you really give yourself is the character of none but that of the chameleon, who appears to be whatever suits the moment.

White expresses his ideas in strong terms, but the underlying concept—lawyer as prostitute—is not new, nor is the moral dilemma it represents. Throughout history there have been countless challenges to the morality of the life of advocate-for-hire.[17] Most lawyers ignore the dilemma, or rationalize it away without much thought. We, however, must address this issue head-on, for it has tremendous significance for the

---

[16] *Id.* at 217.

[17] *See, e.g.,* David Luban, *Introduction,* in *The Ethics of Lawyers* xi, xi (David Luban ed. 1994) ("Moral suspicions about the practice of law are hardly new.").

instruction contained in this book. This book covers advanced strategies in persuasive legal writing. It provides an organized, systematic, and detailed explanation of writing strategies lawyers can use to persuade some reader on behalf of a client. Some critics (like White's Socrates, perhaps) would argue that this book contains nothing more than advanced instruction on manipulation. If White's characterization of lawyers as morally suspect is true of the general legal profession, it must be even more true of those, like the readers of this book, who systematically study and apply *advanced* persuasive writing tactics. Thus, before we end our discussion, we must try to reconcile—if we can—our course of study with such moral criticisms. We must see if we can justify the life of a "professional persuader."

## II.   RESPONSES TO THE CRITICISM AGAINST PROFESSIONAL ADVOCATES

Below are several possible responses to the criticism against professional advocacy expressed above. It is important to note that these responses are not intended to resolve this issue. These responses are a beginning, not an ending.

The questions posed above—questions that have plagued thoughtful professional advocates for centuries—are not susceptible to quick, easy answers. The discussion that follows is merely a summary of some of the responses that have been offered over the years. Some of these responses come from everyday practitioners responding to challenges to their choice of career. Others are the product of deep introspection by ethics and morality scholars. In the end I even offer my own response.

All of these responses seem to come up short in the final analysis. This shortfall, however, is not necessarily a bad thing. No one can answer this question for all of us. What may be a legitimate response for one person will be unconvincing to another. The answer probably lies in a combination of the various responses (with others that are not discussed thrown into the mix). Each of us must come to peace with this issue on our own. The discussion that follows is designed merely to provide some background and structure to your own consideration of this issue. By having an idea of what others have thought and said on this topic, you will be better equipped to contemplate the issue and reach a resolution that works for you.

### A.     *Lawyers as Professional Advocates Use Their Skills Only in Pursuit of Just Causes*

One possible response to the criticism against advocacy is to attempt to refute its basic premise. Some lawyers may argue that they are not indifferent to justice and that they only use their skills of persuasion to promote just and moral causes. This response, however, appears to fail even the most superficial critique.

First, very few attorneys actually believe that they represent only just causes. Rather, one could argue that the following statement by White—spoken through one of the attorneys engaged in the fictitious dialogue with Socrates—represents the position of most attorneys on this issue:

> I know I do not represent only the noble and the good. Most of my clients are good enough in an ordinary way, but basically unthinking and rather selfish;

some are in my view pretty despicable people engaged in pretty despicable enterprises. I help them not only when I think they are in the right, but when I think they are in the wrong, so long as they are not legally wrong or so morally wrong as to be intolerable. In many of the cases I have litigated I am inclined to believe that justice was on the other side, though I have not really asked myself that question in a disciplined way.[18]

As stated above, this statement more than likely reflects the feeling of most attorneys on this issue: namely that (1) they have not really given this issue much thought, and (2) if they were forced to consider the issue, they would conclude that from time to time they represent unjust as well as just causes.

Second, even if some attorneys do believe that they represent only good causes, a strong argument could be made that such a belief is based on misperception and self-denial. When an attorney represents a client in a matter, certain psychological processes come into play that influence the attorney's ability to be objective about what is fair and just in the matter. The psychological phenomena of *projection*, *identification*, and *transference*,[19] in particular, may cause an attorney to become over-sympathetic to the client's cause and to exaggerate the injustice represented by the opposing side. Moreover, in this age of specialization, where attorneys repeatedly represent the same types of clients in the same types of matters, these psychological processes intensify. Linda H. Edwards and Jack L. Sammons explain:

> [T]he limitation of practice to certain client groups brings with it [a] danger. It multiplies the effect of psychological phenomena—such as projection, identification, and transference—long known to cause misperception. These unconscious psychological processes affect lawyers and non-lawyers alike. They are present to one degree or another in many of our interactions with people and our perceptions of situations. They are powerful primarily because they function in the unconscious, where we are largely unaware of them and thus cannot compensate for them.
>
> These phenomena are problematic enough when they operate individually, stemming from and affecting only one relationship or situation at a time. Certainly they were active in the law practices of the past. They affected individual client/lawyer relationships and the accuracy of the lawyer's perspectives. But an insidious multiplier is at work when our practice becomes more and more limited to a certain client group. These phenomena operate cumulatively when the lawyer is confronted over time with the same kinds of objects for transference, projection, and identification. They affect us cumulatively in at least two ways: (1) they cause us to confuse ourselves with our usual client group and thus deprive us of an objective

---

[18] White, *supra* note 14, at 222.

[19] In psychological terms, *projection* refers to "the tendency to ascribe to another person feelings, thoughts, or attitudes present in oneself." *Webster's New Universal Unabridged Dictionary* 1546-47 (1996). Conversely, *identification* is the "process by which one ascribes to oneself the qualities or characteristics of another person." *Id.* at 950. *Transference* is "the shift of emotions . . . from one person or object to another." *Id.* at 2010.

perspective; (2) they cause us to exaggerate or misperceive the negative traits of our usual opponent group, thus distorting our perspective yet again. In fundamental and unfortunate ways, they change who we are.[20]

As this discussion demonstrates, the very process of representing clients can alter an attorney's perception of fairness. Thus, while most attorneys would readily admit that they often represent both just and unjust causes, those few who insist that they represent only just causes are more than likely the unwitting victims of distorted perception. As we can see then, the first response to the criticism against advocacy—the response that denies that advocates use their skills of persuasion to promote just as well as unjust causes—offers no real defense.

## B.      On Occasion, Lawyers as Professional Advocates Use Their Skills to Achieve Justice in Individual Cases

Another response to criticisms against advocacy—and one that is quite popular—is that lawyers, on occasion, participate in "justice being done." That is, a lawyer will occasionally find himself or herself on the morally correct side of an important social issue raised in a specific case. In such cases, the lawyer has the opportunity to use his or her skills of persuasion and advocacy to serve the public good by helping to ensure that justice is done. Some would argue that the occasional "doing of justice" in individual cases justifies the life of a professional advocate generally.

This response is both similar to and different from the first response we considered. Like the first response, this argument points out that advocates use their persuasive skills to achieve justice. However, unlike the first response, this argument does not suggest that lawyers always and exclusively represent just causes; this argument merely points out that attorneys from time to time do have the opportunity to use their skills to achieve justice. Few people outside of the legal profession will ever have the opportunity to actively and directly participate in the achievement of justice. Attorneys, on the other hand, are privileged to have this opportunity, albeit infrequently. Thus, the occasional "doing of justice" is a noble enough accomplishment to justify the life of a lawyer.

The popularity of this rationalization is illustrated by the fact that it served as a fundamental theme in the critically and publically acclaimed lawyer film, *Philadelphia*.[21] In this film, actor Tom Hanks plays Andrew Beckett, a litigator working for a prestigious Philadelphia law firm. When Mr. Beckett is fired, he sues the firm for wrongful termination, alleging that he was a victim of discrimination. Mr. Beckett claims that he was fired because the firm's partners learned that he was homosexual and infected with AIDS. When Mr. Beckett has difficulty finding an attorney to represent him, he is forced to turn to Joe Miller, played by actor Denzel Washington. Mr. Miller is a stereotypical ambulance-chasing plaintiff's attorney who attracts clients through television ads of questionable taste. Mr. Miller takes a break from his typical "slip and fall" clients and represents Mr. Beckett in the case.

---

[20] Jack L. Sammons, Jr. and Linda H. Edwards, *Honoring the Law in Communities of Force: Terrell and Wildman's Teleology of Practice*, 41 Emory L.J. 489, 508-09 (1992).

[21] *Philadelphia* (Tristar Pictures, Inc. 1993).

Mobilizing his skills of advocacy and persuasion, Mr. Miller helps Mr. Beckett receive the justice he deserves.

While the major theme of the film involves the prejudice and ignorance surrounding homophobia, a concurrent theme involves the nobility of the legal profession: that on occasions lawyers—even ambulance chasers—serve an important societal function by helping achieve justice in individual cases. And while this theme is primarily and implicitly presented through the character of Mr. Miller, it is the character of Mr. Beckett that expresses it more directly. In a particularly dramatic scene, Mr. Beckett, while on the witness stand on his own behalf, offers the following statement when asked what he loves about the practice of law:

> What do I love most about the law? Every now and again—not often, but occasionally—you get to be part of justice being done. That really is quite a thrill when that happens.[22]

This theory, too, however, offers only limited justification for the life of a professional advocate. In effect, this rationalization concedes that lawyers for the most part represent clients' interests for compensation, without particular regard for justice. Only sporadically and infrequently (and, arguably, unintentionally) does a lawyer serve justice. This theory offers no justification for the day-to-day practice of law or for being a professional advocate on a daily basis. Under this theory, the majority of a lawyer's practice is spent in disservice of—or at least with indifference to—justice. A lawyer is hard-pressed to justify his or her role as a professional advocate by pointing to the rare instances he or she *does* serve a just cause.

## C.  *A Lawyer Operates Within a Legal Culture that Imposes Constraints on What the Lawyer Can Do in Pursuit of Victory for a Client*

A third response to the criticisms against advocacy is that legal advocates do not operate with impunity. In representing clients, lawyers are subject to many constraints that limit the strategies they can employ in the pursuit of victory. Some of these constraints exist in the form of formal laws or rules of conduct. Others, however, exist only in the form of traditions or customary practices known within the legal culture. Jack L. Sammons explores this argument in some detail in his article "The Radical Ethics of Legal Rhetoricians":

> Why is a rhetorical conception of the practice of law not to be so feared? . . . To begin, legal advocacy is not unbridled rhetoric. (I am not sure that rhetoric is ever unbridled.) It is not unbridled because this particular form of rhetoric is located . . . within a particular rhetorical community with a particular rhetorical culture. If you think of lawyering as a game, . . . you will know that the objective of lawyering is not winning per se, but "winning" in a way consistent with the playing of the game and the maintenance of it.

---

[22] *Id.*

After all, "[i]t is impossible to win a game and at the same time to break one of its rules." In this practice, understood as a game, the rules, the prescribed and proscribed methods of advocacy, and other ethical constraints are inefficiencies as to winning, but they are inefficiencies that are constitutive of the game.

The game of lawyering is a particular conversation about certain social disputes. If lawyers are to continue to play this game, that is, if they are to continue to be lawyers, if they are to continue to enjoy the internal goods of their practice, and if they are to be moved toward the excellences of it, they must accept the responsibility, as all game players must, of maintaining the game. Thus, maintenance of the legal conversation, and the quality of the conversation, is an internal ethic of the practice of law.

Accordingly, I am always obligated, as a lawyer, to speak as persuasively as I can, but I am also obligated to maintain the legal conversation and the quality of it. Part of this constraint is that I can only utilize the means of persuasion available within this particular rhetorical culture, just as a baseball player can only use a bat within a certain size and weight range. My ethical obligation, then, as a good rhetorician, my integrity as a lawyer, if you will, is that I always present myself as honestly offering the best means of persuasion available within this particular rhetorical culture on behalf of my client.

Many of the fears that motivate attacks on rhetoric . . . are greatly reduced when we understand the ethics of lawyering this way. By way of a few examples, none of the following will do for the lawyer as rhetorician: lying, certain forms of deception, perjured testimony, preventing opposing arguments, misstating the law, tempting the judge to make decisions based upon means of persuasion that are not part of the rhetorical culture, and any other conduct that can fairly be described as "not playing the game."[23]

Arguably, however, this response merely begs our original question. In fact, this response highlights the difference between two separate moral inquiries relevant to professional advocacy: (1) the morality of the *causes* an advocate represents (that is, the morality of a client's goals); and (2) the morality of the *tactics* and *strategies* an advocate uses in furtherance of a cause. In this chapter, we are not addressing the morality of the *strategies* of persuasion that advocates employ in their pursuit of victory for their clients. We are addressing the more general question of whether the life of an advocate for hire, frequently called on to facilitate unjust causes, is morally defensible. Pointing to the constraints that the legal culture imposes on the strategies that advocates may employ offers no real response to criticisms against the life of an advocate generally. As White notes, the existence of constraints on advocacy "merely confines and limits the evil; it does not deny it."[24] "[W]hile these constraints to some

---

[23] Jack L. Sammons, *The Radical Ethics of Legal Rhetoricians*, 32 Val. U. L. Rev. 93, 98-99 (1997) (citations omitted).

[24] White, *supra* note 14, at 220.

degree civilize the process, they do not change its fundamental nature."[25] Although a lawyer may be limited in what tactics he or she can employ on behalf of a client, the lawyer still pursues "victory" rather than "justice." A lawyer—even one whose methods and tactics are appropriately within culturally imposed constraints—still operates as an "advocate for hire" who pursues victory irrespective of what fairness and justice may require. Pointing out that a legal advocate operates within constraints does not address the criticisms against the fundamental nature of being a "professional advocate." Thus, despite the constraints that may exist regarding adversarial strategies, the life of an advocate is still subject to the same moral criticisms previously discussed—which leads us to the next response.

### D.      "Role Differentiated Morality" Insulates Professional         Advocates from Criticism for Acting in Ways         Consistent with Their Social Role

Another common response to the moral questions concerning advocacy focuses on what has come to be called "role differentiated morality." According to theorists of role differentiated morality, "social and occupational roles have unique rights and obligations attached to them."[26] Behavior that may be immoral when performed by one person may be acceptable for another person because of the latter's social role. Every social role has its code of conduct, dictating what is acceptable and unacceptable for those in that role. For example, conduct acceptable from someone acting as a "parent" may be unacceptable from a non-parent. Richard Wasserstrom explains:

> In our own culture, and . . . in most, if not all, human cultures, as a parent one is entitled, if not obligated, to prefer the interests of one's own children over those of children generally. That is to say, it is regarded as appropriate for a parent to allocate excessive goods to his or her own children, even though other children may have substantially more pressing and genuine needs for these same items. If one were trying to decide what the right way was to distribute assets among a group of children all of whom were strangers to oneself, the relevant moral considerations would be very different from those that would be thought to obtain once one's own children were in the picture. In the role of a parent, the claims of other children vis-a-vis one's own are, if not rendered morally irrelevant, certainly rendered less morally significant. In short, the role-differentiated character of the situation alters the relevant moral point of view enormously.[27]

Role differentiated morality theory has clear implications for the morality of

---

[25] *Id.* at 222.

[26] Luban, *supra* note 17, at xiii.

[27] Richard Wasserstrom, *Lawyers as Professionals: Some Moral Issues*, in *The Ethics of Lawyers*, *supra* note 17, at 1, 6.

advocacy. The social role of a professional legal advocate is to represent the interests of others in connection with legal disputes. Even when the client's interests are morally questionable, the role of a lawyer qua lawyer is to advance the client's interests. While it may be morally inappropriate for a non-lawyer (such as one acting in the role of a "friend") to assist a person in achieving a morally questionable objective, a lawyer is insulated from criticism because of the social role that lawyers play and the expectations attached to that role. Part of the *obligations* attached to the social role of "lawyer" is the obligation to facilitate a client's interests even when those interests are morally suspect (as long as they are not illegal). And part of the *rights* attached to the social role of "lawyer" is the right to behave this way free from the moral criticism that would exist if the behavior was conducted by a non-lawyer. According to role differentiated morality, a lawyer cannot be morally criticized for behavior that is the quintessence of being a lawyer.[28]

Many ethics experts, however, doubt whether role differentiated morality can adequately justify the life of a professional legal advocate. While there may be some legitimacy to the idea that social and occupational roles have attendant rights and obligations, many ethics experts, nonetheless, feel that role differentiated morality conflicts with a more "universalistic" approach to morality. As Luban states, "[T]he fact that the lawyer's professional ideal condones, even requires, [facilitating injustice on behalf of a client] disturbs our moral consciousness."[29]

In this regard, Professor Wasserstrom argues that all people are members of a broad moral community that has fundamental ideas of right and wrong, good and bad. People operating in specific social roles also operate within the broader moral community. Consequently, behavior that may be conducted in connection with one's social or occupational role is, nevertheless, subject to universalistic moral considerations.[30] Wasserstrom explains the tension between role differentiated morality and the "universalistic dimension of morality" as follows:

> [T]he problem [with role differentiated morality], it seems to me, is that behavior that is potentially criticizable on moral grounds is blocked from such criticism by an appeal to the existence of the actor's role which, it is claimed, makes the moral difference. The appeal to the existence of the role seems to distort, limit, or make irrelevant what might otherwise be morally

---

[28] *See id.* at 1-8; Wasserstrom, *supra* note 5, at 25-28; *see also generally* Arthur Isak Applbaum, *Ethics for Adversaries: The Morality of Roles in Public and Professional Life* (1999). Role differentiated morality is similar to what Murray Schwartz calls the "Principle of Nonaccountability": "When acting as an advocate for a client . . . a lawyer is neither legally, professionally, nor morally accountable for the means used or the ends achieved." Murray L. Schwartz, *The Professionalism and Accountability of Lawyers*, 66 Cal. L. Rev. 669, 673 (1978), *quoted in* David Luban, *The Adversary System Excuse*, in *The Good Lawyer*, *supra* note 4, at 83, 84 (alterations in original).

[29] Luban, *supra* note 4, at 2.

[30] Wasserstrom, *supra* note 5, at 28-29.

relevant, if not decisive, reasons for acting or abstaining from acting.[31]

When we apply this concept to our original question regarding the morality of being an advocate for hire, we begin to see the limitations of a justification based on role differentiated morality theory. A strong argument can be made that facilitating injustice—as advocates are often called on to do—while arguably consistent with the "role" of a lawyer, is inconsistent with a more universalistic sense of morality. Such behavior, in the words of Luban, "disturbs our moral consciousness."[32] Consequently, role differentiated morality theory appears to fall short in its attempt to justify professional advocacy. This conclusion was perhaps best stated by William Whewell in 1845:

> [Every] man is, in an unofficial sense, by being a moral agent, a Judge of right and wrong, and an Advocate of what is right. . . . This general character of a moral agent, he cannot put off, by putting on any professional character. . . . If he mixes up his character as an Advocate, with his character as a Moral Agent . . . he acts immorally. He makes the Moral Rule subordinate to the Professional Rule. He sells his Client, not only his skill and learning, but himself. He makes it the Supreme Object of his life to be, not a good man, but a successful Lawyer.[33]

### E.  The Morality of Lawyering Can Only Be Evaluated from Within Its Defining Culture

As we just saw, some legal scholars believe role differentiated morality theory cannot justify the life of an advocate for hire because this theory fails to justify advocacy in terms of a broad, "universalistic" social ethic. Jack L. Sammons responds to this by arguing that the moral legitimacy of lawyering cannot be evaluated from outside the profession itself.[34]

According to Sammons, every practice, be it lawyering or baseball, is located within a tradition that defines it.[35] Baseball, for example, "is a practice located within the ancient tradition of sports, and it is within that tradition that we pass judgment

---

[31] *Id.* at 28; *see also* W. Bradley Wendel, *Professional Roles and Moral Agency*, 89 Geo. L.J. 667, 710-714 (2001) (reviewing Applbaum, *supra* note 28) (discussing the "Conflicts Between Role Prescriptions and Ordinary Morality" and stating, "If an action is required or permitted by a role prescription . . . but prohibited by ordinary moral duties, then a professional actor may be faced with a tragic choice.").

[32] See *supra* note 29 and accompanying text.

[33] 1 William Whewell, *The Elements of Morality, Including Polity* 258-59 (1845), *quoted in* David Luban, *The Adversary System Excuse*, in *The Good Lawyer, supra* note 4, at 83, 84 (alterations in original).

[34] Sammons, *supra* note 23, at *passim.*

[35] *Id.* at 94.

upon the current practice of baseball."[36] Similarly, the practice of law is located within the ancient tradition of rhetoric. That is, "*legal* rhetoric is a particular form of rhetoric located within a particular rhetorical community with its own particular culture."[37] Thus, when evaluating the morality of lawyering, one must do so in terms of the traditions that define and situate it. As Sammons states, "the practice of law has a formal moral existence"[38] and "any good ethical evaluation of the ethics of lawyering must remain internal to it."[39] "After all, there is no 'context-less' practice of living in which the virtues reside—that must remain God's business."[40]

It necessarily follows from this that one should not evaluate lawyering from a broad social context. Any attempt to do so risks radically altering the practice itself. Sammons offers this analogy:

> [T]ry asking this same "what-good-is-it" question of baseball. The only answers you will be able to give will be the kind you would argue before a city council if you were trying to get a new stadium built to attract a major league team. These answers would have almost nothing to do with the practice of baseball. In fact, as I hope this example makes clear, going beyond the practice itself in search of a justification is to risk corruption of the practice you are seeking to justify. Thinking about baseball, as somehow about those things that would appeal to a city council member, radically changes what baseball is about, and, in doing so, risks its destruction.[41]

Under this view, any attempt to justify advocacy from a broad social context, as we have attempted to do in this chapter, is completely inappropriate. Our only inquiry should be whether the modern practice of advocacy is consistent with the ancient traditions within which it is located. As Sammons pointed out, legal advocacy is a form of rhetoric. Thus, our only inquiry should be whether modern advocacy is consistent with the ancient traditions of rhetoric.

In the introduction to Part II of this text, we learned that classical rhetoric has traditionally involved the art of argumentation and persuasion. Originating around 450 B.C., classical rhetoric involved the comprehensive and systematic study of the art of persuading through written and verbal expression. The genesis of the modern legal advocate lies within that tradition: Lawyering today is essentially the modern version of a noble practice followed for 2500 years. Consequently, when one considers that modern advocacy is a form of rhetoric, and that advocacy and

---

[36] *Id.*

[37] *Id.* (emphasis in original).

[38] *Id.* at 95 (emphasis omitted).

[39] *Id.*

[40] *Id.* at 103 (emphasis omitted).

[41] *Id.* at 102.

persuasion have historically been fundamental aspects of traditional rhetoric, the pursuits of a modern advocate appear to be morally defensible. That is, within the context of the rhetorical culture, advocacy is proper and moral.

It is important to note, however, that we are discussing only the legitimacy of general advocacy. That is, we are discussing the moral legitimacy of being a professional advocate—of being a person who studies, trains, and practices in the art of persuasion. We are not discussing whether specific acts or strategies of persuasion are moral. Individual persuasive strategies themselves would have to be judged against the traditions of rhetoric to determine their legitimacy. Our inquiry here is much more general: whether practicing professional advocacy is morally valid. Considering that modern lawyering is a continuation of a tradition that has existed for some 2500 years, a strong argument can be made that it is justifiable by that standard.

Some readers will end the inquiry here, for Professor Sammons makes a strong argument that lawyering cannot be evaluated from outside of the practice and, judged this way, professional advocacy is morally defensible. Others, however, will insist that we continue with our efforts to justify advocacy in terms of a broader social context. For those readers, we move on to a sixth response.

## F.      Truth and Justice Are Achieved Through Adversarial Clash

The most popular universalistic justification for advocacy is that an adversarial justice system produces as its final product truth and justice. The American adversarial justice system is based on the idea that an impartial and fully informed decision is best achieved where a neutral and passive decision-maker renders a decision based on the involved parties' presentations of opposing evidence and arguments. The parties to a dispute have the greatest incentive to explore a matter thoroughly and to present the strongest arguments possible on both sides of the issue. Thus, the theory goes, the decision-maker in an adversarial system has at his or her disposal all of the evidence and all of the possible arguments based on that evidence necessary to make a just decision.

William Burnham further explains the claimed benefits of what he calls "Adversarial Clash":

> [The presentation of evidence and competing arguments by opposing parties] assures that the *full potential weight and value* of the evidence will be explored. It is simply impossible for a single investigator to develop in her mind, simultaneously and with equal force, completely contradictory theories of a case, and then to maintain those theories in balance until the end of the investigation. While some people are better at this than others, no single person can hold the opposing positions on an issue as well as the opposing parties themselves. . . .
>
>      The simple fact of party presentation of opposing versions and interpretations of the evidence results in a clash before the passive decisionmaker. But the clash is more than a by-product of partisan presentations. It is an essential element of adversary procedure. Partisan presentation of opposing viewpoints serves to counteract the tendency toward premature decisionmaking. . . . As the ABA Report notes:

> The [presentations and] arguments of counsel hold the case, as it were, in suspension between opposing interpretations of it. While the proper classification of the case is thus kept unresolved, there is time to explore all of its peculiarities and nuances.[42]

This relates to the morality of the individual lawyer because, while he or she may be pursuing victory for his or her client rather than justice, the end result to which the individual lawyer contributes is, nevertheless, truth and justice. White explains this argument:

> [A] lawyer does not operate alone, but as a part of a community of lawyers and judges, as one component in a larger system. Since the aim of that system is to do justice, it is justice that the lawyer ultimately serves. . . . Of course he wants to make a good living, and of course he wants his client to prevail—that is part of his function in the system—but above these wants is a larger intention, that of serving justice itself.[43]

Thus, a lawyer can respond to moral criticism and justify his or her social role by pointing to the system in which he or she plays a part. Because the system as a whole produces justice, and because an individual lawyer serves an indispensable role in the system, life as a modern advocate can be seen as morally defensible.

Upon closer examination, however, this argument too has serious flaws. No evidence supports the claim that an adversarial system produces truth and justice. In fact, many legal scholars question the basic assumptions underlying the adversarial system.[44] These doubts arise because the justifications for the adversarial system "are largely based on untested behavioral assumptions and anecdotal evidence."[45] Consequently, lawyers cannot justify their roles as advocates by pointing to the benefits of the adversarial system, generally, when those benefits remain largely

---

[42] William Burnham, *Introduction to the Law and Legal System of the United States* 84-85 (1995) (emphasis in the original) (quoting *Professional Responsibility: Report of the Joint Conference*, 44 A.B.A. J. 1159 (1958), *quoted in* Lon Fuller, *The Forms and Limits of Adjudication*, 92 Harv. L. Rev. 353, 382-85 (1978)) (alterations in the original).

[43] White, *supra* note 14, at 219; *accord* David Luban, *The Adversary System Excuse*, in *The Good Lawyer*, *supra* note 4, at 83, 87-91. Professor White in his essay later rejects this argument as a justification for advocacy. *See* White, *supra* note 14, at 222.

[44] *See, e.g.*, Burnham, *supra* note 42, at 119-31; Luban, *supra* note 43, at 93-97; White, *supra* note 14, at 222.

[45] Burnham, *supra* note 42, at 119; *accord* Luban, *supra* note 43, at 96 ("[Justifications based on adversarial clash], however plausible they sound on paper, are untested speculations from the armchair."); White, *supra* note 14, at 222 ("I do not share [other attorneys'] faith in the perfection of our legal system, whether it is measured by results achieved or standards applied, and I dare say no one else does either who is not forced to such a position by his choice of profession.").

unproven. Moreover, while many lawyers quickly resort to the adversarial clash theory when asked to justify their careers, few actually believe the assumptions upon which the theory is based.[46] Thus, despite its popularity, the adversarial clash theory does little to justify the life of a professional advocate.

## G.  *Professional Legal Advocates Provide Citizens with Access to the Legal System, Thereby Increasing Their Autonomy*

Stephen L. Pepper offers another universalist justification for advocacy. Pepper argues that lawyers serve society by providing citizens with access to an important public good—law.[47]

According to Pepper, law is a public good—that is, a public resource—in three important ways. First, law as a mechanism for resolving disputes is a public good. Law in this sense is like a public utility in that the state, through the legal system, offers citizens a mechanism for dispute resolution. Second, law as substantive knowledge is a public good. That is, knowledge of what the law is and requires (such as criminal law, wage and hour law, and environmental law) is a public good in that such knowledge allows citizens to behave in ways consistent with legal requirements. The third way that law is a public good is that it creates legal mechanisms through which citizens can conduct their affairs and transact business. Legal devices such as contracts, deeds, forms of business organizations (partnerships, corporations, etc.), wills, trusts, leases, licences, are all "goods" created by law that are available to citizens in the handling of their affairs.[48]

Pepper believes that when we view the law this way, the importance of the lawyer's societal function is clear:

> [L]awyers serve the common good by providing access to [all three aspects of] law. Most law cannot be reached or used by laymen without the assistance of a lawyer; a great deal of our law cannot be effective without lawyers. Thus by fulfilling their primary function—acting as a channel by which law becomes known and effective—lawyers serve the common good in a very substantial way.[49]

Pepper's theory has a number of implications, many of which go beyond the scope of this chapter. Before we proceed, then, we must narrow its focus to that part

---

[46] Luban, *supra* note 43, at 96 ("No trial lawyer seriously believes that the best way to get at the truth is through the clash of opposing points of view.").

[47] *See* Pepper, *supra* note 6, at 182-84; Stephen L. Pepper, *The Lawyer's Amoral Ethical Role: A Defense, A Problem, and Some Possibilities*, in *The Ethics of Lawyers*, *supra* note 17, at 57, 57-63 [hereinafter Pepper, *The Lawyer's Amoral Ethical Role*].

[48] See Pepper, *supra* note 6, at 182-83; Pepper, *The Lawyer's Amoral Ethical Role*, *supra* note 47, at 60.

[49] Pepper, *supra* note 6, at 183.

that is relevant to our limited discussion. As we saw, according to Pepper, law is a good in three ways: (1) as a "mechanism for resolving disputes"; (2) as "substantive knowledge" of what conduct is permissible and impermissible; and (3) as "legal devices" through which citizens conduct their affairs and transact business. However, only the first of these is relevant to our discussion. In this chapter we are focusing only on the legitimacy of a lawyer acting in the role of a professional "advocate." Pepper's second category, however, refers to a lawyer, not in the role of an advocate, but in the role of a "counselor," advising clients on what the law requires so that they can behave accordingly. Likewise, the third category refers to a lawyer in the role of a "transactionalist," facilitating clients' transactions by drafting and creating various legal instruments. It is only the first category—law as a mechanism for resolving disputes—that is relevant to our limited inquiry. It is only in regard to this aspect of law that a lawyer functions as an advocate.

Nevertheless, Pepper's argument offers a plausible justification for the life of professional advocates. According to this argument, professional legal advocates function as channels by which citizens gain access to the public resource that is the legal system. As we discussed previously, our system for resolving legal disputes is based on an adversarial model whereby opposing parties present their best arguments to an impartial decision-maker. For the most part (excluding pro se and small claims matters), a citizen's use of (and success within) this system requires the help of a professional legal advocate trained in the substance of the law, the procedures of the system, and the strategies of persuasion. "The system of law is in form available to all, but the lawyer is the only instrument for access to the system, the only instrument through which law becomes actually accessible."[50] Thus, according to Pepper, the life of a professional advocate is moral and justifiable because, first, the legal system for resolving disputes is an important public resource, and second, it is only through professional advocates that this public good is actually available to the public.

Yet, while it may be true that legal advocates provide citizens with access to the legal system, some question whether this is a good thing. As we discussed before, many citizens use the legal system to pursue morally questionable objectives. In light of this, some critics question whether providing those citizens with access to the legal system—in effect facilitating injustice—actually serves the common good. Pepper responds to this objection by pointing out that this theory for the justification for lawyering is based on three important premises. The first premise is that "individual autonomy" is valued in our society. "This premise is founded on the belief that liberty and autonomy are a moral good, that free choice is better than constraint, that each of us wishes, to the extent possible, to make our own choices rather than to have them made for us."[51] The second premise is that "first class citizenship" in a society—that is, being a valuable and productive member of a society—requires personal autonomy.[52] The third premise is that, "in a highly legalized society such as ours,

---

[50] *Id.* at 184 n.4 (quoting Stephen L. Pepper, *A Rejoinder to Professors Kaufman and Luban*, 1986 Am. B. Found. Res. J. 657, 666).

[51] Pepper, *The Lawyer's Amoral Ethical Role*, *supra* note 47, at 60-61.

[52] *See id.* at 61.

autonomy is often dependent on access to the law."[53] That is, for citizens to be autonomous and "act effectively,"[54] they must have access to the legal system; the legal system must be a good available to all citizens. Thus, according to Pepper, the life of a professional advocate is justifiable, even noble, because professional advocates are indispensable to citizens becoming effective and gaining autonomy in society. And this is true even when the client exercises his or her autonomy in morally questionable ways. Pepper states this conclusion this way:

> [T]he resulting conclusion: First-class citizenship is frequently dependent upon the assistance of a lawyer. If the conduct which the lawyer facilitates is above the floor of the intolerable—is not unlawful—then this line of thought suggests that what the lawyer does is a social good. The lawyer is the means to first-class citizenship, to meaningful autonomy, for the client.[55]

Responding to Pepper, some ethics experts argue that the societal good accomplished by providing access to the legal system does not outweigh the bad that results from a lawyer facilitating an immoral or unjust cause. While it may be true that legal advocates serve society by providing access to the law, lawyers nevertheless do a moral disservice to society when they use their skills as advocates to facilitate injustice. Arguably the concrete negative consequences of advocates' behavior (injustice) outweighs and renders meaningless the more abstract general good they provide to society (access to the legal system and enhanced individual autonomy). As David Luban has put it: "[C]lient autonomy is not the only moral value. . . . [W]hen enhancing a client's autonomy injures others, it remains to be shown that the gain in autonomy excuses the wrong."[56]

## H.    *Professional Legal Advocates Engage Clients in Moral Conversations, Thereby Helping Them to Grow Morally*

Another possible justification for the life of a professional legal advocate is that advocates, in the process of representing clients, help clients to exercise moral judgment and grow morally. According to this argument, whenever a client seeks to enforce a legal, yet morally questionable, right (that is, whenever a gap exists between what the law allows and what justice requires), a lawyer has the opportunity to engage the client in a moral conversation. Robert F. Cochran, Jr., John M.A. DiPippa, and Martha M. Peters call this role of advocates the "lawyer as friend" role:

---

[53] *Id.*

[54] Pepper, *supra* note 6, at 184 n.4 (quoting Stephen L. Pepper, *A Rejoinder to Professors Kaufman and Luban*, 1986 Am. B. Found. Res. J. 657, 666).

[55] Pepper, *The Lawyer's Amoral Ethical Role*, *supra* note 44, at 61.

[56] Luban, *supra* note 17, at xix (citing David Luban, *The Lysistratian Prerogative: A Response to Steven Pepper*, 1986 Am. B. Found. Res. J. 637, 639).

In our culture, we generally think of friendship in terms of pleasure, but as sociologist Robert Bellah and his colleagues have suggested, central to the traditional notion of friendship was a moral component:

> For Aristotle and his successors, it was precisely the moral component of friendship that made it the indispensable basis of a good society. For it is one of the main duties of friends to help one another to be better persons; one must hold up a standard for one's friend and be able to count on a true friend to do likewise. Traditionally, the opposite of a friend is a flatterer, who tells one what one wants to hear and fails to tell one the truth.

Of course, lawyers cannot become friends to every client, but they might discuss moral issues with the client in the way that they would discuss moral issues with a friend: not imposing their values on the client, but exploring the client's moral values, and not being afraid to influence the client. Imagine that a close friend comes to you and confesses that he has embezzled something from his employer. You are likely neither to push your friend to confess, nor ignore the wrong that your friend has done. You are likely to try and help your friend think through the matter. You might offer an opinion, but you would be likely to do so in a tentative fashion, respecting the dignity of your friend. The lawyer as friend engages in moral conversations with the client but leaves decisions to the client.[57]

Steven L. Pepper has also discussed the opportunity of advocates to engage clients in moral conversations:

> *When the gap between law and justice is significant, it ought to be part of the lawyer's ethical responsibility to clarify to the client that he or she has a moral choice in the matter.* The lawyer ought to be held responsible for ensuring that the client knows there is, in the lawyer's opinion, a gap between law and justice, and that it is the client—not the law and not the lawyer—who is primarily responsible for injustice if it occurs. It ought to be part of the lawyer's ethical obligation to clarify that merely because one has a legal right to do x, doing x is not necessarily the right thing to do. The lawyer ought to ensure that the client is aware that x, though lawful and otherwise advantageous to the client, may well be morally unjustifiable. Thus, although the lawyer is not directly morally responsible for assisting the client's wrongful or unjust conduct within the bounds of the law, the lawyer ought to be responsible for ensuring that *the client is morally responsible for that conduct*, that the client has chosen it knowing the moral dimension of the

---

[57] Robert F. Cochran, Jr., et al., *The Counselor-At-Law: A Collaborative Approach to Client Interviewing and Counseling* 177-78 (1999) (quoting Robert N. Bellah, et al., *Habits of the Heart: Individualism and Commitment in American Life* 115 (1985)).

choice.[58]

What benefit, you may ask, do such moral conversations between lawyers and their clients provide to society generally? According to Cochran, DiPippa, and Peters, such moral conversations help clients grow morally. "People grow morally through exercising moral judgment. They develop virtues (courage, truthfulness, faithfulness, and mercy) through practice, just as an athlete develops physical skills through practice."[59] Therefore, advocates benefit society by allowing clients to exercise moral judgment. Just as Aristotle saw true friendship as indispensable to a good society, lawyers benefit society by helping clients to become "better persons." In fact, the overall effect of lawyers may be greater than that of friends. It is only infrequently (one hopes) that a person seeks the advice of a friend regarding a moral dilemma. Legal disputes, on the other hand, often have moral implications. Thus, lawyers are in a better position than are others (including other professionals and friends) to influence the moral development of persons; given that, they can contribute greatly to the moral growth of a society's members.

Two problems interfere with this justification for advocacy. First, few legal advocates actually engage their clients in moral conversations of the type described by Professors Pepper, Cochran, DiPippa, and Peters. These writers were describing what, in their opinion, lawyers *should* do when representing clients with immoral aims, not what all, or even most, lawyers currently do.[60] Thus, this argument cannot justify the current state of advocacy, because it remains an aspiration, not a reality.

Second, even if advocates did engage in such moral conversations with their clients, the ultimate decision on how to proceed remains with the client. Thus, when the client still decides to pursue immoral goals, the advocate still uses his or her skills to facilitate injustice. In the end, the amorphous societal good accomplished by engaging clients in moral conversations probably cannot outweigh the more concrete harm resulting from the facilitation of immoral causes.

## I.      *Legal Advocates Safeguard Individuals' Rights Against Governmental Encroachment*

Advocacy is also commonly defended on the grounds that legal advocates safeguard individuals' rights by keeping in check governmental infringement of those rights. This argument is particularly popular in the context of criminal matters and in other matters involving constitutional rights. According to this argument, legal advocates are justified in representing criminals because the zealous representation of a criminal defendant in the legal system (challenging the constitutionality of proffered evidence,

---

[58] Pepper, *supra* note 6, at 190-91 (emphasis in original).

[59] Robert F. Cochran, Jr., et al., *supra* note 57, at 170.

[60] *See* Pepper, *supra* note 6, at 192 ("[E]xplicit consideration of moral issues currently is not common in business or legal conversations."); Robert F. Cochran, Jr., et al., *supra* note 57, at 165-82 (recognizing that the "lawyer as friend" model is only one of four existing models for how lawyers participate in clients' moral decision-making).

aggressively cross-examining witnesses, forcing the government to prove guilt "beyond a reasonable doubt," and so on) keeps state power in check. Even when an individual defendant is guilty, the zealous representation of that defendant assures for all citizens that our constitutionally protected rights are being maintained and observed. David Luban explains this argument this way:

> [Z]ealous adversary advocacy of those accused of crimes is the greatest safeguard of individual liberty against the encroachment of the state. The good criminal defense lawyer puts the state to its proof in the most stringent and uncompromising way possible. Better, we say, that a hundred criminals go free than that one person be wrongly convicted.[61]

The same argument applies to matters involving constitutional challenges to governmental actions. Consider our prior example of a lawyer representing a notorious child pornographer by challenging the constitutionality of an anti-pornography statute. By forcing the government to defend the statute against claims that it infringes on the freedom of speech, the advocate is assuring for all citizens that the government's regulation of such rights is subjected to careful scrutiny. Challenging the government's regulation of constitutionally protected rights, even when the specific client involved is morally suspect, serves society generally by preserving these rights and minimizing governmental intervention.

This argument, however, only justifies advocacy in the contexts of criminal and constitutional law. It is completely irrelevant to civil suits between private individuals and entities. Consider our prior example of an advocate representing a spiteful landlord in connection with the eviction of a needy tenant. An advocate's representation of the landlord does not safeguard "individual liberty against the encroachment of the state." The government is not even involved in the matter. As Luban concludes, this justification for advocacy, as compelling as it is, "pertains only to criminal defense and thus is irrelevant to the enormous number of civil cases tried each year."[62] Thus, while this argument goes a long way toward justifying advocacy when constitutional rights are involved, it falls short of justifying advocacy in a more general sense.

## J.    *Lawyers, as Advocates, Maintain and Improve a "Culture of Argument" that Makes Available to Society Tools of Argumentation and Persuasion that Can Be Mobilized in the Pursuit of Justice*

James Boyd White offers another justification for professional advocacy. According to White, lawyers serve the indispensable and noble function in society of maintaining and improving a "culture of argument" without which it would be

---

[61] Luban, *supra* note 43, at 91.

[62] *Id.*

impossible to even discuss justice or question injustice.[63] This position has many implications, which White explores in depth. For our limited purposes, however, we will consider only one aspect of his argument.

As White states, the legal culture, operating within the tradition of classical rhetoric, is a "culture of argument." Legal advocates in our society maintain a subculture that has as its substance a body of knowledge regarding how to argue, how to challenge, how to reason analytically, and how to persuade. A legal advocate's primary asset is not some encyclopedic knowledge of legal rules and laws; a legal advocate's primary asset is—to use a cliche—his or her ability "to think like a lawyer." And thinking like a lawyer means possessing the skills and training to dissect, analyze, organize, synthesize, communicate, and persuade—skills of argumentation that exist nowhere in purer form than in the legal culture. Thus, legal advocates serve as guardians of an important body of knowledge: the knowledge of critical analysis, argumentation, and persuasion.

And, while lawyers may serve many functions and roles—advisor, counselor, drafter, agent, negotiator—it is their role as advocate that alone produces this "culture of argument." The following scenario makes this point clear. Imagine that the adversarial system for resolving disputes did not exist in our society. Imagine instead that disputes were resolved, not by lawyers as advocates arguing on behalf of the parties involved, but by a single investigator who looks into the facts, considers any applicable rules of law, and then renders an answer. While such a system may or may not produce fair results in any individual case, it would not produce a "culture of argument." In such a society, no profession, no subculture, would exist trained in the art of "arguing." Such a society would have no "professional arguers," because they would not be needed. Thus, it is only by virtue of our adversarial system that we have a sub-culture of advocacy. And this sub-culture maintains and improves an advanced body of knowledge regarding methods of argumentation and persuasion.

The question then becomes, of what importance is it to a society to have an advanced "culture of argument" such as the one created and maintained by legal advocates in our society? The short answer is that such a subculture makes available to our society materials of argumentation and persuasion that can be mobilized in the pursuit of justice, both in individual cases and in more general social issues. The culture of argument provides victims of injustice with professional advocates who can champion their causes. On a larger scale, legal advocates provide our society with tools of argumentation and persuasion that can be employed in pursuit of societal improvement. A review of history reveals that many of the most significant societal advancements have been achieved to a large extent through effective argumentation and persuasion. Consider this, for example, from Edward P. J. Corbett and Robert J. Conners:

> One fact that emerges from a study of the history of rhetoric is that there is usually a resurgence of rhetoric during periods of social and political upheaval. Whenever the old order is passing away and the new order is marching—or stumbling—in, a loud, clear call goes up for the services of the person skilled in the use of spoken or written words. One needs only to

---

[63] White, *supra* note 14, at 223.

hearken back to such historical events as the Renaissance in Italy, the Reformation in England, and the Revolution in America to find evidence of this desperate reliance, in times of change or crisis, on the talents of those skilled in the persuasive arts. As Jacob Burckhardt has pointed out in *The Civilization of the Renaissance in Italy*, the orator and the teacher of rhetoric played a prominent role in the fifteenth-century humanistic movement that was casting off the yoke of the medieval church. After Henry VIII broke with Rome, the Tudor courts of England resounded with the arguments of hundreds of lawyers engaged to fight litigations over confiscated monastic properties. Students of the American Revolution need recall only Tom Paine's incendiary pamphlets, Patrick Henry's rousing speeches, Thomas Jefferson's daring Declaration of Independence, and Hamilton's and Madison's efforts to sell constitutional democracy in the *Federalist Papers* to be convinced that in times of change or upheaval, we rely on the services of those equipped with persuasively eloquent tongues and pens.[64]

Not surprisingly, Thomas Paine, Patrick Henry, Thomas Jefferson, Alexander Hamilton, and James Madison all had training in law and/or traditional rhetoric. Furthermore, in terms of more recent examples, a review of the histories of the civil rights and women's rights movements in the United States reveals that many of their successes have come at the hands of skilled legal advocates.[65] Even Shakespeare recognized the importance of legal advocates in times of major social change when he wrote those famous words, "let's kill all the lawyers." Although this statement is often viewed as a slight to the legal profession, it is actually quite the contrary. Attorney J. B. Hopkins explains:

> To set the record straight, . . . Shakespeare, in the use of the phrase "kill all the lawyers," intended it as anything but criticism.
>
> In Act IV, Scene 2, line 86 of the second part of Henry VI, a play written by Shakespeare in 1591, Dick the Butcher says: "The first thing we do, let's kill all the lawyers."
>
> This play was set in England in the mid-15th century. Young Henry VI was thought to be a weakling, and England was involved in an unsuccessful war with France and was going through some economic depression.
>
> Now, in this background, the Duke of York attempted to incite a rebellion in the laboring class in order to fulfill his own ambitions for obtaining the throne. He did not want to call attention to himself, so he did

---

[64] Corbett and Conners, *Classical Rhetoric for the Modern Student* 16-17 (4th ed. 1999).

[65] *See, e.g.,* Mark V. Tushnet, *Making Civil Rights Law: Thurgood Marshall and the Supreme Court*, 1936-1961 (1994) (discussing how Thurgood Marshall achieved many of his successes in the civil rights movement because of his skills in legal analysis, argumentation, and persuasion); JoEllen Lind, *Symbols, Leaders, Practitioners: The First Women Professionals*, 28 Val. U. L. Rev. 1327 (1994) (discussing the role of women attorneys in the advancement of women's rights).

the planning and orchestration of this rebellion through Jack Cade, who was a warmonger and headstrong Kentishman. Jack Cade ultimately led his riotous followers through the streets of London, damaging and wrecking property, killing noblemen, and attempting to establish the duke as the rightful heir to the throne.

Before the plan was executed, Cade and his followers, among whom was Dick the Butcher, met to discuss the plan of attack and how they should go about gaining the political control of England. It is during this meeting that the sentence involving "kill all the lawyers" occurs.

The exact sentence in the play was, "The first thing we do, let's kill all the lawyers." We see, then, that this sentence was uttered by a riotous anarchist whose intent was to overthrow the lawful government of England. Shakespeare knew that lawyers were the primary guardians of individual liberty in democratic England. Shakespeare also knew that an anarchical uprising from within was doomed to fail unless the country's lawyers were killed.[66]

Thus, as Hopkins explains, this statement from Shakespeare about lawyers is nothing less than a testament to the importance of trained advocates in times of political change.

Thus far, we have discussed the notion that the "culture of argument" maintained by legal advocates makes available to us as a society materials of argumentation and persuasion that can be employed in the pursuit of justice. But—you are probably asking yourself—doesn't it also make possible pursuit of evil? Stated another way, can't the tools of argumentation and persuasion be used for ill, just as easily as they can be used for good?

The answer is "yes." Clearly, in individual lawsuits, tools of argumentation and persuasion are used by the attorneys on both sides of the dispute. Thus, these tools are used in opposition to justice in individual cases just as often as they are used in the furtherance of justice. Furthermore, history shows that tools of argumentation and persuasion have been employed in the pursuit of evil ideals on a societal scale on a number of occasions in a number of cultures.[67] Nevertheless, this does not minimize the importance of a sophisticated "culture of argument" to a society. To borrow another phrase from White, "It is better that the practice itself should exist than that it should not."[68] Evil will always rival good. The important thing is that a society "afford the materials with which one can appeal to its better side, establishing and

---

[66] J. B. Hopkins, *The First Thing We Do, Let's Get Shakespeare Right!*, 72 Fla. B. J. 9 (April 1998). It should be noted, however, that this interpretation is subject to some debate. *See* Gerald T. Bennett, *Let's Kill All The Lawyers!: Shakespeare [Might Have] Meant It*, 72 Fla. B. J. 58 (Dec. 1998).

[67] *See, e.g.*, Richard Weisberg, *Lawtalk in France: The Challenge to Democracy*, in *Poetics and Other Strategies of Law and Literature* 127 (1992) (discussing the role that rhetoric and legal argumentation played in occupied France's legal and social acceptance of Nazi policies during World War II).

[68] White, *supra* note 14, at 230.

reinforcing standards and values that are incompatible with its evils, and thus counteract them."[69] While justice and goodness may not always prevail, the important thing is that we live in a society that makes available to us materials of idealization that enable us to pursue such goals. The existence of positive cultural values that can be appealed to, combined with the "culture of argument" maintained by the legal profession, assures that such materials of idealization are available in our society.

The final question is, then, what does all this mean in terms of the morality of the individual legal advocate? It is the practice of law by individual lawyers in our adversarial system that maintains the "culture of argument" that we have been discussing. Regardless of whose side justice may be on in any specific matter, the process of representing clients and of developing arguments and strategies of persuasion in specific cases, as lawyers routinely do, preserves and maintains the traditions and materials of the culture. The day-to-day practice of law by professional advocates assures that this important body of knowledge is maintained and passed on to future generations and available for mobilization in the pursuit of justice.

The practice of law by individual legal advocates also *improves* the culture of argument. That is, not only do lawyers preserve, maintain, and perpetuate the culture's materials on effective advocacy, they also assist in the creation of new and innovative methods of argumentation and persuasion. Strategies of argumentation and persuasion are not developed in a vacuum. They are developed by real advocates representing real clients in real cases. While academics may identify these strategies and present them in an organized format for further study, such as in articles or books, the strategies themselves are "born" in the heat of battle and through the trial and error of practicing lawyers. New and different types of arguments, new and different types of reasoning, new and different types of stylistic devices are all developed by advocates "doing" advocacy. And just as we as a culture reach the limits of our imagination, a new step is taken: A new strategy is developed, precipitated by the quest for adversarial victory. And it is these strategies, strategies developed by individual attorneys, that eventually become part of the cultural knowledge and as such become available for use by others. In White's terms, "The law as [so described] . . . becomes a repository of shared experiences, a set of experiments and trials and failures, which are by the law made intelligible and shareable."[70]

This argument for advocacy is not meant to suggest that all lawyers directly participate in major social changes of the type we have discussed. This is clearly not the case. Nor is it meant to suggest that individual lawyers always pursue just causes. As we saw in the discussion of the first response above, that also is not true. This

---

[69] *Id.*

[70] *Id.* at 225. It is important at this point to reemphasize that the discussion in this chapter does not address whether specific persuasive strategies or techniques that lawyers may use (or create) are moral or valid. Our discussion is much more general: whether the life of an advocate—even one that operates appropriately within the ethical guidelines of the profession—is morally justifiable. This response argues that professional advocates preserve and improve for society strategies of persuasion and argumentation. This discussion assumes that the strategies in question comply with the ethical constraints of the profession.

argument also should not be taken to mean that lawyering is justifiable based on the occasional "doing of justice" in individual cases. As we saw in the second response above, such a position ignores the value of the day-to-day practice of law by the average attorney. What this response does claim is that lawyers' daily acts of lawyering and advocacy preserve, maintain, improve, and make available to others an important body of knowledge regarding effective argumentation and persuasion. It is not the occasional doing of justice that justifies an advocate's life; it is the fact that professional advocates provide our society with tools of argumentation and persuasion that can be used in the pursuit of just causes. Paradoxically, then, even when an attorney represents a client without regard to which side justice may be on, the attorney nevertheless contributes to justice on a larger scale by contributing to the culture of argument. All professional advocates are the noble guardians of an important body of knowledge—a body of knowledge that can be, and often is, mobilized in the pursuit of justice. Thus, while very few lawyers will ever directly participate in major societal changes, and while individual attorneys may use their skills only occasionally to pursue justice in their cases, all legal advocates nevertheless inherently and continuously contribute to justice as members of the profession that is charged with the responsibility of maintaining and improving the "culture of argument." Viewed this way, the practice of advocacy involves great responsibility and becomes a noble endeavor.

Yet while this argument is quite compelling, it too has its shortcomings. It seems to offer a viable justification for professional advocacy from a "anthropological" standpoint, yet some may feel that this justification is a bit too removed from the day-to-day life of a professional advocate. Granted, a professional advocate, by virtue of his or her profession, may contribute in some small way to the perpetuation and growth of the "culture of argument." However, this benefit to society is measured over generations. It is the *cumulative* effect of all lawyers engaging in advocacy on a society-wide scale that maintains and improves a body of knowledge regarding effective argumentation and persuasion. Each individual lawyer's contribution to this "culture of argument" will be, on average, infinitesimal. Thus, while this response may justify the legal profession in general by demonstrating its importance to a productive society, it seems like a stretch to use this argument to justify the career choice of individual lawyers. An individual lawyer would be hard pressed to justify his or her representation of a morally suspect cause by arguing that the representation, when combined with all other acts of legal advocacy, perpetuates a culture of argument beneficial to the society's development. Such a response seems hollow and desperate.

### K.   *Maybe the First Response Is Correct After All: Professional Advocates Do Use Their Skills in the Pursuit of Just Causes Only*

So far, our efforts to justify professional advocacy have come up short. Perhaps the reason for this is that our approach has been all wrong. Up to now, we have assumed that professional legal advocates sometimes use their skills to promote unjust and immoral causes, and we have attempted to find a commendable function of professional advocacy that outweighs or justifies this negative function. Perhaps, however, we should focus not on finding a justification but on the terms of our basic assumption. That is, perhaps we should more carefully analyze what is and isn't an unjust cause.

In the beginning of this chapter, we saw that professional advocacy is criticized for sometimes requiring advocates to represent and further the interests of clients with immoral or unjust goals. As illustrations of this dilemma, we discussed (1) a lawyer representing a client in the client's attempt to avoid a valid debt; (2) a lawyer assisting a wealthy, spiteful landlord to evict a needy tenant; (3) a lawyer representing a college in its efforts to invalidate a decedent's bequest to his devoted sister; and (4) a lawyer defending the operations of an environmental polluter, among others. We labeled these causes "unjust" and "immoral." But why?

In each of these cases, what the client desires is not illegal. Nevertheless, most people would view these causes as unjust because they are inconsistent with our values and our sense of right and wrong. In short, we consider these causes to be unjust because we have made value judgments based on the brief statements of facts and have concluded that the clients' goals are incompatible with our value systems. Seeing these one-sentence hypothetical situations, we automatically and instinctively engaged in a mental process by which we processed the facts (or "story") presented by the situation and concluded that the "story ending" preferred by the client is inappropriate and improper. This instinctive mental process has a name; it's called "narrative reasoning."

Linda H. Edwards has analyzed "narrative reasoning" and its role in the analysis of legal issues in detail.[71] According to her, people develop moral values by being exposed to cultural narratives. That is, the process "of defining a meaningful world of moral order is accomplished in each culture through the telling and retelling of foundational narratives."[72] "Narrative reasoning" occurs when a person evaluates a factual situation or dilemma by determining what result (or "story ending") is consistent with one's cultural narratives and the values those narratives implicate. As Edwards puts it, "Narrative reasoning evaluates a litigant's story against cultural narratives and the moral values and themes these narratives encode. It asserts, 'X is the answer because that result is consistent with our story.'"[73] In terms of the above hypothetical situations, we deduced through narrative reasoning that the clients' goals are unjust because our cultural narratives and the values encoded by those narratives dictate that avoiding a valid debt (that is, breaking a promise), taking advantage of or being insensitive to the needy, interfering with a dying man's wishes, and polluting the environment are all improper objectives.

As noted, narrative reasoning happens instinctively and automatically. Moreover, it requires no legal training. A person, whether lawyer or lay person, can evaluate a legal issue using narrative reasoning without any legal research or knowledge of the relevant law. The only requirement is that the person know enough of the facts to

---

[71] *See generally* Linda H. Edwards, *The Convergence of Analogical and Dialectic Imaginations in Legal Discourse*, 20 Legal Stud. F. 7 (1996).

[72] *Id.* at 11.

[73] *Id.*

piece together the "story" of the legal dilemma. Once the story is known, one can determine which side of the matter is "in the right" by evaluating the parties' positions against cultural values. This is the primary reason we were so quick to criticize the clients' positions in the above hypotheticals. Based on the brief fact statements, we quickly conjured up stories surrounding these issues and then evaluated these stories against our sense of right and wrong. Thus quickly and instinctively, we concluded that the clients' positions were improper.

Our legal system for resolving disputes, however, is not founded on narrative reasoning. Instead, our legal system is based on a commitment to "the rule of law" and the following of precedent. Legal disputes are not resolved by a decision-maker concluding "instinctively" which side of the dispute appears to be morally right. Legal disputes are resolved by looking to the relevant rule of law and precedent and applying these legal authorities to the facts of the present dispute. Sometimes the rule of law may dictate a result that appears unjust in terms of the specific parties and the emotional aspects of the matter (that is, unjust when evaluated in terms of narrative reasoning). However, the result is nevertheless "just" when evaluated in terms of the rule of law.

The justifications for a legal system based on rules rather than discretionary decision-making go back as far as ancient Greece. As Aristotle said,

> Rightly constituted laws should be the final sovereign; and personal rule, whether it be exercised by a single person or a body of persons, should be sovereign only in those matters on which law is unable, owing to the difficulty of framing general rules for all contingencies, to make an exact pronouncement.[74]

More specifically, political theorists[75] and legal scholars[76] have identified several reasons why a system based on rules and the following of precedent is preferable to an ad hoc system.

> *Fairness and Consistency.* Fairness dictates that similar cases be decided similarly. "We achieve fairness by decisionmaking rules designed to achieve consistency across a range of decisions."[77] Ad hoc decision-making, on the other hand, does not assure consistency.

> *Predictability.* "Rudimentary justice requires that those subject to the law

---

[74] III *The Politics of Aristotle* 127 (Ernest Barker trans. 1946) *quoted in* Antonin Scalia, *The Rule of Law as a Law of Rules*, 56 U. Chi. L. Rev. 1175, 1176 (1989).

[75] *See generally, e.g.*, Friedrich A. Hayek, *The Political Ideal of the Rule of Law* (1955); John Rawls, *A Theory of Justice* (1971).

[76] *See generally, e.g.,* Scalia, *supra* note 74; Frederick Schauer, *Precedent*, 39 Stan. L. Rev. 571 (1987); Kathleen M. Sullivan, *The Justices of Rules and Standards*, 106 Harv. L. Rev. 22 (1992); Eva H. Hanks, et al., *Elements of Law*, 171-85, 212-17 (1994).

[77] Schauer, *supra* note 76, at 595.

must have the means of knowing what it prescribes."[78] A system based on established rules meets this requirement. A system based on ad hoc decision-making does not.

*Efficiency.* A system based on the application of rules and precedent is more efficient than one based on ad hoc decision-making. "[C]ourts are busy enough as it is and . . . it would be intolerably burdensome for them to reinvent the wheel in every case."[79]

*Protection from the Government.* Limiting judges' discretion and having them decide cases based on established rules (particularly rules created by the elected body of a legislature) offers protection against the whim and power of the judiciary. "[It] protects the polity from the judicial leviathan[.]"[80]

*Legitimacy.* Basing decisions on established rules and precedent gives legitimacy to the decision-making institution and insulates the decision-maker from public criticism.

As we can see from this list, compelling reasons exist for having a system for resolving legal disputes based on the application of established legal authority. Granted, sometimes a result dictated by the rule of law or applicable precedent may appear unfair or unjust in terms of the emotional facts of the case and the morals that those facts implicate. But as long as a party's position is legitimate under established rules and precedent, the lawyer representing the party is advocating a just and moral cause. Thus, when a person criticizes a lawyer for furthering a client's immoral aims, what the person is really saying is that, on the surface, the client's position is inconsistent with one's instinctive sense of what is morally right in the situation. Such a judgment, however, is superficial, based on a superficial knowledge of the facts and no knowledge of the applicable law. Like all judgments based on incomplete information, it is (or should be) of little consequence.

It is interesting to note that judges are not subjected to the same amount of criticism as are lawyers. While lawyers are often criticized for representing clients with immoral goals, judges are only rarely criticized for their decisions, even when those decisions favor the immoral party and empower that party's position with the force of law. The public seems to understand that the judge's decision, while unfortunate in terms of narrative reasoning, was nevertheless dictated by the rule of law, and this seems to insulate the judge from moral criticism. Curiously, the same does not hold true for professional advocates. Despite the fact that a lawyer's position may be well founded on established law, the lawyer is nevertheless subject to extreme criticism if the emotional facts of the case suggest that morality favors the other side.

---

[78] Scalia, *supra* note 74, at 1179.

[79] Hanks et al., *supra* note 76, at 178.

[80] *Id.* at 179.

What does all this mean in terms of legitimizing the life of a professional legal advocate? Upon closer examination of how our legal system operates, the criticism against professional advocacy appears to be unfounded. A just and moral position is not merely one for which the emotional facts comport with our sense of right and wrong. A just and moral position is one for which legitimate arguments can be made under the law. Thus, even in cases where the emotional facts suggest that a client's position is immoral, an advocate's representation of that client is justifiable, and just, if the advocate has legitimate arguments under the law in furtherance of that position.[81] Our system for resolving legal disputes is based on a commitment to the rule of law and the following of precedent. As we have seen, many reasons exist why such a system is not only just and valid, but more just and valid than a system based on ad hoc decision-making. Considering the legitimacy of the system in general, a professional advocate is justified in pursuing causes that are legitimate under this system. Just as a judge's life is justifiable for reaching decisions dictated by established law, a professional legal advocate's life is justifiable for representing clients whose positions are viable under the law.

Several questions remain. First, one may wonder whether, under this view of advocacy, a professional legal advocate ever acts immorally. The answer is most assuredly yes. In fact, despite the legitimacy of advocacy in general, professional advocates can act immorally in three ways. First, advocates can act immorally in the tactics and strategies they use to pursue a client's cause. Just because a client's cause may be legitimate does not mean that an advocate is not constrained in the tactics he or she can employ to further that cause. As we saw in connection with the third response above, formal rules of ethics as well as informal traditions within the legal culture impose constraints on what a lawyer can do while pursuing victory for a client. Any lawyer who violates these rules and traditions acts immorally, and this is true even if the client's position is otherwise legitimate.

A second way a legal advocate can act immorally is by pursuing frivolous causes. As we have seen, a lawyer is justified in pursuing causes for which legitimate arguments exist under the law. If, however, an advocate pursues a cause that has no basis under the law and for which no legitimate argument can be made to change existing law, the advocate acts immorally. In fact, the professional rules of ethics codify morality in this regard and specifically provide that, "A lawyer shall not bring or defend a proceeding, or assert or controvert an issue therein, unless there is a basis for doing so that is not frivolous, which includes a good faith argument for an extension, modification or reversal of existing law."[82] A lawyer who violates this rule acts immorally and unethically and is subject to discipline.

---

[81] It is important to note that the emotional facts surrounding a legal dispute (i.e., narrative reasoning) rarely support only one side of the dispute. In most cases, the full facts, if known, would show both sides to be partially in the right and partially in the wrong. Thus, moral criticism of a lawyer's representation of a client is often attributable simply to an incomplete understanding of the facts of the matter. In this discussion, however, we are assuming that the emotional facts of the case do significantly favor the opposing side. Yet, as argued in the text, a lawyer is justified in taking such a case as long as legitimate arguments under the law can be made on behalf of the client.

[82] Model Rules of Professional Conduct Rule 3.1 (2000).

The third way that an advocate may act immorally is a bit more controversial. Arguably, it is possible that the emotional aspects of a case can be so compelling that a lawyer's representation of a client in the matter is morally suspect even if the client's position has legitimacy under the law. That is, a client's goals may be so outrageous as to offend our sense of morality even though some basis exists under the law for the client's position. We saw an allusion to this idea in our discussion of James Boyd White's Socratic dialogue in the first response above. In that dialogue, one of the attorneys defending professional advocacy stated, "I help [clients] not only when I think they are in the right, but when I think they are in the wrong, so long as they are not legally wrong or so morally wrong as to be intolerable."[83] As this statement suggests, in some situations, a client's goal may be so morally wrong as to be unworthy of representation. Arguably, a lawyer who represents a client under such circumstances acts immorally. Granted, this point has the potential to unravel the entire argument made in this response. On the one hand, this response argues that a lawyer acts morally as long as the position advocated has basis in the law. On the other hand, this response states that a lawyer may be subject to moral criticism for representing a legal, yet intolerably offensive position. The difference, however, is a matter of degree. Despite the legitimacy of advocacy based on colorable legal arguments, on some occasions, facilitation of a client's cause unjustifiably shocks our conscience. Furthermore, this is the exception rather than the rule. The discussion under this response justifies representation in the large majority of the cases, for most morally suspect clients are not so morally wrong as to be "intolerable." Yet, in those cases in which the client's position *is* intolerable, the advocate should have the moral right (if not the moral obligation) to reject the representation.[84]

Another lingering question is whether narrative reasoning, which seems to be inconsistent with our system's commitment to the rule of law, has any legitimate role in legal decision-making. The answer to this, too, is yes. Despite the commitment to deciding cases based on established rules and the application of precedent, narrative reasoning plays an essential role in legal analysis. Edwards explores the roles of narrative reasoning in the legal decision-making process in some detail in her article *The Convergence of Analogical and Dialectic Imaginations in Legal Discourse*[85] and her book *Legal Writing: Process, Analysis, and Organization*.[86] Most of Edwards' discussions are beyond the scope of our discussion here, but, in a nutshell, she asserts that narrative reasoning has two important functions in legal decision-making. First, it supplements reasoning based on legal authorities; while legal authorities may *justify*

---

[83] White, *supra* note 14, at 222.

[84] For general discussions regarding the ethical and moral implications of an attorney rejecting the representation of a repugnant client, see generally Charles W. Wolfram, *A Lawyer's Duty to Represent Clients, Repugnant and Otherwise*, in *The Good Lawyer*, *supra* note 4, at 214; Teresa Stanton Collett, *The Common Good and the Duty to Represent: Must the Last Lawyer in Town Take Any Case?*, 40 S. Tex. L. Rev. 137 (1999).

[85] *See supra* note 71.

[86] Linda Holdeman Edwards, *Legal Writing: Process, Analysis, and Organization* 4-8, 337-38, 341-43 (2d ed. 1999).

a result in a decision-maker's mind, narrative reasoning, with its appeal to emotions and values, can help motivate the decision-maker to *want* to decide the case in a particular way.[87] The most effective arguments combine justifying arguments based on legal authorities with motivating arguments based on narrative reasoning. Second, narrative reasoning can be very instrumental in convincing a judge (or a member of the legislature) to create new law or change existing law. Law is created to resolve legal disputes. Very often the substance of the law is determined by the values and policies that the law maker wants to further. Thus, narrative reasoning plays an important role in the original creation of law and its subsequent modification.[88]

The final question we must address is what relevance does all this have to the instruction in this text? In this book, we have studied advanced strategies of persuasive writing, attempting to add weapons to the arsenal of strategies available to you as a "professional persuader." As we discussed at the outset of this chapter, however, such a course of study is legitimate only if the profession of "profession persuader" is itself legitimate. In this chapter, we analyzed various responses to the criticisms leveled against professional advocates. In the end, we have justified advocacy as a way of life by pointing out that, despite the common criticisms of uninformed outsiders, professional legal advocates act morally when they represent causes for which just arguments can be made under the law. As this is the essence of being a professional legal advocate, the life of a professional advocate is just and moral. Thus, we should feel justified in our course of study and in our efforts to become better persuasive writers. Because the life of a professional legal "persuader" is morally worthy, one acts morally when he or she endeavors to master the skills of the trade.

---

[87] *See id.* at 337-38; Edwards, *supra* note 71, at 9-17; *see also* Richard K. Neuman, Jr., *Legal Reasoning and Legal Writing: Structure, Strategy, and Style* 271-72 (3d ed. 1998).

[88] *See* Edwards, *supra* note 71, at 17-23.

# *Appendix A*

Below is the dissenting opinion of Pennsylvania Supreme Court Justice Michael Musmanno in the case of *DaPra v. Pennsylvania Liquor Control Board*, 227 A.2d 491 (Pa. 1967), for use in completing Exercise 10.1.

Musmanno, J., dissenting.

1     There should be no rule which declares, with the finality of doom on the
2    Day of Judgment, that no explanation will be permitted to show that something
3    is not what it seems. The defendant in this case, Clement DaPra, has been
4    convicted of performing an obviously innocent act. He was fooled, deceived, and
5    imposed upon, and, because he was subjected to indignity and harm through no
6    fault of his own, the law, speaking through this Court, comes along to push him
7    off the ledge of the window to which he fell from a higher floor without
8    negligence on his part.

9     It is not correct to say, as the Majority Opinion does, that there are certain
10   laws which have no exception. There is not a rule in the law books of the
11   country which may not be set aside when it can be shown that the serpent of
12   fraud had spoken with forked tongue. When deceit and wickedness tie a guiltless
13   person to the stake, the law will cut the bonds and release him. But not,
14   according to the Majority, in this case. Why not?

15    Clement DaPra and his wife, Antoinette DaPra, own a modest tavern in
16   Canonsburg, Washington County. One day, a young man came in and asked for
17   beer. Clement DaPra, fearing this customer might not be an adult, asked him his
18   age. The youth replied that he was over 21 and, in documentation of this
19   assertion, presented a West Virginia draft card which showed he was 26.
20   Washington County borders on the State of West Virginia and many West
21   Virginians come into Washington County on business and for social reasons.
22   DaPra was convinced that there was nothing unusual about the youth's visit and
23   accordingly sold him, in accordance with the youth's request, four bottles of
24   beer, which he took away with him.

25    The Liquor Control Board served a citation on DaPra and, after a hearing
26   before an examiner of the Board, suspended his restaurant liquor license. DaPra
27   appealed to the Court of Quarter Sessions of Washington County which went
28   into an extensive hearing and found that DaPra had not violated the law. In its
29   decision the Court said: "Since Smith had a West Virginia draft card, it would
30   have been idle to have asked him for Pennsylvania type identification, either that
31   furnished by the Liquor Control Board or voter's registration."

32    The Court said further that the description on the card fitted Charles Smith
33    "almost perfectly and Smith certainly looks like an Anglo-Saxon hillbilly from
34    the Appalachian region."

35    The Liquor Control Board appealed the decision of the Washington Court
36    to the Superior Court of Pennsylvania, which, after argument and study, affirmed
37    the decision of the Washington Court. The Liquor Control Board then appealed
38    to this Court, and this Court reversed the previous two courts. On what basis?

39    The Court of Washington County was the fact-finder. What do we know
40    about the facts? Who are we, sitting here higher than the Appalachians, to train
41    our jurisprudential telescope on a humble fellow-man and declare that there is
42    no Balm in Gilead for him because he sold four bottles of beer? Certainly DaPra
43    didn't become wealthy by that sale. He is a poor tradesman trying to eke out a
44    living in what the laws of the Commonwealth declare to be a honorable
45    business. DaPra is not a man of means, but he possesses one wealth which the
46    decision of the Majority would take away from him, and that is his good name.

47    The Lieutenant of Police in Canonsburg, Patrick Matrogran, as well as a
48    reputable businessman in the community, testified to DaPra's "good reputation,
49    as a licensee, a citizen and a church member." He had never been in trouble
50    before. No one pictured him other than an honest, straightforward person
51    without guile or misdemeanor.

52    This Court now allows a shadow to darken his name, in spite of the fact that
53    two other Courts of record, closer to the facts, more familiar with the entire
54    episode than we, have given him a clean slate. This Court, in its interpretation
55    of decisions coming down from the Supreme Court of the United States, has
56    released, or in some way mitigated the punishment due confessed burglars,
57    robbers and established killers. It seems to me that it might be a little considerate
58    of a man who honestly sells a few thimblefuls of beer to put some bread on his
59    table for himself and family. The lower Court said that DaPra was "not
60    particularly successful." DaPra would not be the first honest man who failed to
61    become rich.

62    In reversing the two other Courts, this Court goes into a learned discussion
63    between laws malum in se and laws malum prohibitum, taking me back
64    nostalgically to my law school days, but I think that this erudite dissertation
65    could be saved for something a little more substantial than what is involved here.
66    Suppose someone, without the knowledge of the proprietor, turned back the
67    clock in a tavern, and the proprietor sold beer after the official closing hour,
68    according to Eastern Standard Time. Would this Court say that, regardless of
69    clock, calendar, chronometer, or compass, regardless of deception, imposture,
70    and trickery, regardless of common sense and arithmetic, the proprietor was
71    guilty of violating the criminal code?

72    This is a little case. I should not be writing a Dissenting Opinion about it.
73    Why should I care? The Majority of the Court has spoken. It has spoken bad

74    law, it has jettisoned logic, equity and sapience, but it has spoken, and it should
75    not be my concern to complain about it. I have other cases of far more
76    importance than this one awaiting my attention, study, and midnight lamp, but
77    I am compelled to express my dissent against the decision of the Majority of this
78    Court because I am disturbed about Clement DaPra, an honest citizen and a good
79    church member, who is being stigmatized because someone blindfolded him and
80    pushed him into a pit of undeserved prosecution.

81        When DaPra learned that Charles Smith was not 21 years of age, he hurried
82    to the police station to notify the authorities of what had occurred. He was
83    concerned with the dignity of the law and he was disturbed about young Smith
84    who, he felt, was starting on the wrong path of life. DaPra gave of his time,
85    attention and concern to the law. And for this he is now branded a law-breaker.

86        I cannot help stating with all candor that this case should never have come
87    to the Supreme Court. We had no business to touch it. The Court of Common
88    Pleas, after listening to numerous witnesses, after considering all the evidence,
89    and after taking judicial notice of the West Virginia-Pennsylvania boundary line
90    and the traffic which passes back and forth over that line, found no violation in
91    the law on the part of DaPra and released him. The Liquor Control Board
92    appealed to the Superior Court, and the Superior Court, after studying the
93    record, after hearing arguments, and after due deliberation, affirmed the decision
94    of the Washington County Court of Quarter Sessions and released DaPra as
95    being without fault.

96        Then the Liquor Control Board, with a Javert persistence, all the while
97    spending the money of the Pennsylvania taxpayers, petitioned this Court for an
98    allocatur. This Court could well have turned down this request for allocatur, as
99    it turns down hundreds. But it allowed the petition. The Liquor Board then again
100   spent large sums of the taxpayers' money to print the record and brief; its
101   lawyers, again using taxpayers' money, gave of their expensive time to this
102   monumental litigation, one or more of them traveled to the seat of judgment and
103   delivered themselves of their extensive learning about a little case involving a
104   little tradesman, who had been twice told by the Courts of the Commonwealth
105   to go home and forget about the hard luck which had visited him when someone
106   tripped him and sent him reeling into a brier patch of legal entanglement.

107       This Court then, the Supreme Court of Pennsylvania, the Court of last resort
108   in the Keystone State of the Union, sat in exalted session, listened to the
109   attorneys, went into deliberation, and finally, after months of study, analysis and
110   profound cerebration, produced the decision which overruled the Court of
111   Quarter Sessions, overruled the Superior Court, and overruled the law of
112   common sense, which is as much a part of the jurisprudence of American justice
113   as formalistic codes.

114       But it is possible I am unfair in complaining. The Majority Opinion has been
115   good to me by providing me with a magic carpet transporting me back in fancy
116   to my halcyon days at Georgetown Law School where I learned with bated

117  breath the distinction between laws malum in se and those malum prohibitum.
118  The Majority Opinion has revived for me those ivy-clad days of my youth when
119  I was joyously drinking in the lesson being taught me that law was the
120  "distillment of reason."

121      Alas, I have since found out that that distillation is occasionally diluted by
122  stale beer.

# *Appendix B*

The following materials form part of Exercise 12.2. These fictitious cases, decided by the courts of the state of Lincoln, address the issue of whether a criminal suspect is in "custody" for the purposes of Miranda warnings.

Case 1. *State v. Ellis* (Lincoln's highest appellate court, 1994):

> We find that the defendant was not in "custody" at the time that he made his incriminating statements. The defendant was found by police walking dazed and confused in a remote field. He was initially brought into the police station to assure his safety and to determine his identity. The purpose and intent of the officers in questioning the defendant was to determine who he was so that relatives could be contacted. At the time of the questioning, the defendant was not a suspect in any crime. Furthermore, the manner of the questioning was caring and courteous, not aggressive like interrogations often are. These facts indicate that the defendant was not in custody during the questioning. Thus, his incriminating statements can be used against him even though he did not receive a Miranda warning before the questioning began.

Case 2. *State v. Lewis* (Lincoln intermediate appellate court, 1994):

> The fact that the interrogation at issue took place in the defendant's own house supports the State's position. Nevertheless, we find that the defendant was in custody for the purposes of Miranda. The police considered the defendant to be their primary suspect before they went to the defendant's house. At the house, the police aggressively interrogated the defendant and even presented incriminating pictures to the defendant and asked for an explanation. Moreover, the interview lasted over three hours and policeman were stationed at all exits preventing the defendant from leaving. The defendant should have received a Miranda warning and the motion to suppress the defendant's statements should have been sustained.

Case 3. *State v. Black* (Lincoln's highest appellate court, 1996):

> In this case, the defendant was initially called into the police station to provide general information as a witness to an armed robbery under investigation. However, while the defendant was in the station, separate evidence became available that implicated the defendant in the robbery. At that point, the purpose of the questioning changed—the defendant was seen as a suspect. Moreover, the incriminating statements at issue here were made subsequent to this discovery by the officers. We find that the defendant was in custody at the point he became a suspect and that he should have been advised of his Miranda rights at that time. The defendant's

incriminating statements must be excluded.

Case 4. *State v. Gamble* (Lincoln intermediate appellate court, 1997):

> The defendant in this case was summoned to the police station to provide evidence as a witness. While some evidence implicated the defendant and while the police may have considered the defendant to be one of a number of possible suspects in the crime at the time he was summoned, they did not present him with any evidence of his involvement at the time of this initial interview. The police were cordial and polite, and their questions were general in nature and not accusatory. Finally, there is nothing in the record that suggests that the defendant was not free to leave the interview at any time he wished. In view of these facts, we find that the defendant was not in custody at the time of his initial interview. Thus, Miranda warnings were not necessary and his incriminating statements made during this interview can be used against him at trial.

Case 5. *State v. Harris* (Lincoln intermediate appellate court, 1997):

> The defendant was not summoned to the police station, he was forcibly taken there in a police car. If a police station by itself is not intimidating enough, the defendant was placed in a locked conference room during his interview. Furthermore, the defendant was subjected to aggressive questioning for over two and one-half hours. Clearly the defendant was in "custody" during his questioning. He should have been Mirandized.

Case 6. *State v. Lee* (Lincoln intermediate appellate court, 1999):

> In this case, the police asked the defendant to meet them at a public diner to discuss what he had witnessed relevant to the crime under investigation. During this meeting, the defendant made some statements that would later seal his fate. The defendant claims that these statements are inadmissible because the police officers did not advise him of his Miranda rights before the questioning at the diner. The questioning at the diner, however, was not of a custodial nature. Thus, Miranda warnings were unnecessary. The defendant's statements are admissible.

# Index